**MANHATTAN** PREP

POWERED BY KAPLAN

GMAT™

All the Quant + DI

This guide provides comprehensive coverage of all question types tested
on the Quant and Data Insights sections of the exam, as well as all of
the quant- and logic-based content.

Acknowledgements

A great number of people were involved in the creation of the book you are holding.

Our Manhattan Prep resources are based on the continuing experiences of our instructors and students. The overall vision for this edition was developed by Stacey Koprince, who determined what strategies to cover and how to weave them into a cohesive whole.

Stacey Koprince and Chris Gentry were the primary authors; they were supported by a number of content experts. Mario Gambino, David Mahler, and Helen Tan served as sounding boards during the writing phase, identifying and editing content that needed to be updated for the new version of the GMAT. Paul Fisher and Mark Sullivan wrote a number of new problems for the guide, and David Mahler and Jeff Vollmer proofed them all. The handwritten solutions were the work of Helen Tan, and Mario Gambino produced all the images. Helen and Mario also proofed the entire book from cover to cover.

Prakash Jagannathan managed the production work for this guide, with the help of editors Shaheer Husanne Anwar Ali, Arunsanthosh Kannan, and Chitra Shanmugam. Once the manuscript was done, Mary Jo Rhodes edited and Rebecca Berthiaume proofread the entire guide from start to finish. Carly Schnur and Andrea Repole designed the covers.

GMAT® Strategy Guides

GMAT All the Quant + Data Insights

GMAT All the Verbal

GMAT Foundations of Math

GMAT Advanced Quant

July 2, 2024

Hello!

Thank you for picking up a copy of *All the Quant + DI*. I hope this book provides just the guidance you need to get the most out of your GMAT studies.

At Manhattan Prep, our goal is to provide the best instructors and resources possible. If you have any questions or feedback, please do not hesitate to contact us.

Chat our Student Services team on our website, email us at gmat@manhattanprep.com or give us a shout at 212-721-7400 (or 800-576-4628 in the United States or Canada). We try to keep all our books free of errors, but if you think we've goofed, please visit manhattanprep.com/GMAT/errata.

Our Manhattan Prep Strategy Guides are based on the continuing experiences of both our 99th percentile instructors and our students. The primary authors of the 8th Edition All the Quant + DI guide were Stacey Koprince and Chris Gentry and the primary editors were Stacey Koprince and David Mahler. Project management and design were led by Prakash Jagannathan, Mario Gambino, and Helen Tan.

Finally, we are indebted to all of the Manhattan Prep students who have given us excellent feedback over the years. This book wouldn't be half of what it is without their voice.

And now that *you* are one of our students too, please chime in! I look forward to hearing from you. Thanks again and best of luck preparing for the GMAT!

Sincerely,

Stacey Koprince

Stacey Koprince
Director, Content & Curriculum
Manhattan Prep

TABLE OF CONTENTS

The GMAT Mindset

The GMAT is a complex exam. It feels like a strictly academic test—math, reading comprehension, data analysis, logical reasoning—but at heart, the GMAT is really a test of your *executive reasoning skills.*

Executive reasoning is the official term for your ability to make decisions in the face of complex and changing information. It makes sense, then, that graduate management programs would want to test these skills. But *how* does the GMAT test executive reasoning skills? Understanding this will impact both how you study for the GMAT and the decisions you make as you're taking the test.

Here's the first big difference compared to school tests: Your teachers tested you on material they fully expected you to know how to handle. They never put something on the test that they *expected* you to get wrong.

But the GMAT will actually do this! The GMAT wants to know how well you make decisions regarding when to invest your limited time and mental energy *and* when *not* to. When you see something that will take too long or be too hard, do you let yourself get sucked in? Or do you say, "No, thanks!" and walk away?

In other words, the GMAT is testing you on how well you make business decisions. No good businessperson invests in every single opportunity that comes along. Rather, an effective businessperson evaluates each opportunity, saying yes to some and no to others.

That's what you're going to do on the GMAT, too. You will invest in a majority of the problems presented to you, but you *will also* say no to some—the ones that look too hard or seem like they'll take too long to solve. These are literally bad investments.

The GMAT is Adaptive

Here's the next big difference compared to school tests: The GMAT adapts to you as you take it, offering easier or harder questions based on how you're doing on the test. Ideally, you'll do well on the material that you know how to answer in a reasonable amount of time. Your reward? Eventually, you'll earn questions that are too hard—either they'll take too long, or they'll be so hard that you wouldn't get them even if you had unlimited time.

Then what? If you use a "school mindset" on the test, you'll keep trying to answer these questions even though you really can't do them. You'll waste a bunch of time and have to rush on other questions. As a result, you'll start to miss questions that you actually do know how to answer and your score will go down. This is the business equivalent of spending most of your annual budget by month 8...and then not having enough money left to run the business effectively for the last 4 months of the year. Not a good look.

Instead, use your business mindset to carry you through the exam. When the test finds your limit (and it will), acknowledge that! Call it a bad investment and let that problem go, ideally before you've spent very much time on it. Choose an answer, any answer, and move on.

Extend the business mindset to your studies as well. If there are certain topics that you really hate, don't study them. Seriously! Instead, on your next practice test, guess quickly and move on when one of those "bad investment opportunities" comes up. After your next practice test, you can see what your score is like and decide whether to study those topics in the future.

You might get to your goal score without ever having to master the content that you find the most annoying. Even those of us who score in the 99th percentile on the test have "guess fast on this" lists.

One caveat: You can't give up immediately on huge swaths of content. For example, don't bail on all of algebra; that represents too great a portion of the Quant and Data Insights sections. You can, though, choose a subset of algebra—say, absolute value problems.

Start orienting yourself around your business mindset today. You are *not* going to do every problem or master everything. Rather, you're going to focus on the best investment opportunities (aka, problems) for you, as you see them throughout the test. When you decide not to pursue a particular investment, pick a random answer and move on as quickly as you can—don't waste precious time on a poor investment opportunity. And feel good about the fact that you're doing exactly what you're supposed to do on the GMAT: making sound investment decisions about what to do *and* what *not* to do.

How to Organize Your Quant and Data Insights Studies

The Quant section of the exam tests primarily Quant skills. The Data Insights (DI) section of the exam tests quant, verbal, and formal logic skills.

This book covers all of the question types found in the DI and Quant sections, as well as all of the quantitative and formal logic skills tested on the exam. It also touches on the most important verbal reasoning skill, inference.

All of the verbal-based skills are covered in our *All the Verbal* book; these skills are tested on the Verbal section of the exam and can show up on the DI section of the exam as well. As such, we do recommend using our *All the GMAT* book set, as these books together will cover all of the content and all of the question types found across the GMAT.

How to Use This Book

There are four units in this book:

1. Unit One: Quant and DI Intro; FDPRs

2. Unit Two: Algebra

3. Unit Three: Stories and Stats

4. Unit Four: Number Properties and More

Separately, we also have a free *GMAT Foundations of Math* e-book. If, while working your way through anything in this book, you realize that you would like more foundational help, find the corresponding chapter in *Foundations of Math*. Spend some time building your foundation in the needed area(s), then come back to *All the Quant + DI*.

If you find yourself frequently consulting the *Foundations of Math* book, then you may want to complete that entire book before continuing with this book.

You'll learn about time management, as well as other test details, both in this guide and in the online resources associated with this guide. You can also test your skills using official GMAT problems that are published by the test makers in *The GMAT Official Guide* (also known as "the OG"). These problems appeared on the official GMAT in the past, so they're a fantastic resource to help you get ready for the real test. (Note: The OG is published by the official test makers. It is sold separately from the Manhattan Prep books.)

Book Purchasers: Read Me!

If you are taking a live course or complete self-study program with us, you can skip this section. Your syllabus in Manhattan Prep's online study platform will give you all of the needed assignments from all of your program resources throughout your studies.

If you have purchased books from us on Amazon or a similar site, then you will need to do some organization of your studies yourself. If you haven't already, create your account on the Manhattan Prep website and register your purchase of this book and any other books you may have bought from us. This will give you access to a Starter Kit syllabus, containing resources both for this book and for the test overall. Take 15 minutes right now to explore your syllabus and understand how it works.

If you purchased our *All the GMAT* book set, you will have access both to the Starter Kit syllabus and to a more extensive syllabus on our online study platform. Just register your book set on our website to unlock the *All the GMAT* syllabus and get started.

We also recommend purchasing your own copy of the most recent edition of *The GMAT Official Guide* (also known as "the OG"). The OG is published by the official maker of the GMAT and contains problems that appeared on the official GMAT in the past. It's a fantastic resource for your studies (which is why we include it in all of our live course and self-study programs). One more note: Don't buy any OG editions from 2022 or earlier; those were all built for the classic GMAT, not for the new GMAT.

Use OG problems to train yourself under official test conditions. We recommend following the below guidelines when you devise problem sets for yourself. (If you are taking one of our courses or complete self-study programs, ignore this! You already have OG problem sets assigned in your online syllabus.)

When	What
Early in your studies	At first, try a single problem at a time: 1. Time yourself; it's perfectly fine to go up to a minute over average time for that question type. 2. If you're approaching 1 minute of *extra* time, pick an answer (any answer!); you'll have to do this on the real test, too, so practice that from the beginning. Then either try the problem again or decide that you'd rather guess immediately on the real test. If you try it again, don't time yourself and look up anything you want in your study materials. 3. Review each problem thoroughly before trying the next one.
In the middle of your studies	Add a couple of layers of complexity: 1. Try two to four problems in one straight block before stopping and analyzing the problems. Set a timer for the whole block of time and have an answer for every problem by the time the timer runs out (even if you have to guess). 2. Include some problems from lessons or assignments you completed in earlier weeks (do some new problems *and* retry some problems that you did before). These two additional layers will allow you to practice your time management and keep your skills fresh on material you studied earlier.

(Continued)

When	What
Later in your studies	Add some more complexity: 1. Graduate to longer sets of problems (either four or eight for the Quant or DI sections). 2. Mix question types for DI—include at least three of the five DI problem types in any set. 3. Choose problems randomly out of the OG—so that even *you* don't know what you're about to do! After all, the real test will never tell you what kind of problem you're about to get. If you can mimic the randomness of the test, you'll train yourself to be prepared for anything.

One word of caution: Don't create problem sets that consist of many problems of the exact same type—for example, don't do four Exponents questions in a row. The real test will always mix things up, so do the same with your own practice.

One last—and very important—note: Manhattan Prep's online study platform contains a host of additional resources associated with this book. These aren't "extra" or optional materials; they're integral components of your GMAT study plan.

Online, you'll find materials that explain how to manage your time during the test and what to do if you find yourself too far ahead or behind on time. You'll also find resources to help you analyze your practice test results and figure out your study priorities going forward. You'll even find more practice problems. Register your guide today to get access to all of these materials!

Quant and DI Intro; FDPRs

In this unit, you will learn about the major question types given in the Quant and Data Insights (DI) sections of the GMAT. You'll also gain a strong grounding in estimation and using real numbers to test cases, use smart numbers, and work backwards, skills that are crucial to your success on the GMAT. And you'll learn all of the facts, rules, and relationships governing fractions, decimals, percents, and ratios (FDPRs), as well as how to manipulate and solve for all four number forms.

In This Unit

CHAPTER 1

How Quant and DI Work

In This Chapter...

- The Six Problem Types

- Data Sufficiency

- Table Analysis

- Graphics Interpretation

- Multi-Source Reasoning

- Two-Part Analysis

- Content and Strategy on the GMAT

- Understand, Plan, Solve

In this chapter, you will learn the basics about all six of the problem types that appear in the Quant and Data Insights (DI) sections of the exam. You'll also learn Understand, Plan, Solve (UPS), a process you'll use to tackle every Quant and DI problem.

CHAPTER 1 How Quant and DI Work

Quant and Data Insights make up two of the three sections of the GMAT. (The third section is the Verbal section.)

Both sections are 45 minutes long (default timing*) but the details differ from there. The Quant section focuses on math skills and consists of a single problem type, called Problem Solving. This section includes 21 problems to answer in your given 45 minutes.

*The GMAT has default (1x) timing and, for those who qualify, extended timing. The most common extended time multiplier is 1.5x (or 50% extended time); the second most common is 2x (or 100% extended time). This book will provide all timing on the 1x scale. If you are granted extended time, multiply any timing by the multiplier you were granted to know your timing for each section or problem type.

The Data Insights (DI) section is a bit more complicated. It asks you to do math, verbal, *and* logical analysis across 20 problems in 45 minutes. The DI section includes 5 different types of problems that you'll learn about in this chapter.

The good news: The math content and logic skills tested on the GMAT are the same for both the Quant and DI sections of the GMAT. And the verbal reasoning skills tested are the same for the Verbal and DI sections of the exam. So, while the three sections have different problem types to learn, you don't have to learn all different content for each section of the exam.

Scoring on the GMAT

Each section of the GMAT is scored on a scale of 60 to 90. Your performance on the three sections is then combined into one Total score on a scale of 205 to 805.

Schools typically place the most weight on your Total score. Most programs will post the average scores for their incoming/accepted students, as well as the range of scores earned by the "middle 80%" of their incoming students. (They lop off the top 10% and the bottom 10% of the dataset as outliers.)

Schools will also look at your individual section scores. And this is your chance to bolster any weaker spots in your application. For example, if you have an undergrad degree that didn't require any quantitative classes, you can use your Quant and DI scores as evidence that you can handle the quant-heavy curriculum in business school.

Or maybe you did your undergraduate degree in a language other than English. Your Verbal and DI scores can help demonstrate that your communication skills are at the level needed for an English-language-based graduate program.

If you find yourself getting nervous about analyzing data or solving math or figuring out the best conclusion to a logical scenario…consider this an opportunity! These are all skills you'll use every day in business school. So the investment you're making right now to build these skills for the GMAT will also help you feel a lot more comfortable from day one of your grad school program.

1

Changing Your Answers

On all sections of the GMAT, you must first answer the problems in the order they appear. You will need to put in an answer in order to get to the next problem, and you cannot—at first—go back to problems you've already answered.

But, when you reach the end of each section, you will be allowed to go back to review your work and change up to 3 answers—as long as you still have time left in that section. In general, assume that you won't spend much time reviewing problems, but there are a few circumstances in which it can be helpful to go back to a problem:

What happens	What to do
You submit your answer . . . and *then* realize you made a careless mistake.	Jot down the problem number on your scratch paper and write RETURN next to it.
You know how to do it, but it's going to take a long time to do.	Bookmark the problem and make a random guess now. If you have enough time left at the end, you can solve it then.
You "know you know it," but you're blanking on something right now.	Bookmark the problem. If you later remember what you're blanking on, you can come back to the problem at the end.

Content

The Quant section of the exam can test pure math or applied math, and this section doesn't include a calculator, so you're going to have to do some actual number-crunching on paper in the Quant section.

The one problem type in the Quant section, Problem Solving, is just a plain, choose-one multiple-choice problem type—the most basic problem type on the GMAT. If you've ever taken a multiple-choice math test of any kind, that's what Problem Solving looks like. So, the Quant section feels the most like a "school math" test.

The DI section is different. It was built to mimic case studies—true histories of difficult business situations that include vast amounts of real information (quant and verbal) that you must sort through and analyze to glean insights and make decisions. Case studies are very commonly used in business school, so it makes sense that the GMAT includes a case-study-like section.

The DI section is designed to mirror two key aspects of case analysis that the Quant and Verbal sections of the GMAT don't address:

1. Math–verbal integration
2. The flood of real-world data

Problems on the Quant section of the test typically give you only what you need in order to solve and no more; the numbers often simplify cleanly, leaving you with an integer solution. In addition, the Quant section does not typically incorporate logical reasoning or other verbal skills, although it does require you to translate words into math. On the Verbal section, while Critical Reasoning (CR) and Reading Comprehension (RC) problems can include some quantitative concepts, you're not solving math.

In contrast, problems in the DI section may give you giant tables or graphics of ugly numbers or complex situations—but you'll never actually use most of the information (much like data in the real world). Further, you'll have to integrate quantitative concepts with the kind of reasoning and analysis more typically found on the Verbal section of the exam. You'll be using your math and reasoning skills simultaneously—again, very much like the real world and business school.

The Six Problem Types

In this section, you'll learn how the six problem types on the Quant and Data Insights (DI) sections of the exam work.

Well, really, you'll learn how five of them work, because you already know how the sixth works. The Problem Solving (PS) type, which is the only problem type in the Quant section of the exam, is a basic, boring multiple-choice problem. You'll always have five answer choices and you'll always choose exactly one answer. It looks like every regular multiple-choice math problem you've ever seen.

The other five problem types appear on the DI section of the exam and were invented specifically for the GMAT. Most of them are multi-part problem types—you may have to answer two or even three parts in order to answer the "whole" question. You're given a **Prompt** (or upfront information to process), and you use that information to answer one or more questions.

There are five types of DI problems:

1. Data Sufficiency (aka DS)
2. Table Analysis (aka Table)
3. Graphical Interpretation (aka Graph)
4. Multi-Source Reasoning (aka MSR)
5. Two-Part Analysis (aka Two-Part)

DS, Table, Graph, and Two-Part prompts always have exactly one associated question. That is, for each Data Sufficiency prompt, you'll answer one question, and the same is true for each Table prompt, each Graph prompt, and each Two-Part prompt. Some of these questions, though, will be multi-part questions—you will have to answer two or three parts in order to fully answer that question.

The MSR prompt works more like Reading Comprehension: A single prompt typically comes with three separate associated questions (and some of those individual questions will also be multi-part).

The mix of questions on the DI section will vary:

Prompt type	Typical # of problems	Details
DS	4 to 8	1 prompt with a one-part (single answer) question
Table	2 to 4	1 prompt with a three-part question
Graph	2 to 4	1 prompt with a two-part question
MSR	3	1 prompt with 3 separate questions (some of which are multi-part)
Two-Part	4 to 6	1 prompt with a two-part question

1

DI is complex, just like the real world. And just like the real world, once you gain some experience with DI, it will start to seem normal.

Data Sufficiency

Data Sufficiency (DS) problems test how you think logically about mathematical and analytical concepts. These problems are essentially a cross between math and logic. Imagine this scenario:

> Boss: Should we raise the price on this product? (Dumps a bunch of data on your desk)
>
> You: (after looking through it all) Yes, we should raise the price by 6%.
>
> Boss: Why?
>
> You: (justify your position from the data)
>
> Boss: Great! Let's do it.

This kind of logical reasoning is exactly what you use when you answer DS questions. You're going to answer a specific question that was asked ("Should we raise the price?") and you're going to indicate which specific data points are needed in order to arrive at that answer.

Here's another question: How old is Farai?

Imagine that you're also told a fact: Farai is 10 years older than Dmitry.

But you don't know anything about Dmitry's age, so that doesn't help to figure out how old Farai is. The GMAT would say that this fact—Farai is 10 years older than Dmitry—is *not sufficient* (i.e., not enough) to answer the question.

But suppose you were also given another fact: Dmitry is 8 years old. Given *all* of these facts, Farai would have to be 18.

If you know *both* that Farai is 10 years older than Dmitry *and* that Dmitry is 8 years old, then you have *sufficient* (i.e., enough) information to answer the question. How old is Farai? Farai is 18.

Every DS problem has the same basic form. It will ask you a question. It will provide you with two separate facts, called *Statements*. And it will ask you to figure out what combination of these two facts is *sufficient* to answer the question.

You'll learn more about how DS works in Chapter 3.

Table Analysis

The **Table Analysis (Table)** prompt is made up of two things: a sortable table and some additional text—also known as a **Blurb**—that gives you context about the information contained in the table. The blurb can be quite basic (e.g., a title); other times, the blurb may contain information necessary to answer the associated question.

The table will always appear on the left-hand side of the screen, and the question will always appear on the right-hand side. The blurb is sometimes above the table and sometimes above the question. In this example, the prompt is made up of the blurb, right above the table, and the table itself:

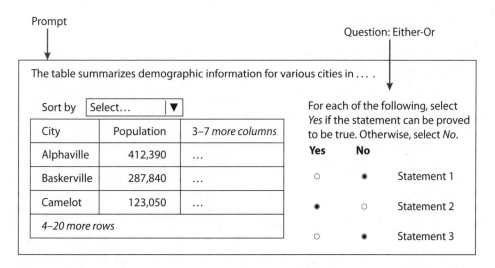

You will be able to sort the table by its columns; sorting will usually help you to save time and minimize careless mistakes.

Table prompts are always accompanied by one **Either-Or** question with three parts. The three parts will be in the form of three statements for which you will choose *either* the answer in the first column *or* the answer in the second column. In the example shown above, the choice is either Yes or No.

One more thing: There is no partial credit on the test. In order to get credit for a multi-part problem, you'll have to answer all parts of the question correctly.

This has implications for test strategy. If you realize, for example, that you can answer one statement but you have no idea how to do the other two, then your best move might be to guess on all three and move on. Alternatively, if you feel confident that you can answer two parts in reasonable time but don't know how to do the third, you would likely still want to do that problem. A guess on the third part will still give you a 50/50 chance of answering the entire question correctly.

Essentially, the Data Insights (DI) section is setting up the kinds of strategic decisions people have to make in the business world every day. You'll learn more about how to handle Tables in Chapter 8.

Graphics Interpretation

Graphics Interpretation (Graph) problems will present you with some kind of a graphic—anything from a classic pie chart or bar graph to a flowchart to an unusual diagram created specifically for this test.

The graph will usually be accompanied by a blurb describing the visual. As with tables, the blurb may describe only the visual, or it may provide additional information that you'll need to use to answer the question. Here is an example:

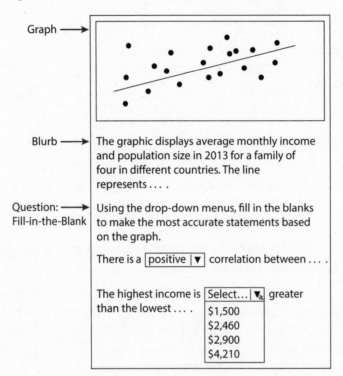

Graph →

Blurb → The graphic displays average monthly income and population size in 2013 for a family of four in different countries. The line represents . . . .

Question: → Using the drop-down menus, fill in the blanks
Fill-in-the-Blank to make the most accurate statements based on the graph.

There is a [positive |▼] correlation between . . . .

The highest income is [Select... |▼] greater
than the lowest . . . .
$1,500
$2,460
$2,900
$4,210

Graph problems are accompanied by a **Fill-in-the-Blank** question with two separate parts to complete. You'll be given one or two sentences with two drop-down menus placed somewhere in the text, offering you multiple-choice options to fill in the blanks. As the image shows, the answers could be numerical or verbal. You may have anywhere from three to five answer choices for each blank, and you will need to answer both parts correctly in order to earn credit for that graph problem.

You'll learn more about Graphs in Chapter 10.

Multi-Source Reasoning

Like Reading Comprehension (RC) prompts on the Verbal section, **Multi-Source Reasoning (MSR)** prompts on the DI section will present you with a bunch of text along with a *set* of questions based on that text. Unlike RC passages, however, the information in MSR can include tables, charts, graphs, or other diagrams along with the text, and all of the information provided is spread across two or three tabs that can only be viewed one at a time. In order to answer the accompanying questions, you will often have to use information from at least two different tabs.

MSR will feel like an RC passage: The prompt will stay on the left-hand side of the screen the whole time, but you will see a series of different questions on the right-hand side of the screen, one after another. Most of the time, you'll have a total of three separate accompanying questions.

MSR questions come in one of two formats. First, they can be standard five-answer multiple-choice questions; your goal is to choose one answer:

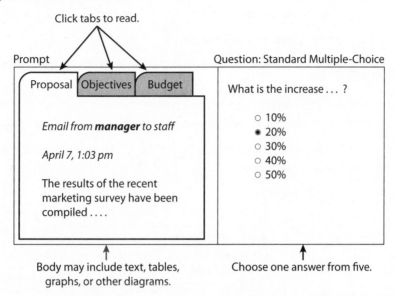

The second type of MSR question is the same either-or question type that appears with Table prompts:

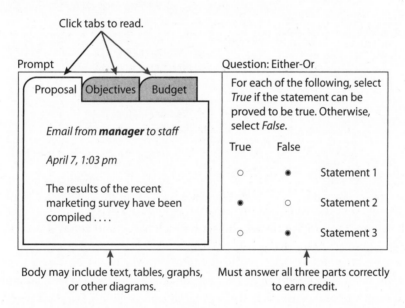

MSR questions always come in one of these two forms:

1. Choose-one multiple choice

2. Either-or with three statements

As in Table problems, the either-or question type is considered a single question; all three parts must be answered correctly in order to earn credit for that question.

After you answer your first MSR question, the prompt will stay on the left side of the screen, and a new question will appear on the right side of the screen.

1

Most often, an MSR prompt will come with three total questions: one standard multiple-choice question and two either-or questions. Since there are three separate questions for an MSR prompt, you have the chance to earn credit for each of the three questions.

You'll learn more about Multi-Source Reasoning in Chapter 18.

Two-Part Analysis

Superficially, **Two-Part Analysis (Two-Part)** problems look very similar to multiple-choice problems from the Quant and Verbal sections of the test—until you get to the answers.

The example below fairly closely resembles a standard Quant problem. The prompt appears first, typically in paragraph form, and the question is always below that:

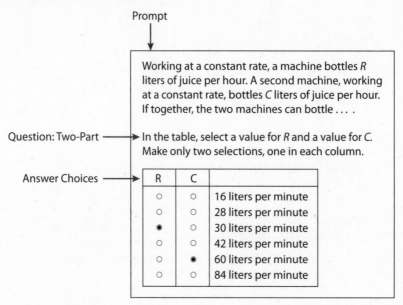

Prompt

Working at a constant rate, a machine bottles *R* liters of juice per hour. A second machine, working at a constant rate, bottles *C* liters of juice per hour. If together, the two machines can bottle . . . .

Question: Two-Part → In the table, select a value for *R* and a value for *C*. Make only two selections, one in each column.

Answer Choices →

R	C	
○	○	16 liters per minute
○	○	28 liters per minute
●	○	30 liters per minute
○	○	42 liters per minute
○	●	60 liters per minute
○	○	84 liters per minute

At the bottom, though, things start to look different. First, you're asked two questions, not just one. And then you'll see a little table that contains your available answer choices in the right-hand column, along with *two* labeled columns on the left side. Those first two columns will be the two parts of the question you need to answer.

The answer choices are the same for both parts of the question; this will always be the case. It's even possible, though rare, for the correct answer to be the same one for both parts. As with all multi-part questions, you'll need to answer both parts correctly in order to earn credit on Two-Part problems.

Two-Parts can also closely resemble classic Critical Reasoning problems—perhaps they'll ask you to both strengthen and weaken an argument. You may also see a logic-based problem, in which you're given a series of constraints and asked a scenario-based question. For example, you may be given various criteria for setting a time for a meeting (times that certain people are or are not available, people who must attend versus those whose attendance is optional, and so on), and then be asked to select both the time that the greatest number of people can attend and the time that the fewest number of people can attend.

Two-Part prompts will often feel the least real-world and the most standardized-test-like of the DI question types. Two-Parts tend to be primarily quant-based, verbal-based, or logic-based; the test doesn't often mix the three topic areas in a single question. You'll learn more about Two-Parts in Chapter 21.

Content and Strategy on the GMAT

Throughout the Quant and DI sections, you'll need to know a variety of facts, formulas, rules, and quantitative concepts.

You'll also need to know a variety of strategies for answering questions as efficiently as possible, without sacrificing accuracy. For example, estimation can be used across most Quant and DI question types on the GMAT.

This book will teach you all of the math-based content and strategies you need for both the Quant and DI sections of the GMAT.

A basic on-screen calculator is available during the DI section but *not* during the Quant section. The calculator can be a blessing and a curse; it's important to learn when and how to use this tool—and when *not* to use it.

In the test screen window, click the link in the upper left corner to pull up the calculator. The calculator will float above the problem on the screen; you can move it around on the screen.

The calculator includes the following limited functions:

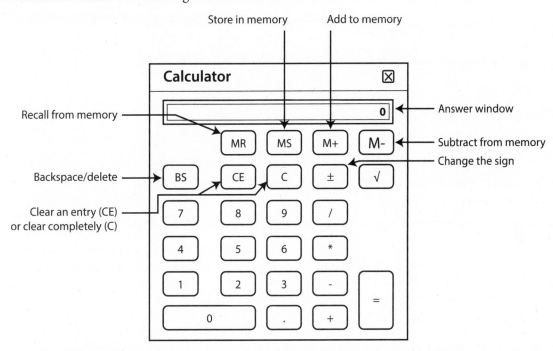

Have you ever panicked on a math problem during a test, picked up a calculator, and punched in some numbers, hoping inspiration would strike? If you ever find yourself doing this during the DI section, stop immediately, pick any random answer, and move on. The calculator is not going to save you when you don't know what you're doing.

That said, don't hesitate to pull up the calculator when you do need it. The Quant section of the test often provides numbers that work pretty cleanly in calculations; the DI section, by contrast, won't hesitate to give you messy numbers. As long as you know what steps you want to take, the calculator can be a very helpful tool.

1

Understand, Plan, Solve

On all Quant and DI problems, use a universal, three-step process to keep track of your thinking and your work:

> Step 1: Understand the question

> Step 2: Plan your approach

> Step 3: Solve the problem

At first glance, the process might seem pretty simple. Most test-takers, though, jump straight to solving and pay minimal attention to the earlier steps. If you want to get through the GMAT with a minimum of stress and a good score, follow the process!

Step 1: Understand the Question

Your first goal is just to comprehend the given information.

First, glance at the entire problem. What type is it? Do any clues jump out at you that tell you what this problem is testing? For example, if you see a pie chart, then there's a good chance you'll need to do some work with percentages or maybe fractions. If you see any type of problem with answer choices in sentence or word form, then you know you've got a more verbal- or logic-focused problem.

Next, as you scan the given data, ask yourself *what* and *so what* questions:

What **is this?**

- What is the question stem, title, or accompanying text indicating?
- What is in this tab, this row, or this column?
- What kind of graph is this and what do these points on the graph represent?
- What kinds of numbers are these—percents or other relative values? Or absolute quantities, such as dollars or barrels?
- What form are the answer choices in? Words or numbers? Real numbers, relative number, variables?

So what **about this?**

- How is this information organized?
- Why is this part here? What purpose does it serve, relative to everything else?
- How does it all fit together? What connections can you draw?

Finally, articulate the question to yourself in your own words. If you can do this confidently, you understand the question well enough to move to the next step.

And if you don't, then this is an excellent time to cut your losses on a bad investment opportunity. Pick a random answer and move on. Use the time you save to do another problem later in the section.

Step 2: Plan Your Approach

Assuming you understand the problem, you'll next figure out what to *do* in order to solve the problem:

- What do you want to jot down? Which portions, if any, should you reread?
- What pieces of information do you need to combine?
- What formulas or rules will you need to use?
- What strategies or shortcuts can you use? Can you eyeball a figure or a list of numbers? Can you estimate?
- How do you want to organize your work?

You won't be able to determine every last step of your plan before you start to solve, but you do want to get far enough in your planning that you feel fairly confident about what you need to do.

If you aren't confident in your plan, this is another great opportunity to guess and move on. Get out now, before you lose time on this problem and find yourself having to rush elsewhere.

Step 3: Solve the Problem

Understand? Have a plan? Great: Now execute your plan of attack. If you've done the first two steps well, you'll be able to solve more efficiently and effectively.

Think about how to organize your work before you dive in. Be methodical; write notes and calculations clearly to minimize the chance of careless mistakes. Finally, if you get stuck at any step along the way, don't dwell on it. Go back and try to unstick yourself *once*. If you're still stuck, guess and move on to the next question.

If you think you might be able to figure out the problem with more time, bookmark it before moving on. If you do have extra time at the end of the section, you can come back and try again.

As you work your way through the rest of this book, you'll learn how to apply the Understand, Plan, Solve process to all of the problem types.

Math Fundamentals

In This Chapter...

- Subtraction of Expressions

- Fraction Bars as Grouping Symbols

- Fractions, Decimals, and Percents

- Common FDP Equivalents

- Converting among Fractions, Decimals, and Percents

- When to Use Which Form

In this chapter, you will learn the basic usage of fractions, decimals, and percents, as well as how to move back and forth quickly among the three. You'll also learn what kinds of calculations are most easily performed in which form.

CHAPTER 2 Math Fundamentals

When simplifying an expression, you have to follow a specific order of operations: Parentheses Exponents (Multiplication/Division) (Addition/Subtraction), or **PEMDAS** as it's referred to in the United States. If you learned math in other English-speaking countries, you may have memorized slightly different acronyms, but the rules are still the same.

Multiplication and division are in parentheses because they are on the *same* level of priority. This is also true for addition and subtraction. When two or more operations are at the same level of priority, work from left to right. For example:

Simplify: $5 + (2 \times 4 + 2)^2 - |7(-4)| + 18 \div 3 \times 5 - 8$

P = PARENTHESES. First, perform all of the operations that are *inside* parentheses. For PEMDAS, absolute value signs fall under the parentheses category. In this expression, there are two groups at the P level:

$(2 \times 4 + 2)$ and $|7(-4)|$

In the first group, there are two operations to perform, multiplication and addition. According to PEMDAS, multiplication must come before addition:

$(2 \times 4 + 2) = (8 + 2) = 10$

In the second group, perform the operation inside first (multiplication), then take the absolute value of that number:

$|7(-4)| = |-28| = 28$

Now, the original expression looks like this:

$\mathbf{5 + 10^2 - 28 + 18 \div 3 \times 5 - 8}$

E = EXPONENTS. Second, take care of any exponents in the expression:

$10^2 = 100$

Now, the expression looks like this:

$\mathbf{5 + 100 - 28 + 18 \div 3 \times 5 - 8}$

M&D = MULTIPLICATION & DIVISION. Next, perform all the multiplication and division. When only multiplication and division are involved, you can do the work in any order. If that seems complicated, keep it simpler by working left to right:

$\underline{18 \div 3} \times 5$

$6 \times 5 = 30$

Now, the expression reads:

$\mathbf{5 + 100 - 28 + 30 - 8}$

A&S = ADDITION & SUBTRACTION. Lastly, perform all the addition and subtraction. Always work from left to right when doing a mix of addition and subtraction:

$5 + 100 - 28 + 30 - 8$

$105 - 28 + 30 - 8$

$77 + 30 - 8$

$107 - 8$

The answer: **99**

2

Subtraction of Expressions

One of the most common errors involving the order of operations occurs when an expression with multiple terms is subtracted. The subtraction must occur across *every* term within the expression. Each term in the subtracted part must have its sign reversed. For example:

$x - (y - z) = x - y + z$ The signs of both y and $-z$ have been reversed. Note that "minus a negative" turns into a positive.

$x - (y + z) = x - y - z$ The signs of both y and z have been reversed.

$x - 2(y - 3z) = x - 2y + 6z$ The signs of both y and $-3z$ have been reversed.

Try this example:

What is $5x - [y - (3x - 4y)]$?

Both expressions in parentheses must be subtracted, so the signs of each term must be reversed for *each* subtraction, working from the inside out. Note that the square brackets are just fancy parentheses, used so that you avoid having double parentheses right next to each other:

$$5x - [y - (3x - 4y)] =$$
$$5x - (y - 3x + 4y) =$$
$$5x - (5y - 3x) =$$
$$5x - 5y + 3x = \mathbf{8x - 5y}$$

Fraction Bars as Grouping Symbols

In any expression with a fraction bar, pretend that there are parentheses around the numerator and denominator of the fraction. This may be obvious as long as the fraction bar remains in the expression, but it is easy to forget if you eliminate the fraction bar or add or subtract fractions. For example:

Simplify: $\frac{3x - 3}{6} - \frac{4x - 2}{6}$

Treat the numerators $3x - 3$ and $4x - 2$ as though they were enclosed in parentheses. Once you combine them, actually put these numerators in parentheses. Then, reverse the signs of *both* terms in the second numerator when you distribute the subtraction:

$$\frac{(3x - 3) - (4x - 2)}{6} = \frac{3x - 3 - 4x + 2}{6} = \frac{-x - 1}{6} = -\frac{x + 1}{6}$$

The last two forms are both acceptable as the answer. You can leave the negative sign in each of the two terms in the top of the fraction. You can also pull a negative out of both terms and put that negative sign out front.

Fractions, Decimals, and Percents

F, D, and P stand for fractions, decimals, and percents, respectively. These three forms are different ways to represent the exact same number. For example:

A **fraction** consists of a numerator and a denominator:	$\frac{1}{2}$
A **decimal** uses place values:	0.5
A **percent** expresses a relationship between a number and 100:	50%

All three are equal to each other and represent the same number: $\frac{1}{2} = 0.5 = 50\%$

Ratios are closely related to fractions but not quite the same; you'll learn more about ratios a little later in this book.

The GMAT often mixes fractions, decimals, and percents (and sometimes even ratios) in a single problem, and certain kinds of math operations are easier to perform on one form compared to the others. In order to achieve success with FDP problems, you need to shift among the three accurately and quickly. Try this problem:

> A sum of money is divided among three sisters. The first sister receives $\frac{1}{2}$ of the total, the second receives $\frac{1}{4}$ of the total, and the third receives the remaining $10. How many dollars do the three sisters split?
>
> (A) $10
> (B) $20
> (C) $30
> (D) $40
> (E) $50

To solve, you have to figure out what proportion of the money the first two sisters get so that you know what proportion the third sister's $10 represents. The information is provided in fractions but, in general, adding fractions is annoying because you have to find a common denominator. It's not too difficult to add up the relatively simple fractions $\frac{1}{2}$ and $\frac{1}{4}$. However, harder fractions would make the work a lot more cumbersome. So, find a better way to solve, one that would work well even on a harder problem.

Numbers that are in decimal or percent form are much easier to add. Because this problem talks about parts of a whole, convert to percentages. The first sister receives 50% of the money and the second receives 25%, leaving 25% for the third sister. That 25% represents $10, so 100% of the money is 4 times as much, or $40. The correct answer is (D).

In order to do this kind of math quickly and easily, you'll need to know how to convert among fractions, decimals, and percents. Luckily, certain common conversions are used repeatedly throughout the GMAT. If you memorize these conversions, you'll get to skip the calculations. The next two sections of this chapter cover these topics.

Common FDP Equivalents

Save yourself time and trouble by memorizing the following common equivalents:

Fraction	Decimal	Percent
$\frac{1}{1}$	1	100%
$\frac{1}{2}=\frac{2}{4}=\frac{3}{6}=\frac{4}{8}=\frac{5}{10}$	0.5	50%
$\frac{3}{2}$	1.5	150%

Fraction	Decimal	Percent
$\frac{1}{4}=\frac{2}{8}$	0.25	25%
$\frac{3}{4}=\frac{6}{8}$	0.75	75%
$\frac{5}{4}$	1.25	125%
$\frac{7}{4}$	1.75	175%

Fraction	Decimal	Percent
$\frac{1}{8}$	0.125	12.5%
$\frac{3}{8}$	0.375	37.5%
$\frac{5}{8}$	0.625	62.5%
$\frac{7}{8}$	0.875	87.5%

Fraction	Decimal	Percent
$\frac{1}{5}=\frac{2}{10}$	0.2	20%
$\frac{2}{5}=\frac{4}{10}$	0.4	40%
$\frac{3}{5}=\frac{6}{10}$	0.6	60%
$\frac{4}{5}=\frac{8}{10}$	0.8	80%

Fraction	Decimal	Percent
$\frac{1}{10}$	0.1	10%
$\frac{3}{10}$	0.3	30%
$\frac{7}{10}$	0.7	70%
$\frac{9}{10}$	0.9	90%

Fraction	Decimal	Percent
$\frac{1}{3}=\frac{2}{6}$	$0.\overline{3}\approx0.333$	$\approx33.3\%$
$\frac{2}{3}=\frac{4}{6}$	$0.\overline{6}\approx0.667$	$\approx66.7\%$
$\frac{4}{3}$	$1.\overline{3}\approx1.333$	$\approx133.3\%$

Fraction	Decimal	Percent
$\frac{1}{6}$	$0.1\overline{6}\approx0.167$	$\approx16.7\%$
$\frac{5}{6}$	$0.8\overline{3}\approx0.833$	$\approx83.3\%$
$\frac{1}{9}$	$0.1\overline{1}\approx0.111$	$\approx11.1\%$

Fraction	Decimal	Percent
$\frac{1}{100}$	0.01	1%
$\frac{1}{50}$	0.02	2%
$\frac{1}{25}$	0.04	4%
$\frac{1}{20}$	0.05	5%

Converting among Fractions, Decimals, and Percents

If you see a number that isn't on the Common Equivalents list to memorize, you can convert among fractions, decimals, and percents. The table below shows how:

FROM ↓ TO→	Fraction	Decimal	Percent
Fraction $\frac{1}{4}$		Divide the numerator by the denominator: $$1 \div 4 = 0.25$$ Alternatively, multiply the top and bottom to get the denominator to equal 100: $$\frac{1}{4} \times \frac{25}{25} = \frac{25}{100} = 0.25$$ Note: These operations are hard if the fraction is annoying; in that case, see whether you can estimate.	Divide the numerator by the denominator and move the decimal two places to the right: $$1 \div 4 = 0.25 \rightarrow 25\%$$
Decimal 0.375	Put a 1 plus zeros in the denominator; use the same number of zeros as places to the right of the decimal point (in this case, 3 zeros). Put the decimal's digits in the numerator. Then, simplify: $$\frac{375}{1,000} = \frac{3}{8}$$		Move the decimal point two places to the right: $$0.375 \rightarrow 37.5\%$$
Percent 65%	Use the digits of the percent for the numerator and 100 for the denominator. Then, simplify: $$\frac{65}{100} = \frac{13}{20}$$	Find the percent's decimal point and move it two places to the left: $$65.0\% \rightarrow 0.65$$	

Think before you convert, though. If the conversion is annoying—for example, if you have to do long division—don't do it. Instead, see whether you can estimate or use some other approach. For example, converting 0.65 to a percent or fraction isn't too bad. But converting $\frac{7}{13}$ to a decimal or percent would be very annoying. Instead, can you estimate? The fraction is almost $\frac{7}{14}$, or 0.5.

Pop quiz: Is $\frac{7}{13}$, a little larger or a little smaller than $\frac{7}{14}$? Play around with that a little bit. Later in this guide, you'll learn how to estimate this quickly.

You'll get plenty of practice with these skills throughout this book, but if you'd like some more practice, see Manhattan Prep's *GMAT Foundations of Math*.

2

When to Use Which Form

As you saw in the "three sisters" problem, when you have to add or subtract, percentages (or decimals) tend to be easier. By contrast, fractions work very well with multiplication and division.

If you have already memorized the given fraction, decimal, and percent conversions, you can move among the forms quickly. If not, you may have to decide between taking the time to convert from one form to the other and working the problem using the less convenient form (e.g., in order to add, you could convert fractions to decimals or you could leave them in fraction form and find a common denominator).

Try this problem:

> What is 37.5% of 240 ?

If you convert the percent to a decimal and multiply, you will have to do a fair bit of arithmetic, as shown on the left:

$$\begin{array}{r} 0.375 \\ \times\ 240 \\ \hline 0 \\ 15000 \\ \hline 75000 \\ 90.000 \end{array}$$

Alternatively, recognize that $0.375 = \dfrac{3}{8}$.

$$(0.375)(240) = \left(\frac{3}{8}\right)\overset{30}{240} = 3(30) = 90$$

This is much faster!

Try something a bit harder:

> A dress is marked up 16.7% to a final price of $140. What was the original price of the dress?

16.7% is on the memorization list; it is equal to $\dfrac{1}{6}$. In order to increase a number by $\dfrac{1}{6}$, add a sixth of the number to itself: $1 + \dfrac{1}{6} = \dfrac{7}{6}$. Call the original price x and set up an equation to find x:

$$x + \frac{1}{6}x = 140$$

$$\frac{7}{6}x = 140$$

$$x = \left(\frac{6}{7}\right)140 = \left(\frac{6}{7}\right)\overset{20}{140} = 120$$

Therefore, the original price was $120.

Decimals and percents work very well with addition and subtraction because you don't have to find common denominators. For this same reason, decimals and percents are often preferred when you want to compare numbers or perform certain estimations. For example, which is greater, $\dfrac{3}{5}$ or $\dfrac{5}{8}$?

You could find common denominators, but both fractions are on the "conversions to memorize" list:

$$\frac{3}{5} = 60\% \qquad \frac{5}{8} = 62.5\%$$

The greater fraction is $\dfrac{5}{8}$.

In some cases, you may decide to stick with the given form rather than convert. If you do have numbers that are easy to convert, though, then use fractions for multiplication and division, and use percents or decimals for addition and subtraction, as well as for estimating or comparing numbers.

Problem Set

Now that you've finished the chapter, try these problems. On the GMAT, Quant problems will always provide five answer choices. In this guide, you will sometimes have fewer than five answer choices (and sometimes none at all).

1. Express the following as fractions and simplify: 0.4   0.008

2. Express the following as fractions and simplify: 420%   8%

3. Express the following as decimals: $\dfrac{9}{2}$ $\dfrac{3{,}000}{10{,}000}$

4. Evaluate: $(4 + 12 \div 3 - 18) - [-11 - (-4)]$

5. Evaluate: $-|-13 - (-17)|$

6. Express the following as percents: $\dfrac{83}{1{,}000}$ $\dfrac{25}{8}$

7. Express the following as percents: 80.4   0.0007

8. Order from least to greatest: $\dfrac{8}{18}$ 0.8   40%

9. Evaluate: $\left(\dfrac{4 + 32}{2 - (-6)}\right) - (4 + 8 \div 2 - (-6))$

10. Simplify: $x - (3 - x)$

11. 20 is 16% of what number?

12. What number is 62.5% of 96 ?

13. Simplify: $(4 - y) - 2(2y - 3)$

Solutions

1. $\frac{2}{5}$ and $\frac{1}{125}$: To convert a decimal to a fraction, write it over the appropriate power of 10 and simplify:

$$0.4 = \frac{4}{10} = \frac{2}{5}$$

$$0.008 = \frac{8}{1000} = \frac{1}{125}$$

2. $\frac{21}{5}$ or $4\frac{1}{5}$ and $\frac{2}{25}$: To convert a percent to a fraction, write it over a denominator of 100 and simplify:

$$420\% = \frac{420}{100} = \frac{21}{5} \text{ (improper)} \quad \text{OR} \quad 4\frac{1}{5} \text{ (mixed)}$$

$$8\% = \frac{8}{100} = \frac{2}{25}$$

3. **4.5 and 0.3:** To convert a fraction to a decimal, divide the numerator by the denominator:

$$\frac{9}{2} = 9 \div 2 = 4.5$$

It often helps to simplify the fraction *before* you divide:

$$\frac{3,000}{10,000} = \frac{3}{10} = 0.3$$

4. **−3:**

$(4 + 12 \div 3 - 18) - (-11 - (-4)) =$	Division before addition/subtraction
$(4 + 4 - 18) - (-11 + 4) =$	Subtraction of negative = addition
$(-10) - (-7) =$	Arithmetic—watch the signs!
$-10 + 7 = -3$	

5. **−4:**

$-\lvert -13 - (-17) \rvert =$	Subtraction of negative = addition
$-\lvert -13 + 17 \rvert =$	
$-\lvert 4 \rvert = -4$	

Note that the absolute value *cannot* be made into $13 + 17$. You must perform the arithmetic inside grouping symbols *first*, whether inside parentheses or inside absolute value bars, *then* remove the grouping symbols.

6. **8.3% and 312.5%:** To convert a fraction to a percent, rewrite the fraction with a denominator of 100:

$$\frac{83}{1,000} = \frac{8.3}{100} = 8.3\%$$

Alternatively, convert the fraction to a decimal and shift the decimal point two places to the right:

$$\frac{25}{8} = 25 \div 8 = 3\frac{1}{8} = 3.125 = 312.5\%$$

7. **8,040% and 0.07%:** To convert a decimal to a percent, shift the decimal point two places to the right:

$$80.4 = 8,040\%$$
$$0.0007 = 0.07\%$$

8. **40% $< \dfrac{8}{18} <$ 0.8:** To order from least to greatest, express all the terms in the same form (your choice as to which form!):

$$\frac{8}{18} = \frac{4}{9} = 0.4444\ldots = 0.\overline{4}$$
$$0.8 = 0.8$$
$$40\% = 0.4$$
$$0.4 < 0.\overline{4} < 0.8$$

9. **-9.5:**

$$\left[\frac{4+32}{2-(-6)}\right] - [4 + 8 \div 2 - (-6)] =$$

$$\left(\frac{4+32}{2+6}\right) - (4 + 8 \div 2 + 6) =$$

$$\left(\frac{36}{8}\right) - (4 + 4 + 6) =$$

$$4.5 - 14 = -9.5$$

10. **$2x - 3$:** Reverse the signs of every term in the parentheses:

$$x - (3 - x) = x - 3 + x = 2x - 3$$

11. **125:** The sentence translates as $20 = (16\%)x$. Fraction form is better for multiplication or division, so convert 16% into a fraction first: $16\% = \dfrac{16}{100} = \dfrac{4}{25}$. Then solve for x:

$$20 = \frac{4}{25}x$$
$$20\left(\frac{25}{4}\right) = x$$
$$(5)(25) = x$$
$$x = 125$$

12. **60:** The sentence translates as $x = (62.5\%)(96)$. The figure 62.5% is one of the common FDPR equivalents to memorize; the fraction form is $\frac{5}{8}$. Solve for x:

$$x = \left(\frac{5}{8}\right)96$$
$$x = (5)(12)$$
$$x = 60$$

13. $-5y + 10$ **(or $10 - 5y$):** Reverse the signs of every term in the subtracted parentheses:

$$(4 - y) - 2(2y - 3) = 4 - y - 4y + 6 = -5y + 10 \text{ (or } 10 - 5y)$$

Data Sufficiency 101

In This Chapter...

- How Data Sufficiency Works

- The Answer Choices

- Starting with Statement (2)

- Value vs. Yes/No vs. Choose One Questions

- The DS Process

- Testing Cases

- Test Cases Redux

- The C-Trap

- Avoid Statement Carryover

- Guessing Strategies

In this chapter, you will learn how to tackle Data Sufficiency (DS) problems, including an overall process to help you solve the problems efficiently. You'll also learn how to test cases on DS; this strategy will help you handle more complicated problems as you advance in your studies.

CHAPTER 3 Data Sufficiency 101

As discussed in Chapter 1, every DS problem has the same basic form. It will ask you a question. It will provide you with some facts. And it will ask you to figure out what combination of facts is *sufficient* to answer the question.

Take a look at this example, in full DS form:

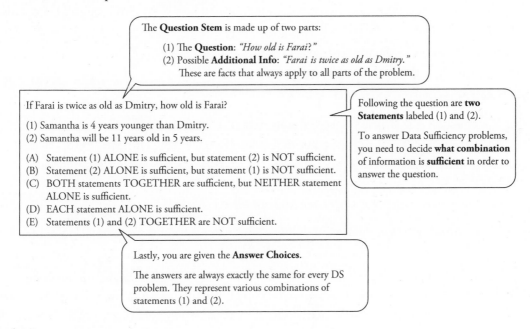

The **Question Stem** is made up of two parts:

(1) The **Question**: *"How old is Farai?"*
(2) Possible **Additional Info**: *"Farai is twice as old as Dmitry."*
These are facts that always apply to all parts of the problem.

If Farai is twice as old as Dmitry, how old is Farai?

(1) Samantha is 4 years younger than Dmitry.
(2) Samantha will be 11 years old in 5 years.

(A) Statement (1) ALONE is sufficient, but statement (2) is NOT sufficient.
(B) Statement (2) ALONE is sufficient, but statement (1) is NOT sufficient.
(C) BOTH statements TOGETHER are sufficient, but NEITHER statement ALONE is sufficient.
(D) EACH statement ALONE is sufficient.
(E) Statements (1) and (2) TOGETHER are NOT sufficient.

Following the question are **two Statements** labeled (1) and (2).

To answer Data Sufficiency problems, you need to decide **what combination** of information is **sufficient** in order to answer the question.

Lastly, you are given the **Answer Choices**.

The answers are always exactly the same for every DS problem. They represent various combinations of statements (1) and (2).

Now what?

How Data Sufficiency Works

The **Question Stem** always contains the question you need to answer. It may also contain **Additional Info** (also known as *givens* or *facts*) that you can use to help answer the question.

Below the question stem, the two **Statements** provide additional facts or given information—and you are specifically asked to determine what combination of those two statements would be sufficient to answer the question.

The **Answer Choices** describe various combinations of the two statements: For example, one answer says that statement (1) is sufficient, but statement (2) is not sufficient. The answer choices don't contain any possible ages for Farai. DS questions aren't asking you *to* solve; they're asking *whether* it's possible to solve. (By the way: No need to try to figure out what all of those answer choices mean right now; you'll learn as you work through this chapter.)

DS questions look strange but you can think of them as deconstructed Problem Solving (PS) questions—the "regular" type of multiple-choice math problem. Take a look at this PS-format problem:

> Samantha is 4 years younger than Dmitry, and Samantha will be 11 years old in 5 years. If Farai is twice as old as Dmitry, how old is Farai?

This is actually the same question as the DS-format one. The PS form puts all of the givens as well as the question into the question stem. The DS problem moves some of the givens down to statement (1) and statement (2).

The DS statements are always givens—that is, they are always true. In addition, the two statements won't contradict each other. In the same way that a PS question wouldn't tell you that $x > 0$ and $x < 0$ (that's impossible!), the two DS statements won't do that either.

In the PS format, you would need to calculate Farai's age. In the DS format, you typically will *not* need to calculate that value; on DS, you only need to go far enough to know *whether* Farai's age can be calculated. Since every DS problem works in this same way, it is critical to learn how to work through all DS questions using a systematic, consistent process. Take a look at how this plays out:

> If Farai is twice as old as Dmitry, how old is Farai?

(1) Samantha is 4 years younger than Dmitry.

(2) Samantha will be 11 years old in 5 years.

(A) Statement (1) ALONE is sufficient, but statement (2) alone is not sufficient.
(B) Statement (2) ALONE is sufficient, but statement (1) alone is not sufficient.
(C) BOTH statements TOGETHER are sufficient, but NEITHER statement ALONE is sufficient.
(D) EACH statement ALONE is sufficient.
(E) Statements (1) and (2) TOGETHER are NOT sufficient.

The goal: Figure out which pieces of information *would* allow you to answer the question (How old is Farai?).

Your first task is to understand what the problem is saying and jot down the information in math form. Draw a T on your page to help keep the information organized. Write information from the question stem above the horizontal line. Include a question mark to indicate the question itself (later, you'll learn why this is important):

$$\boxed{?} \quad F = \underline{\quad} \, ?$$

$$F = 2D$$

(1)	(2)

Hmm. Reflect for a moment. If they tell you Dmitry's age, then you could just plug it into the given equation to find Farai's age. Jot that down!

Take a look at the first statement. Also, write down $\frac{AD}{BCE}$ off to the right of your scratch paper, above the line (you'll learn what this is as you work through this chapter):

(1) Samantha is 4 years younger than Dmitry.

$$\boxed{?} \quad F = \underline{\hphantom{xx}}?$$

$$F = 2D$$

$$\begin{array}{l} AD \\ BCE \end{array}$$

$$(1) \quad S = D - 4 \quad \bigg| \quad (2)$$

Translate the first statement and jot down the information below the horizontal line, to the left of the T. (Not confident about how to translate that statement into math? Use Manhattan Prep's *GMAT Foundations of Math* to practice translating.)

The first statement doesn't allow you to solve for either Samantha or Dmitry's real age. Statement (1), then, is *not sufficient*. Cross off the top row of answers, (A) and (D).

Why? Here's the text for answers (A) and (D):

(A) Statement (1) ALONE is sufficient, but statement (2) is NOT sufficient.

(D) EACH statement ALONE is sufficient.

These two answers indicate that statement (1) *is* sufficient to answer the question. But statement (1) is *not* sufficient to find Farai's age, so both (A) and (D) are wrong.

The five answer choices will always appear in the order shown for the above problem, so any time you decide that statement (1) is not sufficient, you will always cross off answers (A) and (D) at the same time. That's why the $\frac{AD}{BCE}$ answer grid groups these two answers together on the top row.

Next, consider statement (2), but wait! First, forget what statement (1) told you. Because of the way the DS answers are constructed, you must evaluate the two statements *separately* before you look at them together. So here's just statement (2) by itself:

(2)   Samantha will be 11 years old in 5 years.

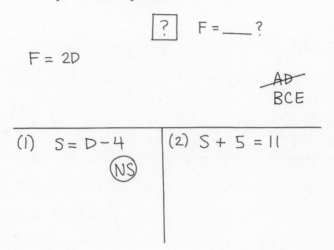

In your T diagram, write the information about statement (2) below the horizontal line and to the right. It's useful to separate the information this way in order to help remember that statement (2) is separate from statement (1) and has to be considered completely by itself first.

You'll always organize the information in this way: The question stem goes above the T, statement (1) goes below and to the left of the T, and statement (2) goes below and to the right.

Back to statement (2). This one allows you to figure out how old Samantha is now, but *alone* the info doesn't connect back to Farai or Dmitry. By itself, statement (2) is *not* sufficient. Of the remaining answers (BCE), answer (B) says that statement (2) is sufficient by itself. This isn't the case, so cross off answer (B).

When you've evaluated each statement by itself and haven't found sufficient information, *then* look at the two statements together. Statement (2) allows you to figure out Samantha's age. Statement (1) allows you to calculate Dmitry's age if you know Samantha's age. Finally, the question stem allows you to calculate Farai's age if you know Dmitry's age!

$$? \quad F = \_\_\_ ?$$

$$F = 2D$$

~~AD~~
~~B~~C~~E~~

(1)   S = D − 4
(NS)

(2) S + 5 = 11
(NS)

(1 + 2)   (S)

As soon as you see that you *can* find Farai's age, write an S with a circle around it to indicate *sufficient*. Don't actually calculate Farai's age; you only need to know that you *can* calculate it. Save that time and mental energy for other things on the test.

The correct answer is (C): Both statements together are sufficient to answer the question, *but* neither statement alone is sufficient.

The Answer Choices

On the real test, the five Data Sufficiency answer choices will always be exactly the same (and presented in the same order), so you won't even need to read them on the real test. By then, you'll have done enough DS problems to have them memorized. (In fact, to help you memorize, this book won't even show the DS answer choices in end-of-chapter problem sets.)

Here are the five answers written in an easier way to understand:

(A) Statement (1) *does* allow you to answer the question, but statement (2) *does not*.

(B) Statement (2) *does* allow you to answer the question, but statement (1) *does not*.

(C) Neither statement works on its own, but you can use them *together* to answer the question.

(D) Statement (1) works by itself *and* statement (2) works by itself.

(E) Nothing works. Even if you use both statements together, you still can't answer the question.

Answer (C) specifically says that neither statement works on its own. For this reason, you are required to look at each statement by itself first *and decide that neither one works alone* before you evaluate the two statements together.

Here's an even shorter way to remember the five answer choices, the "12-TEN" mnemonic (memory aid):

1	only statement 1
2	only statement 2
T	together
E	either one
N	nothing works

As you practice DS over the next couple of weeks, make an effort to memorize the five answers. If you do a couple of practice DS problems every day in that time frame, you'll likely memorize the answers without conscious effort—and you'll solidify the DS lessons you're learning right now.

Speaking of solidifying the lessons you're learning, set a timer for two minutes and try this problem:

All dogs are mammals, and all mammals are vertebrates. Is this animal a vertebrate?

(1) This animal is a dog.

(2) This animal is a mammal.

(A) Statement (1) ALONE is sufficient, but statement (2) alone is not sufficient.

(B) Statement (2) ALONE is sufficient, but statement (1) alone is not sufficient.

(C) BOTH statements TOGETHER are sufficient, but NEITHER is sufficient ALONE.

(D) EACH statement ALONE is sufficient.

(E) Statements (1) and (2) TOGETHER are NOT sufficient.

Ready? What did you get? (If you got stuck and didn't get to an answer, pick one anyway. That's what you'll have to do on the real test, so you might as well practice that now.)

Start with the question. Take a moment to understand how any given facts relate to the question stem itself. How are dogs, mammals, and vertebrates related?

dog → mammal → vertebrate

If the animal is a dog, then it's a vertebrate. And if the animal is a mammal, then it's a vertebrate.

Congratulations! You just completed a rephrase of a DS question. Is this animal either a dog or a mammal? See the image below for one example of how to notate this on scratch paper.

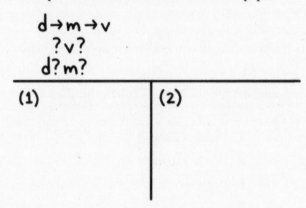

Now, assess the statements.

(1) This animal is a dog.

This statement matches the rephrased question: *Is this animal a dog?*. It's sufficient to answer the question. Which row should you cross off in the grid, AD or BCE?

Think of statement (1) as associated with answer choice (A). If statement (1) is sufficient, then answer (A) needs to stay in the mix. Therefore, cross off the bottom row, BCE.

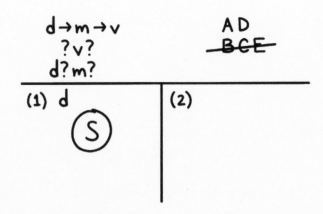

What's next? Pause and try to remind yourself before you keep reading.

The next step is to forget about statement (1) and take a look at statement (2):

> (2)   This animal is a mammal.

This statement asserts the other variation of the rephrased question: *Is this animal a mammal?* So, it's also sufficient by itself.

Cross off answer (A) and circle answer (D): Either statement alone is sufficient to answer the question. Do actually take the time to do this on your scratch paper before you select your answer on screen. It won't take you more than a second and this action will help to minimize careless mistakes on the test.

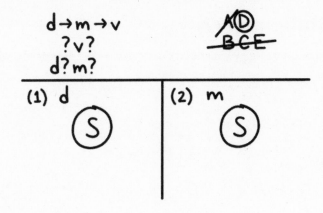

To help you visualize each step, here's a summary of the answer choice process when starting with statement (1):

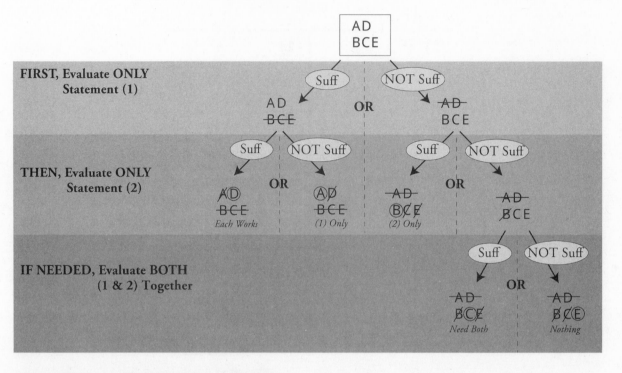

Starting with Statement (2)

If statement (1) looks hard or annoying, you can start with statement (2) instead. Your process will be the same; you'll just make one small change in your answer grid.

Try this problem:

> If Farai is twice as old as Dmitry, how old is Farai?
>
> (1)   Two years ago, Dmitry was twice as old as Samantha.
>
> (2)   Samantha is 6 years old.

```
1
2
T
E
N
```

(From now on, the full answer choices won't be shown. Start memorizing! You can also glance back at earlier pages until you know the answers by heart.)

First, what to do with that question stem? You can write it down the same way you did before, but now that you've learned about rephrasing, add one more thing. If you found D's age, you could find F's age, so the question can be rephrased as "$D = ?$"

Next, statement (1) is definitely more complicated than statement (2), so start with statement (2) this time. Lay out your scratch paper in the same way—statement (1) on the left and statement (2) on the right—but this time write $\frac{BD}{ACE}$ for your answer grid (you'll learn why in a minute):

(2) Samantha is 6 years old.

$$F = 2D \qquad \boxed{?} \begin{array}{l} F = \underline{\quad} \; ? \\ D = \underline{\quad} \; ? \end{array} \quad \begin{array}{l} BD \\ ACE \end{array}$$

$$\underline{\hspace{5cm}}$$

(1) \qquad (2) $S = 6$

Statement (2) is not sufficient to determine Farai's age. Think of this statement as associated with answer (B). Since the statement is *not* sufficient, you *don't* want to keep (B), so cross off the row that contains that answer: the top row (BD).

Whenever you decide to start with statement (2), you'll always use the $\frac{BD}{ACE}$ answer grid, and you'll always cross off either the entire top row or the entire bottom row, depending on whether statement (2) is sufficient.

Now, forget about statement (2) and assess statement (1):

(1) Two years ago, Dmitry was twice as old as Samantha.

$$F = 2D \qquad \boxed{?} \begin{array}{l} F = \underline{\quad} \; ? \\ D = \underline{\quad} \; ? \end{array} \quad \begin{array}{l} \cancel{BD} \\ ACE \end{array}$$

$$\underline{\hspace{5cm}}$$

(1) $D - 2 = 2(S-2)$ | (2) $S = 6$ \quad (NS)

That translation is tricky. Since it's talking about the time period 2 years ago, subtract 2 from each of D and S. Then translate and write the rest of the equation. By itself, is statement (1) sufficient?

Nope! This isn't enough to find a specific age for Farai, Dmitry, or Samantha. Cross off (A), the first of the remaining answers in the bottom row, and now assess the two statements together:

3

$$F = 2D$$

$$\boxed{?}\quad F = \underline{\quad} ?$$
$$D = \underline{\quad} ? \quad \cancel{BD}$$
$$\cancel{ACE}$$

(1) $D - 2 = 2(S-2)$ (2) $S = 6$

(NS)   (NS)

(1 + 2) $D = \#$

(S)

You can plug Samantha's age (from the second statement) into the formula from statement (1) to find Dmitry's age, and Dmitry's age is sufficient to answer the question. Together, the statements are sufficient.

The correct answer is (C): Neither statement works alone, but *together* the information is sufficient to answer the question.

Here's a summary of the answer grid process when starting with statement (2):

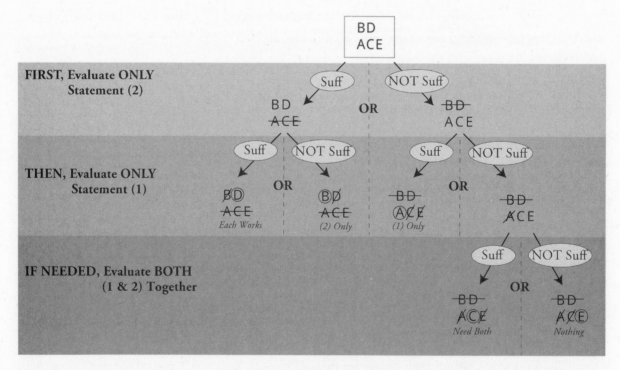

The two answer grids work the same way, regardless of which one you use. When starting with statement (1), always use the AD/BCE grid. Think of statement (1) as associated with the first answer letter in that grid, (A).

When starting with statement (2), always use the BD/ACE grid and think of this statement as associated with the first answer letter, (B).

In either case, when assessing your starting statement, you will get to cross off an entire row:

- If the first statement you try *is* sufficient, cross off the *bottom row* (the row that does *not* contain the letter associated with that statement).
- If the first statement you try is *not* sufficient, cross off the *top row* (the row containing the letter associated with that statement).

Once you've crossed off an entire row and have just one row left, assess the answers in the remaining row, one answer at a time.

Finally, you must assess the statements separately before you can try them together—and you'll only try them together if neither one is sufficient on its own. In other words, you will only consider answers (C) and (E) if you have already crossed off answers (A), (B), and (D).

Value vs. Yes/No vs. Choose One Questions

Data Sufficiency questions come in three "flavors": Value, Yes/No, or Choose One.

Value questions are usually math-based. On these, it is necessary to find a single value in order to answer the question. If you can't find any value or you can find two or more values, then the information is not sufficient.

Here's an example of a Value question with one accompanying statement:

> How old is Farai?
>
> (1) Farai's age is a multiple of 4.

Farai could be 4 or 8 or 12 or any multiple of 4. Because it's impossible to determine one particular value for Farai's age, the statement is not sufficient to answer the Value question: How old is Farai?

Now, consider this question:

> Is Farai's age an even number?
>
> (1) Farai's age is a multiple of 4.
> (2) Farai is between 19 and 22 years old.

This question is fundamentally different. It's not asking for a value; it's asking a yes/no question.

There are three possible sufficiency outcomes for a Yes/No question:

1. Always Yes: Sufficient!
2. Always No: Sufficient!
3. Maybe (or Sometimes Yes, Sometimes No): Not Sufficient

It may be a surprise that Always No is sufficient to answer the question. Imagine that you ask a friend to go to the movies with you. If she says, "No, I'm sorry, I can't," then you did receive an answer to your question (even though the answer is negative). You know she can't go to the movies with you.

Apply this reasoning to the Farai question. Is statement (1) sufficient to answer the question: Is Farai's age an even number?

    (1)   Farai's age is a multiple of 4.

If Farai's age is a multiple of 4, Farai could be 4, 8, 12, … but in *every* case, the answer to the question is Yes. Even though you don't know how old Farai is, the information is sufficient to answer the specific question asked: Yes, Farai must be an even number of years old.

Because statement (1) is sufficient, keep answer (A) in the mix. Cross off the bottom row of answers (BCE).

In the sample notes above, the question is jotted down with the question mark included: *Is F even?* It's crucial to include both the starting "question word" (*Is*) and the question mark; if you omit these, then later you might mistakenly think that the problem is telling you that *F is even*—and, if that happens, you're much more likely to get this question wrong.

While you might not make that mistake on this particular problem, this is a potential source of error on *any* DS problem, so get into the habit of writing that question mark every time. Always distinguish between *facts* (things you know to be true) and *questions*.

Okay, back to the problem. Next, check statement (2):

    (2)   Farai is between 19 and 22 years old.

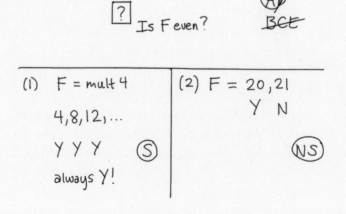

Farai could be 20, in which case the age is even. However, Farai could also be 21, in which case the age is odd. The result here is Sometimes Yes, Sometimes No, so the information in statement (2) is *not* sufficient to answer the question. Cross off answer (D).

The correct answer is (A): The first statement is sufficient but the second is not.

There are two common traps to note. First, for statement (2), someone might think that Farai must be 20, not 21, because the age is even. But the problem doesn't *tell* you that Farai's age is even; rather, it *asks* whether Farai's age is even.

Answer (C) is also a trap answer on this problem. If you think that you need to find one specific value for Farai's age, then you'll think that you need both pieces of information: If Farai is *between* 19 and 22 *and* the age is a multiple of 4, then Farai must be 20 years old.

But the problem doesn't ask how old Farai is. It asks only whether the age is an even number—and the first statement is sufficient to answer that question.

As soon as you see what kind of question you have (Value, Yes/No, or Choose One), jot down a reminder on your scratch paper. That will help you to avoid traps and to make sure you're answering the right question.

Consider one more example:

> Three people—Adlai, Bhavin, and Callisto—are standing in line. Who is first in line?
>
> (1) Callisto is last in line.
> (2) Neither Bhavin nor Callisto is first in line.

This question is the third type: Choose One. Instead of asking for a mathematical value, the question asks for a definitive choice from among a short list of options. In this problem, the question specifically asks which of the three given options is first.

Start drawing this out. List the three options, and draw three slots for those options. Label the first slot, and mark that slot as the focus of the question. For example, you might put a question mark in that slot or draw a box around it:

For this question, there is no effective rephrase. Other than the list of options, the question stem gives no facts that could be used to reinterpret the question itself. Dive into the statements!

    (1)   Callisto is last in line.

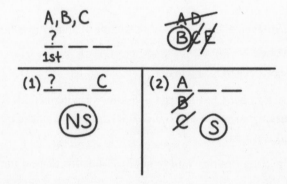

Redraw the slots in the statement (1) area, adding the information given in this statement. Callisto is last in line, but either of the other two people could be first in line. This statement is *not* sufficient to determine who is first. Cross off answer choices (A) and (D).

    (2)   Neither Bhavin nor Callisto is first in line.

Notate the diagram to reflect that neither Bhavin nor Callisto can be first. Eliminating those two options leaves only one remaining option, Adlai, so this statement is sufficient to know who is in the first slot. Cross off answer choices (C) and (E).

The correct answer is (B): The second statement is sufficient alone but the first is not.

On DS, one of your first tasks is to determine whether it's a Value, Yes/No, or Choose One problem:

Question Type	Characteristics	Sufficiency
Value	Asks for a specific numeric value	Suff: A *single* value works Not Suff: Multiple values work
Yes/No	Asks a yes/no question	Suff: Always yes *or* Always no Not Suff: Sometimes yes, sometimes no
Choose One	Asks to choose one from a short list	Suff: A single option is valid Not Suff: More than one option is valid

The DS Process

This section summarizes each step that you've learned in one consistent DS process. You can use this on every DS problem on the test.

Your process consists of three distinct stages: Understand, Plan, and Solve. Most people dive straight into the third step, Solve, but this can create all kinds of issues. You may find yourself halfway through a solution and it then falls apart on you. Or you'll realize most of the way through that there was some easier, faster way you could have approached this problem.

The Understand and Plan steps help you to make sure that you actually want to do this problem in the first place (business mindset—don't do them all!) and they help you to settle on a solution process that is efficient and effective.

Step 1: Understand

First, just *glance* at the problem to note the overall type—in this case, it's a DS. Where does it look messy or complex? Include the question stem and both statements in your glance.

Next, *read* the problem and decide: Is this math or logic-based? Is it Value, Yes/No, or Choose One?

Value:	Usually math-based; the question asks for the specific value of an unknown (e.g., "What is x?").
	A statement is **Sufficient** if it provides **exactly one possible value**.
	A statement is **Not Sufficient** if it provides **more than one possible value**.
Yes/No:	Either math or logic-based. The question asks whether a given piece of information is true (e.g., "Is x even?" or "Is Sam chosen for the team?").
	A statement is **Sufficient** when the answer is **Always Yes** *or* **Always No**.
	A statement is **Not Sufficient** when the answer is **Sometimes Yes, Sometimes No** or **Maybe**.
Choose One:	Usually logic-based. The question asks you to choose the answer from a short list of options (e.g., Given five types of coffee, "Which type is most expensive?").
	A statement is **Sufficient** if it points to **exactly one possible answer**.
	A statement is **Not Sufficient** when **more than one answer** is possible.

Jot down both the given information and the question itself. If the information is straightforward, it's fine to jot down notes as you read. If the information is at all complex (especially if it's a story!), you may want to read the whole thing before you go back to jot down the information.

Finally, *given* information—that is, any information in the question stem other than the question itself—is true information. These are facts. Write this information separately from the question itself. It's important to distinguish between what you were *told* is true and what you were *asked* to find.

Step 2: Plan

Reflect on the question and the givens, and rephrase the question if you can. If you have a lot of information, you may also need to decide how to *organize* your work.

At the least, you'll usually be able to simplify what is written on screen. For example, if the question stem asks, "What is the value of *x*?" then you might write down something like $x =$ _____?

For more complicated question stems, you will likely have more work to do to rephrase the question—but rephrasing will make your job easier when you get to the next step. Ideally, before you go to the statements, you will be able to articulate a fairly clear and straightforward question (or, at least, one that's a little more clear than the original question).

Consider this problem:

> Store M sells exactly one product for a price of $20 per unit. On each of the past 5 days, Store M sold at least 6 units of the product. Was yesterday's profit greater than $100 ?
>
> (1) Store M's profit per unit is $17.
> (2) Yesterday, Store M sold 8 units of the product.

The question itself seems pretty straightforward: Was yesterday's gross profit greater than $100?

But what else would you need to know in order to calculate profit?

$$\text{Profit} = \text{Revenue} - \text{Cost}$$

Hmm. First, the question is asking whether the profit was greater than 100. Plug that into the formula:

$$R - C = P$$

$$\text{Is } R - C > 100 \text{ ?}$$

Next, revenue is the cost per item times the number of items. In this case, the cost per item is $20 and at least 6 items were sold every day, so revenue was at least $120 yesterday:

$$\text{Is } R - C > 100 \text{ ?}$$

$$\text{Is } (\geq 120) - C > 100 \text{ ?}$$

But there's no way to tell what the profit might have been without knowing something about the cost. So, the first question to answer is really: What is the *cost*? Now, you have a plan!

It might seem like a waste of time to keep writing *Is* and the question mark on each line, but don't skip that step or you'll be opening yourself up to a careless error. By the time you get to the end, you don't want to forget that this is still a *question*, not a statement or a given.

Step 3: Solve

Now that you know what you need to figure out, use the answer grid to evaluate the statements.

If you start with statement (1), then write the AD/BCE grid on your scrap paper. If you start with statement (2), then write BD/ACE instead.

Here is the rephrased problem:

> $\text{Is } (\geq 120) - C > 100 \text{ ?}$
>
> (1) Profit *per unit* = $17
> (2) Yesterday, sold 8 units

Statement (1) indicates that the per-unit profit is $17. Since per-unit revenue is $20, the per-unit *cost* is $3. If 6 units were sold yesterday, the cost would be only $18 for a revenue of $120. So, total profit would be greater than $100.

What if you sold more than 6 units yesterday? For each unit sold, you make another $17, so profit would just keep increasing. Therefore, statement (1) is sufficient to answer the question: Yes, yesterday's profit was more than $100. Keep answer (A) in the mix, so cross off the bottom row of answers:

AD
~~BCE~~

Statement (2) might have looked more promising before you rephrased the question. Exactly 8 units were sold, so revenue was $160.

But what were the costs? No idea. (Forget about the first statement right now!) Without any information about the cost, it's impossible to conclude anything about profit.

Statement (2) is not sufficient to answer the question. Cross off answer (D) and circle correct answer (A) on your grid:

Ⓐ ~~D~~
~~BCE~~

If you decide to start with statement (2), your overall process is almost identical, but you'll use the BD/ACE grid instead. The answer will still turn out to be (A), even if you use this grid.

Whether you use AD/BCE or BD/ACE, you will always:

- Cross off the *top* row if the first statement you try is *not* sufficient
- Cross off the *bottom* row if the first statement you try *is* sufficient

Finally, when moving to the next statement, put the first statement out of your mind! Always try each statement by itself first. Only evaluate the two statements together if you've already crossed off answers (A), (B), and (D), so that only answers (C) and (E) are left.

Here's a summary of the 3-step process:

Step 1: **Understand**

Glance at the problem. Note that it's DS and also notice which parts look annoying or complex. (Don't think about this yet. Just notice.)

Read the problem. Don't rush it. Your goal right now is just to understand what it's saying. Math or Logic? Value, Yes/No, or Choose One?

Jot down information. Don't do anything with this info yet.

Step 2: **Plan**

Reflect on what you know so far. Do you have any ideas about how to translate or rephrase (simplify) the complex parts in the question stem or the statements?

Organize your information, if needed, and organize your thoughts. How do you want to set up your scratch paper? Do you have a decent idea for how to solve in a reasonable amount of time?

If so, proceed. If not, make the call to bail: Pick a random answer and move on.

Step 3: **Solve**

If you understand and have a plan, go ahead and do whatever work is needed to solve this problem. Note that even the best laid plans sometimes fail. If things aren't working the way you thought they would or you're realizing that this is taking a lot more time than you'd planned, get out of the problem. Have a business mindset—don't use up too many of your resources on any one business opportunity!

Testing Cases

Data Sufficiency problems often allow for multiple possible scenarios, or cases. For example, if you know that $x + y = 1$, there are an infinite number of possible values for x and y, as long as the pair of values makes that equation true.

When a statement is set up to allow multiple cases, you can use the **Test Cases** strategy to determine whether a statement is sufficient or not sufficient. This process can feel a little different for Value vs. Yes/No vs. Choose One questions, so you'll get a chance to try all three in this section.

When you're testing cases, your goal is to try to prove the statement *insufficient*, if possible. Why? As soon as you find two contradictory answers, you're done! Then it's a Maybe answer, or a not-definitive answer, which is not sufficient to answer the question.

If, on a Yes/No question, you keep getting a Yes answer every time, even when you're actively trying hard to find a No answer (or vice versa), then you can feel pretty confident that this statement is giving you a definitive answer—that is, that the statement is sufficient to answer the question.

Consider this problem:

> If x and y are positive integers, is the sum of x and y between 50 and 60, inclusive?
>
> (1) $x - y = 6$

First, **Understand**. This is a DS Yes/No problem. It tells you that x and y are positive integers and asks whether $x + y$ is between 50 and 60, inclusive. (*Inclusive* is math-speak for *include the endpoints—50 and 60—in the range*.)

Glance at the statement. You aren't given enough information to be able to solve definitively for specific values of x and y; there are many possible values. So you can test cases on this problem to try to find contradictory answers: You'll be trying to prove or disprove a sum in the 50–60 range.

Use that understanding to **Plan**. You also need to follow any constraints given in the statement. In this case, the two numbers have to be positive integers and $x - y$ must equal 6. Go ahead and try any two numbers that fit these constraints, then see what happens.

Solve. Case 1: $x = 10$ and $y = 4$.

These numbers are both positive integers and are valid, based on the constraint from the first statement ($10 - 4 = 6$). Now, try to answer the Yes/No question: $10 + 4 = 14$, so in this case No, the sum is not between 50 and 60, inclusive.

You now have a No answer. Go back to the Plan step for a second. Can you think of another set of numbers that will give you the opposite, a Yes answer? What kind of numbers would you need?

Think about what a Yes answer means. The sum would have to be in the 50–60 range, so you'll need larger starting numbers. You might have to play with the numbers a bit to find a good pairing.

Solve. Case 2: $x = 30$ and $y = 24$.

These numbers are both positive integers and valid for the first statement ($30 - 24 = 6$). Now, answer the Yes/No question: $30 + 24 = 54$, so in this case, Yes, the sum is between 50 and 60, inclusive.

Because you have found both a Yes case and a No case (contradictory cases!), you have proved that this statement is not sufficient to answer the question.

One note: The last problem and the next two are on the line between "pure" math and applied (story) math. In all three cases, you're using your knowledge of math theory and terminology to solve, rather than crunching a bunch of pure-math steps; this type of thinking is fair game on GMAT DS.

Here's a summary of the process:

1. In the **Understand** phase of the DS process, notice that you *can* test cases on a particular problem. You can do this whenever the problem and the statement allow for multiple possible values. Also think to yourself, "What would contradictory answers look like on this problem?" For instance, in the previous problem, a sum between 50 and 60 (inclusive) would be a Yes, while any other sum would be a No.

2. Come up with a **Plan**. Consider two things:

   • First, what kinds of numbers are you *allowed* to pick? Any numbers you use must fit the facts given in the question stem and in the statement that you're testing right now.

   • Second, what kinds of numbers would be likely to give you a *different* or contradictory answer?

3. **Solve**. Process your first case:

   • Choose your first set of numbers.

   • Double-check that the numbers work with all of the given facts. If you accidentally chose numbers that do not fit all of the given facts, *discard* that case. Cross out that case on your scratch paper and start again. You're only allowed to try numbers that follow the facts of the problem.

   • Solve and find the specific answer for this case. On a Yes/No problem, you'll get either Yes or No. On a Value problem, you'll get a numerical value. On Choose One problems, you'll narrow down to a single option.

4. Then, solve again! Try to find a second case that gives you a *different* outcome. Before you choose numbers, remind yourself of what a contradictory answer looks like for this problem.

On a:	First case:	Second case:
Yes/No	If you found a Yes...	...Look for a No
Value	If you found a value of 3...	...Look for any value other than 3
Choose One	If, from a list of 5 fruits, apple was the answer...	...Look for any one of the other four types of fruit

If you can find two contradictory answers, you're done! That statement is not sufficient to provide one consistent answer, so you can cross off the relevant answer(s) on your grid and move to the next step in your DS process.

What if you try to find a different answer but it doesn't work—you keep finding the same answer? Try this problem:

If x and y are positive integers, is the product of x and y greater than 20 ?

(1) x is a multiple of 11 and y is divisible by 2.

Math vocab alert: *Product* means *multiply*. A *multiple* of a number is that number multiplied by a series of integers. For example, the positive multiples of 4 are 4, 8, 12, 16, and so on. And *divisible by 2* means that you'll get an integer when you divide that number by 2.

Understand. The two variables are positive integers and the question is a Yes/No: Is $xy > 20$?

Plan. Many possible values are allowed, so test cases. Look for contradictory answers.

Solve. Case 1: Test $x = 11$ and $y = 2$. The product is $(11)(2) = 22$, which is greater than 20. The answer to the question in this case is Yes. Now, can you find a No answer?

Solve. Case 2: How about $x = 11$ and $y = 4$? Then xy will be 44…hmm. Increasing the value of either variable just makes the product even greater. Can you go smaller?

It's not possible. The smallest multiple of 11 is 11 and the smallest positive integer divisible by 2 is the number 2, so the smallest product of the two is 22.

You've just proved the statement sufficient. The given information leads to an Always Yes answer; it is impossible to find a No case, no matter what you try. The Test Cases strategy can help you figure out the "theory" behind the answer, or the mathematical reasoning that proves the statement is sufficient.

This won't always work so cleanly. Sometimes, you'll keep getting all Yes (or all No) answers, but you won't be able to figure out the theory behind it all. If you test three or four different cases, and you're actively seeking out a contradictory answer but never finding it, then go ahead and assume that the statement is sufficient, even if you're not completely sure why.

Here's how testing cases would work on a Value problem:

> If x and y are prime numbers, what is the product of x and y?
>
> (1)   The product xy is even.

Math vocab alert: *Prime* numbers are numbers that are divisible by exactly two numbers: themselves and 1. The number 2 is the smallest prime number (and the only even prime!). Other examples include 3, 5, 7, 11, 13, and 17.

Understand. Theory problem—no real numbers given. Can only choose primes for x and y. What is the value of xy? The statement contains the word *even*…

Plan. Think about even and odd—*and* prime. The only even prime number is 2. All other prime numbers are odd. Whenever you multiply anything by 2, the result is even, so if the product xy is even and those numbers are both prime, one of those numbers has to be 2.

Solve. Case 1: $x = 2$ and $y = 3$. Both numbers are prime numbers and their product is even, so these are legal numbers to try. In this case, the product is 6. Are you allowed to choose numbers that will give a different product?

Solve. Case 2: $x = 2$ and $y = 5$. Both numbers are prime numbers and their product is even, so these are legal numbers to try. In this case, the product is 10.

The statement is not sufficient because there are at least two different values for the product of x and y.

Try this problem:

> When Adrian and her two siblings go to the candy store, they always choose from among the following options: bubble gum, a chocolate bar, rock candy, and taffy. Adrian always chooses something different from her siblings. Which candy does Adrian choose?
>
> (1) Adrian's siblings do not choose the same candy.
>
> (2) Adrian does not choose bubble gum.

Understand. There are three people and four candy options in a logic-based question. Diagram to organize the information given and the question asked:

Plan. With only three people, a diagram showing which person chooses which options would be effective. Test multiple cases to show options for Adrian.

Solve. Build out the cases for the statements individually:

For Statement (1), make a notation that s_1 and s_2 cannot be the same. Then choose two different options for each sibling. In this case, the notes show G and R, although you could have chosen a different pair. Then make a selection for Adrian. In this case, Adrian cannot choose either G or R, but she could choose either of C or T. Since there are two options for Adrian, it's not possible to tell which candy she chose. Statement (1) is not sufficient.

Drawing out both options for Adrian may seem like more work than needed for this problem. But it only takes a few seconds to prove on paper that there are multiple options for Adrian. Systematic work will help you avoid careless mistakes on the test.

Next, examine the second statement:

$$G, C, R, T \qquad \cancel{A} \; \cancel{D} \; \cancel{B} \; C \; E$$

$$\frac{?}{A} \; \frac{}{S_1} \; \frac{}{S_2}$$

$$(1) \qquad\qquad (2)$$

$$\frac{}{A} \; \frac{\ne}{S_1} \; \frac{}{S_2} \qquad \frac{}{\cancel{A}} \; \frac{}{S_1} \; \frac{}{S_2}$$

$$\boxed{\text{NS}}$$

$$\frac{C}{A} \; \frac{}{S_1} \; \frac{}{S_2}$$

$$\frac{R}{A} \; \frac{}{S_1} \; \frac{}{S_2}$$

Adrian did not choose *G*, but she could have chosen any of the other three types of candy. As with the first statement, don't just do this in your head; record your analysis on your scratch paper. Since Adrian could have chosen multiple types of candy, statement (2) is not sufficient.

Finally, combine the two statements:

$$G, C, R, T \qquad \cancel{A} \; \cancel{D} \; \cancel{B} \; \cancel{C} \; \boxed{E}$$

$$\frac{?}{A} \; \frac{}{S_1} \; \frac{}{S_2}$$

$$(1) \qquad\qquad (2)$$

$$\frac{}{A} \; \frac{\ne}{S_1} \; \frac{}{S_2} \qquad \frac{}{\cancel{A}} \; \frac{}{S_1} \; \frac{}{S_2}$$

$$\boxed{\text{NS}}$$

$$(1+2) \quad \frac{}{\cancel{A}} \; \frac{\ne}{S_1} \; \frac{}{S_2} \qquad \frac{C}{\cancel{A}} \; \frac{G}{S_1} \ne \frac{R}{S_2}$$

$$\frac{T}{\cancel{A}} \; \frac{G}{S_1} \ne \frac{R}{S_2}$$

Include all of the given information so far (the two siblings do not choose the same candy, Adrian does not choose gum). When you combine statements (1) and (2), first check to see whether you can reuse any of your prior cases. Luckily, in this instance, both of the cases tested for statement (1) are also allowed for (1) and (2) together. Since Adrian still has multiple options, the two statements together are still not sufficient.

The correct answer is (E): Even using both statements, you still can't answer the question.

When you're testing cases on DS, take an "I'm going to try to find different answers" mindset:

- After you try your first case, think about how the problem worked. What kind of number or setup would be a good one to try for your second case in order to try to get a different answer?
- If you do find two contradictory answers, then immediately declare that statement not sufficient.
- If, after several tries, you keep finding the same answer despite actively trying to set up cases that will give a different answer, that statement is likely sufficient. By now, you may even be able to say why (because you've seen why different kinds of numbers or setups keep giving the same result). Even if you can't articulate why, go ahead and assume that the statement is sufficient.

Here's a summary of the sufficiency rules for each type of DS problem:

Type	Sufficiency
Value	Suff: Only one *single* value is possible (e.g., 3).
	Not Suff: *More than one* value is possible (e.g., 3 and 4).
Yes/No	Suff: There is *one* definitive answer: either always Yes *or* always No.
	Not Suff: Some cases are Yes and some cases are No.
Choose One	Suff: Exactly *one* item from the list is possible.
	Not Suff: More than one item from the list is possible.

Test Cases Redux

Here's a summary of the Test Cases strategy for DS problems:

Understand: First, **recognize** that you can test cases. The question stem and the statement will allow for multiple possible values or scenarios; it doesn't lock you into using one set of values or one scenario.

Articulate the *facts* given in the problem and separate them from the *question* that is being asked. Remind yourself of your goal when testing cases on DS: Try to find two different/contradictory answers so that you can call that statement Not Sufficient and move on.

Plan: First, **think about** any **constraints** you're given. The constraints are the facts given in the problem and can be found in *two* places: (1) the question stem and (2) the two statements. You are only allowed to try numbers or test scenarios that fit the given facts. (Also, as you work on one statement alone, ignore any facts given in the *other* statement.)

Next, use the given facts as clues to figure out what kinds of numbers or scenarios you *do* want to try. These clues will help you to find the kinds of cases that can give you different answers.

Solve: Then, **test one case**. Choose one set of values or scenarios, write them down, then check your inputs against the facts in the problem to make sure that you have set up a valid case. For example, if your chosen numbers "break" any of the facts—that is, make a given fact false—*discard* that case. The given facts are always true.

When you're working on statement (1) alone, follow the facts given for the question stem and statement (1). When you're working on statement (2) alone, follow the facts given for the question stem and statement (2). When you're working on both statements together, follow all facts given everywhere in the problem.

If you realize that you chose numbers that contradict any of those facts, cross off that case on your scratch paper and start again.

When you have a valid case (you haven't contradicted any facts!), solve to find an answer to the question. On a Value question, you will get a particular value. On a Yes/No question, you will get either a Yes or a No. On a Choose One question, you will get one particular outcome from the available list.

Then, try to find a second case that gives you a *different* answer. Ask yourself what a different answer will look like for this problem. For example, if the question is "Is $b > 5$?" and your first answer is Yes, then you would want to find a No case. For this particular question, a No case would only occur when b is equal to or less than 5, so try to choose accordingly when you set up your second case.

If you can find two different answers, you're done! That statement has a Maybe/Who Knows? answer, so you can cross off the relevant answer(s) on your grid and move to the next step in your DS process.

If you keep getting the same answer, try to articulate *why* this is happening. If you are trying the same kind of number (e.g., positives) on a math-based problem, then you may need to try a different kind of number (e.g., negatives) to find that opposite case.

If you are starting with the same basic setup on a logic-based problem, you may need to examine your constraints again to see whether you can try a different starting point. Trying to articulate what's happening can lead you to realize that you need to try a specific kind of case that will get you to a different answer.

Alternatively, articulating what's happening with the math or logic may allow you to realize that you will always get that same answer—in other words, that this statement is sufficient.

At times, you may get the same answer after a few cases but not be able to articulate why. If you're not sure why, but you also don't see how to get a different answer after actively trying to find different kinds of cases, don't keep sitting on this problem. Go ahead and call this statement sufficient and move on.

The C-Trap

Set a timer for 4 minutes and try these two DS problems.

A basket contains more apples than bananas; there are no other pieces of fruit in the basket. How many bananas are in the basket?

(1) There are 16 apples in the basket.

(2) There are 28 pieces of fruit in the basket, and there are 4 more apples than bananas.

A concession stand sells chips, dip, pretzels, and soda. If Vikram buys either chips or a pretzel, he will buy a soda. If he does not buy chips, then he will not buy dip. Does Vikram buy chips?

(1) Vikram buys exactly three different items from the concession stand.

(2) Vikram buys at least a pretzel and a soda from the concession stand.

What did you get for the first one?

> A basket contains more apples than bananas; there are no other pieces of fruit in the basket. How many bananas are in the basket?
>
> (1) There are 16 apples in the basket.
>
> (2) There are 28 pieces of fruit in the basket, and there are 4 more apples than bananas.

Step 1: **Understand**. It's a DS Value question, asking for the number of bananas. It also indicates that there are only apples and bananas in the basket and that there are more apples than bananas.

Glance at the statements. Statement (2) is more complex because it includes both types of fruit. It's also providing two pieces of information, not just one.

Step 2: **Plan**. Since statement (1) is a lot less complex, start there.

Step 3: **Solve**. Statement (1) indicates the number of apples (16), but provides no information about bananas. There's no information in the question stem that can be used with the number of apples to determine the number of bananas, so this statement is not sufficient. Eliminate answers (A) and (D). So far, so good (you haven't hit the trap yet).

Here's where the trap closes: You now know that statement (1) gives you the number of apples. Look at statement (2): There are 28 pieces of fruit, and four more pieces are apples than bananas. That might not seem like enough information at first glance. So, your brain might immediately jump to combining with the first statement, and arriving at an answer of (C)…but you just fell into the C-Trap. Answer (C) is *not* the correct answer!

Evaluate statement (2) completely and on its own before you think about combining it with statement (1).

There are 28 pieces of fruit, and four more pieces are apples than bananas. Translate these pieces of information into math. Two different equations are hidden in this statement:

$$A + B = 28$$
$$A = B - 4$$

The second equation can be plugged into the first equation, resulting in a new equation with just a single variable, B. Then, you can solve for the number of bananas. (It's DS, though, so don't actually solve!)

The correct answer is (B): Statement (2) alone is sufficient to answer the question, but statement (1) alone is not.

The C-Trap occurs when you (mistakenly) think that you need *both* statements to answer the question, but it turns out that *just one* of those statements is enough all by itself. The text for answer (C) states that you have to use both pieces of information and that *neither one alone is sufficient*.

It is certainly true that, if you have both pieces of information, you can find the number of bananas—but you don't *need* both pieces together. Statement (2) will do the job by itself.

If you ever find yourself thinking, "Oh, it's *completely* obvious that using the two pieces of information together will get me to the answer," pause for a moment! This test isn't often super-obvious—so double-check. Ask yourself whether you might be falling for the C-Trap. It may be the case that one of the pieces of information is sufficient on its own.

Here's the second problem. Did you get (C) as your answer? If so, try it again right now:

> A concession stand sells chips, dip, pretzels, and soda. If Vikram buys either chips or a pretzel, he will buy a soda. If he does not buy chips, then he will not buy dip. Does Vikram buy chips?
>
> (1) Vikram buys exactly three different items from the concession stand.
> (2) Vikram buys at least a pretzel and a soda from the concession stand.

Step 1: **Understand**. It's a Yes/No question. Vikram has options; does he buy chips? According to the question stem:

- If he buys chips, then he'll buy a soda.
- If he buys a pretzel, then he'll buy a soda.
- If he does not buy chips, then he won't buy dip.

The negative wording of the third fact is hiding another meaning: If he *does* buy dip, then he must also buy chips. Why? Because if he didn't buy the chips, then he couldn't get the dip. You'll learn more about formal logic later in this book.

Step 2: **Plan**. The two statements each provide additional constraints, so plan to test cases to see whether you can get a definitive answer from the statements.

Step 3: **Solve**, starting with statement (1). On its face, statement (1) seems insufficient, since it doesn't mention any specific items to buy. It would be easy to move immediately to statement (2), thinking that you must have information about specific items to answer the question. *This is a trap*. Don't assume; test out the cases!

There are only four items total and Vikram has to buy three of them. There are not that many ways to buy exactly three out of four different items—each item can be left out only once. Pick any item and test out what happens when that item is included and when that item is not included.

Case 1: Vikram buys dip. Then he must buy chips. If he buys chips, he must buy soda. Since he buys these three items, he doesn't buy the fourth (a pretzel). So, this is the only possible case in which Vikram buys the dip.

Case 2: Vikram does not buy dip. He has to buy three items, so he must buy chips, a pretzel, and a soda. This is the only possible case in which Vikram does not buy dip.

Since there are two valid cases, is this statement not sufficient? *Here's another trap!* This problem has a Yes/No question: Did Vikram buy chips? In both possible cases, he did, so statement (1) is sufficient.

When testing cases, always finish each case with the explicit answer to the question asked:

Case 1: V buys dip, chips, and soda. Did he buy chips? Yes.

Case 2: V does not buy dip. He buys chips, a pretzel, and a soda. Did he buy chips? Yes.

No other cases are possible, so yes, Vikram definitely bought chips. Statement (1) is sufficient to answer the question; eliminate answers (B), (C), and (E).

Test cases again for statement (2): He buys *at least* a pretzel and a soda.

Case 1: Vikram only buys a pretzel and a soda. Did he buy chips? No.

Case 2: Vikram buys a pretzel, a soda, and chips. Does he buy chips? Yes.

One Yes and one No is a Maybe answer, so statement (2) is not sufficient to answer the question. Eliminate answer (D); the correct answer is (A).

If you overlook the fact that the first statement is sufficient on its own, you'll eventually get to the step of combining statements (1) and (2)—and you'll fall into the C-Trap. Vikram bought exactly three items and those items had to include at least a pretzel and a soda. Since Vikram got a soda, he also had to have bought chips, so using both statements, you'd know exactly what he bought. That seems sufficient—but that isn't what the question asked. The question merely wants to know whether he bought chips, and statement (1) is enough to tell you that.

The correct answer is (A): the first statement is sufficient but the second statement is not.

Avoid Statement Carryover

The Data Sufficiency process includes this step: Evaluate each statement individually before evaluating the two statements together.

The GMAT likes to set a certain trap that plays off of this step (and you may have already fallen for this trap). Take a look at this problem, which is similar to an earlier one in this guide:

> If Farai is twice as old as Dmitry, how old is Farai?
>
> (1) Samantha will be 11 years old in 5 years.
> (2) Samantha is 4 years younger than Dmitry.

The question asks how old F is and provides a relationship: $F = 2D$. The rephrased question is "What is F or D?" since the equation provides a direct relationship between the two variables.

Here's how the trap works. You can find S's age from statement (1), but that's not enough to get to D or F, so you cross off answers (A) and (D).

On to statement (2). Since you know how old S is, you can find D, and if you know D, you can find F's age! So the answer is (B).

The answer is actually *not* (B). What happened?

In the logic written above, when working on statement (2), you used the information about S's age, but that information is from statement (1). At this stage, you're required to evaluate each statement individually! You're not allowed to carry over information from one statement to the other (not right now, anyway).

This mistake is literally called the **Statement Carryover** trap. In the heat of the test, it's very easy to do this, even when you know that you're not supposed to—especially as the math becomes more complicated (and therefore distracting).

To help avoid this trap, use the T-diagram consistently when solving DS problems. When you are working on each statement, you are not allowed to "cross the vertical line" of the T. Keep the two statements completely separate. You can only look "up the T" and use the information on top of the horizontal line:

If you have eliminated answers (A), (B), and (D), you are *then* allowed to evaluate the two statements together. In this circumstance, put your scratch work below the two prior statements—and right below the "Do Not Cross" line. Now (and only now!), you're allowed to use the information from both statements at the same time.

Guessing Strategies

There are several strategies that can help you guess effectively. And these strategies can also help you to avoid certain traps or careless mistakes, even when you don't need to guess.

Situation 1: The Identical Twins. Two statements provide *exactly* the same information.

Here is an example:

> The unit cost of a certain product is an integer value that is a multiple of 4. (Blah blah distraction text, and then here's a question.)
>
> (1)   The unit cost is $8.
>
> (2)   The unit cost is between $5 and $10

The first statement contains a clear piece of information. But the second statement actually resolves to that same piece of information, too, once it's combined with the information from the question stem. The only multiple of 4 between $5 and $10 is $8. The statements are identical.

When the statements are identical, only two answers are possible. If the information in one statement is sufficient to answer the question, then that same information is also sufficient in the other statement. So, the correct answer is (D).

Alternatively, if the information in one statement is *not* sufficient to answer the question, then the second statement also won't be sufficient. Further, that second statement adds no *new* information to the first one, so even together, the statements are not sufficient. In this case, the answer must be (E).

If you see that the two statements are identical twins, immediately cross off answers (A), (B), and (C)—even if you are still working on the problem. That will forestall any careless mistakes. The answer must be either (D) or (E).

Situation 2: The Cannibal. One statement completely includes or incorporates the information given by the other.

Here is an example:

> (1) There are more than 20 computers in the lab.
> (2) The lab has between 80 and 142 computers.

The first statement indicates that the number of computers (let's call it C) is greater than 20. The second statement indicates that C is between 80 and 142.

If C is between 80 and 142, then C must be greater than 20. Statement (2) tells you everything that statement (1) told you (C is greater than 20), plus additional information (C is between 80 and 142). Statement (1) has been cannibalized by statement (2). Statement (2) includes everything that statement (1) gives you, plus statement (2) gives you additional information.

If Statement (1) has been cannibalized, then the answer cannot be (A), statement (1) alone, because statement (2) also provides that same piece of information. If the fact that C is greater than 20 is sufficient, then the answer must be (D): *Each* statement works alone.

The answer also cannot be (C). In order for answer (C) to be correct, each statement must contribute a *separate* piece of useful information (since neither statement works alone). In the example above, statement (1) doesn't provide any *new* information relative to statement (2), so the answer cannot be (C).

When statement (1) has been cannibalized, cross off answers (A) and (C).

Here is another example:

> (1) $x = 10$
> (2) x is even.

This time, statement (1) is the Cannibal: If you know that $x = 10$, then you already know that x is even. In this case, statement (2) gets cannibalized, so the answer cannot be (B) or (C).

If, at any point, you become aware that the information given in one statement is already 100% covered by the other statement, identify which statement provides *less* information. For example, statement (1) indicates both that x is even and that x equals 10, while statement (2) indicates only that x is even, so statement (2) provides less information. The statement that provides *less* information is the statement that gets cannibalized.

As soon as you determine which statement got cannibalized, immediately cross off two answers:

- If statement (1) gets cannibalized, cross off answers (A) and (C).
- If statement (2) gets cannibalized, cross off answers (B) and (C).

If you end up having to guess, you'll be down to just three answers. Of the three remaining answers, the best guess is the one associated with the Cannibal—either (A) or (B)—since that statement provides at least two pieces of relevant information.

Situation 3: You suspect a C-Trap.

If it seems very clear to you that using the two statements together would be sufficient—it would have been obvious when you were 12 and first learning this math!—then be on the lookout for a possible C-Trap. If you suspect there may be a C-Trap even though you can't figure out why or which statement does work alone, then don't guess answers (C) or (E).

Next, decide which of the two statements contains the more complicated information. This statement is the one more likely to work on its own (similar to the Cannibal), so choose the corresponding answer. For example, if statement (1) has the more complicated info, choose answer (A). If, on the other hand, statement (2) looks more complex, choose choice (B).

As you continue to work through the chapters in this book, you can also continue practicing DS via *GMAT Official Guide* problems (if you have that book). Start with lower-numbered problems first, in order to practice the process, and work your way up to more difficult problems as you gain expertise. (If you are in one of our study programs, your online syllabus already contains these types of assignments.)

3

Problem Set

As you solve each problem, focus on solidifying your DS process. Before you check your answers, review your work. Did you write down (and use) your answer grid? Did you look at each statement separately before looking at them together? Did you mix up or skip any of the steps of the process? You may want to rewrite your work before you review the answers.

The five answer choices for every problem are as follows. (Note: In future problem sets, the answer choices for DS problems will *not* be given.)

(A) Statement (1) ALONE is sufficient, but statement (2) alone is not sufficient

(B) Statement (2) ALONE is sufficient, but statement (1) alone is not sufficient

(C) BOTH statements TOGETHER are sufficient, but NEITHER statement ALONE is sufficient.

(D) EACH statement ALONE is sufficient.

(E) Statements (1) and (2) TOGETHER are NOT sufficient.

3

1. Lora purchased 2 pounds of apples and 1 pound of oranges for $7. What was the cost per pound of apples?

　　(1) The cost per pound of oranges was $3.

　　(2) Had Lora purchased one more pound of apples, she would have spent $9 in total.

2. If Val always carries at least one book in his backpack, how many books did he carry in his backpack today?

　　(1) The number of books Val carried in his backpack today was a multiple of 8.

　　(2) The number of books Val carried in his backpack today was less than 15.

3. Tino purchased three types of flowers—dahlias, sunflowers, and zinnias—to create a bouquet. On which of the three types of flowers for this bouquet did Tino spend the greatest amount of money?

　　(1) Half of the flowers in the bouquet were zinnias.

　　(2) The prices per flower for dahlias, sunflowers, and zinnias were in the ratio 3:2:4, respectively.

4. At a certain clothing store, a sweater, a jacket, and a hat cost $300 in total. What is the price of the sweater?

　　(1) The price of the jacket is the average of the prices of the sweater and the hat.

　　(2) The price of the sweater is the average of the prices of the jacket and the hat.

5. Along a stretch of highway running from east to west, there are four rest stops marked *A*, *B*, *C*, and *D*. Is rest stop *A* more than 5 miles to the west of rest stop *C* ?

    (1) Rest stop *A* is more than 5 miles to the west of rest stop *D*.

    (2) Rest stop *A* is more than 5 miles to the west of rest stop *B*.

6. A certain bag contains only red and blue marbles. Are there at least 25 red marbles in the bag?

    (1) Fewer than 40% of the marbles in the bag are red.

    (2) There are at least 90 marbles in the bag.

Solutions

1. **(D):** First, understand. This is a DS Value problem. The question stem provides a total cost for two pounds of apples and one pound of oranges and asks for the price of one pound of apples. What would you need to know in order to be able to find the one and only one value for that price?

    Plan. If you let A be the price of one pound of apples and O be the price of one pound of oranges, then the given information in the question stem can be translated into the equation $2A + O = 7$. You can find A if you know the value for O. Jot that down on your scratch paper. Also, statement (1) looks easier, so start there.

    (1) SUFFICIENT: If you know the value of O, then you can plug it into the equation given in the question stem to find the value of A. Eliminate answers (B), (C), and (E).

    (2) SUFFICIENT: The question stem provides one linear equation (no squares or similar complications). The statement can be translated into a different linear equation: $3A + O = 9$. You can use the two equations to solve for the individual values of the two variables. Eliminate answer (A). Alternatively, you could use logic. If Lora's original purchase totaled $7 and adding one more pound of apples would bring the total to $9, then the price of one pound of apples must be $2, the difference between those two totals.

    The correct answer is **(D):** Each statement works alone.

2. **(C):** First, understand. Let V be the number of books Val carried in his backpack today. The question stem indicates that $V \geq 1$; jot that down. Value question: What is the value of V?

    Plan. For each statement, look to see if multiple values for V are valid. If only one value is valid, the statement is sufficient.

    (1) INSUFFICIENT: V could be 8, but V could also be 16. Since there are two different answers, this statement is not sufficient; cross off answers (A) and (D).

    (2) INSUFFICIENT: V could be any value from 1 to 14. Since there are multiple different answers, this statement is not sufficient; cross off answer (B).

    (1) AND (2) SUFFICIENT: Return to the Plan step and remind yourself of the combined constraints. Positive integers only. Multiple of 8. Less than 15. What cases can you test?

    V could be 8, but the next multiple of 8 is 16...but this fails the constraint that $V < 15$. There's no other case to test; the only answer is 8, so together, the two statements work.

    The correct answer is **(C):** The two statements work together but neither one works alone.

3 **(C):** First, understand the question stem. This is a DS Choose One problem; the answer can be dahlias, sunflowers, or zinnias—whichever type of flower had the greatest total cost.

Plan. What will determine the total cost? For each flower type, the total cost will be the number of flowers of that type times the price per flower for that type. The question does not ask for the total cost itself, but you need to see which flower type has the greatest product of price per flower and number of flowers.

(1) INSUFFICIENT: This tells you nothing about the price per flower for any type. Eliminate answers (A) and (D).

(2) INSUFFICIENT: While this statement does tell you that zinnias were the most expensive per flower, it tells you nothing about the number of flowers of any type. Eliminate answer (B).

(1) AND (2) SUFFICIENT: You know that zinnias were the most expensive per flower and that there were more zinnias than either of the other two types of flowers (if half of the flowers were zinnias, then dahlias and sunflowers must each be less than half of the flowers). So, together the two statements tell you that Tino spent more money in total on zinnias than on either of the other two types of flowers.

The correct answer is **(C)**: Both statements together are sufficient, but neither one alone is sufficient.

4. **(B):** The question stem tells you that the total for all three items is $300, but asks you specifically for the price of the sweater. What else could you be given that would narrow down the price of the sweater to one value? If you know the combo price of a jacket and a hat, you could subtract that value from $300 to find the price of only the sweater. So the rephrased question is: What is the price of a jacket and a hat?

(1) INSUFFICIENT: It's possible that each of the three items costs $100. But it could also be the case that the jacket costs $100 and the prices of the sweater and hat just average $100, so, for example, the sweater could cost $50 and the hat could cost $150.

(2) SUFFICIENT: At first it may look like you have too many variables and too few equations, but try translating what you know into equations. Let S, J, and H be the prices of the sweater, jacket, and hat, respectively. The question stem indicates that $S + J + H = \$300$ and statement (2) could be translated as:

$$S = \frac{(J + H)}{2}$$
$$2S = J + H$$

Plug that simplified equation back into the given equation from the question stem to get:

$$S + 2S = 300$$
$$3S = 300$$
$$S = 100$$

So the correct answer is **(B)**: Statement (2) is sufficient, but statement (1) is not.

5. **(B):** When the GMAT provides a number line with a specific ordering of variables, you can assume that the variables do appear in that order on the line. In this case, A is farther west than the other three rest stops. It's a Yes/No question: Is A more than 5 miles west of C?

    (1) INSUFFICIENT: It's possible that A is 10 miles west of D and 6 miles west of C; in this case, Yes, A is more than 5 miles west of C. Alternatively, A could be 10 miles west of D but only 4 miles west of C; in this case, No, A is not more than 5 miles west of C.

    (2) SUFFICIENT: This statement is almost identical to the first one—so although you still generally want to ignore statement (1) at this point, do pay attention to the similarity. Statement (2) changes just one thing: Rest stop D becomes rest stop B. Look at the number line and compare what the two statements indicate: (1) says that the A-to-D distance is more than 5 miles and (2) says that the A-to-B distance is more than 5 miles.

    The distance from A to D is greater, so if the A-to-B distance is already more than 5 miles, then the A-to-D distance must be more than 5 miles as well. In other words, statement (2) is a Cannibal: It already fully incorporates statement (1). As a result, the answer cannot be either (A) or (C). Cross those off on your answer grid. (Answer (A) is already crossed off, but (C) isn't crossed off yet.)

    Now, process statement (2). The question asked about the A-to-C distance, which you know from the picture is greater than the A-to-B distance. If the A-to-B distance is more than 5 miles, then the A-to-C distance must be more than 5 miles as well.

    The correct answer is **(B):** Statement (2) is sufficient, but statement (1) is not.

6. **(E):** First, understand. There are only red and blue marbles in the bag—but there's no indication in the question stem as to the number of each color or the total number of marbles. The question is Yes/No: Is red ≥ 25?

    Glance at the statements. One contains a percent sign and one has a real number.

    Plan. Remind yourself of an important point on the GMAT when dealing with percents vs. real numbers. If you only know information about a percentage of something, you can't figure anything out about the real numbers associated with that something.

    (1) INSUFFICIENT: This statement provides information about the percentage of red marbles. Percentages alone cannot give you the real number. Eliminate answers (A) and (D).

    (2) INSUFFICIENT: This statement does provide a real number: There are 90 marbles total. But there could be only 1 red marble or 89 red marbles. This isn't enough to know whether at least 25 are red. Eliminate answer (B).

    (1) AND (2) INSUFFICIENT: The combined information is complicated; time to do a little calculation. Fewer than 40% of the marbles are red. There are at least 90 marbles total. To simplify testing cases, use 90 as the total for now. To find 40% of 90, take 10% and multiply by 4; 10% is 9, so 40% is $(9)(4) = 36$.

    Fewer than 36 marbles are red. There could be 35 red marbles, in which case the answer is Yes. But there could also be 20 red marbles, in which case the answer is No. Even together, the two statements aren't enough to solve.

    The correct answer is **(E):** Even together, the two statements aren't sufficient to answer the question.

Fractions and Ratios

In This Chapter...

- Ratio Labels

- Types of Fractions

- Numerator and Denominator Rules

- Simplifying Fractions and Ratios

- Simplify Before You Multiply

- Add and Subtract Fractions: Use a Common Denominator

- Dividing Fractions: Use the Reciprocal

- Split Up Double-Decker Fractions

- The Unknown Multiplier

- Comparing Fractions: The Double-Cross

- Multiple Ratios: Make a Common Term

- Complex Fractions: Don't Split the Denominator

- Relative Values and Data Sufficiency

In this chapter, you will learn the relationship between fractions and ratios and how to use either form to solve problems. You'll also learn all of the needed computation skills to manipulate fractions and ratios.

CHAPTER 4 Fractions and Ratios

Fractions are most often used to express numbers that fall in between integers. For example, the fraction $\frac{13}{2}$, which equals 6.5, falls between the integers 6 and 7:

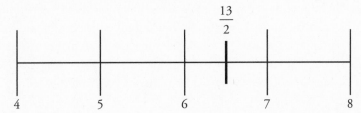

All fractions express what's called a **part-to-whole relationship**. The top number (the numerator) is the *part* and the bottom number (the denominator) is the *whole*. For example, if you eat 5 of the 8 slices in a pizza, you have eaten 5 parts out of 8 (the whole pizza), or $\frac{5}{8}$ of the pizza. You left $\frac{3}{8}$ of the pizza for your friend Sam.

Ratios, on the other hand, express what's called a **part-to-part relationship**. In the pizza example, you ate 5 parts and Sam ate 3 parts. The ratio of pizza that you ate to pizza that Sam ate is 5 to 3.

Something interesting happens here: Notice that the 5 and the 3 are the numerators of the two fractions from the prior paragraph. A ratio consists of all the parts of a whole—and you can actually create the whole by adding up the parts! In this case, $5 + 3 = 8$, which is the whole, or the denominator, of the fractions. When talking about ratios, this *whole* is called the **ratio total**.

You can convert any fraction to a ratio and vice versa. If a bouquet of flowers has 1 rose for every 3 tulips, then the ratio of roses to tulips is 1 : 3. The *whole* is $1 + 3 = 4$. Therefore, $\frac{1}{4}$ of the bouquet consists of roses and $\frac{3}{4}$ consists of tulips.

Ratios can be written in three different ways:

1. 1 to 3

2. 1 : 3

3. $\frac{1}{3}$

In the third case, you'll need to learn how to read the sentence to know whether it's talking about a fraction or a ratio. The following are examples of ratios:

- The ratio of dogs to cats is $\frac{3}{4}$.

- This bouquet contains $\frac{3}{4}$ as many roses as daisies. (For every 3 roses, there are 4 daisies.)

- For every 3 blue cars sold, there are 4 red cars sold. (The ratio of blue cars sold to red cars sold is 3 : 4.)

In the first example, the sentence outright tells you that the number that looks like a fraction is really a ratio. The second and third examples, though, make you interpret the information. In each case, the information conveyed is part-to-part. If you can write a sentence that fits the pattern "For every X of the first thing, there are Y of the second thing," then you know you have a ratio.

Fractions will always have two portions (with the *part* on top and the *whole* on the bottom), but ratios can have two or more portions. For example, you could have 2 horses to 3 rabbits to 7 llamas, or a ratio of 2 : 3 : 7.

Finally, fractions and ratios both express a *relationship* between two (or more, for ratios) items, but by themselves they do not tell you the exact quantities in question. For example, knowing that someone ate $\frac{1}{2}$ of a pizza does not indicate how many slices that person ate. If the pizza had 8 slices, then that person ate 4 of them, but if the pizza had 10 slices, then that person ate 5.

Similarly, knowing that the ratio of dogs to cats is 2 to 3 does *not* indicate the actual number of dogs and cats. There could be 2 dogs and 3 cats, or 6 dogs and 9 cats, or any other combination that works out to 2 dogs for every 3 cats. (Note: If the problem is talking about something that can't reasonably come in non-integer quantities, such as dogs and cats, then the problem is assuming what's called an *integer constraint*: Only integer values are allowed for the real number of dogs and cats.)

Ratio Labels

It's vital to jot down the order in which the ratio information is given. After all, "the ratio of dogs to cats is 2 : 3" is very different from "the ratio of dogs to cats is 3 : 2."

It is very easy to accidentally reverse the order of a ratio—especially on a timed test like the GMAT. In order to avoid these reversals, write units on either the ratio itself or on the variables you create, or on both.

Thus, if the ratio of dogs to cats is 2 : 3, you might write any of the below:

D : C 2 : 3	$\dfrac{D}{C} = \dfrac{2}{3}$	$\dfrac{2 \text{ dogs}}{3 \text{ cats}}$

However you choose to jot down this information, label the ratio on your scratch paper carefully—every time.

Types of Fractions

It's useful to know certain terms in order to study for the GMAT, but you don't need to memorize these names for the test. You just need to know that these different categories exist.

Proper fractions are those that fall between 0 and 1. In proper fractions, the numerator is always smaller than the denominator. For example:

$$\frac{1}{4}, \frac{1}{2}, \frac{2}{3}, \frac{7}{10}$$

Improper fractions are greater than or equal to 1. In improper fractions, the numerator is always greater than or equal to the denominator. For example:

$$\frac{5}{4}, \frac{13}{2}, \frac{11}{3}, \frac{101}{10}$$

An improper fraction can be rewritten as a mixed number (an integer and a proper fraction together). For example:

$$\frac{5}{4} = \frac{4}{4} + \frac{1}{4} = 1\frac{1}{4} \qquad\qquad \frac{11}{3} = \frac{9}{3} + \frac{2}{3} = 3\frac{2}{3}$$

Most of the time, you'd only need to convert to a mixed number at the end of the problem, in order to match the format of the answers. If you are still in the middle of the problem, don't convert to a mixed number unless you absolutely have to, because you can't use mixed numbers easily in normal math operations (e.g., multiplying by another number).

Numerator and Denominator Rules

In fractions, certain key rules govern the relationship between the **numerator** (the top number) and the **denominator** (the bottom number) of proper fractions. The following rules apply only to positive numbers.

If you increase the numerator of a fraction, while holding the denominator constant, the value increases:

$$\frac{1}{8} < \frac{2}{8} < \frac{3}{8} < \frac{4}{8} < \cdots$$

You are increasing the *part*, while keeping the *whole* constant. Increasing only the numerator is like eating more slices of the same pizza: You eat 1 out of 8 slices, then 2 out of 8 slices, and so on.

If you increase the denominator of a fraction, while holding the numerator constant, the value gets smaller and smaller as it approaches 0:

$$\frac{1}{2} > \frac{1}{3} > \frac{1}{4} > \frac{1}{5} \cdots > \frac{1}{1,000} \cdots \to 0$$

This time, you're increasing the *whole* but leaving the *part* constant. Imagine that you have one slice of a whole pizza and, magically, the rest of the pizza (but not your slice!) keeps getting bigger and bigger. Your one part (one slice) becomes a smaller and smaller portion of the entire pizza.

Pop quiz: Is $\frac{7}{13}$ a little greater or a little less than $\frac{7}{14}$, or 0.5? The denominator gets a little *smaller* in this example, not larger.

When you *increase* the denominator, the fraction gets *smaller*. So when you *decrease* the denominator, the opposite happens: The value of the fraction *increases* a little. Therefore, $\frac{7}{13}$ is a little greater than 0.5.

Finally, consider this lesser-known rule that the GMAT likes to employ (still for positive numbers only): Adding the exact same number to *both* the numerator and the denominator brings the fraction *closer* to 1, regardless of the fraction's value.

If the starting fraction is *less* than 1, the fraction gets closer to 1 (it *increases*) as you add the same number to the top and bottom:

$$\frac{1}{2} < \frac{1+1}{2+1}, \text{ or } \frac{1}{2} < \frac{2}{3}$$

$$\frac{2}{3} < \frac{2+9}{3+9}, \text{ or } \frac{2}{3} < \frac{11}{12}$$

$$\frac{11}{12} < \frac{11+988}{12+988}, \text{ or } \frac{11}{12} < \frac{999}{1,000}$$

$$\text{Thus: } \frac{1}{2} < \frac{2}{3} < \frac{11}{12} < \frac{999}{1,000} \cdots \to 1$$

And if the starting fraction is *greater* than 1, the fraction gets closer to 1 (it *decreases*) as you add the same number to the top and bottom:

$$\frac{3}{2} > \frac{3+1}{2+1}, \text{ or } \frac{3}{2} > \frac{4}{3}$$

$$\frac{4}{3} > \frac{4+9}{3+9}, \text{ or } \frac{4}{3} > \frac{13}{12}$$

$$\frac{13}{12} > \frac{13+988}{12+988}, \text{ or } \frac{13}{12} > \frac{1,001}{1,000}$$

Thus: $\frac{3}{2} > \frac{4}{3} > \frac{13}{12} > \frac{1,001}{1,000} \cdots \rightarrow 1$

Simplifying Fractions and Ratios

Simplifying a fraction is a way to express a fraction or ratio in its lowest terms. Answers in fraction or ratio form on the GMAT will always be presented in fully simplified terms. If you multiply or divide both the numerator and the denominator by the same number, you don't actually change the value of the fraction because you're multiplying or dividing by 1. You're always allowed to do this as long as you do the same thing to the top and bottom of the fraction, or to all parts of the ratio. For example:

Fraction:

$$\frac{24}{30} = \frac{24 \div 6}{30 \div 6} = \frac{4}{5}$$

Ratio:

$$4 : 12 : 16$$
$$\frac{4}{4} : \frac{12}{4} : \frac{16}{4}$$
$$1 : 3 : 4$$

You can simplify (or reduce) a fraction or ratio by dividing both the numerator and the denominator by any common factors until no common factors remain (either one at a time, or in a single step):

Two steps: $\dfrac{75}{45} = \dfrac{75 \div 5}{45 \div 5} = \dfrac{15}{9} = \dfrac{15 \div 3}{9 \div 3} = \dfrac{5}{3}$

One step: $\dfrac{75}{45} = \dfrac{75 \div 15}{45 \div 15} = \dfrac{5}{3}$

Simplify Before You Multiply

When multiplying fractions, you could first multiply the numerators together, then multiply the denominators together, and finally simplify the resulting product. For example:

$$\frac{8}{15} \times \frac{35}{72} = \frac{8(35)}{15(72)}$$

Next step? You don't have a calculator on the Quant section, so time to do long multiplication . . .

$$\frac{8(35)}{15(72)} = \frac{280}{\cdots}$$

Wait! Stop! Don't even do that first step. If the math is that annoying, pause and think about what else you could do. In this case, you'd eventually have to simplify that fraction, so why not do that first?

In general, always try to simplify before you multiply: Cancel common factors from the top and bottom of the fractions.

For example, the **8** in the numerator and the **72** in the denominator both have 8 as a factor. Thus, the 8 can be simplified to 1 and the 72 can be simplified to 9:

$$\frac{\overset{1}{\cancel{8}}}{15} \times \frac{35}{\underset{9}{\cancel{72}}}$$

It doesn't matter that the numbers appear in two different fractions. When multiplying fractions together, you can treat all of the numerators as one group and all of the denominators as another. You can cancel anything in the top group with anything in the bottom. (You can't do this when you're adding or subtracting two fractions—just when you're multiplying.)

What next? The **35** and **15** both have 5 as a factor, so simplify those two numbers as well:

$$\frac{\overset{1}{\cancel{8}}}{\underset{3}{\cancel{15}}} \times \frac{\overset{7}{\cancel{35}}}{\underset{9}{\cancel{72}}} = \frac{1(7)}{3(9)} = \frac{7}{27}$$

Make your life easier: Always simplify before you multiply! These numbers are a lot nicer than what you would have gotten by multiplying first.

Add and Subtract Fractions: Use a Common Denominator

If you're asked to add or subtract fractions, first consider whether it would be better to convert to percents or decimals instead. If you see common conversions that you have memorized, it's likely going to be easier to convert from fractions to percents or decimals first.

If you do decide to add or subtract in fraction form, follow these steps:

1. Find a common denominator.

2. Rewrite each fraction so that it is expressed using this common denominator.

3. Add up the numerators only.

Here's an example:

$$\frac{3}{8} + \frac{7}{12}$$

$$\frac{9}{24} + \frac{14}{24}$$ A common denominator is 24. Thus, $\frac{3}{8} = \frac{9}{24}$ and $\frac{7}{12} = \frac{14}{24}$.

$$\frac{9}{24} + \frac{14}{24} = \frac{23}{24}$$ Finally, add the numerators to find the answer.

Why don't you also add up the denominators? Think back to the pizza you shared with your friend Sam at the beginning of this chapter. You ate 5 of the 8 slices, or $\frac{5}{8}$ of the pizza, and Sam ate 3 of the 8 slices, or $\frac{3}{8}$ of the pizza. Together, you ate $\frac{8}{8}$ of the pizza—that is, the whole thing!—not $\frac{8}{16}$, or half of the pizza.

In this example, you have to simplify the fraction at the end:

$$\frac{11}{15} - \frac{7}{30}$$

$$\frac{22}{30} - \frac{7}{30}$$ A common denominator is 30: $\frac{11}{15} = \frac{22}{30}$. Leave $\frac{7}{30}$ the same.

$$\frac{22}{30} - \frac{7}{30} = \frac{15}{30}$$ Subtract the numerators.

$$\frac{15}{30} = \frac{1}{2}$$ Simplify $\frac{15}{30}$ to find the answer: $\frac{1}{2}$.

Dividing Fractions: Use the Reciprocal

What if you're asked to do the following math?

$$\frac{1}{2} \div \frac{3}{4}$$

If you're asked to divide by a fraction (in this case, you're asked to divide by $\frac{3}{4}$), instead multiply by the reciprocal. The reciprocal of a fraction is the *flip* of that fraction. For example:

The reciprocal of $\frac{3}{4}$ is $\frac{4}{3}$.   The reciprocal of $\frac{2}{9}$ is $\frac{9}{2}$.

What is the reciprocal of an integer? Think of an integer as a fraction with a denominator of 1. For example, the integer 5 is the fraction $\frac{5}{1}$. To find the reciprocal, flip it:

The reciprocal of 5, or $\frac{5}{1}$, is $\frac{1}{5}$.   The reciprocal of 8 is $\frac{1}{8}$.

In order to divide by a fraction, follow these steps:

1. Change the divisor (the second number) into its reciprocal.

2. Multiply the fractions.

For example:

$$\frac{1}{2} \div \frac{3}{4}$$ First, change the divisor $\frac{3}{4}$ into its reciprocal $\frac{4}{3}$.

$$\frac{1}{2} \times \frac{4}{3}$$ Rewrite the problem as multiplication.

$$\frac{1}{2} \times \frac{\cancel{4}^{2}}{3} = \frac{2}{3}$$ Solve. Simplify before you multiply!

Split Up Double-Decker Fractions

The division of fractions can be shown by putting the fractions themselves into a **double-decker fraction**. Consider one of the previous examples:

$\frac{1}{2} \div \frac{3}{4}$ can also be written as a double-decker fraction this way: $\dfrac{\frac{1}{2}}{\frac{3}{4}}$

You can rewrite this as the top fraction divided by the bottom fraction. Then, solve normally by using the reciprocal of the second fraction and then multiplying:

$$\frac{\frac{1}{2}}{\frac{3}{4}} = \frac{1}{2} \div \frac{3}{4} = \frac{1}{\cancel{2}} \times \frac{\cancel{4}^{2}}{3} = \frac{2}{3}$$

In addition, you can often simplify more quickly by multiplying both top and bottom by a common denominator of the "fractions within the fraction":

$$\frac{\frac{1}{2}}{\frac{3}{4}} = \frac{\frac{1}{2} \times 4}{\frac{3}{4} \times 4} = \frac{2}{3}$$

In this case, the common denominator of 2 and 4 is 4, so multiply both the top and bottom by 4 to make the fractions within the fraction drop out.

The Unknown Multiplier

You've already learned that if you multiply the top and the bottom of a fraction by the same number, you will end up with an equivalent fraction. For example:

$$\frac{4}{7} = \frac{8}{14} = \frac{12}{21}$$

A ratio is equivalent to the most-reduced fraction, $\frac{4}{7}$, in the above example. For example, you might be told that there are 4 dogs for every 7 cats. That ratio doesn't (necessarily) tell you the actual number of dogs and cats, though. You could have exactly 4 dogs and 7 cats, but you could also have 8 dogs and 14 cats, or 12 dogs and 21 cats, and so on.

The $\frac{8}{14}$ fraction is the result of multiplying the top and bottom of the base ratio, $\frac{4}{7}$, by 2.

The $\frac{12}{21}$ fraction is the result of multiplying the base ratio by 3.

The number by which you multiply the ratio to find the actual number of things is called the **unknown multiplier**. Every ratio has an unknown multiplier, and that multiplier is the same for every part of the ratio.

Recall from earlier in this chapter that every ratio has a ratio total, calculated by adding up the parts of the ratio.

If the ratio of dogs to cats is 4 to 7, and there are 8 actual dogs, what else can you figure out? Lay out the information in a table—and always include the ratio total as one column in the table:

	Part	Part	Whole
	Dogs	Cats	Total
Ratio	4	7	
Multiplier			
Actual	8		

The multiplier for dogs must be $\frac{8}{4} = 2$. Since the multiplier is always the same for all parts of a ratio, write 2 in all of the multiplier boxes. (Note: The multiplier needs to be an integer for this problem, because you must have whole numbers of dogs and cats.)

	Dogs		Cats		Total
Ratio	4	+	7	=	11
	×		×		
Multiplier	**2**	=	**2**	=	**2**
	=		=		
Actual	8	+		=	

Now, you can determine that there are 14 cats. You can even calculate the total number of animals, either by adding dogs and cats ($8 + 14 = 22$) or by multiplying the ratio total ($4 + 7 = 11$) by the multiplier, 2.

If you know the ratio and you know any one of the actual values, then you can calculate everything in the table.

Try this problem:

A display holds 56 devices, all of which are either phones or tablets. If the ratio of phones to tablets is 3 : 4, how many of the devices in the display are phones?

Draw a table and begin to fill it in:

	Phones	Tablets	Total
Ratio	3	4	
Multiplier			
Actual	⬭		56

Add the top row to obtain a total of 7. The ratio of phones to tablets to total is $3 : 4 : 7$. The multiplier for the total is $\frac{56}{7} = 8$, so 8 is the multiplier across the board.

	Phones	Tablets	Total
Ratio	3	4	7
Multiplier	8	8	8
Actual	(24)		56

There are $3 \times 8 = 24$ phones in the display. (Again, the multiplier must be an integer for this problem.)

If you prefer, you can also solve algebraically. Call the unknown multiplier x. The ratio is $3 : 4$ and the actual numbers of phones and tablets are $3x$ and $4x$, respectively.

The problem indicates that the total number of devices equals 56:

$$\text{Phones} + \text{Tablets} = \text{Total}$$
$$3x + 4x = 56$$
$$7x = 56$$
$$x = 8$$

Plug the multiplier into the expression for phones ($3x$) to determine how many phones are in the display: $(3)(8) = 24$. There are 24 phones in the display.

The unknown multiplier is particularly useful with three-part ratios. For example:

A recipe calls for amounts of lemon juice, orange juice, and water in the ratio of $2 : 5 : 7$. If the mixture yields 35 milliliters of liquid, how much orange juice was included?

First, set up the given information, including the total for the base ratio:

	L	O	W	Tot
R	2	5	7	14
M				
A		( )		35

Next, begin calculating what you need in order to find the value for the Orange-Actual cell. Compare the actual total to the ratio total to find the multiplier.

	L	O	W	Tot
R	2	5	7	14
M		2.5		2.5
A		(12.5)		35

In this problem, the unknown multiplier turns out not to be an integer. This result is fine, though, because the problem deals with continuous quantities (milliliters of liquids).

Here's how to set up the problem algebraically:

$$\text{Lemon} + \text{Orange} + \text{Water} = \text{Total}$$
$$2x \quad + \quad 5x \quad + \quad 7x \; = 14x$$

Now, solve: $14x = 35$, or $x = 2.5$. Thus, the amount of orange juice is $5x = 5(2.5) = 12.5$ milliliters.

Comparing Fractions: The Double-Cross

Which fraction is greater, $\frac{7}{9}$ or $\frac{4}{5}$?

The traditional method for comparing fractions involves finding a common denominator and comparing the two fractions. The common denominator of 9 and 5 is 45.

Thus, $\frac{7}{9} = \frac{35}{45}$ and $\frac{4}{5} = \frac{36}{45}$. In this case, $\frac{4}{5}$ is slightly greater than $\frac{7}{9}$.

Why? Because the numerator 36 is greater than the numerator 35. Once you find a common denominator, the only thing you need to compare is the numerator—so take advantage of that fact to make the work go faster:

$(7 \times 5) = 35 \qquad (4 \times 9) = 36$

$$\frac{7}{9} \diagup\!\!\!\!\diagdown \frac{4}{5}$$

Set up the fractions next to each other. Multiply the numbers across the arrows and put each answer by the corresponding numerator (*not* the denominator!).

$$35 < 36$$
$$\frac{7}{9} < \frac{4}{5}$$

Since 35 is less than 36, the first fraction must be less than the second one.

Essentially, you have done the same thing as before—you just didn't bother to write down the common denominator of 45. This process can save you time when comparing fractions on the GMAT.

You can even use the double-cross method to add or subtract fractions, with one more step: Draw a third arrow straight across the bottom. All three arrows mean *multiply*. For example:

$$\frac{7}{9} + \frac{4}{5}$$

$$+$$

$$\frac{7}{9} \diagup\!\!\!\!\diagdown \frac{4}{5}$$

$(7)(5) = 35 \qquad \frac{7}{9} \diagup\!\!\!\!\diagdown \frac{4}{5} \qquad (9)(4) = 36$

$(9)(5) = 45$

$$35 \;\; \frac{7}{9} \diagup\!\!\!\!\diagdown \frac{4}{5} \;\; 36 = \frac{71}{45}$$

Essentially, multiply across all three arrows, as shown. Add the two results for the numerators (or subtract, if the problem asks you to subtract). For the denominator, just use the single number from the bottom multiplication.

Since this method involves multiplying, check the numbers before you start. If they're too large and annoying, you might want to use the traditional method for finding a common denominator.

Multiple Ratios: Make a Common Term

You may encounter two separate ratios containing a common element (e.g., dogs to cats and cats to birds). To combine the ratios, you can use a process remarkably similar to creating a common denominator for fractions.

Consider the following problem:

> In a box containing action figures from Game of Thrones, there are 3 figures of Arya for every 2 figures of Brienne, and 5 figures of Arya for every 4 figures of Daenerys. What is the ratio of Daenerys figures to Brienne figures?

Jot down the given info as you try to understand the story:

$$A : B \qquad A : D$$
$$3 : 2 \qquad 5 : 4$$

The question asks for the ratio of D to B, but neither of the given ratios contains both of these variables. What now?

Just as you can change *fractions* to have common *denominators*, you can change ratios so that the common *terms* correspond to the same quantity. Once you do this, you can put everything together in one big three-part ratio.

The two ratios have Arya in common, but the two values for Arya are different. In order to combine the two ratios, the values for Arya must be the same.

$A : B : D$		$A : B : D$
$3 : 2 : ?$	$\rightarrow$ Multiply by 5 $\rightarrow$	$15 : 10 : ?$
$5 : ? : 4$	$\rightarrow$ Multiply by 3 $\rightarrow$	$15 : ? : 12$
	This is the combined ratio:	$\boxed{15 : 10 : 12}$

Once the A's are the same (15), combine the two ratios into one big three-part ratio. Note: Do not add the two A's together. Just use the base number, 15.

Now, answer the question. Pull out just the parts that you are asked for: D and B. The ratio D to B is 12 to 10, which simplifies to 6 to 5.

Try this same problem but with a different question:

> In a box containing action figures from Game of Thrones, there are 3 figures of Arya for every 2 figures of Brienne, and 5 figures of Arya for every 4 figures of Daenerys. What is the least number of action figures that could be in the box?

First, you still want to combine the two separate ratios into one big ratio, as you did for the first version of the problem. So $A : B : D$ is $15 : 10 : 12$.

Next, what could the *actual* number of action figures be, not just the ratio? The actual values for the action figures are the ratio numbers multiplied by an unknown multiplier (which must be a positive integer, since you need whole action figures). The question asks for the *least* number of action figures, so use the least possible multiplier, 1. In other words, the ratio itself represents the least number of action figures.

Therefore, the least possible number of action figures is $15 + 10 + 12 = 37$.

Complex Fractions: Don't Split the Denominator

A complex fraction is a fraction in which there is a sum or a difference in the numerator or the denominator. For example:

$$\frac{x + y}{z}$$

When simplifying fractions that incorporate sums or differences, remember this rule: You may split up the terms of the numerator, but you may *never* split the terms of the denominator.

For example, you can add up the two terms in the numerator in this example, but you may decide it's easier to split it into two fractions first and add after:

$$\frac{480 + 165}{10} = \frac{480}{10} + \frac{165}{10} = 48 + 16.5 = 64.5$$

By contrast, the terms in this example may *not* be split:

$$\frac{5}{15 + 10} \neq \frac{5}{15} + \frac{5}{10} \quad \textbf{NO!}$$

Instead, simplify the denominator first:

$$\frac{5}{15 + 10} = \frac{5}{25} = \frac{1}{5}$$

Often, GMAT problems will involve complex fractions with variables. On these problems, it is tempting to split the denominator. Do not fall for it!

$$\frac{5x - 2y}{x - y} \neq \frac{5x}{x} - \frac{2y}{y} \quad \textbf{NO!}$$

Unfortunately, $\frac{5x - 2y}{x - y}$ cannot be simplified further, because neither of the terms in the numerator shares a factor with the entire denominator.

On the other hand, the expression $\frac{6x - 10}{10}$ can be simplified by splitting the numerator. Both terms in the numerator share a factor with the denominator, and by splitting into two fractions, you can write each part in simplified form:

$$\frac{6x - 10}{10} = \frac{6x}{10} - \frac{10}{10} = \frac{3}{5}x - 1$$

Relative Values and Data Sufficiency

Some problems will give you concrete values, while others will provide only relative values:

Concrete values are actual amounts (number of tickets sold, liters of water, etc.).

Relative values relate two quantities using fractions, ratios, percents, or decimals (twice as many, ratio of 2 : 3, 60% less, etc.).

Try this Data Sufficiency problem:

A company sells only two kinds of pie: apple pie and cherry pie. What fraction of the total pies sold last month were apple pies?

(1)   The company sold 460 pies last month.

(2)   The company sold 30% more cherry pies than apple pies last month.

When a question asks for a relative value, not a concrete or actual value, you don't need as much information in order to solve.

The question asks what fraction of the total pies sold were apple pies:

$$\frac{\text{apple pies}}{\text{total pies}} = ? \quad \text{or} \quad \frac{a}{a+c} = ?$$

Statement (1) indicates that the total number of pies sold was 460, so $a + c = 460$:

$$\frac{a}{460} = ?$$

The value of a is still unknown, so this statement is not sufficient. Eliminate answer choices (A) and (D).

Statement (2) indicates that the company sold 30% more cherry pies than apple pies; in other words, the number of cherry pies sold was 130% of the number of apple pies sold:

$$1.3a = c$$

On the surface, this may not seem like enough information. But watch what happens when you replace c with $1.3a$ in the rephrased question.

$$\frac{a}{a+c} = ?$$

$$\frac{a}{a + 1.3a} = ?$$

$$\frac{\cancel{a}}{2.3\cancel{a}} = \frac{1}{2.3}$$

The a variables drop out. Statement (2) actually does provide enough information to find the value of the fraction. The correct answer is (B).

How could you recognize that statement (2) is sufficient without having to do that algebra?

This DS question stem was asking for a relative value (*What* fraction *of the total pies . . .*). Relative values are really just ratios in disguise. The ratio in this question is as follows:

apple pies sold : cherry pies sold : total pies sold

The question asks for the ratio of apple pies sold to total pies sold, or apple : total. Statement (2) provides the ratio of apple pies sold to cherry pies sold. You could write it this way:

a : c
10 : 13

The number 13 is 30% greater than the number 10, so this ratio fits the given information. And, if you know the two parts of the ratio, then you can find the ratio total:

a : c : t
10 : 13 : 23

As a result, the ratio of apple pies to total pies (a : t) is 10 : 23. Statement (2) is sufficient to answer the question.

If you know a ratio, you can find a fraction using the ratio total. For example, 10 out of 23 total pies are apple, so the fraction of apple pies is $\frac{10}{23}$.

Also note that, although statement (2) allows you to determine the *relative* value, it does not provide enough information to calculate the *actual* number of pies. If the question had asked for a concrete number, such as the number of apple pies, you would have needed to use both statements to solve.

4

Problem Set

Note: On Quant problems, the GMAT will always provide exactly five answer choices. In this guide, however, you will sometimes encounter multiple-choice problems with fewer than five answer choices.

For problems 1–5, decide whether the given operation will cause the original value to **increase**, **decrease**, or **stay the same**.

1. Multiply the numerator of a positive fraction by $\frac{3}{2}$.

2. Add 1 to the numerator of a positive fraction and subtract 1 from its denominator.

3. Multiply both the numerator and denominator of a positive fraction by $3\frac{1}{2}$.

4. Multiply a positive fraction by $\frac{3}{8}$.

5. Divide a positive fraction by $\frac{3}{13}$.

For problems 6–10, assume that all variables do not equal 0.

6. If $48 : 2x$ is equivalent to $144 : 600$, what is x?

7. Simplify: $\dfrac{8(3)(x)^2(3)}{6x}$

8. Simplify: $\dfrac{\frac{3}{5}+\frac{1}{3}}{\frac{2}{3}+\frac{2}{5}}$

9. Simplify: $\dfrac{12ab^3 - 5a^2b}{3ab}$

10. Initially, the markers and pens in a drawer were in the ratio of 5 : 7. Then, 6 pens were removed. If there are 35 markers in the drawer, how many pens are left?

    (A) 29
    (B) 43
    (C) 49

Save the problem set below for review after you finish this entire guide.

11. Which of the following fractions has a value between $\frac{3}{5}$ and $\frac{2}{3}$?

    (A) $\dfrac{9}{14}$

    (B) $\dfrac{8}{18}$

    (C) $\dfrac{16}{21}$

12. A cleaning solution mixture calls for a ratio of 1 part bleach for every 4 parts water. When mixing the solution, Aki made a mistake and mixed in half as much bleach as was required by the ratio. The total solution consisted of 27 milliliters. How much bleach did Aki put into the solution, in milliliters?

    (A) 3

    (B) 4

    (C) 6

13. The amount of time that three people worked on a certain project was in the ratio of 2 : 3 : 5. If the project took 110 hours, what is the difference between the number of hours worked by the person who worked for the longest time and the person who worked for the shortest time?

    (A) 22

    (B) 33

    (C) 55

14. DS Challenge! Every game of chess that Artem played this month resulted in a win, a loss, or a tie. What fraction of the chess games that Artem played this month did he win?

    (1) The number of games that resulted in a tie was $\frac{1}{4}$ of the number of games that Artem won.

    (2) Artem lost $\frac{2}{5}$ of the games.

Solutions

1. **Increase:** Multiplying the numerator of a positive fraction by a number greater than 1 increases the numerator. As the numerator of a positive fraction increases, its value increases.

2. **Increase:** As the numerator of a positive fraction increases, the value of the fraction increases. As the denominator of a positive fraction decreases, the value of the fraction also increases. Both actions will work to increase the value of the fraction.

3. **Stay the same:** Multiplying or dividing the numerator and denominator of a fraction by the same number is equivalent to multiplying by 1, so doing this will not change the value of the fraction.

4. **Decrease:** Multiplying any positive number by a positive, proper fraction (a fraction between 0 and 1) decreases the number.

5. **Increase:** Dividing a positive number by a positive, proper fraction (a fraction between 0 and 1) increases the number.

6. **100:** Consider the first given, $48 : 2x$, the ratio, and the second given, $144 : 600$, the actual. Put the info in a ratio table and find the multiplier:

	Part 1	Part 2
R	48	2x
M		
A	144	600

Try some numbers to see what you'd need to multiply 48 by to get to 144. How about 48×2? Not enough; that's only 96. What about 48×3? Because $50 \times 3 = 150$, the value of 48×3 has to be 6 less... Yes, that's 144! Plug the info into the table and solve for x:

	Part 1	Part 2
R	48	2x
M	3	3
A	144	600

For the second part, the ratio number times the multiplier gives the actual value: $(2x)(3) = 600$, so $x = 100$.

7. **12x:** First, cancel terms in both the numerator and the denominator. Then, combine terms:

$$\frac{8(3)\,(x)^2(3)}{6x}$$

$$= \frac{8(\overset{1}{\cancel{3}})\,(x)^2(3)}{\underset{2}{\cancel{6}}x}$$

$$= \frac{\overset{4}{\cancel{8}}\,(x)^2(3)}{\underset{1}{\cancel{2}}x}$$

$$= \frac{4\,(x)^{\cancel{2}}(3)}{\cancel{x}}$$

$$= 4(x)(3)$$

$$= 12x$$

8. $\dfrac{7}{8}$: To get rid of the fractions within fractions, first find the common denominator of all the fractions within fractions. The denominators are all 5 or 3, so the common denominator is 15. Next, multiply everything by the fraction $\dfrac{15}{15}$:

$$\left(\frac{\frac{3}{5}+\frac{1}{3}}{\frac{2}{3}+\frac{2}{5}}\right)\left(\frac{15}{15}\right) = \frac{9+5}{10+6} = \frac{14}{16} = \frac{7}{8}$$

Alternatively, add the fractions in the numerator and denominator:

$$\frac{\frac{14}{15}}{\frac{16}{15}} = \frac{\overset{7}{\cancel{14}}}{\underset{1}{\cancel{15}}} \times \frac{\overset{1}{\cancel{15}}}{\underset{8}{\cancel{16}}} = \frac{7}{8}$$

9. $4b^2 - \dfrac{5}{3}a$: Split the numerator. Then, cancel terms in both the numerator and denominator:

$$\frac{12ab^3 - 5a^2b}{3ab} = \frac{12ab^3}{3ab} - \frac{5a^2b}{3ab} = 4b^2 - \frac{5}{3}a$$

10. **(B) 43:** Find the unknown multiplier, then use it to calculate the initial number of pens in the drawer. Include the Total column when you make the table, but only use it if the problem requires you to. (Note: The given information is shown in bold; the calculated information is not bold.)

	M	P	Total
R	5	7	
M	7	7	
A	35	49	

There were initially 49 pens in the drawer but 6 were removed, so 43 pens remain.

11. **(A)** $\frac{9}{14}$**:** The two starting fractions are both on the "common conversions" list, so consider converting to percentages or decimals:

$$\frac{3}{5} = 0.6 = 60\% \text{ and } \frac{2}{3} = 0.6\overline{6} = 66\frac{2}{3}\%$$

Take a look at the answers. Are there any that are well below or above that range?

Answer (B), $\frac{8}{18}$, is less than 0.5 (since $\frac{9}{18}$ is 0.5), so eliminate this answer. What about the other two?

Answer (C), $\frac{16}{21}$, is close to $\frac{15}{20}$, which is 0.75. But is $\frac{16}{21}$ greater than or less than 0.75? In order to go from $\frac{15}{20}$ to $\frac{16}{21}$, you have to add 1 to both the numerator and denominator. If you start with a positive fraction less than 1 and add the same positive number to both the top and bottom, the fraction will get closer to 1—that is, it will increase. Therefore, $\frac{16}{21}$ must be greater than 0.75. It cannot be correct; the only answer remaining is **(A)**.

12. **(A) 3 mL:** The proper ratio of bleach to water is 1 : 4. However, Aki accidentally put in half as much bleach as the ratio called for. Sketch out the given info in a ratio box and think about how to proceed:

	B	W	Total
R	orig: 1 oops: 0.5	4	
M			
A	?		27

The actual ratio Aki used was 0.5 : 4, and the total volume of the mixture was 27 milliliters. This would be a lot easier to solve if you knew the unknown multiplier or if you knew how much bleach or water Aki actually used. In fact, you (sort of) do: The answer choices represent three possible values for the amount of bleach used. Work backwards!

If Aki used 4 milliliters of bleach, then the mixture would have had 23 milliliters of water (since the whole thing is 27 mL). The ratio, then, would be 4 : 23. Does that reduce to a ratio of 0.5 : 4?

$$4 : 23 \rightarrow 0.5 : \frac{23}{8}$$

Divide 4 by 8 to get 0.5. Do the same thing to the 23. Nope, that value is not 4. Eliminate answer (B).

Is that answer too big or too small? $\frac{23}{8}$ is just a bit smaller than $\frac{24}{8}$, or 3. But the water part of the ratio is supposed to be 4, not 3, so there isn't enough water in this mixture. In order for more of the 27 milliliters of mixture to be water, you need less bleach, so the answer must be the smaller number, 3 milliliters.

If you're not sure, you can check (but don't do more math than you need to do!). If Aki used 3 milliliters of bleach, then the mixture contained $27 - 3 = 24$ milliliters of water. The ratio 3 : 24 does reduce to the ratio 0.5 : 4.

13. **(B) 33:** The ratio is $2 : 3 : 5$. Call x the unknown multiplier, so the actual number of hours for each person are $2x$, $3x$, and $5x$. Use this to set up an equation and solve for x:

$$2x + 3x + 5x = 110$$
$$10x = 110$$
$$x = 11$$

Therefore, the person who worked for the longest time put in $5(11) = 55$ hours, and the person who worked for the shortest time put in $2(11) = 22$ hours. This represents a difference of $55 - 22 = 33$ hours.

14. **(C):** There are three possible outcomes for each game: W, L, or T. The question asks for the fraction of games won, or $\dfrac{W}{W + L + T}$. Note that the question is asking for a relative value, not the actual numbers involved; it may be possible to find this fraction without knowing the actual number of wins and the total number of games.

The first statement mentions both ties and wins, while the second mentions only losses. Since the second statement is less complex, start there and write $\begin{smallmatrix}BD\\ACE\end{smallmatrix}$ on your scratch paper.

(2) INSUFFICIENT: Artem lost 2 out of every 5 games. At most, then, Artem won 3 out of every 5 games, but he could have won fewer. All you can tell for sure is that Artem won or tied 3 out of 5 games. Eliminate answers (B) and (D).

(1) INSUFFICIENT: This statement can be interpreted as a ratio. For every 1 game tied, Artem won 4 games. The ratio of ties to wins is $1 : 4$. No information is given about losses, however, so this information is not enough to determine the fraction of games won out of the total number of games. Eliminate answer (A).

(1) AND (2) SUFFICIENT: Set up a partial ratio box. Since the question asks for a fraction and never provides real numbers, you only need the first row (the Ratio row). The ratio of $T : W$ is $1 : 4$.

	T	W	L	Total
R	1	4	L	$5 + L$

The second statement indicates that L represents 2 parts out of a total of 5 parts. That information is the equivalent of providing a second equation so that you can solve for the two unknowns (L and the ratio total). If you like, you can just memorize the idea that if there is only one unknown part of the ratio (L in this case) *and* you're also told the relationship between that unknown and the ratio total, then you can always find the relationship between any of the three individual parts and the total. If you want to understand why this is true, read on (understanding why may help you to remember this fact).

Statement (2) can be written algebraically as $\dfrac{L}{Total} = \dfrac{2}{5}$. The ratio box indicates that the total is $5 + L$. You can substitute that into the statement (2) equation to solve for the L part of the ratio. (This is DS, so don't actually solve. Just know that you can.) If you know the ratio value of L, you know all three parts of the ratio, so you can find $\dfrac{W}{W + L + T}$.

The correct answer is **(C):** Both statements together are sufficient, but neither one works alone.

Strategy: Estimation

In This Chapter...

- How to Estimate

- When to Estimate

- Using Benchmarks to Estimate

In this chapter, you will learn how to identify when to estimate on the GMAT, as well as how to stay within reasonable bounds and minimize errors in your estimations. For the rest of this book, keep an eye out for opportunities to estimate!

CHAPTER 5 Strategy: Estimation

You can estimate your way to an answer on problems with certain characteristics. Try these two problems:

1. $\frac{7}{13} + \frac{5}{11}$ is approximately equal to

    (A) 0

    (B) 1

    (C) 2

2. Of 450 employees at a company, 20% are managers and the rest are not managers. If 60% of the managers work in the engineering department, how many managers do not work in the engineering department?

    (A) 36

    (B) 54

    (C) 90

    (D) 180

    (E) 216

Before you look at the solutions in the next section, try to figure out how you would recognize that you *can* estimate on these two problems.

How to Estimate

As in the previous chapters, this chapter will follow the UPS process:

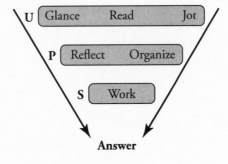

Step 1: **Understand**. Glance at the problem. First, what kind of problem is it? Since it's Problem Solving (PS), glance at the answers. The first one has whole, "easy" values in the answers.

1. $\frac{7}{13} + \frac{5}{11}$ is approximately equal to

   (A) 0

   (B) 1

   (C) 2

Then, read the problem. This problem contains the word *approximately*. It's literally telling you to estimate! When you see this kind of language, do not even try to do exact calculations. Take the problem at its word and estimate. Also, jot down the given expression.

Step 2: **Plan**. First, converting to common denominators here would be pretty annoying, as would converting the fractions to decimals or percents. Second, it's telling you to estimate and the answers are 0, 1, and 2. So, here's the plan: Round the annoying fractions to easier ones and estimate whether the sum is closest to 0, 1, or 2.

Step 3: **Solve**. $\frac{7}{13}$ is very close to $\frac{7}{14}$, or $\frac{1}{2}$, so call that first fraction 0.5.

Note that $\frac{7}{13}$ is a little *greater* than $\frac{7}{14}$ because increasing only the denominator makes a positive fraction smaller. In other words, you rounded down, so your answer will be a little too small. The next time you need to estimate, if possible, round up so that you are minimizing the amount of error that you introduce.

Since $\frac{5}{11}$ is a little bit less than $\frac{1}{2}$, you can round up this time. Call the second fraction 0.5 as well.

The approximate sum is $0.5 + 0.5 = 1$, so the answer is (B).

2. Of 450 employees at a company, 20% are managers and the rest are not managers. If 60% of the managers work in the engineering department, how many managers do not work in the engineering department?

   (A) 36

   (B) 54

   (C) 90

   (D) 180

   (E) 216

The second problem doesn't say that you can estimate; nevertheless, it contains an important clue that points toward estimation.

In the **Understand** step, your first task is to glance at the problem:

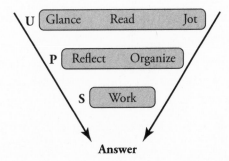

On all problems, get in the habit of glancing at the answers, too. In this case, the answers are pretty far apart. When that's true, you can often estimate. (Note that sometimes the numbers only need to be far apart in relative terms—in the first problem, the numbers are only 1 apart, but 2 is twice as big as 1, and there's a big relative difference between 1 and 0.)

Step 1: **Understand**. The answers are decently far apart, so plan to estimate wherever it makes sense in the process. Also, the question asks for the number of *managers* who do *not* work in engineering. Jot that down on your scratch paper.

Step 2: **Plan**. The problem provides information about percentages of certain categories of employees, as well as the total number of employees, so your task is going to be to take percentages of that 450 total. But save yourself some time by using the answers to estimate as you go.

Step 3: **Solve**. First, find the number of managers, which is 20% of 450. Hmm. Well, 10% of 450 is 45, so 20% is twice as many, or 90.

There are 90 *total* managers, so a fraction of that group will be less than 90. Cross off answers (C), (D), and (E).

Next, what percentage of these 90 managers do *not* work in engineering? If 60% of those managers *do* work in engineering, then 40% do not. You could find 40% of 90 ... but you don't have to. Glance at the remaining answers and estimate accordingly. Half of 90 is 45, so the number of managers not in engineering must be less than 45. The only possible answer is (A).

The four wrong answers are all traps built into the problem. The value for total managers, 90, is given. The value 54 represents 60% of the managers (instead of 40%). The value 180 represents 40% of the entire 450 employees rather than 40% of only the managers. And the value 216 represents mistakenly taking 80% and then 60% of the total number of employees, rather than 20% and then 40%.

When to Estimate

On any new problem that includes math, always examine whether there are opportunities to estimate. Ask yourself this during all three stages—Understand, Plan, and Solve.

If the problem explicitly asks for an approximate answer, of course, go ahead and estimate. If the answer choices are relatively spread out, also go ahead and estimate. In both cases, pay attention to the answer choices as you solve; that will help you figure out how aggressively to estimate.

In addition, consider estimating whenever the answers are "divided" into different groupings. Consider these possible answers:

(A) −6
(B) −3
(C)   0
(D)   1
(E)   2

These answers can be divided into three groups: negative, positive, and zero. Can you estimate enough to tell which group the answer should fall into? If so, you'll be down to just 1 or 2 answers.

Here's another example:

(A) $\frac{1}{5}$
(B) $\frac{1}{3}$
(C) $\frac{1}{2}$
(D) $\frac{3}{5}$
(E) $\frac{2}{3}$

Let's say that, on this problem, you figure out that the answer is less than $\frac{1}{2}$. Can you take it any further? Well, $\frac{1}{5} = 20\%$ and $\frac{1}{3} = 33.3\%$. Can you tell whether the answer should be greater or less than $\frac{1}{4}$ (25%), which falls between the two remaining answer choices? If so, you're down to a single answer.

Other examples of a divided or grouped characteristic: Some answers are greater than 1 and others are less than 1. Some answers are clustered around 50 and some answers are clustered around 400.

Whenever you run into these divided or grouped characteristics, you may be able to estimate. Train yourself to look for opportunities to estimate as you Understand, as you Plan, and as you Solve.

Using Benchmarks to Estimate

The Benchmark method is a way to use easier numbers to estimate or figure out harder numbers. You're benchmarking the harder numbers against easier ones.

For example, when dealing with percents, the easiest benchmarks are 50%, 10%, and 1%. If you need to find 60% of a number, you can first find 50% and 10%, and then add those two values together to get 60%.

You can also use easy fraction benchmarks to estimate. The easiest fraction benchmarks are $\frac{1}{2}$, the quarters $\left(\frac{1}{4}, \frac{3}{4}\right)$, and the thirds $\left(\frac{1}{3}, \frac{2}{3}\right)$.

Try this problem:

A television originally priced at $700 was offered at a 12% discount. What was the sale price of the television?

(A) $650

(B) $616

(C) $560

Because 10% of 700 is 70, the discount is something more than $70. The new price, then, must be somewhat less than $700 - 70 = 630$. Answer (A) can't be correct.

Next, the answer does need to be somewhat smaller than 630, but not very much smaller—the difference between 10% and 12% is not that much. So answer (B) looks better than answer (C).

And, indeed, a 20% discount would result in another $70 off, for a total $140 discount, or a sale price of $560. Answer (C) is definitely too small. The correct answer must be (B).

(If you check the math: $10\% + 1\% + 1\% = 70 + 7 + 7 = \$84$, and $700 - 84 = \$616$. But don't do precise math on the test unless it's absolutely necessary!)

You can also use benchmark values to compare fractions:

Which is greater: $\frac{127}{261}$ or $\frac{162}{320}$?

Definitely don't try to solve yet. First, **Understand** and **Plan**. It would be seriously annoying to try to figure out precise values without a calculator. It would be even more annoying to find common denominators. And there's your clue! When they give you math that clearly won't be done in 2 minutes without a calculator, there must be another way to approach it.

Each fraction is smaller than 1. Hmm. How does each fraction compare to $\frac{1}{2}$? It turns out that 127 is *less* than half of 261 and 162 is *more* than half of 320, so $\frac{162}{320}$ must be the greater fraction.

You can also use benchmark values to estimate computations involving fractions:

What is $\frac{10}{22}$ of $\frac{5}{18}$ of 2,000 ?

Again, that math is annoying, so estimate. What nicer fractions are these fractions close to?

The fraction $\frac{10}{22}$ is a little bit less than $\frac{1}{2}$ and $\frac{5}{18}$ is a little bit more than $\frac{1}{4}$. Use these to estimate:

$$\frac{1}{2} \text{ of } \frac{1}{4} \text{ of } 2{,}000 = 250$$

Therefore, $\frac{10}{22}$ of $\frac{5}{18}$ of $2{,}000 \approx 250$.

Notice that the rounding errors compensated for each other:

$\frac{10}{22} \approx \frac{10}{20} = \frac{1}{2}$ The denominator decreased, so you rounded up: $\frac{10}{22} < \frac{1}{2}$.

$\frac{5}{18} \approx \frac{5}{20} = \frac{1}{4}$ The denominator increased, so you rounded down: $\frac{5}{18} > \frac{1}{4}$.

If you had rounded $\frac{5}{18}$ to $\frac{6}{18} = \frac{1}{3}$ instead, then you would have rounded both fractions up. This would lead to a slight but systematic overestimation:

$$\frac{1}{2} \times \frac{1}{3} \times 2{,}000 \approx 333$$

That might be good enough, depending on how far apart the answer choices are, but it's a little risky. If possible, try to make your rounding errors cancel out. If you round up in one part of the calculation, try to round down in another (or vice versa).

Problem Set

Directions: On some problems, try doing the official math *and* estimating to see how much time and effort estimation can save you. When you're done, analyze your work. How did you know you could estimate? At which point in the problem did the estimation come into play? Could you have streamlined the process or made better estimates at any step along the way? Should you have estimated more, or less, aggressively (and how do you know)? Finally, continue to look for opportunities to estimate on every GMAT problem you do from now on!

1. All of a certain company's employees are either right-handed or left-handed. If 115 of the company's 540 employees are left-handed, then approximately what percent of the company's employees are right-handed?

    (A) 17%
    (B) 21%
    (C) 71%
    (D) 79%
    (E) 83%

2. At a particular school, 65% of the students have taken language classes. Of those students, 40% have studied more than one language. If there are 300 students at the school, how many have studied more than one language?

    (A)   78
    (B) 102
    (C) 120
    (D) 150
    (E) 195

3. A total of 9,180 people participated in a research study on the genetics of eye color. Of the participants, $\frac{4}{9}$ had two parents with blue eyes, and of the remaining participants, $\frac{8}{17}$ had one parent with blue eyes. How many participants, in total, had at least one blue-eyed parent?

    (A)   780
    (B) 2,700
    (C) 4,320
    (D) 6,480
    (E) 8,400

4. Every elementary school student in a certain town attends one of two schools, and at both schools, each student is assigned to a specific classroom. Broad River Academy has 29 classrooms with an average of 17 students per classroom, and Lakeside School has 19 classrooms with an average of 18 students per classroom. Approximately what percent of the town's elementary school students attend Broad River Academy?

    (A) 29%

    (B) 41%

    (C) 48%

    (D) 59%

    (E) 82%

5. Which of the following fractions is the greatest?

    (A) $\frac{51}{95}$

    (B) $\frac{103}{190}$

    (C) $\frac{149}{285}$

    (D) $\frac{209}{380}$

    (E) $\frac{253}{475}$

Solutions

1. **(D) 79%:** First, Understand. This is a Problem Solving (PS) question that asks for an approximate answer. If the question says to approximate, it's okay (advisable, even) to do so. Note that the question gives information about left-handed employees but then asks about right-handed employees. Don't get them mixed up!

   Next, Plan. Since the question calls for approximation, start by approximating the percentage of the employees that are left-handed by approximating 115 as a percent of 540. Then subtract that number from 100% to find the percentage of employees who are left-handed.

   Finally, Solve. A tenth of 540 is 54, so two-tenths (20%) would be 108. The number of left-handed employees (115) is a little *more* than 108, or a little more than 20%. That means the number of right-handed employees must be a little *less* than 80% of the total. Choice (E) is too big. Eliminate it. Choice **(D)** is the closest. Choice (C) is the next closest, at 71%, but it's not that close. If 71% of the employees were right-handed, that would mean that almost 30% were left-handed. Thirty percent is 3×54, which is more than 150; choice (C) is too far away!

2. **(A) 78:** First, Understand. Glance at the problem: Problem Solving. Percentages in the question. Numerical answers. Not very close together.

   Jot:

   $$65\% = L \qquad \rightarrow 40\% \text{ OF } L > 1 \text{ lang}$$
   $$300 = T$$

   Next, Plan. Reflect on the info. The starting point is 300, but 65% is a bit annoying. You *can* figure out that number. Do you want to take the time to do so?

   If you've noticed that the answers are decently far apart, you know you can estimate. Since 65% is very close to $\frac{2}{3}$, that's the way to go (especially with 300 as the starting point!).

   Finally, Solve:

   $$\frac{2}{3} \text{ of } 300 \text{ is } 200$$

   Note that you rounded up, so your estimate will be a little higher than the official number.

   Benchmark to calculate 40% of that number. Find 10% of the number, then multiply by 4 to get 40%:

   $$10\% \text{ of } 200 = 20, \text{ so } 40\% = 20 \times 4 = 80$$

   Approximately 80 students have studied more than one language. The closest answer is 78.

3. **(D) 6,480:** The ugly fractions jump out. The first fraction isn't too bad, but $\frac{8}{17}$ is really annoying.

   Couple that with the starting number of 9,180 people and no calculator and this looks like a terrible problem.

   But wait! During your Understand phase, when you did your first glance, did you glance at the answer choices? If not, start making that a part of your glance on PS problems and notice this: The answers are spread very far apart. What does that mean?

Estimate your way to the answer. Both fractions are near 50%, so you might round to that benchmark, but aim to make your rounding errors balance across all of the steps.

Of the 9,180 people, $\frac{4}{9}$ had two parents with blue eyes. If you round the number of people down to 9,000, you don't need to approximate the $\frac{4}{9}$ fraction at all: $\frac{4}{9}$ of 9,000 is 4,000. This is a slight underestimation of the number of people who had two parents with blue eyes.

Next, how many people remain? About $9,000 - 4,000 = 5,000$. Of these people, $\frac{8}{17}$ or approximately 50%, had one parent with blue eyes. Half of 5,000 is 2,500, which is a slight overestimation of the number of people who had one parent with blue eyes.

In total, about $4,000 + 2,500 = 6,500$ people had at least one parent with blue eyes. The only close answer is 6,480.

4. **(D) 59%:** Glance at those answers. They contain pretty annoying percentages. If only they'd given nicer numbers—they wouldn't even have had to change them very much.

That's your big clue! The answers are basically 30%, 40%, 50%, 60%, and 80%—so estimate on this problem.

The question asks for *B* students as a percentage of all students. The number of *B* students is $(29)(17) =$ yuck. And the number of *L* students is $(19)(18)$. It's easy to round 29 up to 30, and 19 up to 20, but what about that 17 and 18? Can you just round everything up? Write out the math that needs to happen, but don't do anything; just examine it:

$$\frac{(29)(17)}{(29)(17) + (18)(19)}$$

The 17 on the top can cancel with the one 17 on the bottom, but it also has to cancel with something in the (18)(19) term. Why not have it cancel the 18? That's close enough:

$$\frac{(29)\cancel{(17)}}{(29)\cancel{(17)} + \cancel{(18)}(19)} \approx \frac{29}{29 + 19} \approx \frac{30}{30 + 20} = \frac{30}{50} = \frac{60}{100}$$

And estimate once again at the middle step. On a fraction, estimate in the *same* direction to balance out your estimations: If you estimate up on the top, also estimate up on the bottom. The closest match is 59%.

5. **(D) $\frac{209}{380}$:** First, Understand. Look at these ugly fractions. It's unlikely that the best way to do this problem is to calculate the decimal equivalents of these fractions, since that would be a lot of unwieldy work.

Another option when comparing fractions is a common denominator. Is that possible here? Look at the denominators. The denominator in choice (B) is twice the denominator in choice (A), and the denominator in choice (D) is twice the denominator in (B). What's going on? Keep investigating. Choice C's denominator is 95 more than (B)'s, and (E)'s is 95 more than (D)'s. These denominators are just successive multiples of 95: 95, 190, 285, 380, 475.

Next, Plan. If these denominators are all multiples of 95, then 95 can be factored out of the denominators to make the numbers easier to compare. Then, estimate the values of the answer choices one at a time, always eliminating any values lower than another value.

Finally, Solve. Rewrite them as:

$$\frac{51}{1(95)} \quad \frac{103}{2(95)} \quad \frac{149}{3(95)} \quad \frac{209}{4(95)} \quad \frac{253}{5(95)}$$

Get rid of the 95s, since they are common to each denominator:

$$\frac{51}{1} \quad \frac{103}{2} \quad \frac{149}{3} \quad \frac{209}{4} \quad \frac{253}{5}$$

Now it's time to compare them: Choice (A) is 51, and (B) is 51.5, so eliminate (A). Choice (C) would be less than 50, so eliminate it too. Choice (D) is greater than 52, so keep it and eliminate (B). Choice (E) is less than 51, eliminate (E). Choice **(D)** is the last choice remaining, so it must be the greatest.

Percents

In This Chapter...

In this chapter, you will learn how to translate and solve percent problems, as well as how to approach more advanced percent topics such as percent increase and decrease. You'll also learn how to benchmark percents—a strategy that will allow you to perform computations much more quickly.

CHAPTER 6 Percents

Percent literally means "per one hundred." You can think of a percent as a special type of fraction (or decimal) that involves the number 100:

> Of the students, 75% like chocolate ice cream.

This means that, out of every 100 total students, 75 like chocolate ice cream.

In fraction form, this is written as $\frac{75}{100}$, which simplifies to $\frac{3}{4}$.

In decimal form, this is written as 0.75.

One common mistake is the belief that 100% equals 100. In fact, 100% means $\frac{100}{100}$. Therefore, 100% = 1.

A multiplier greater than 1, in percent terms, is greater than 100%. For example, if your salary this year is 1.2 times your salary last year, then your salary is now 120% of what it was last year. (Nice!)

A multiplier less than 1 is less than 100%. For example, if your expenses this year are 0.78 of last year's expenses, then your current expenses are 78% of the previous year's expenses.

Percents as Decimals: Move the Decimal

You can convert percents into decimals by moving the decimal point two spaces to the left:

$$525\% = 5.25 \qquad 52.5\% = 0.525 \qquad 5.25\% = 0.0525 \qquad 0.525\% = 0.00525$$

A decimal can be converted into a percent by moving the decimal point two spaces to the right:

$$0.6 = 60\% \qquad 0.28 = 28\% \qquad 0.459 = 45.9\% \qquad 1.3 = 130\%$$

> **Strategy Tip:** Remember, the percent always looks "bigger" than the decimal!

Percent, Of, Is, What

These four words are by far the most important when translating percent questions. In fact, many percent word problems can be rephrased in terms of these four words:

Percent	=	divide by 100	$\overline{100}$
Of	=	multiply	$\times$
Is	=	equals	=
What	=	unknown value	x, y, or any variable

For example, try this problem:

What is 70 percent of 120 ?

First, as you read left to right, translate the question into an equation:

x	=	70	$\overline{100}$	×	120
What	is	70	percent	of	120 ?

Now, solve the equation:

$$x = \frac{70}{100} \times 120$$

$$x = \frac{7}{10} \times 120$$

$$x = 7 \times 12$$

$$x = 84$$

This translation works no matter what order the words appear in. Try another example:

30 is what percent of 50 ?

This statement can be translated directly into an equation:

30	=	x	$\overline{100}$	×	50
30	is	what	percent	of	50 ?

In the examples above, x represents the unknown value that you have been asked to find. If you have a Data Sufficiency problem, you might be done already; because the equation has only one variable, and that variable is not a square or in any kind of weird form, you can find a single value for x. That would be sufficient if, for example, the problem asked you to find x.

If you are doing a Problem Solving or a non-DS Data Insights problem, you may need to solve for x, which means "get x by itself on one side." For example:

$$30 = \frac{x}{100} \times 50$$

$$30 = \frac{x}{2}$$

$$60 = x$$

Look for *percent*, *of*, *is*, and *what* as you translate percent problems into equations; those four words should provide the necessary structure for each equation.

As you get better with translation, you may eventually feel comfortable using a shortcut. Take a look at this example:

30 is what percent of 50 ?

First, note that this problem *gives* you two real numbers and asks you to *find* a percent. When this is the setup, you can use the following shortcut.

Think of the *what percent of 50* portion as saying *what percent **out of** 50*. Put the *out of* number in the denominator. Put the other number in the numerator. The *what percent* part goes by itself on the other side of the equation as shown here:

$$\frac{30}{50} \times 100 = x\%$$

Whenever you see *what percent of a number*, you can think of this as "percent out of" that number and go straight to writing a fraction for the left side of the equation. Put the *out of* number on the bottom and the other number on the top. Then, multiply by 100 to go from the decimal form of the number to the percent form.

Fast Math: Percent Benchmarks

You can calculate most percentages quickly using some combination of 50%, 10%, 5%, and 1% of the original number. These percentages are **benchmark** percentages, or common building blocks for other numbers.

For example, the previous section asked you to find 70% of 120. Note that 70% is the equivalent of 50% + 10% + 10%. Calculate 50% and 10% of the number and add up the building blocks:

100% (original number)	50%	10%	50% + 10% + 10% = 70%
120	60	12	60 + 12 + 12 = 84

Here's another way: 70% is equivalent to 10% × 7, as shown here:

100% (original number)	10%	10% × 7 = 70%
120	12	12 × 7 = 84

There are typically multiple ways to compute an ugly percent from a combination of benchmark percents. The numbers you're dealing with may mean that, one time, you'd rather do the 50% + 10% + 10% version, but another time, you'd rather do the 10% × 7 version. Pause and think about the numbers involved before rushing to do the calculation.

Try this problem:

What is 15% of 90 ?

100% = 90
10% = 9
5% = 4.5
15% = 9 + 4.5 = 13.5

Now, try this one:

What is 6% of 50 ?

$$100\% = 50$$
$$1\% = 0.5$$
$$6\% = (1\%)(6) = (0.5)(6) = 3$$

You can also find 5% and 1% and add them up—whatever seems easier to you. Just take a moment to think about your approach and make the best choice for you.

Test your skills on these drills:

1. What is 18% of 50 ?

2. What is 40% of 30 ?

3. What is 75% of 20 ?

Here are the answers:

1. $100\% = 50$

    $20\% = (10\%)(2) = (5)(2) = 10$

    $2\% =$ move the decimal from $20\% = 1$

    $18\% = 20\% - 2\% = 10 - 1 = 9$

2. $100\% = 30$

    $10\% = 3$

    $40\% = (4)(10\%) = (4)(3) = 12$

3. Don't forget about your fraction-conversion skills! Sometimes, it's easier to convert to fractions and cancel. $75\% = \frac{3}{4}$, so:

$$\frac{3}{\cancel{4}_1}(\cancel{20}^5) = (3)(5) = 15$$

Why is it (arguably) easier to use the benchmark method on the first two problems, but easier to use fractions on the third problem?

Most people don't memorize the fraction conversion for 18%, so converting to fractions for the first problem would be annoying.

The second problem could go either way, but because 40% is a multiple of 10%, and 10% is very easy to find, building the answer is still quick.

In the third problem, 75% would take multiple steps to build via the percent method, plus 75% also converts to a very nice fraction: $\frac{3}{4}$. In this case, it will probably be easier to use the fraction here (especially because the starting number, 20, is a multiple of 4, so the denominator will cancel entirely).

Percent Increase and Decrease

Consider this example:

> The price of a cup of coffee increased from 80 cents to 84 cents. By what percent did the price change?

If you want to find a change, whether in terms of percent or of actual value, use the following equation:

$$\text{Percent Change} = \frac{\text{Change in Value}}{\text{Original Value}}$$

In the coffee example, you want to find the *change* in terms of percent. Write $\frac{x}{100}$ to represent an unknown percent:

$$\text{Percent Change} = \frac{\text{Change}}{\text{Original}}$$

$$\frac{x}{100} = \frac{4}{80} = \frac{1}{20}$$

Cross-multiply to get rid of the fractions and solve:

$$\frac{x}{100} = \frac{1}{20}$$
$$20x = 100$$
$$x = 5$$

Therefore, the price increased by 5%.

If you feel comfortable thinking in percents, you can also use the benchmark approach to answer that question. The price went from 80 cents to 84 cents, an increase of 4 cents. That additional 4 cents represents what percentage of the original price, 80 cents?

Ten percent of 80 cents is 8 cents. Halve the 8 cents to get 4 cents. And this figure is half of 10%, or 5%. The percent increase is equivalent to 5%.

Alternatively, a question might ask:

> If the price of a $30 shirt is decreased by 20%, what is the final price of the shirt?

In this case, the question didn't tell you the new percent; rather, it gave the percent decrease. If the price decreases by 20%, then the new price is $100\% - 20\% = 80\%$ of the original. Use the new percent, not the decrease in percent, to solve for the new price directly. You can use this equation:

$$\text{New Percent} = \frac{\text{New Value}}{\text{Original Value}}$$

Once again, use x to represent the value you want, the new price:

$$\frac{80}{100} = \frac{x}{30}$$
$$\frac{4}{5}(30) = x$$
$$24 = x$$

The new price of the shirt is $24.

Alternatively, you can solve directly without setting up a proportion. The starting price is $30 and this price is decreased by 20%. Find 20% of $30 and subtract:

$$\$30 - (20\%)(\$30) \qquad 20\% \text{ of } 30 \text{ is } 6$$

$$\$30 - \$6 = \$24$$

Increasing or Decreasing from the Original

When dealing with percent change, how you calculate depends on what is considered the "original" number, or starting point. For example, if a problem asks how much *smaller* the population was in 1980 than in 1990, which is the original number—the population in 1980 or that in 1990?

Don't try to do math yet. Just think. The question says the number gets smaller, with the population in 1990 as the high point. In this case, the 1990 population is the starting point, or original number—it's the starting point of the story.

Next, when talking about a percent change made to a number, always think of the original number as 100%, or your baseline for future calculations.

For example, if you increase the number 100 by 10%, you'll get $100 + 10 = 110$. The new number will be 110% of the original number, regardless of your starting number. Here are some common language cues for this concept:

> 10% increase = 110% of the original
>
> 10% greater than = 110% of the original

If you decrease a number, then you subtract from 100%:

> 45% decrease = 55% of the original
>
> 45% less than = 55% of the original

Use this conversion to save steps on percent problems. For example:

> What number is 50% greater than 60 ?

Fifty percent greater than is the same as *150% of*. So one path is to rewrite the question:

> What number is 150% of 60 ?

Translate into an equation, using 1.5 or $\frac{3}{2}$ to represent 150%:

$$x = \frac{3}{2} \times 60$$

$$x = 90$$

Another path is to use benchmarks. What number is 50% greater than 60? Well, 50% of 60 is 30. So 50% greater than 60 is $60 + 30 = 90$.

Successive Percent Change

Some problems will ask you to calculate successive percents. For example:

> If a ticket increased in price by 20%, and then increased again by 5%, by what percent did the ticket price increase in total?

Although it may seem counterintuitive, the answer is *not* 25%. When you have *successive* percent changes, the answer will never be to just add or subtract the percentages.

Walk through this with real numbers. If the ticket originally cost $100, then the first increase would bring the ticket price up to 100 plus 20% of 100 (or $20) for a total of $120.

The second increase of 5% is now based on this *new* ticket price, $120:

$$120 + (0.05)(120) = \$126$$

The price increased from $100 to $126, so the percent increase is the change divided by the original, or $\frac{26}{100} = 26\%$.

Why is it 26% and not 25%? Because the second calculation is based on a larger starting number—you're taking 5% of 120, not 100. This will always be true when you are doing two percent increases in a row, so the total percent increase will always be more than the number you'd get if you just added the two percentages together.

In short, successive percents *cannot* simply be added together; instead, you have to calculate each piece separately. This holds for successive increases, successive decreases, and for combinations of increases and decreases.

Try this problem:

> The cost of a plane ticket is increased by 25%. Later, the ticket goes on sale and the price is reduced 20%. What is the overall percent change in the price of the ticket?

You can *multiply* these changes together; you can't just add or subtract them. A 25% increase followed by a 20% decrease is the same as 125% of 80% of the original number:

$$\left(\frac{125}{100}\right)\left(\frac{80}{100}\right)x = ?$$

$$\left(\frac{5}{4}\right)\left(\frac{4}{5}\right)x = x$$

The 20% decrease entirely offsets the 25% increase. The new price is exactly the same as the original price. You can also work through the math using a real number, as shown in the previous problem:

$$\$100 + (25\% \text{ of } \$100) = \$125$$

$$\$125 - (20\% \text{ of } \$125) = \$100$$

Finally, remember how two successive percent increases will result in a percent change that is greater than the number you'd get if you added the two numbers together? (In that problem, the answer was 26%, not 25%.)

If you have two successive percent decreases, the overall percent decrease will be less than the number you'd get if you just added the two together. For example, if the price of a TV decreased by 10% and then decreased by another 10%, look what happens:

$$\$100 - (10\% \text{ of } \$100) = 100 - 10 = \$90$$

$$\$90 - (10\% \text{ of } \$90) = 90 - 9 = \$81$$

Why does it work that way? By definition, the second number in the calculation, $90, is smaller than the original number, $100. So 10% of that number is going to be smaller. Instead of a total decrease of 10% + 10% = 20%, the total decrease is actually 10% + 9% = 19%.

Problem Set

1. A stereo was marked down by 30% and sold for $84. What was the presale price of the stereo?

    (A) $100

    (B) $120

2. A car loan is offered at 8% annual interest, compounded annually. After the first year, the interest due is $24. What is the principal amount of the loan?

3. If x is 40% of y and 50% of y is 40, then 16 is what percent of x ?

4. The price of a shirt was increased by 25%. After using a coupon that applied a certain percent discount, a customer paid the original price for the shirt. What was the percent discount?

    (A) 15%

    (B) 20%

    (C) 25%

5. Last year, Company Y was profitable. For that year, what percent of the company's total revenue was its total profit?

    (1) Company Y's total cost last year was $4,000,000.

    (2) Company Y's total revenue last year was three times its total cost last year.

Save the below problem set for review after you finish this entire guide.

6. A bowl is half full of water. Four cups of water are then added to the bowl, filling the bowl to 70% of its capacity. How many cups of water are now in the bowl?

7. Challenge problem! (Data Sufficiency answers not given; check the DS chapter if needed.)

    Company X has exactly two product lines and no other sources of revenue. If the consumer product line experiences a k% increase in revenue (where k is a positive integer) in 2015 from 2014 levels, and the machine parts line experiences a k% decrease in revenue in 2015 from 2014 levels, did Company X's overall revenue increase or decrease in 2015 ?

    (1) In 2014, the consumer products line generated more revenue than the machine parts line.

    (2) $k = 8$

8. If 800 is increased by 50% and then decreased by 30%, what is the resulting number?

9. If 1,500 is increased by 20% and then reduced by y%, yielding 1,080, what is y ?

    (A) 20

    (B) 30

    (C) 40

10. A bottle is 80% full. The liquid in the bottle consists of 60% guava juice and 40% pineapple juice. The remainder of the bottle is then filled with 200 milliliters of rum. How much guava juice is in the bottle?

    (A) 360 ml

    (B) 480 mL

    (C) 600 mL

    (D) 720 mL

    (E) 900 mL

11. Challenge problem! Company Z sells only chairs and tables. What percent of its revenue in 2008 did the company derive from its sales of chairs?

    (1) In 2008, the price of tables sold by Company Z was 10% higher than the price of chairs sold by the company.

    (2) In 2008, Company Z sold 20% fewer tables than chairs.

Solutions

1. **(B) $120:** Understand and Plan before you try to Solve. This problem is worded in a very annoying way: It provides the answer after 30% is taken, but not the original or starting number. The original number, though, is what you want to take 30% of. What to do?

    Luckily, the GMAT is a multiple-choice test. The answers represent the starting number—so just try them to see which one matches the information given in the problem.

    (A) $100. Take 30%: $30. In this case, the new price would be $100 - 30 = 70$, but the problem says the new price is $84. This one's incorrect and (B) is the only remaining answer, so that one must be correct.

    Here's how to do the math, but note that on the GMAT, if you have only one answer left, stop solving. Go ahead and pick it.

    (B) $120. Take 30%: $(10\%)(3) = (12)(3) = 36$.

    $120 - 36 = 84$. Bingo! Answer **(B)** is indeed correct.

    Alternatively, you could rephrase the given information to say the following:

    $84 is 70% of the original price of the stereo.

    You could then translate this statement into an equation and solve:

    $$84 = \left(\frac{70}{100}\right)x$$
    $$84 = \left(\frac{7}{10}\right)x$$
    $$840 = 7x$$
    $$120 = x$$

2. **$300:** Although this looks like an interest problem, you can think of it as a percent change problem. The percent change is 8%, and the change in value is $24:

    $$\text{Percent Change} = \frac{\text{Change in Value}}{\text{Original Value}}$$
    $$\frac{8}{100} = \frac{24}{x}$$
    $$\frac{2}{25} = \frac{24}{x}$$
    $$2x = (24)(25)$$
    $$x = (12)(25) = 300$$

    The principal amount of the loan is $300.

    Alternatively, you could use benchmarks. $24 represents a change of 8%:

    $$8\% = 24$$
    $$1\% = \frac{24}{8} = 3$$
    $$10\% = 30$$
    $$100\% = 300$$

Examine those two solution methods. Which one works better for you? If you would have naturally thought of the first one, but you like the second better, what do you need to practice in order to get comfortable enough with benchmarks that next time you think of that solution method first?

3. **50%:** You can translate the first two sentences directly into equations. Just slow down and Reflect/Plan for a moment. Use the simplest versions of the equivalent fractions:

$$x \text{ is } 40\% \text{ of } y \rightarrow x = \left(\frac{2}{5}\right) y$$

$$50\% \text{ of } y \text{ is } 40 \rightarrow \left(\frac{1}{2}\right) y = 40$$

Reflect again. The second equation has only one variable, so solve for y:

$$\left(\frac{1}{2}\right) y = 40$$

$$y = 80$$

Now, replace y with 80 in the first equation to solve for x:

$$x = \left(\frac{40}{100}\right)(80)$$

$$x = \frac{4}{10} \times 80$$

$$x = 4 \times 8 = 32$$

Be careful now. The question asks, *16 is what percent of* x? You figured out that $x = 32$, so this question is really asking, *16 is what percent of 32?*

Create a new variable (z) to represent the unknown value in the question and solve:

$$16 = \frac{z}{100} \times 32$$

$$\frac{100}{32} \times 16 = z$$

$$\frac{100}{2} \times 1 = z$$

$$50 = z$$

Alternatively, use the translation shortcut. Place the "percent of" number on the bottom of the fraction and the other number on the top:

$$\frac{16}{32} \times 100 = 0.5 \times 100 = 50\%$$

Or, if you feel *really* comfortable with percents, think logically. What percent of 32 is 16? Sixteen is half of 32, so 16 is 50% of 32.

4. **(B) 20%:** Since no real numbers are given, you can use a smart number for the original price. In general, choosing 100 as a smart number when only percents are given is a good idea. Note, though, that the given percent (25%) has a nice fraction equivalent $\left(\frac{1}{4}\right)$, so you could work with a much smaller number than 100 by setting the original price equal to $4.

After the 25% price increase, the shirt costs $5. If the customer's coupon took the price back to the original $4, then the percent change was $\frac{4-5}{5} = -\frac{1}{5} = 20\%$ decrease.

The correct answer is **(B)**.

5. **(B):** This is a DS Value question asking for the company's profit as a percent of revenue. Jot down the relevant equation: $P = R - C$, where P is profit, R is revenue, and C is cost. The question can be rephrased as the fraction $\frac{P}{R}$, which can be further rephrased:

$$\frac{P}{R} = \frac{R - C}{R} = 1 - \frac{C}{R}$$

So the real question is: What is $\frac{C}{R}$, the ratio of cost to revenue?

(1) INSUFFICIENT: Having a value for cost does not tell you the ratio of cost to revenue. Eliminate answers (A) and (D).

(2) SUFFICIENT: This statement tells you that the ratio $\frac{C}{R}$ is $\frac{1}{3}$, which is exactly what the rephrased question asked for.

The correct answer is **(B):** Statement (2) alone is sufficient, but statement (1) alone is not sufficient.

6. **14 cups of water:** Understand and Plan before you Solve. If the bowl was already half full of water, then it was originally 50% full. Adding 4 cups of water increased the percentage by 20% of the total capacity of the bowl.

Use benchmarks to solve. The measurement 4 cups is equivalent to 20%. What else can you figure out?

$$20\% = 4 \text{ cups}$$
$$10\% = 2 \text{ cups}$$
$$70\% = (2)(7) = 14 \text{ cups}$$

There are 14 cups of water in the bowl.

Alternatively, you can set up a proportion. You know 4 represents 20% of the capacity. Let x represent 70% of the capacity. Set up the proportion and solve for x:

$$\frac{4}{x} = \frac{20}{70}$$
$$\frac{4}{x} = \frac{2}{7}$$
$$28 = 2x$$
$$14 = x$$

7. **(A):** This question requires you to employ logic about percents. No calculation is required, or even possible, since no real numbers are given.

Here's what you know so far (use new variables c and m to keep track of your information):

2014:

*   Consumer products makes c dollars
*   Machine parts makes m dollars
*   Total revenue $= c + m$

2015:

- Consumer products makes c dollars increased by $k\%$
- Machine parts makes m dollars decreased by $k\%$
- Total revenue = ?

What would you need to answer the question *did Company X's overall revenue increase or decrease in 2015?* Certainly, if you knew the values of c, m, and k, you could achieve sufficiency, but the GMAT would never write such an easy problem. What is the *minimum* you would need to know to answer definitively?

Since both changes involve the same percent (k), you know that c increases *by the same percent* by which m decreases. As a result, whichever number is greater (c or m) will constitute a bigger change to the overall revenue. Why?

If c started off greater, then a $k\%$ increase in c means more new dollars coming in than you would lose due to a $k\%$ decrease in the smaller number, m. On the other hand, if c is smaller, then the $k\%$ increase would be smaller than what you would lose due to a $k\%$ decrease in the larger number, m.

So you really need to know whether c or m is greater. You don't actually need to know k at all!

The question can be rephrased, *Which is greater,* c *or* m*?*

(1) SUFFICIENT: This statement indicates that c is greater than m. Thus, a $k\%$ increase in c is greater than a $k\%$ decrease in m, so the overall revenue went up.

(2) INSUFFICIENT: Knowing the percent change doesn't help, since you don't know whether c or m is bigger.

Note that you could try some real numbers, although this problem is probably faster with logic. Using statement (1) only:

2014:

- Consumer products makes $200
- Machine parts makes $100
- Total revenue = $300

2015: if $k = 50$

- Consumer products makes $300
- Machine parts makes $50
- Total revenue = $350

This one case yields an answer of Yes—the overall revenue did increase. However, you might have to test several sets of numbers to establish that this will always be true. (That's the main reason that logic is faster here!) You can experiment with different values for c and m, and you can change k to any positive integer (you don't need to know what k is). As long as c is greater than m, you will get the same result. The increase to the larger c will always be greater than the decrease to the smaller m.

The correct answer is **(A)**: Statement (1) is sufficient to answer the question, but statement (2) is not.

8. **840:** This is a successive percent question. Since the numbers in the problem are fairly nice, one approach is to calculate step-by-step.

    Start with 800. Increase by 50%, or 400. Now, you have $800 + 400 = 1,200$.

    From 1,200, decrease by 30%. Benchmark: 10% is 120, so 30% is 360. Subtract: $1,200 - 360 = 840$.

    Alternatively, set up the math as follows. Increasing by 50% is the same as *150% of* something. Decreasing by 30% is the same as *70% of* something. So the full problem translates to *What is 150% of 70% of 800?*

    $$\frac{150}{100} \times \frac{70}{100} \times 800 =$$
    $$\frac{3}{2} \times \frac{7}{10} \times 800 =$$
    $$\frac{21}{20} \times 800 =$$
    $$21 \times 40 = 840$$

9. **(C) 40:** Break the question into two parts. First, 1,500 is increased by 20%. Find 20% percent of 1,500.

    If 10% of 1,500 is 150, then 20% is 300. The new number is $1,500 + 300 = 1,800$.

    Next, 1,800 is reduced by y% to get to 1,080. The answer choices represent y, so try them to see which one works. Start with the middle of the three answers.

    (B) 30%. Find 30% of 1,800: 10% of 1,800 is 180, so 30% is $(180)(3) = 540$. Next, $1,800 - 540 = 1,260$. The answer is supposed to be 1,080, not 1,260, so answer (B) is incorrect.

    The other two possibilities for y are 20% and 40%. Think about what happened with the math when trying 30%. Do you need a larger or smaller percentage?

    When using 30%, the number to subtract was 540, yielding an answer of 1,260. In order to get down to 1,080, you'd need to subtract a larger number. So you're looking for a larger percentage decrease than 30%.

    Only answer **(C)** is larger than 30%, so it must be correct. (You can try the math to make sure—but the GMAT is a timed test. If you feel confident in the logic, don't try the math; just select the answer and move on.)

10. **(B) 480 mL:** If the bottle was 80% full, and adding 200 milliliters of rum filled it to capacity, then 200 milliliters is equal to 20% of the bottle's total capacity.

    The figure 80% is 4 times 20%, so the other 80% of the bottle represents $(200 \text{ mL})(4) = 800 \text{ mL}$.

    The guava juice represents 60% of that 800 milliliters. Use benchmarks to figure out how much guava juice there is:

    $$100\% = 800 \text{ mL}$$
    $$10\% = 80 \text{ mL}$$
    $$60\% = (80 \text{ mL})(6) = 480 \text{ mL}$$

    The bottle contains 480 milliliters of guava juice.

Alternatively, you could work backwards to solve this problem. The answer choices represent the amount of guava juice in the mixture; also, the answers are relatively "clean" numbers, making working backwards less cumbersome.

Start with answer (B) or (D), your choice. This solution will start with (B) since that number is smaller.

(B) 480 mL. This represents 60% of the liquid currently in the bottle. This problem has some intricate details. The answers represent the guava juice, which is 60% of the liquid that's currently in the bottle—but that liquid only fills 80% of the bottle. Lay out separate steps for each of these circumstances.

First, find the amount of liquid in the bottle. That represents 80% of the bottle's capacity, so find the value for the 20% that's empty and see whether it matches the figure given in the problem:

Guava = 60% of liquid	100% of liquid	Liquid = 80% of capacity	20% of capacity = 200 ?
(B) 480	60% = 480 10% = 80 100% = (80)(10) = 800	80% = 800 divide both by 4 20% = 200	Yes!

It's a match, so this is the correct answer. If you had started with answer (D) and done the same math, you'd get the following:

Guava = 60% of liquid	100% of liquid	Liquid = 80% of capacity	20% of capacity = 200 ?
(D) 720	60% = 720 10% = 120 100% = (120)(10) = 1,200	80% = 1,200 10% = 150 20% = (150)(2) = 300	No!

Using answer (D), 20% of the capacity is 300 milliliters, but the problem said that it was 200 milliliters, so this is not the correct answer. Further, 300 is too much, so the answer has to be smaller. At this point, you'd cross off answers (D) and (E), then try answer (B) next.

11. **(C):** First, notice that the question is asking only for the *percent* of its revenue the company derived from chairs. The question is asking for a relative value, so you may not need to know any actual values in order to solve.

The question asks for the revenue from chairs as a fraction of the total. Also, total revenue is made up of the revenue from chairs and the revenue from tables:

$$\frac{R_C}{\text{Total Rev}} \qquad\qquad \text{Total Rev} = R_C + R_T$$

If you know the ratio of chair revenue to total revenue, you can find the requested percentage. But note also that, if you're given relationships involving table revenue, you might also be able to find the requested percentage, since that second equation is true, too.

Also, note that the GMAT will expect you to know that Revenue = Price × Quantity Sold.

The revenue derived from tables is the price per table multiplied by the number of tables sold. The revenue derived from chairs is the price per chair multiplied by the number of chairs sold. You can create some variables to represent these unknown values:

$$R_T = P_T \times Q_T$$
$$R_C = P_C \times Q_C$$

(1) INSUFFICIENT: This statement provides the relative value of the price of tables to the price of chairs. If the price of tables was 10% higher than the price of chairs, then the price of tables was 110% of the price of chairs:

$$\frac{P_T}{P_C} = 1.1$$

However, no information is given on quantity sold, so it's not possible to determine anything about the relative value of their revenues.

(2) INSUFFICIENT: If the company sold 20% fewer tables than chairs, then the number of tables sold is 80% of the number of chairs sold:

$$\frac{N_T}{N_C} = 0.8$$

However, no information is given about price, so it's not possible to determine anything about the relative value of their revenues.

(1) AND (2) SUFFICIENT: Hmm. The first statement was about price, but not quantity. The second statement was about quantity, but not price. Could they work together to find a consistent *relative* value?

$$R_T = P_T \times N_T$$

The formula above is for revenue of tables. The first statement provided information about how the price of tables relates to the price of chairs (or how P_T relates to P_C). The second statement provided information about how the number of tables relates to the number of chairs (or how N_T relates to N_C).

When you know those relative relationships for the right side of the equation, then it's possible to calculate the relative relationship for the left side of the equation—that is, how table revenue relates to chair revenue.

If you know how table revenue relates to chair revenue, then you can always figure out what percentage each represents out of total revenue. For example, if you knew that table revenue was three times as much as chair revenue, then table revenue would have to be 75% of total revenue and chair revenue would have to be 25% of total revenue, because 75% is three times as much as 25%.

In other words, you don't have to calculate anything further (since this is Data Sufficiency). You can just know that, if you know the relative relationship between price and the relative relationship between quantity, then you can find the relative relationship between revenue.

The correct answer is (**C**): The two statements together are sufficient, but neither one alone is sufficient.

If you really want to see how this works from a textbook math perspective, read on. But it's strongly recommended to stop right here!

6

Replace P_T with $1.1\,P_C$ and replace N_T with $0.8\,N_C$:

$$R_T = P_T \times N_T$$
$$R_T = 1.1\,P_C \times 0.8\,N_C$$
$$R_T = (0.88)(P_C \times N_C)$$

On the right-hand side, $P_C \times N_C = R_C$, so substitute that in:

$$R_T = 0.88\,R_C$$

Taken together, the two statements provide the relative value of the revenues for tables and chairs.

You can use that to find the relative value of chair revenue to total revenue. Rearrange the equation so that you can write a ratio:

$$\frac{R_T}{R_C} = \frac{0.88}{1}$$

RevChair : RevTable : RevTotal

$$1 : 0.88 : 1.88$$

Finally, use the needed parts of the ratio to solve:

$$\frac{R_C}{\text{Total Revenue}} = \frac{1}{1.88} \approx 53\%$$

Save time on DS problems by avoiding unnecessary computation. Once you know you can find the needed figure, choose your answer and move on to the next problem.

Strategy: Arithmetic vs. Algebra 101

In This Chapter...

In this chapter, you will learn three strategies for avoiding textbook algebra and using real numbers (arithmetic) instead. Real numbers are easier to manipulate than variables/algebra. You can use these strategies on both the Quantitative and Data Insights sections of the GMAT.

CHAPTER 7 Strategy: Arithmetic vs. Algebra 101

When you first learned how to do math, you started with arithmetic—that is, you did math with real numbers. In later classes, you learned about variables (or unknowns) and started to do algebra.

Which of these problems is easier for you to solve?

What percent of a number is 50% of 10% of that number?	What percent of 100 is 50% of 10% of 100 ?
(A) 1%	(A) 1%
(B) 5%	(B) 5%
(C) 10%	(C) 10%

The setup of the two problems is identical—but the second one has real numbers throughout. What percent of 100 equals 50% of 10% of 100? First, find 50% of 10% of 100:

$$\text{Step 1:} \quad 10\%(100) = 10$$

$$\text{Step 2:} \quad 50\%(10) = 5$$

Now plug that value back into the sentence from the problem. What percent of 100 is 5? It's 5%. Done!

In the first problem, though, the question asks *What percent of a number is 50% of 10% of that number.* Now what? You would need to do an extra step: Assign a variable to the unknown *number* mentioned and then use algebra to solve. If you are strong with algebra, you may not find that extra step particularly onerous in this version, but *it's still an extra step.* No matter how good your algebra is, it's faster to work with the real number given in the second problem.

In general, arithmetic is easier than algebra—for everyone. Our brains just work better and faster with real numbers.

So take this mantra into the test with you: Don't just do the math presented to you, in the form it is presented. Pause to evaluate—make a conscious choice! If the algebra on a particular problem is really easy for you, go for it. Often, though, using real numbers will be faster and easier—and that means more time and mental energy to spend elsewhere on the test.

Here's the exciting thing: There are a number of ways to turn GMAT algebra into arithmetic. You've already learned about one strategy in the Data Sufficiency (DS) chapter: Test Cases.

In those DS problems, some theoretical question was asked, and multiple possible values were allowed to be used in the problem…in other words, the question involved some algebra. But algebra is annoying—so, where possible, try some real numbers (Test Cases) to see whether you can get different answers (not sufficient!) or whether you keep getting the same answer (sufficient!).

This general principle (try some real numbers/do arithmetic instead of algebra) can apply to Problem Solving (PS) problems, as well as the rest of the Data Insights (DI) problem types. The details just change a bit in terms of how you execute. This chapter will use PS and DS as the examples. Later chapters will expand into other DI problem types.

There are three main strategies that you can use to turn algebra into arithmetic on PS problems:

1. Test Cases (TC)

2. Choose Smart Numbers (SN)

3. Work Backwards (WB)

In this chapter, you'll learn the basics for each question type. As you continue your studies, you'll continue to learn more about these strategies until you're an expert for the real test.

Test Cases

You can actually **Test Cases** (TC) on non-DS math problems, too—in one specific circumstance. When the problem asks which answer choice *must be* or *could be* a certain characteristics (usually must be *true* or must be *false*), you can use this strategy.

Consider this problem:

If *x* and *y* are integers and *xy* = 6, which of the following must be true?

(A) *x* is even.

(B) *x* equals either 2 or 3.

(C) Either *x* or *y* is even.

Understand. Both variables are integers. The product *xy* equals 6. *Must be* signals that you could test cases. According to this question stem, one (and only one) of the answers *must be true* all the time.

Plan. If the numbers are both integers and multiply to 6, then they could be 2 and 3, or 1 and 6, or... anything else? They could also be negative, such as −2 and −3. Feel free to start with a positive case, but see how the math plays out; you may want to try a negative later.

Solve. Case 1: *x* = 2 and *y* = 3. In this case...hmm, all of the answers are true. Can you think of a case to test that would give you a different response for answer (A)? In other words, can you choose a value for *x* that is *not* even?

Case 2: Swap the two numbers. If *x* = 3 and *y* = 2, then you can eliminate answer (A). Answers (B) and (C) are still in, though. Take a look at the text of those two answers; what case do you want to try next?

Case 3: Try something other than 2 and 3. If *x* = 1 and *y* = 6, then you can eliminate answer (B).

The correct answer is (C), the only remaining answer.

You'll test cases most often on DS problems—but it's good to know that you can use this strategy on certain other problems, too, usually Problem Solving (PS), Two-Part, and Multi-Source Reasoning (MSR).

Let's summarize that process.

U: First, during the Understand step, **recognize** that you can test cases on a non-DS problem. The question will ask what *must* or *could be* a certain characteristic (e.g., true, false, even, and so on).

P: During the Plan step, **think about** any **constraints** you're given; this determines what kinds of numbers you are allowed to try. Also think about what kinds of numbers might give you a different answer. You'll learn more strategies for this step throughout this book.

S: Then, test your first case. **Choose one set of numbers,** following any constraints given in the problem, and test the answers. Cross off any answers that fail the test. **Decide what to test next:** Look at the remaining answer choices and think about what kind of case might help you to knock out one (or more) of those choices. Repeat until you're down to one answer (or you get stuck; in that case, guess from the remaining answers and move on).

Choose Smart Numbers

The next two strategies, **Choose Smart Numbers** (SN) and **Work Backwards** (WB) apply only to non-DS math problems. You can use these on Problem Solving and on the other math-based Data Insights problem types.

When the problem asks you to find either a *variable* expression or a *relative* number (such as a percentage, a fraction, or a ratio), you can choose your own real numbers. This strategy is very similar to testing cases, but you will probably only have to test one case.

Remember this problem?

> What percent of a number is 50% of 10% of that number?
>
> (A) 1%
> (B) 5%
> (C) 10%

Understand. The problem keeps referring to *a number* but never offers a real value for that number. Even the answer choices aren't actual values—they're just percentages, or relative values. Whenever you see a problem that never gives you a real value for whatever it's describing, you can pick your own value for the problem.

So far, this probably feels similar to testing cases. Here's the great part: Unlike DS, you only need to try one case (most of the time) when you use SN. That one case will lead to a single one of the answers and then you're done!

Plan. Since the problem deals with percentages, 100 is a "smart" number to pick.

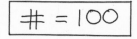

Jot this down and put a big box around it—you may need to use it multiple times, so you want to find it again easily.

Now, anywhere the problem talks about *that number*, you're going to use 100 instead:

What percent of ~~a number~~ 100 is 50% of 10% of ~~that number~~ 100?

Solve. Start with the concrete numbers in the question:

$$\boxed{\# = 100}$$

$$(50\%)(10\%)100$$

10

5

Note: Since it's all multiplication, you can do that math in either order. It's your choice whether to take 10% first, or 50% first. Either way, 50% of 10% of 100 equals 5.

The starting number is 100 and the *50% of 10% of that number* portion of the question now equals 5. Plug this information into the original question:

Original: What percent of a number is *50% of 10% of that number?*

Rephrased: What percent of 100 is 5?

The value 5 represents 5% of 100. If you're not sure, put the *of* number on the bottom of a fraction and the other number on top: $\frac{5}{100} = 5\%$.

The correct answer is (B).

Let's summarize that process.

U: During the Understand step, **recognize** that you can use smart numbers. It's a non-DS math problem. The problem keeps talking about a certain value but never gives a real number for that value, in the question stem or in the answer choices. The answers contain either variables or relative values, such as fractions, percents, or ratios.

P: During the Plan step, think about **what kind of number will work nicely** in the problem—in other words, try to find a *smart* number. You'll learn more strategies for this step as you work your way through this book.

S: Finally, **use your chosen number to work through the math** until you find a numerical answer, then find the choice that matches your numerical answer.

Work Backwards

What if the problem *does* give you real values for the items mentioned? In that case, you can't choose your own real number. But you *might* be able to use the real numbers given in the answer choices!

Consider this problem:

> Flannery is 28 years old and Harumi is 11 years old. In how many years will Flannery's age be twice Harumi's age?
>
> (A) 3
> (B) 4
> (C) 6
> (D) 8
> (E) 9

There are ways to solve this problem algebraically, but that's a lot more annoying than doing some arithmetic. But this problem has real numbers already...so now what?

Glance at the answers. The numbers are all "nice" numbers—they look pretty easy to work with. Read the question to see what the answers represent. They represent a single variable in the problem (the number of years before a specific fact will be true). If you have these two characteristics, you can just try the numbers in the answer choices until you find the one that works.

Hmm. What if you have to try all five answers?

The good news: You won't have to. The GMAT will put numerical answers in increasing order or decreasing order (so, in this case, either 3, 4, 6, 8, 9 or 9, 8, 6, 4, 3). This little feature means that you'll likely never have to try more than two answer choices when working backwards. Here's how it works.

Understand. $F = 28$ and $H = 11$. In how many years will $F = 2H$? The answer choices represent that actual number of years and they're "nice" numbers, so work backwards.

Plan. When working backwards, start with answer (B) or (D). In this case, answer (B) is smaller, so start there. (Why not answer (C)? You'll learn a little later.) Start a chart on your scratch paper showing answer (B) and what it represents. You're going to keep adding new columns to this chart as you perform each step.

Solve. Work through the problem, using answer (B). When you get to the last piece of information given in the question stem, check whether your math matches what the problem says:

Flannery is 28 years old and Harumi is 11 years old. In how many years will Flannery's age be twice Harumi's age?

$$F = 28 \text{ now}$$
$$H = 11 \text{ now}$$

Yrs from now:	F will be:	H will be:	F is 2H ?
(B) 4	32	15	No

The very last piece of given information is that F will be twice H's age. But this isn't what happens with answer (B) because 15 times 2 is 30, not 32. So this answer cannot be correct. Cross it off.

Next, look at the way that math played out. Do you need a larger value for "years from now" or a smaller one? How can you tell?

If you aren't sure (it's not easy to tell on this problem!), try answer (D) next:

Yrs from now:	F will be:	H will be:	F is 2H?
(B) 4	32	15	No, $H < \frac{1}{2}$
(D) 8	36	19	No, $H > \frac{1}{2}$

In 8 years, H will be 19 and F will be 36. Once again, F is not double H's age. This answer is still not the right one. But something's different this time. Using choice (B), H was *less* than half of F. That is, answer (B) was too small. But using answer (D), H is now *more* than half of F. Answer (D) goes too far! What does that mean?

You need a number that's greater than 4 and less than 8. Only answer choice (C) qualifies. You can check the math if you're not sure—but the GMAT is a timed test, so don't do work unless you really need to.

The correct answer is (C).

The fact that the answers are in order is exactly what allows you to "follow the pattern" when working backwards. You'll always start with either answer (B) or answer (D).

Imagine you have the same problem (and the correct answer is still 6) but the five answers given are (A) 6, (B) 8, (C) 9, (D) 10, and (E) 12. You'd try (B), 8, first and, as above, you'd figure out that 8 was incorrect. What would that mean?

If you were able to analyze the math, you'd realize that (B) was *too large*, so the correct answer must be (A), the only smaller choice. You'd never have to try answer (D).

It's tough to spot the pattern, though, when you have only one data point. If you don't see a quick way to tell whether you need to go larger or smaller, just test (D) and compare it to (B) to find the pattern. Here's what would happen for the new answer choices:

(B): In 8 years, F will be 36 and H will be 19. Double H should be 38, but F is only 36. So this is two years short of what's needed.

(D): In 10 years, F will be 38 and H will be 21. Double H should be 42, but F is only 38. This is now *four* years short of what's needed. Choosing a bigger answer choice made things worse!

So, you now know the pattern—you need a value that's in the opposite direction, something less than (B). Choice (A) must be the correct answer.

Consider these three possible patterns of answers; what does each one mean? For each example, assume you've tried answers (B) and (D) and determined that they're incorrect.

Example 1	Example 2	Example 3
(A) 1	(A) 1	(A) 5
(B) 2 too small	(B) 2 too small	(B) 4 not right; can't tell which way to go
(C) 3	(C) 3	(C) 3
(D) 4 too big	(D) 4 too small, but closer	(D) 2 wrong in the same 'direction' as (B), but closer to right
(E) 5	(E) 5	(E) 1

In the first example, answer (B) is too small, but (D) is too big. The correct answer must be in between, so the only possible choice is answer (C).

In the second example, answers (B) and (D) are both too small, but answer (D) gets *closer* to the right answer. The pattern is sending you to answer (E).

The third example is more complex. You can tell answer (B) is wrong, but you're not sure which way to go, so you try answer (D) next. Once you've tried (D), you can see the pattern: Answer (D) is still "off" in the same way as (B), but answer (D) is at least getting closer. In this case, the pattern is pointing you to go further to answer (E).

This pattern idea is why you want to try answers (B) and (D) vs. answer (C). Starting with answers (B) and (D) will show you the "spaced-out" pattern among all five answers, so that you can then figure out which of (A), (C), and (E) is correct without actually having to try them.

Here's a summary of the working backwards process.

U: First, **recognize** that you can work backwards. It's a non-DS math problem and the answers represent a single variable in the problem (for example, they represent one person's age, not the difference between the ages of two people). The answers contain actual values—no variables or relative values—and those values are pretty "nice" to work with for that type of problem, whatever it is.

P: Second, glance at the answers; do they increase or decrease? **Start with answer (B) or (D).** Note: This summary will assume that the answers increase and that you start with answer (B).

Set up a little table on your scratch paper. **Organize to make it easier** to run through the math again with another answer, just in case.

S: **Do the math** from the beginning of the problem to the last fact given in the problem. If the answer you started with, (B), is correct, you're done. If it doesn't match, cross off answer (B) and figure out what to try next.

Is there an easy way to tell whether to go larger or smaller?

If you can tell that you need a *smaller* number, then the answer must be (A). Pick it and move on. If you can tell that you need a *larger* number, cross off answer (A) and try answer (D).

If you can't tell which way to go, still try (D) next. If you try (D) and it's correct, you're done. If not, cross it off. Then, **examine the pattern created by answers (B) and (D)** and make your choice among the remaining answers accordingly.

Note: As you practice working backwards, you will get better at being able to decipher the pattern shown by answers (B) and (D).

Occasionally, on a harder problem, you may not be able to decipher the pattern. In that case, you'll have to decide between trying more answers and just guessing and moving on. If you've already spent 2+ minutes, it's probably best just to guess and move on unless the math is very fast. You've eliminated two answers, so your chances of guessing correctly are pretty good.

Summary: TC, SN, WB

At first, you may find yourself avoiding these "use real numbers" approaches and instead defaulting to the textbook approaches that worked for you in school. You've practiced algebra for years; you've only been using these GMAT techniques for a short period of time.

Keep practicing; you'll get better! Every high scorer on the Quant and DI sections will tell you that using these strategies where appropriate is invaluable to getting through on time and with a sufficiently consistent performance to reach a top score.

Here's a summary of what you've learned so far:

Test Cases

- Data Sufficiency: Use when the problem allows multiple possible values for the unknowns. Try at least two different cases to see whether you can get a different answer (Yes *and* No; two *different* values; two *different* items from a list).

- Other math problem types: Use when the problem asks a *must be* or *could be* question. Keep testing cases until only one answer choice remains.

Choose Smart Numbers

- Use on any math-based problem type *except* DS.

- Glance at the answers first. Do they have variable expressions or relative values (such as percents, fractions, ratios)? If so, check the problem to see whether you can use smart numbers.

- If the problem never gives you a *real* number for a particular variable or relative value, you can choose your own real (and smart!) number.

- This strategy is very similar to Test Cases but, most of the time, you will only need to try a single case.

Work Backwards

- Use on any math-based problem type *except* DS.

- Glance at the answers first. Are they relatively "nice" real numbers? If so, check the problem to see whether you can work backwards.

- If the problem asks you to solve for what would be a single variable (if you were to set things up algebraically), you can work backwards.

- Start from answer (B) or (D). Then try the other one. If neither (B) nor (D) is correct, use the pattern to figure out whether the answer is (A), (C), or (E).

Working backwards allows you to use the numbers given in the answer choices, but for the first two strategies, you'll need to decide yourself what numbers to use—and the guidelines can vary based on the strategy and on what that problem is testing. Knowing how to pick good numbers will save you time and mental effort on the GMAT. Read on to learn how.

Good Numbers for Test Cases

When using the Test Cases (TC) strategy, your goal depends on whether this is a PS or DS problem:

- PS: Test as many *valid* cases as needed to prove four answers incorrect.
- DS: For each statement, find at least two *valid* cases that result in *different* answers (e.g., Yes and No) to prove that statement insufficient.

Valid cases are cases that follow all facts given in the problem. For example, if the problem says that x is a positive integer, then $x = 3$ would be valid, but $x = -3$ would not be valid. So, don't try any cases in which $x = -3$.

When testing cases, it's often a good idea to start with a small integer, such as 1 or 0 (as long as this is a valid case). After that first case, it can be useful to test numbers that have "weird" properties—negatives, primes, odds and evens, fractions between 0 and 1, and so on—as long as those weird cases are also valid for this problem.

Weird properties often give you a different answer to the question—for example, a positive integer might give you a Yes answer but a negative integer might give a No answer.

Consider this problem:

If $c + d > 0$, which of the following must be true?

(A) $c > 0$

(B) $d > 0$

(C) $d > 1$

(D) $c - d < 0$

(E) at least one of c and d is greater than 0

Step 1: **Understand**. This problem asks which answer *must be true*. Jot down the given facts:

$$c + d > 0$$

This is a "theory" problem; it uses variables to ask something about certain relationships, but c and d could be lots of possible values—as long as $c + d > 0$. Choose your own numbers to test out what would happen in various scenarios (or cases). In short, test cases!

Step 2: **Plan**. Look at the given facts. What kinds of cases might do weird things? For example, since the fact contains > 0, consider trying both positives and negatives—and even 0 itself.

Step 3: **Solve**. First, you're only allowed to try numbers that make the *facts* in the problem true.

Second, try numbers that make your job easier. Glance at the answers while keeping the facts in mind. The first answer, for example, says that $c > 0$. To break that answer, you'd have to find a valid case where c is not greater than 0.

Start with the simplest *valid* numbers you can think of. For example, you could try $c = 0$ and $d = 2$. (Check: Is $c + d > 0$? Yes. This is a valid case. Carry on.)

In this case, $c = 0$, so c does not have to be greater than 0. Cross off answer (A). Run down the other answer choices. No others can be eliminated from this case, but as you evaluate them, consider what values you may want to try next.

Answer to test	Case 1: $c = 0$, $d = 1$	Case 2: $c = 2$, $d = -1$
Check facts: $c + d > 0$	Valid: $c + d > 0$	Valid: $c + d > 0$
(A) $c > 0$	False: $c = 0$ Eliminate (A)	
(B) $d > 0$	True: $d = 1$	False: $d = -1$ Eliminate (B)
(C) $d > 1$	False: $d = 1$ Eliminate (C)	
(D) $c - d < 0$	True: $0 - 1 = -1$	False: $2 - (-1) = 3$ Eliminate (D)
(E) at least one of c and d is greater than 0	True: $d = 1$	True

The first case, $c = 0$ and $d = 1$, knocks out answers (A) and (C). The other three answers are true, so try another case. Examine those remaining answers as you decide what to try next. Since choice (B) says that d is positive, try a negative value for d. This then forces c to be something big enough that the sum of the two will still be positive, so try $d = -1$ and $c = 2$.

You don't need to try the answers that have already been knocked out. This second case eliminates answers (B) and (D).

Answer (E) is the only one left, so pick it and move on, even if you're not sure why it's always true. Afterwards, though, try to understand. The question stem establishes $c + d > 0$. In order for the sum of these two values to be greater than 0, at least one must start out as a positive value. If both c and d were negative values, they could never add up to a positive number.

The correct answer is (E).

It doesn't matter in which order you try different cases, as long as you're trying valid numbers. Try the first valid case you think of and see what answer you get. Then pause to think about what kinds of numbers might give you a different result and try that case next.

Let's recap. When testing cases, your goal is to try to either disprove the answer choice (on PS) or prove the statement insufficient (on DS). As such, you want to try numbers that have different characteristics that might serve to help you disprove the answer or statement. What kinds of numbers? That will depend on clues you find in the specific problem you're trying to solve.

For example, if a problem has an absolute value symbol, try negatives and positives. If a problem mentions that something is divisible by two, try evens and odds. If you have x^2, consider trying 0 or 1 for x, as those values don't change when you square them. (And consider trying fractions between 0 and 1. As you'll learn in Chapter 12, the exponents chapter later in this book, those fractions do funny things when you square them.)

Start keeping a list or make flash cards to help you remember the clues that will point you toward certain numbers to test.

When testing cases, when I see...	I'll try... for x
$|x|$	$|x|$: + and −
x^2	x^2: 0, 1, fractions

7

Good Numbers for Smart Numbers

The considerations for "good" numbers are different when you **choose smart numbers**. For this strategy, you usually *don't* want to go for the weird numbers (unlike testing cases).

When choosing smart numbers, follow these guidelines:

- Avoid 0 and 1.
- Avoid numbers that appear in the problem.
- If picking two or more values, choose different values for each variable.
- When appropriate, pick numbers that have different characteristics (e.g., one even and one odd, if you think the problem is testing even/odd concepts).

When you become very practiced, you may decide to break one of these rules for some very good reason—but for now, follow these guidelines.

Finally, think about what's going on in the problem and try to choose numbers that will make your task easier.

Try this problem:

> A store sold a packet of 10 identical pens for a total of *x* dollars. The store originally purchased the packet of pens for 80% of the amount for which it sold the packet. In terms of *x*, how much profit did the store make on a single pen?
>
> (A) $\frac{x}{5}$
>
> (B) $\frac{x}{10}$
>
> (C) $\frac{4x}{5}$
>
> (D) $\frac{x}{50}$
>
> (E) $\frac{4x}{50}$

Step 1: **Understand**. The answers contain variables. Also, the problem talks about a price for the pens but never mentions a real number for price anywhere along the way, so you can use smart numbers. The question asks how much *profit* was made on *one* pen. Finally, note that Profit = Revenue − Cost (the GMAT expects you to know this formula).

Step 2: **Plan**. Choose a number that will work nicely in the problem. You bought 10 pens for *x* dollars. The problem asks for the profit in terms of just 1 pen, not all 10, so you're going to need to divide by 10 at some point. Choose something that is a multiple of 10. Make this small but not 10 itself (in general, avoid choosing numbers that already appear in the problem). Try *x* = $20.

Step 3: **Solve**. The store sold the 10 pens for a total of $20, or $2 per pen. The store earned revenue of $2 per pen.

Its *cost* for the pens was 80% of the sales price, so its *profit* is 20% of the sales price. Use benchmarks to find 20% of $2:

$$100\% = \$2$$
$$10\% = \$0.20$$
$$20\% = \$0.40$$

The profit for one pen was $0.40.

None of the answers say $0.40 though—they still have that pesky variable. Plug $x = 20$ into the answers and look for the one that matches $0.40. At any point that you can tell that a particular answer will *not* equal $0.40, stop and cross off that answer:

(A) $\frac{x}{5} = \frac{20}{5} =$ not 0.4

(B) $\frac{x}{10} = \frac{20}{10} =$ not 0.4

(C) $\frac{4x}{5} = \frac{4(20)}{5} =$ too big

(D) $\frac{x}{50} = \frac{20}{50} = 0.4 =$ a match!

(E) $\frac{4x}{50} = \frac{4(20)}{50} = \frac{80}{50} =$ too big

The correct answer is (D).

Here's the algebraic solution:

The store sold 10 pens for a total of x dollars, or $\frac{x}{10}$ dollars per pen. The store bought the pens for 80% of that sale price. Profit equals revenue minus cost:

(Profit per pen) = (Revenue per pen) − (Cost per pen)
$$P = \frac{x}{10} - \frac{4}{5}\left(\frac{x}{10}\right)$$
$$P = \frac{x}{10} - \frac{4x}{50}$$
$$P = \frac{5x}{50} - \frac{4x}{50}$$
$$P = \frac{x}{50}$$

The correct answer is (D). That may seem like fewer steps, but it's harder to set up. And take a look at some of the wrong answers:

(A) $\frac{x}{5}$ Mistake: Assume x is cost per pen, instead of $\frac{x}{10}$.

(C) $\frac{4x}{5}$ Mistake: Assume x is cost per pen, instead of $\frac{x}{10}$, *and* solve for cost rather than profit.

(E) $\frac{4x}{50}$ Mistake: Solve for cost rather than profit.

It's very easy, when doing algebra, to make either of those mistakes—or both. And the most common algebraic mistakes are *always* built into the answers on this test. You have a much better chance of avoiding those mistakes when you are working with real numbers—both because everybody is better at arithmetic than algebra and because the trap answers assume you are doing algebra, not arithmetic.

As a general rule, if you find the algebra very easy, go ahead and solve that way. As the algebra becomes harder for you, though, switch to smart numbers. If you realize you made a careless mistake with the algebra, that may be a signal to try smart numbers instead.

You can, of course, make careless mistakes whether using algebra or real numbers. Whichever approach you choose to use, do make sure to write down what your variables stand for (in the above, $x =$ total $) and double-check what you're solving for (profit for *one* pen).

PS Pop Quiz: Smart Numbers or Test Cases?

On Data Sufficiency, you can use only Test Cases. But on Problem Solving, you can use smart numbers or test cases. The strategies are similar…but not the same. When do you use which? And how do you execute on each strategy?

Pop Quiz! Take about 30 seconds to determine the strategy for each problem. Then go ahead and try the two problems:

1. The price of a certain computer is increased by 10%, and then the new price is increased by an additional 5%. The new price is what percent of the original price?

    (A) 120%

    (B) 119.5%

    (C) 117%

    (D) 115.5%

    (E) 115%

2. If $ab > 0$, which of the following must be negative?

    (A) $a + b$

    (B) $|a| + b$

    (C) $b - a$

    (D) $\dfrac{a}{b}$

    (E) $-\dfrac{a}{b}$

7

Ready? What did you think?

Use...	When you see...
Test Cases	Data Sufficiency "theory" problem OR Problem Solving with a *must be* or *could be* question.
	For both types, test as many cases as needed until you get to one answer. Try 0, 1, and other weird values.
Smart Numbers	Problem Solving with variables or relative values (percents, fractions, ratios) in the answers and *no* real numbers given for the variables or for items mentioned in the problem (e.g., number of cats, cups of sugar, dollars).
	Test just one case. Avoid 0, 1, and annoying values; use easy numbers.
Work Backwards	Problem Solving with real values in the answers. The answer choices represent a single variable in the problem.
	We didn't give you one of these in this set.

The first problem is a Smart Numbers problem and the second one is a Test Cases problem.

> The price of a certain computer is increased by 10%, and then the new price is increased by an additional 5%. The new price is what percent of the original price?
>
> (A) 120%
> (B) 119.5%
> (C) 117%
> (D) 115.5%
> (E) 115%

Step 1: **Understand**. Glance at the answers: They're percentages. Check the problem: No real values are given anywhere for the price. You can use smart numbers or solve algebraically.

Step 2: **Plan**. Think through what's going on. First, the price goes up 10%, and then that new price goes up another 5%. This is successive percent increase, so the increase is *not* just 10% + 5% = 15%. Further, it has to be *more* than 15% because the second (5%) increase is based on a larger starting number. Cross off answer (E).

Working algebraically on this problem is likely to be pretty annoying. Try choosing a smart number instead. Since this is a percent problem, use 100. (On percent problems in general, unless the number 100 shows up in the problem, it's a good idea to use 100 as your smart number.)

Step 3: **Solve**. Starting price is $100.

First increase: $100 + 10% = $100 + $10 = $110

Second increase: $110 + 5% = $110 + $5.50 = $115.50

Use benchmarks when calculating percents. To get 5% of a number, take 10% and divide that by 2. In this case, 10% of $110 is $11, and 5% is half of that, or $5.50. Finally, calculate the percentage:

$$\text{Percentage: } \frac{\text{new}}{\text{orig}} \times 100 = \frac{115.5}{100} \times 100 = 115.5\%$$

Notice, at the end, how you both divide and multiply by 100, so they just cancel out? This is why choosing 100 on a percent problem is a good idea.

The correct answer is (D).

The second problem was the Test Cases problem.

> If $ab > 0$, which of the following must be negative?
>
> (A) $a + b$
> (B) $|a| + b$
> (C) $b - a$
> (D) $\dfrac{a}{b}$
> (E) $-\dfrac{a}{b}$

Step 1: **Understand**. Asks a *must be* "theory" question, so test cases. Jot down the fact: $ab > 0$.

Step 2: **Plan**. Think about the kinds of numbers that you could try: 0 and 1, fractions, negatives, etc. What would be good to try here?

Since the question asks what must be negative, include negatives in the mix. Also, what does the inequality $ab > 0$ signify? Two variables multiply together to be positive. First, that means neither variable can be 0, so don't try 0. It also means that the two numbers have to have the same sign, either both positive or both negative.

Step 3: **Solve**. Go straight for a negative-negative case:

$$a = -1$$
$$b = -2$$

(A) $a + b$	neg
(B) $|a| + b$	neg
(C) $b - a$	neg
~~(D) $\dfrac{a}{b}$~~	~~pos~~
(E) $-\dfrac{a}{b}$	neg

The question wants to know what must be negative, so cross off anything that's positive. When you're done, review any answers still in the mix to see what you might want to change in your next case in order to get a positive answer next time.

For example, choice (A) is negative for the first set of numbers, but you're allowed to choose positive numbers, too. And if you do, choice (A) will drop out. So will choice (B). You may even notice some of these things as you work through your first case; if so, jot down a reminder for what to use for your second case.

$$a = -1 \qquad a = 2$$
$$b = -2 \qquad b = 1$$

		$a=-1,\ b=-2$	$a=2,\ b=1$
~~(A) $a+b$~~		~~neg~~	~~pos~~
~~(B) $|a| + b$~~		~~neg~~	~~pos~~
(C) $b - a$		neg	neg
~~(D) $\dfrac{a}{b}$~~		~~pos~~	
(E) $-\dfrac{a}{b}$		neg	neg

Choices (C) and (E) both stayed negative. If you're going to use positive values, then you need variable *b* to be greater than variable *a* in order to get choice (C) to drop out. Prove it to yourself with a concrete case:

$$a = -1 \qquad a = 2 \qquad a = 1$$
$$b = -2 \qquad b = 1 \qquad b = 2$$

	$a=-1,\ b=-2$	$a=2,\ b=1$	$a=1,\ b=2$
~~(A) $a+b$~~	~~neg~~	~~pos~~	
~~(B) $|a| + b$~~	~~neg~~	~~pos~~	
~~(C) $b-a$~~	~~neg~~	~~neg~~	~~pos~~
~~(D) $\dfrac{a}{b}$~~	~~pos~~		
(E) $-\dfrac{a}{b}$	neg	neg	neg ✓

Finally! The correct answer is (E). No matter what you try, this one stays negative.

As you worked through the problem, you might have begun to "see" the theory. For instance, on that last step, you might have felt comfortable that answer (C) would drop out as soon as you made variable *b* greater than variable *a*. Any time you feel confident in your reasoning, it's okay not to plug in actual values to test. You're still testing the case—you're just using number properties rather than specific numbers.

One more thing. If you know that you're prone to careless mistakes on any specific kinds of math (e.g., absolute values or fractions), then write out the math itself, not just the "pos" and "neg" designations.

Everyone makes careless errors with some kinds of seemingly simple math. Know your own patterns to help you minimize mistakes!

7

Avoid 0 or 1 When Choosing Smart Numbers

For the Smart Numbers strategy, you've learned to avoid using 0, 1, or a number that appears elsewhere in the problem. Here's why. Try this example:

> A truck can carry x shipping containers and each container can hold y gallons of milk. If one truck is filled to capacity and a second truck is half full, how many gallons of milk are they carrying, in terms of x and y?
>
> (A) $x + 0.5y$
>
> (B) $x + y$
>
> (C) $0.5xy$
>
> (D) $1.5xy$
>
> (E) $2xy$

Step 1: **Understand**. Glance at the answers: There are variables. Check the problem: There are no real numbers given. You can use smart numbers.

What's the actual story? One truck holds some number of shipping containers and each shipping container holds some number of gallons of milk. And there are two trucks. Sketch something out. It doesn't need to be pretty! Just use the sketch to help understand the story.

There are two trucks. One's full and the other is half full. Each one has the same number of shipping containers (how about 1?) and each container can carry…how about 3 gallons of milk?

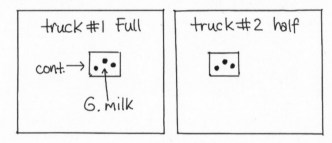

Don't worry at this stage about whether those are the right numbers to pick (it turns out that what's sketched above doesn't quite fit all the facts in the story—so you will have to adjust later). Just focus on understanding the story first. (Bonus points if you've already figured out why those numbers in the sketch don't quite fit the story. No worries if you haven't.)

Step 2: **Plan**. Once you understand, you can decide what to do. The drawing shows $x = 1$ and $y = 3$. At this stage, you'd normally tell yourself, "Whoops, I'm not supposed to use 1 on smart numbers," but keep going so that you can see what could happen when you do.

Step 3: **Solve**. Okay, $x = 1$ and $y = 3$. Each truck has one shipping container. The first truck is filled to capacity, so it carries a total of 3 gallons of milk. The second is half full, so it carries 1.5 gallons…ugh, decimals are annoying.

That's okay! Just go back and tweak your drawing/numbers to give you integer values instead. What if $x = 1$ and $y = 2$, instead? Now, here's the scenario: The first truck is filled to capacity, so it has 2 gallons of milk. The second is half full, so it carries 1 gallon, and together, the two trucks carry 3 gallons of milk.

Plug $x = 1$ and $y = 2$ into the answers to find the one that equals 3:

(A) $x + 0.5y = 1 + (0.5)(2) = 2$

(B) $x + y = 1 + 2 = 3$ Match!

(C) $0.5xy = (0.5)(1)(2) = 1$

(D) $1.5xy = (1.5)(1)(2) = 3$ Wait a second—this one matches, too!

(E) $2xy = 2(1)(2) = 4$

In rare circumstances, when using the Smart Numbers strategy, the number you choose could work for more than one answer choice. The odds are greatly increased if you choose 0, 1, or a number that already appears in the problem—so that's why you want to avoid those numbers when using the Smart Numbers strategy. (Incidentally, this is the same reason why you *do* want to use 0 or 1 when testing cases on "must be true" PS problems—because that can make multiple answers drop out at once!)

If you do get two answers that work, now what? If you think you've spent too much time already, guess between those two answers that worked; you still have a 50/50 chance. Alternatively, if you have time, try a second case—and you only need to check answers (B) and (D) for this case.

Try $x = 2$ containers and $y = 3$ gallons of milk per container instead.

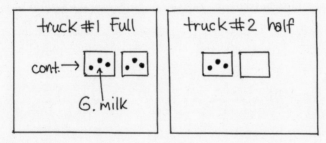

The first truck is now carrying $(2)(3) = 6$ gallons of milk. The second carries half that, or 3 gallons. Together, they carry 9 gallons of milk.

Try (B) and (D):

(B) $x + y = 2 + 3 = 5$ Not a match

(D) $1.5xy = (1.5)(2)(3) = 9$ Match!

The correct answer is (D).

If you follow the guidelines for choosing smart numbers, then the "two answers work" situation is much less likely to occur:

- Avoid 0 and 1.
- Avoid numbers that appear elsewhere in the problem.
- If you have to choose multiple numbers, choose different numbers.

If you do accidentally find yourself in this situation and you have the time, then try a second case. Go back, change one or both of the numbers in your problem, and do the math again. If you don't have time, just choose one of the two answers that did work and move on.

Finally, this is important enough to repeat: At first, you may find yourself always choosing the textbook, or algebraic, approach. You've practiced algebra for years, after all, and you've only been using these test-taking techniques for a short period of time. Keep practicing; you'll get better! And you'll find these arithmetic strategies are lifesavers in terms of both time and mental energy during the test.

Problem Set

Practice your test-taking strategies: Smart Numbers, Test Cases, Work Backwards. Try the algebraic/textbook way as well to compare methods. When you're done, ask yourself which way you prefer to solve *this* problem and why.

On the real test, you won't have time to try both methods; you'll have to make a decision and go with it. Learn *how* to make that decision while studying; then, the next time a new problem pops up in front of you, you'll be able to make a quick (and good!) decision about what to do.

1. If $a < 0$ and $b < c$, which of the following must be true?

    (A) $ab < c$

    (B) $ac > b$

    (C) $ab > 0$

    (D) $ac < 0$

    (E) $ab > ac$

2. At the beginning of the day, the ratio of \$5 bills to \$10 bills in Thom's wallet was 2 to 3. Thom then paid for a purchase with one \$5 bill and four \$10 bills, and did not receive change. Afterwards, Thom observed that the ratio of \$5 bills to \$10 bills in the wallet was 3 to 2. How many \$5 bills were in Thom's wallet at the beginning of the day?

    (A) 4

    (B) 6

    (C) 8

    (D) 10

    (E) 12

3. Seamus has 3 times as many marbles as Ronit, and Taj has 7 times as many marbles as Ronit. If Seamus has s marbles, then, in terms of s, how many marbles do Seamus, Ronit, and Taj have together?

    (A) $\frac{3}{7}s$

    (B) $\frac{7}{3}s$

    (C) $\frac{11}{3}s$

    (D) $7s$

    (E) $11s$

4. Machine X produces cartons at a uniform rate of 90 every 3 minutes, and Machine Y produces cartons at a uniform rate of 100 every 2 minutes. Working simultaneously, the two machines would produce a total of 560 cartons in how many minutes?

    (A) 7

    (B) 6

    (C) 5

    (D) 4

    (E) 3

Save the next problems for review after you finish this entire guide.

5. If $x = a + b$ and $y = a + 2b$, then what is $a - b$, in terms of x and y ?

    (A) $2y - 3x$

    (B) $3y - 2x$

    (C) $2x - 3y$

    (D) $2x + 3y$

    (E) $3x - 2y$

6. Two libraries are planning to combine a portion of their collections into one new space. The new space will house $\frac{1}{3}$ of the books from Library A, along with $\frac{1}{4}$ of the books from Library B. If there are twice as many books in Library B as in Library A, what proportion of the books in the new space will have come from Library A?

    (A) $\frac{1}{3}$

    (B) $\frac{2}{5}$

    (C) $\frac{1}{2}$

    (D) $\frac{7}{12}$

    (E) $\frac{3}{5}$

7. If $x < y$, which of the following must be true?

    (A) $x < y^2$

    (B) $x^2 < y$

    (C) $x^2 < y^2$

    (D) $(x - y)^2 > 0$

    (E) $x^3 > y$

8. A train travels at a constant rate. If the train takes 13 minutes to travel m kilometers, how long will the train take to travel n kilometers?

   (A) $\frac{13m}{n}$

   (B) $\frac{13n}{m}$

   (C) $13mn$

   (D) $\frac{n}{13}$

   (E) $\frac{m}{13}$

9. A manager split a bonus award among four employees. The first employee received $\frac{1}{3}$ of the total, the second received $\frac{1}{4}$ of the total, the third received $\frac{1}{5}$ of the total, and the fourth received the remaining $195. What was the total bonus amount awarded to the four employees?

   (A) $500

   (B) $600

   (C) $750

   (D) $900

   (E) $1,000

7

Solutions

1. **(E)** $ab > ac$: The question stem asks a *must be* question, so test cases on this problem. The stem also indicates that a is negative and that b is less than c. Since the first piece of information makes a distinction between positive and negative, think about the second piece of information in that same context. If b is less than c, then they could both be positive or both be negative, or b could be negative, while c is positive.

    Glance at the answers. They all involve multiplication of various combinations of the variables. Answers (C) and (D) also include > 0 or < 0, which are shorthand for positive and negative, respectively. What do you know about rules around positive and negative when multiplying two numbers together? If you're not sure, try a couple of small numbers to see what happens.

    If the two numbers have the same sign, such as $(1)(2) = 2$ or $(-1)(-2) = 2$, then the product will be positive. If the two numbers have opposite signs, such as $(1)(-2) = -2$, then the product will be negative.

    Given that, test answers (C) and (D) first.

    (C) $ab > 0$. The variable a is negative, but b could be negative or positive. If b is positive, then this choice is false; that is, it is not always true. Eliminate.

    (D) $ac < 0$. The variable a is negative, but c could be negative or positive. If c is negative, then this choice is false; that is, it is not always true. Eliminate.

    For the other three choices, try real values. Remember: a must be negative and $b < c$. Try whatever comes to mind for your first test, then think about how to alter the first test in order to get another answer to drop out.

	Test 1 $a = -1$ $b = -2$ $c = 3$	Test 2 $a = -1$ $b = -2$ $c = -1$
(A) $ab < c$	$(-1)(-2) < 3$ $2 < 3$ True	$(-1)(-2) < -1$ $2 < -1$ False
(B) $ac > b$	$(-1)(3) > -2$ $-3 > -2$ False	(already eliminated)
(E) $ab > ac$	$(-1)(-2) > (-1)(3)$ $2 > -3$ True	$(-1)(-2) > (-1)(-1)$ $2 > 1$ True

    Answer (B) drops out in the first test. In order to choose values for the second test, look at how the math worked. You can make the value for c negative, so it cannot be greater than the positive ab product, making choice (A) false.

    The correct answer is **(E)**.

2. **(A) 4:** Thom started with a certain ratio of bills, used some of those bills, and then finished with a different ratio of bills. Annoyingly, the problem doesn't offer any real numbers as a starting point. You could solve algebraically—but you could also just use the answer choices as your starting point and work backwards. Start with answer (B):

$5 at start	Start ratio $5 : $10 2 : 3	Pay −1 $5 −4 $10	New ratio $5 : $10 = 3 : 2 ?
(B) 6	Actual 6 : 9	New 5 : 5	No

If Thom started with six $5 bills, and the starting ratio was 2 : 3, then the unknown multiplier is 3 and there were nine $10 bills to start. After paying out the given amounts, Thom would be left with a new ratio of 5 : 5, or 1 : 1, but the problem specifies that the new ratio should be 3 : 2, so (B) is not correct. Try (D) next:

$5 at start	Start ratio $5 : $10 2 : 3	Pay −1 $5 −4 $10	New ratio $5 : $10 = 3 : 2 ?
(B) 6	Actual 6 : 9	New 5 : 5	No
(D) 10	Actual 10 : 15	New 9 : 11	No

This time, the new ratio would be 9 : 11, which still doesn't match the given ratio of 3 : 2, so answer (D) is also incorrect.

Now, what's the pattern between the two choices? It might help to view the ratios as fractions (you can always "read" ratios as fractions without literally rewriting them):

Answer (B) ratio	Answer (D) ratio	Desired new ratio
$\frac{5}{5}$ or $\frac{1}{1}$	$\frac{9}{11}$	$\frac{3}{2}$

The ratio given by answer (B) is 1. Answer (D) got smaller. But the desired ratio, $\frac{3}{2}$, is larger than both, so moving from answer (B) to answer (D) was the wrong direction. The answer must be **(A)**.

If you don't feel confident in that reasoning, go ahead and try answer (A). It will work!

3. **(C)** $\frac{11}{3}s$: The problem will be easier to solve if you can choose smart numbers that will give you all integers as you solve. Both Seamus and Taj have a multiple of the number of marbles that Ronit has, so begin by picking for Ronit, not for Seamus.

    If Ronit has 2 marbles, then Seamus has $(3)(2) = 6$ marbles and Taj has $(7)(2) = 14$ marbles. Together, the three have 22 marbles.

    Plug $s = 6$ into the answers (remember that the problem asks about Seamus's starting number, not Ronit's!), and look for a match of 22:

    (A) $\frac{3}{7}s$ = not an integer

    (B) $\frac{7}{3}s = \frac{7}{3}(6) = 14$. Not a match.

    (C) $\frac{11}{3}s = \frac{11}{3}(6) = 22$. Match!

    (D) $7s = 42$. Not a match.

    (E) $11s$ = too large

    Alternatively, you can use an algebraic approach. Begin by translating the first sentence into equations:

    $$s = 3r$$
    $$t = 7r$$

    The question asks for the sum of the three:

    $$s + r + t = ?$$

    The answers use only s, so figure out how to substitute to leave only s in the equation:

    $$r = \frac{s}{3}$$
    $$t = 7r = 7\left(\frac{s}{3}\right)$$

    Substitute for r and t in the original question:

    $$s + r + t$$
    $$= s + \frac{s}{3} + 7\left(\frac{s}{3}\right)$$
    $$= \frac{3s}{3} + \frac{s}{3} + \frac{7s}{3}$$
    $$= \frac{11s}{3}$$

    The correct answer is **(C)**.

7

4. **(A) 7:** The answer choices are real numbers and they represent a single variable in the problem (how long it would take the two machines together to produce 560 cartons). Work backwards from the answers. Start with answer (B) or (D).

Minutes	X 90 cart in 3 min	Y 100 cart in 2 min	Total cartons produced	= 560 ?
(B) 6	180	300	480	No

Answer (B) is incorrect; in 6 minutes, the two machines will have produced only 480 cartons, not 560. Further, the number of minutes must be greater than 6 (in order for more cartons to be produced).

Only answer (A) is greater than 6, so it must be correct.

If you're not sure about that reasoning, try answer (D) next. In 4 minutes, the two machines produce 320 cartons, even fewer! This confirms the trend that a lower number of minutes will produce fewer cartons, so the answer must be **(A)**.

5. **(E) $3x - 2y$:** With so many variables, choosing smart numbers will probably be more efficient. Because x and y can be found by certain sums of a and b, pick for a and b, then calculate x and y.

If $a = 5$ and $b = 2$, then $x = 5 + 2 = 7$ and $y = 5 + 2(2) = 9$. The difference is $a - b = 5 - 2 = 3$.

Plug $x = 7$ and $y = 9$ into the answers and look for a match of 3:

(A) $2y - 3x = 2(9) - 3(7) = 18 - 21 =$ negative

(B) $3y - 2x = 3(9) - 2(7) = 27 - 14 =$ not 3

(C) $2x - 3y = 2(7) - 3(9) = 14 - 27 =$ negative

(D) $2x + 3y = 2(7) + 3(9) =$ too big

(E) $3x - 2y = 3(7) - 2(9) = 21 - 18 = 3$. Match!

The correct answer is **(E)**.

You can also use an algebraic approach.

Given: $x = a + b$

Given: $y = a + 2b$

What is $a - b$?

The answers use only x and y, so figure out how to rewrite the given equations to plug into the question, using only x and y.

If you subtract the two equations, you'll get x and y in terms of b alone:

$$\begin{aligned} y &= a + 2b \\ -(x &= a + b) \\ \hline y - x &= b \end{aligned}$$

Multiply the $x = a + b$ equation by 2 and perform the same operation to get x and y in terms of a alone:

$$2x = 2a + 2b$$
$$\underline{-(y = a + 2b)}$$
$$2x - y = a$$

Then, find $a - b$:

$$(2x - y) - (y - x)$$
$$= 2x - y - y + x$$
$$= 3x - 2y$$

6. **(B)** $\frac{2}{5}$: The answers are in relative form, so you can use smart numbers. When working with fraction problems, choose a common denominator of the fractions given in the problem, in case you have to divide by either of those denominators. In this case, the problem contains the fractions $\frac{1}{3}$ and $\frac{1}{4}$, so use the common denominator of 12. Any multiple of 12 will work, but keep things simple and use 12 itself.

Assign the value 12 to the total for the *smaller* library—in this case, Library A—because the other library has twice as many books. As a result, Library B's capacity, 24, is also a multiple of the denominators 3 and 4:

$$(12)\left(\frac{1}{3}\right) = 4 \text{ of Library A's books will move to the new space.}$$

$$(24)\left(\frac{1}{4}\right) = 6 \text{ of Library B's books will move to the new space.}$$

The new space will therefore contain 10 books total. Because 4 out of 10 of those books came from Library A, 40%, or $\frac{2}{5}$, of the books in the new space will have come from Library A.

The correct answer is **(B)**.

Bonus Exercise: Take a look at the wrong answers. Can you figure out how someone would have gotten to any of them?

Answer (A), $\frac{1}{3}$, is one of the numbers given in the question. Also, it's the proportion of the books in the combined original libraries that are Library A's (that is, all books, not just the moved books).

Answer (D), $\frac{7}{12}$, represents the sum of $\frac{1}{3}$ and $\frac{1}{4}$, which is a simple—too simple!—arithmetic combination of two of the given numbers.

Answer (E), $\frac{3}{5}$, represents the proportion of Library B's books in the new space. If you calculated this answer, then you may have solved correctly, but for the wrong thing. How can you avoid making that kind of mistake in future?

7. **(D)** $(x - y)^2 > 0$: The *must be* language signals that you can (and probably want to) test cases on this problem. The only constraint given is that x is less than y. The answers contain exponents and one contains > 0, so test negatives and fractions between 0 and 1, as well as 0 and 1 themselves.

Answer	$x = 0$ $y = 1$	$x = -1$ $y = 0$	$x = \frac{1}{4}$ $y = \frac{1}{2}$
(A) $x < y^2$	$0 < 1$ True	$-1 < 0$ True	(A) $\frac{1}{4} < \frac{1}{4}$ False
(B) $x^2 < y$	$0 < 1$ True	$1 < 0$ False	already eliminated
(C) $x^2 < y^2$	$0 < 1$ True	$1 < 0$ False	already eliminated
(D) $(x - y)^2 > 0$	$1 > 0$ True	$1 > 0$ True	(D) $\left(-\frac{1}{4}\right)^2 = \frac{1}{16} > 0$ True!
(E) $x^3 > y$	$0 > 1$ False	already eliminated	

Try the easiest combo first, something involving 0 and 1. That only knocks out one answer, but it helps you to think about what's going on with the math. Sometimes x is squared, sometimes y is squared, so next put a negative number into the mix. (Note: You no longer have to try answer (E); it drops out after the first case.)

When x is -1 and y is 0, two more answers drop out, but two are still left. Fractions between 0 and 1 do interesting things when squared, so try those next. In this final case, answer (A) is false. Answer **(D)** is true throughout all of the tests, so it's the correct answer.

8. **(B)** $\frac{13n}{m}$: The problem never provides a real number for the distance that the train travels, just the variables m and n, so you can choose your own smart number. A small number like 2 is often a good one to choose—but that turns out not to be a great number in this case. Why?

The train takes 13 minutes to travel 2 kilometers, so the train's rate is 2 kilometers per 13 minutes. That's not a nice number. Choose something that will result in an integer, such as $m = 26$ kilometers. Now, the train is going $\frac{26 \text{ km}}{13 \text{ min}} = 2$ km/min.

Next, how long will the train take to go n kilometers? If $n = 10$, then the train will take 5 minutes to go 10 kilometers.

Find a match in the answers. Plug $m = 26$ and $n = 10$ into the answers. Your goal is to find an answer choice that equals 5. If you can tell that a certain answer will *not* equal 5, cross it off without calculating exactly what it does equal:

(A) $\frac{13m}{n} = \frac{13(26)}{10} =$ too big

(B) $\frac{13n}{m} = \frac{13(10)}{26} =$ maybe. Simplify to confirm: $\frac{1(10)}{2} = 5$. Match!

(C) $13mn = 13(10)(26) =$ too big

(D) $\frac{n}{13} = \frac{10}{13} =$ fraction

(E) $\frac{m}{13} = \frac{26}{13} = 2$. Not a match.

The correct answer is **(B)**.

9. **(D) $900:** You can solve this problem algebraically or you can work backwards. You'd have to find a common denominator across three fractions to solve algebraically, so it may be faster to work backwards, since the fractions are relatively easy ones and the numbers in the answers are pretty nice. Start with answer (B).

	#1$\left(\frac{1}{3}\right)$	#2$\left(\frac{1}{4}\right)$	#3$\left(\frac{1}{5}\right)$	#4 ($195)	Sum to the choice?
(B) 600	200	150	120	195	NO

To find a third, divide by 3. To find a fourth, divide by 2 twice. To find a fifth, or 20%, take 10% and double it.

The total won't be $600 because three of the numbers end in a 0 and the fourth ends in a 5, so answer (B) isn't correct. Is this answer too big or too small? Examine the first three figures—the ones that can actually change from answer choice to answer choice.

The first three figures add up to 470. If the total is 600, then the fourth person would get a bonus of 130. But the fourth person's bonus is actually 195, so this answer choice falls short. You need a larger number. Cross off answers (A) and (B), and try (D) next.

	#1$\left(\frac{1}{3}\right)$	#2$\left(\frac{1}{4}\right)$	#3$\left(\frac{1}{5}\right)$	#4 ($195)	Sum to the choice?
(B) 600	200	150	120	195	NO
(D) 900	300	225	180	195	Yes!

This could be correct, since two of the answers end in 5 now. Add them up, but make your job easier; 195 is an annoying value, so take 5 from the 225 and add it to the 195.

Don't do: $300 + 225 + 180 + 195$

Instead, do: $300 + 220 + 180 + 200 = 300 + 400 + 200 = 900$

The total matches the starting point, so **(D)** is the correct answer.

Table Analysis

In This Chapter...

- UPS for Tables

- Sort, Eyeball, and Estimate

- Review and Improve on Tables

In this chapter, you will learn how Table problems are constructed and what they test. You'll also learn how to use UPS (Understand, Plan, Solve) and the SEE (sort, eyeball, estimate) approach to solve Table problems.

CHAPTER 8 Table Analysis

Table Analysis (Table) problems, unsurprisingly, require you to analyze tables of information.

The table appears on the left side of the screen; the question appears on the right side of the screen. Table prompts are always accompanied by one three-part **Either-Or** question (e.g., true/false, yes/no).

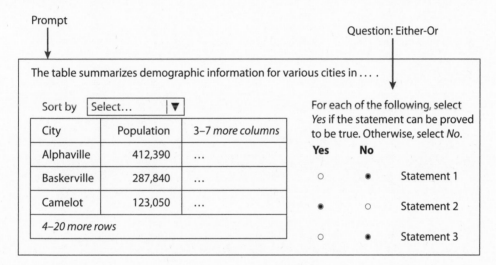

The table can be presented alone or with an associated blurb, which can range from a simple title to a full paragraph of information that you must understand in order to fully process the data in the table. The blurb is sometimes placed on the left side, above the table, and sometimes on the right side, above the question.

You'll be able to sort the Table by column, but if you're an experienced Excel user, you'll find the sorting very limited. The sorts will always be ascending, and you can perform only one sort at a time (no secondary sorts).

UPS for Tables

Table problems usually have a quantitative focus, often testing general Statistics (mean, median, standard deviation, range, correlation, and so on), Fractions, Decimals, Percents, and Ratios. They might ask you to look something up in the table, perform some calculations based on data presented in the table, or make inferences based on the data in the table.

Take a look at the following Table problem:

The table displays data from the different divisions of Company X in 2011. Market shares are computed by dividing a division's total sales (in dollars) by the total sales (in dollars) made by all companies selling products in that category. Market shares are separately calculated for the world (global market share) and for the United States (U.S. market share). Ranks are based on Company X's position relative to other companies competing in the same market.

Division	Global market share	Global market rank	U.S. market share	U.S. market rank
Agriculture & Food	8%	6	12%	4
Health Care & Medical	12%	4	18%	2
Household Goods & Personal Care	5%	5	10%	4
Performance Plastics	30%	1	26%	1
Water & Process Solutions	19%	1	26%	1

Select *Yes* if the statement can be proved true for Company X in 2011 based on the information provided in the table. Otherwise, select *No*.

Yes	No	
O	O	There is a positive correlation between global market share and U.S. market share.
O	O	The same division of Company X is the median of Company X's five divisions by both U.S. market rank and global market rank.
O	O	The Performance Plastics division had a greater market share in at least one other country than it had in the United States.

Step 1: Understand the Prompt and Question

The table and the blurb accompanying it are the prompt; focus on understanding that information first.

First, **Glance** at the table title (if applicable) and at the column and row headers. In this case, there is no title. The first column shows *divisions* that appear to be categories for different types of products. The next two columns provide global market data, and the final two columns provide U.S. market data. That data has to do with market share (in percent form) and market rank.

Next, **Read** the blurb (if any) given with the table. If the blurb explains specific parts of the table, examine the relevant parts as you read:

- The blurb indicates that the table contains data about the divisions of one specific company. Now you have the full context for the first column of the table.

- Next, the blurb explains how market share is calculated. Glance again to reinforce the message: The *Global market share* column shows market share for the entire global market and the *U.S. market share* column shows market share for just the U.S. They are both in percentage form. (Note: The U.S. market is a subset of the global market, since the global market is comprised of the markets of all countries.)

- Finally, the blurb indicates that the table shows how each division ranks against all other companies in that geographic region; again, glance at the table to reinforce the message.

Time to **Jot**. Take another glance over the full table to make sure you know the kind of data you have and how it is presented, then consider what you want to jot down. Your goal is not to make an inventory of everything you read. Rather, jotting at this stage can help to reinforce the major messages and keep you oriented properly as you try to solve the problem.

In this case, you might jot down something like this:

> Global vs. U.S.
> Share % + Rank for each

If you are not completely sure that you fully understand what you just reviewed, pick a cell or group of cells in the table and then articulate to yourself what the value or values represent. For example, the Household Goods & Personal Care division has a global market share of 5% and is ranked fifth in the global market in that category. So, there must be four other companies that outrank this division of Company X in the global market (i.e., four other companies each make at least 5% of the global sales in that category).

If you can do this, great! Move on to the question. If you can't, consider whether you want to do this problem at all. It may be better to guess randomly—and immediately—and move on.

It is possible that a table blurb will contain complex additional information—that is, information about something other than the specific data in the table. For instance, in this example, the blurb provides some extra detail regarding how those numbers are calculated.

When this happens, you may not be able to fully understand or process this information until later. That's okay. You don't have to bail now if you don't understand that type of information. As long as you understand the basic information contained in the table, keep going.

Let's move to the question. It will first provide directions and then give you a box with three statements. Here is the question text for this problem again:

> Select *Yes* if the statement can be proved true for Company X in 2011 based on the information provided in the table. Otherwise, select *No*.

Yes	No	
○	○	There is a positive correlation between global market share and U.S. market share.
○	○	The same division of Company X is the median of Company X's five divisions by both U.S. market rank and global market rank.
○	○	The Performance Plastics division had a greater market share in at least one other country than it had in the United States.

This is an either-or problem; Table prompts always use this problem type. You will be asked to select one of two answers in either X or Y form: in this case, either *Yes* or *No*.

Three statements accompany the question; your task is to choose either Yes or No for each statement. In order to earn credit for this problem, you have to answer all three statements correctly.

As with the prompt, your first goal is to understand the question asked. In this case, the question is whether you can *prove* each statement *true* based on the information provided. The *for Company X in 2011* language is given in order to avoid having to specify those details in each statement. This language signals that they aren't going to try to trick you by asking a question about a random Company Y or a different year, for which no data is given, just to see whether you're paying attention.

Next, glance through the three statements.

First, are they more quant-based (you're asked about some actual math concept) or verbal/analytical-based (you're asked to infer or otherwise analyze in a way that doesn't involve computation)?

The first statement mentions correlation, a math topic, but the other two are focused on your ability to read the table properly, so they are more verbal or analytical in nature.

Also note that the three statements look fairly different, so you will probably need to solve each one separately. This is often the case on Table problems, but sometimes the statements are very similar and can be solved using the same process—sometimes even simultaneously.

Next, read the first statement. If it seems straightforward, go ahead to the next step in the process (Plan). If not, skip that statement for now and read the second one. You can always start with whichever statement seems easiest to you. (If you read all three statements and realize you don't want to start with any of them, guess immediately and move on.)

Step 2: Plan Your Approach

Assume that you decide to start with the first statement:

Yes	No	
○	○	There is a positive correlation between global market share and U.S. market share.

First, what does *positive correlation* mean?

Two sets of data have a positive correlation when the two sets of numbers increase together or decrease together. For example, the age of a tree and the circumference of its trunk have a positive correlation: As age increases, so does the circumference of the trunk.

Next, on a Table problem, it is usually the case that sorting the table in some way will make it easier for you to find the answer. What kind of sort would be useful for this question?

The two relevant columns are *Global market share* and *U.S. market share*. Should you sort by the former or the latter? Sometimes, this will be obvious. Other times, you may have to think about this a bit or even try a couple of different sorts.

In this case, you can sort by either column. You'll be looking to see whether they "go in the same direction"—that is, they both generally increase or they both generally decrease.

Step 3: Solve the Problem

Here's the table sorted by *Global market share*:

Division	Global market share	Global market rank	U.S. market share	U.S. market rank
Household Goods & Personal Care	5%	5	10%	4
Agriculture & Food	8%	6	12%	4
Health Care & Medical	12%	4	18%	2
Water & Process Solutions	19%	1	26%	1
Performance Plastics	30%	1	26%	1

As global market share increases, U.S. market share does increase, indicating a positive correlation.

The answer to the first statement is *Yes*.

Evaluate the second and third statements in the same manner, repeating the Plan and Solve steps. Here's the second statement:

Yes	No	
◯	◯	The same division of Company X is the median of Company X's five divisions by both U.S. market rank and global market rank.

The median for five divisions is the division in the third position when the numbers are placed in increasing order. You can sort first either by global rank or by U.S. rank; the order you check doesn't matter. Here is the sort by *U.S. market rank*:

Division	Global market share	Global market rank	U.S. market share	U.S. market rank
Performance Plastics	30%	1	26%	1
Water & Process Solutions	19%	1	26%	1
Health Care & Medical	12%	4	18%	2
Agriculture & Food	8%	6	12%	4
Household Goods & Personal Care	5%	5	10%	4

The Health Care & Medical division falls into the third-highest position for the U.S. rankings. Now, take a look at the *Global market rank* column. In a longer or more jumbled list, you might have to sort again by this column. In this case, though, eyeball (glance at) that column first. The numbers are almost in order already; only the 5 and the 6 would need to be swapped. The Health Care & Medical division is again in the third position of the five divisions within Company X.

The answer to the second statement is *Yes*.

Here is the third statement:

Yes	No	
○	○	The Performance Plastics division had a greater market share in at least one other country than it had in the United States.

In this case, you don't need to sort any columns; you can answer using just the Performance Plastics row:

Division	Global market share	Global market rank	U.S. market share	U.S. market rank
Performance Plastics	30%	1	26%	1

U.S. market share is 26% and global market share is 30%. In other words, this division had a higher market share globally than it did in the United States.

The U.S. market is a subset of the global market, so U.S. sales contribute to the company's global sales. What is the relationship between global market share and market share in just one country?

If this market exists only in the U.S.—that is, these products were sold nowhere else in the world by any company—then the division's U.S. market share and global market share would be identical (because the two markets would be the same). The U.S. and global market shares are *not* the same, though, so there must be at least one other country in which the Performance Plastics division has sales.

Next, imagine that the division has 26% market share in every country where it sells these products. If that were the case, the company would have exactly 26% of the global market share as well. Its global share is greater, though—it has 30% of the market share globally. So it must have a greater share of the market somewhere other than the United States.

That scenario is what the third statement says: Company X's global market share, at 30%, is greater than its U.S. market share, so it must have a greater market share in at least one other country than it does in the United States.

The answer to the third statement is *Yes*.

The answers are as follows:

Yes	No	
●	○	There is a positive correlation between global market share and U.S. market share.
●	○	The same division of Company X is the median of Company X's five divisions by both U.S. market rank and global market rank.
●	○	The Performance Plastics division had a greater market share in at least one other country than it had in the United States.

Sort, Eyeball, and Estimate

On any Table problem, don't do any work at all until you've considered how to **SEE: Sort, Eyeball,** and **Estimate**. These steps will save you a lot of time and mental effort on the exam.

Try this problem:

> The table presents the Q1 medical equipment sales figures for 9 regional sales teams, as well as the forecast changes in sales for each quarter (relative to the prior quarter). Q1 figures are in thousands of dollars.

Sales team	Q1 sales (in thousands)	Forecast		
		Q2 (change from Q1)	Q3 (change from Q2)	Q4 (change from Q3)
A	$902	−13.2%	8.6%	−8.3%
B	$1,301	−10.4%	−11.6%	−6.0%
C	$1,793	17.0%	−7.4%	13.2%
D	$877	−6.8%	−5.1%	−4.6%
E	$3,866	1.2%	3.5%	3.7%
F	$2,576	4.9%	4.2%	1.4%
G	$2,140	−5.4%	3.3%	2.2%
H	$3,214	15.6%	8.5%	−7.6%
I	$4,325	12.4%	−12.4%	16.8%

For each of the following statements, select *True* if the statement can be shown to be true using the information provided. Otherwise, select *False*.

True	False	
○	○	According to the forecasts, the team with the median sales in Q1 will also have the median sales in Q2.
○	○	Of the teams that are projected to see a quarterly increase in Q3, more than half are expected to see an additional quarterly increase in Q4.
○	○	The number of teams projected to see a quarterly decrease in both Q2 and Q3 is greater than the number of teams projected to see a quarterly decrease in both Q3 and Q4.

How did it go? Before continuing to read here, review your work to look for opportunities to answer any of the statements more efficiently. Pay close attention to any steps that seemed cumbersome—any ideas for how to streamline or entirely avoid that part?

Step 1: Understand the Prompt and Question

The blurb is pretty basic; it just explains what's in the table.

Interestingly, actual quantities are given only in the Q1 column. The other three are all percentage increases or decreases from the immediately preceding quarter (the column to the left). Pick a row and follow the numbers to the right to see how they work.

How about row G? This team had Q1 sales of $2,140,000. Since all given numbers are in thousands, you can ignore the final three zeros and just call it $2,140. In Q2, sales are projected to decline: The forecast for Team G is a negative percent change. If you wanted to find the forecast sales figure for Q2, you would either take 5.4% of the Q1 figure and subtract, or you would multiply the Q1 figure by $(100 - 5.4)\% = 94.6\%$. Sales are projected to increase in Q3 and Q4, though, so the forecast for Team G is a positive percent change in both these quarters.

So you can see at a glance whether the team is predicted to do better or worse than the immediately previous quarter, based on whether the percentage change is positive or negative. However, you would have to crunch the numbers to know the actual sales figures for Q2, Q3, and Q4.

Mini Math Lesson

Percentages do funny things. For example, in the final row, Sales Team I is forecast to have a 12.4% increase in Q2 and a 12.4% decrease in Q3. Does that mean that their sales figure in Q3 ends up back where it started in Q1, at $4,325K?

If you're not sure, calculate the steps to see what happens.

First, if you take any number and increase it by a certain percentage, then decrease the resulting number by the same percentage, you will never end up back at the same starting point (unless your starting point was 0 or your percentage was 0%). Why?

Try some real numbers to see. If you have $100 and increase by 20%, you'll have $120. Now, take that new figure and decrease by 20%: $120 - $24 = $96.

For the second calculation, you're taking 20% of $120, which is a greater value than $100. So 20% of $120 will be a greater figure than 20% of 100.

In fact, it will always be the case that 20% of a smaller number is less than 20% of a greater number, so when you increase by a certain percentage and then decrease by that same percentage, you'll always end up *lower* than where you started. The same is true for Sales Team I: For Q3, they are forecast to have sales *below* their Q1 starting point of $4,325K.

By the way, do you think Team G did better or worse in Q4 than in Q1? Make your best guess, then do the math to check. The answer is at the end of this section.

Back to the problem. Here's the question stem again:

> For each of the following statements, select *True* if the statement can be shown to be true using the information provided. Otherwise, select *False*.

Essentially, can the statement be proven true using the data in the table? If so, call that one true. If you can't prove it true *using the given data*, call it false—even if you don't have enough information to tell that it's truly false.

Here's the first statement:

True	False	
○	○	According to the forecasts, the team with the median sales in Q1 will also have the median sales in Q2.

Did the same team have the median sales in both Q1 and Q2?

Glance back up at the blurb; how many sales teams are there? Nine. (You don't have to count—the blurb says that there are nine teams. Always check the blurb first before you try to count the total number of rows; if it's a longer table, chances are the blurb will tell you.)

Step 2: Plan Your Approach

To find the median, the numbers have to be listed in order, so you're definitely going to use the first step in SEE, *sort*, on this table. Finding the median for Q1 will be easy, since the Q1 column shows the actual sales figures.

Q2, though, is trickier, as it shows only the percentage increase or decrease from Q1. You do have a calculator, so maybe you just have to calculate the forecast sales for each sales team in Q2?

There are nine rows. That's a lot of work.

So stop! Don't do annoying math. This is why you Plan before you Solve. First, sort by Q1 sales to find that median, then examine the data to think about the best approach for the Q2 values.

Step 3: (Start to) Solve the Problem

Here's the table sorted by Q1 (and without Q3 or Q4, since they don't matter for this statement):

Sales team	Q1 sales (in thousands)	Q2 (change from Q1)
D	$877	−6.8%
A	$902	−13.2%
B	$1,301	−10.4%
C	$1,793	17.0%
G	$2,140	−5.4%
F	$2,576	4.9%
H	$3,214	15.6%
E	$3,866	1.2%
I	$4,325	12.4%

The median for Q1 is the fifth one from the top or the bottom: Team G.

Review the question: Does Team G have the median for *both* Q1 and Q2? In other words, does Team G stay in the fifth position or does its position change?

Team G's sales will decrease a little bit, but not that much—a little over 5%. The numbers for each team are far enough apart that you can use benchmarks to *estimate* the change:

10% of $2,140 = $214

Half of that = 5% = $107

$2,140 − $107 ≈ $2,000

So Team G will be at about $2,000 in Q2. Next, eyeball the data to see which other teams *might* change positions relative to Team G. (To *eyeball* is to look and think logically about the data; you won't be doing any actual calculations, even at an estimation level.)

Teams D, A, and B are already below $2,000 in Q1 and they all decrease further in Q2, so they will still stay below Team G in the Q2 list. No need to calculate anything for them.

Team C, by contrast, increases, so it could jump past Team G. You might have to do some calculations, so jot down Team C on your scratch paper as a reminder.

Next, eyeball the teams that have Q1 sales greater than those of Team G. They are already higher than $2,000 and all four increase in Q2, so they will stay above Team G in that quarter.

The only possibility is that Team C will swap places with Team G. Eyeballing the data saves a lot of time that would have been wasted on unnecessary calculations!

Jot down the numbers you need, then figure out how to do the calculations. Finally, plug the calculations into the on-screen calculator to solve:

	Q1 value	Q2 % change	Q2 value (rounded)
Team C	1,793	+17.0%	$(1,793)(1 + 0.17) = \$2,098$
Team G	2,140	−5.4%	$(2,140)(1 − 0.054) = \$2,024$

Team C does indeed pass Team G in Q2, so Team C is now the team with the median sales volume. It is *not* true that the same team is in the median position for both quarters.

The correct answer for statement 1 is *False*.

Here is statement 2:

True	False	
○	○	Of the teams that are projected to see a quarterly increase in Q3, more than half are expected to see an additional quarterly increase in Q4.

This time, the statement focuses on Q3 and Q4. When you see something like *of the teams that* (fall into a certain category), the statement is giving you a qualifier: It wants you to consider *only* this subset of the categories given in the table.

In this case, the desired subset is those teams that will have a Q3 increase. You don't technically have to sort in order to see which teams have positive percentages in Q3, but do so anyway. Sorting by Q3 will group those teams together so that you don't inadvertently include teams that you don't want. SEE starts with *sort* for a reason—it's easy to do and it will save you both time and careless mistakes.

8

Before you do that, though, jot down what the statement wants you to find. Here's one way to do that:

Do > 50% of teams that ↑ in Q3 *also* ↑ in Q4?

Jot this down in any way that makes sense to you. Here's the data sorted by the Q3 column:

Sales team	Q3 (change from Q2)	Q4 (change from Q3)
I	−12.4%	16.8%
B	−11.6%	−6.0%
C	−7.4%	13.2%
D	−5.1%	−4.6%
G	3.3%	2.2%
E	3.5%	3.7%
F	4.2%	1.4%
H	8.5%	−7.6%
A	8.6%	−8.3%

Only five of the teams are projected to have a quarterly increase in Q3: Teams G, E, F, H, and A. Of just those teams, three are also projected to have an increase in Q4: Teams G, E, and F.

Therefore, three out of five of the teams increase in both quarters. This is greater than 50%, so this statement is true.

The correct answer for statement 2 is *True*.

Here is the third statement:

True	False	
○	○	The number of teams projected to see a quarterly decrease in both Q2 and Q3 is greater than the number of teams projected to see a quarterly decrease in both Q3 and Q4.

This is very similar to statement 2: You're looking for two adjacent quarters with the same trend. You have to do it for two groupings this time, not just one. Jot this down in a form that makes sense for you; here's one way to do that:

Is # (Q2 and Q3) ↓ more than # (Q3 and Q4) ↓ ?

Make sure to evaluate each part separately so that you don't, for example, mistakenly carry over Q2 data into the examination of Q3 and Q4. And you'll again minimize your chances of a careless error if you *sort* as you go. First, sort by Q2:

Sales team	Q2 (change from Q1)	Q3 (change from Q2)
A	−13.2%	8.6%
B	−10.4%	−11.6%
D	−6.8%	−5.1%
G	−5.4%	3.3%
E	1.2%	3.5%
F	4.9%	4.2%
I	12.4%	−12.4%
H	15.6%	8.5%
C	17.0%	−7.4%

Two teams are projected to have a decrease in both Q2 and Q3: Teams B and D.

Next, sort by Q3:

Sales team	Q3 (change from Q2)	Q4 (change from Q3)
I	−12.4%	16.8%
B	−11.6%	−6.0%
C	−7.4%	13.2%
D	−5.1%	−4.6%
G	3.3%	2.2%
E	3.5%	3.7%
F	4.2%	1.4%
H	8.5%	−7.6%
A	8.6%	−8.3%

Again, two teams are projected to have a decrease in both Q3 and Q4; Teams B and D again.

It is *not* the case that the number of teams with decreased sales in both Q2 and Q3 is greater than that in both Q3 and Q4.

The correct answer for statement 3 is *False*.

8

The answers are:

True	False	
○	●	According to the forecasts, the team with the median sales in Q1 will also have the median sales in Q2.
●	○	Of the teams that are projected to see a quarterly increase in Q3, more than half are expected to see an additional quarterly increase in Q4.
○	●	The number of teams projected to see a quarterly decrease in both Q2 and Q3 is greater than the number of teams projected to see a quarterly decrease in both Q3 and Q4.

Whenever you have to solve a Table problem, don't do any real work until you consider how you can SEE (sort, eyeball, estimate) to save yourself time and effort. On this problem, all three of these strategies made a big difference for the first statement. For the other two statements, sorting saved a small amount of time and—perhaps more important—helped to minimize the chances of a careless error.

Don't hesitate to pop up the on-screen calculator when you need it; just make sure that you know what you need to calculate before you start punching in numbers. It's a good idea to write out the calculations you want to do before you start using the calculator.

Mini Math Lesson Redux

So, what happened with Team G?

Most people will guess that Team G ends up with greater sales in Q4 than in Q1 . . . but it doesn't! Why do people think this and why are they wrong?

Nobody wants to do tedious calculations, so most people will just compare the percentages. Sales are forecast to decrease by 5.4% in Q2, but then increase by 3.3% and 2.2% in Q3 and Q4, respectively. That seems like a 5.5% increase, since 3.3% + 2.2% = 5.5%, and 5.5% is greater than 5.4%, right?

Maybe. Would you rather have 5.5% of $10 or 5.4% of $1,000,000?

Why?

Here's how the calculations play out:

$$\begin{aligned} &\text{Q1:} &&2{,}140 \\ &\text{Q2: } -5.4\% = (2{,}140)(1 - 0.054) = 2{,}024 \\ &\text{Q3: } +3.3\% = (2{,}024)(1 + 0.033) = 2{,}091 \\ &\text{Q4: } +2.2\% = (2{,}091)(1 + 0.022) = 2{,}137 \end{aligned}$$

Since the first step is a decrease, that lowers the base figure that Team G is working from; in Q2, they're making just 2,024. The Q3 forecast is for an increase of 3.3%, but the increase is calculated from that lower base (2,024). The same is true for the 2.2% increase—it's 2.2% of a lesser number than the starting point of $2,140.

So, for the same reason that you would much rather have 5.4% of a greater number than 5.5% of a smaller one, Team G finished the year a bit lower than it started.

Alternatively, since this is the DI section, you could use the calculator to find the cumulative change for Q4 in one combined step: cumulative change from Q1 to Q4 = (0.946)(1.033)(1.022) = 0.9987 = 99.87%.

In other words, the Q4 sales forecast is 99.87% of the Q1 sales figure. This is less than 100%, so Q4 sales will be less than Q1 sales.

Review and Improve on Tables

Review every problem you do, regardless of whether you got it right or wrong.

If you answered a question incorrectly—or aren't fully confident about something you answered correctly—review each step of the UPS process. Did you overlook, misunderstand, or fail to comprehend any information in the prompt? Did you inadvertently answer a different question than the one that was asked? Was there a better way to approach the problem? Did you make any mistakes at the solution stage?

If you answered it correctly, ask yourself whether there are any opportunities to do things better next time. Where could you streamline any steps of the process? (Consider both time and mental energy.) What if it took a long time to solve and you don't see a way to make it faster—do you really want to do this on the real test? It might be better to guess quickly and spend your time elsewhere.

Grab a timer and give yourself approximately 2 minutes to try this problem:

> The table summarizes total sales information for a large production company for the first six months of 2014. The table also provides percent of total sales from the company's only three divisions (Electronics, Housewares, and Automotive). The company acquired the automotive division in March of 2014.

2014 Monthly Sales by Product Line

Month	Total ($, thousands)	% Electronics	% Housewares	% Automotive
January	3,890	47.09	52.91	0.00
February	4,204	49.75	50.25	0.00
March	6,561	34.19	33.00	32.81
April	6,982	36.44	34.03	29.53
May	6,613	37.97	33.34	28.69
June	7,028	34.58	34.00	31.42

For each of the following statements, select *Would help explain* if the statement would, if true, help explain some of the information in the table. Otherwise, select *Would not help explain*.

Would help explain	Would not help explain	
○	○	Consumer purchases of electronics typically drop just after the month of December, but they revive within two to three months after that.
○	○	Companies that have electronics, housewares, and automotive product lines tend to have higher total sales in housewares than do companies that sell only one or two of these product lines.
○	○	The housewares division took a $1.1 million loss in March due to an accounting change.

Before reading the explanations below (or even checking whether you got it correct), ask yourself whether you're generally happy with how things went. If you want to try any part of the problem again, go ahead; you don't need to time yourself, and you can look up anything you want elsewhere in this guide.

Then, take a look at the correct answers (scroll to the end of this section—the answers are not immediately below so that you aren't "spoiled" while you are working the problem). Does knowing the correct answer make you want to check or redo anything? Go ahead.

Finally, work your way through the official solution—but stop whenever you get a good idea about what to do next. See how far you can push that idea yourself before you continue reading the official solution. Make yourself work for it! You'll learn better that way.

Step 1: Understand the Prompt and Question

The accompanying blurb explains that the table provides total and percent of sales numbers across six months. It also explains why the Automotive division seemingly had no sales in January and February: because that division was acquired in March.

The Total column shows a significant jump in March, corresponding with the acquisition of the new division. Other than that, sales are generally increasing, though May shows a drop. The percentages for Electronics and Housewares drop in March, but this occurs because a third division is added; *sales in dollars* haven't necessarily dropped in the other two divisions, just their *share* of total sales.

This fact—that a new division was acquired partway through the period—means the data is going to be a little odd. Make a note to yourself to be especially careful with any questions that ask you to bridge the pre- and post-acquisition periods—perhaps jot down "Mar = acq!" on your scratch paper as a reminder. You may have to do some number crunching in order to be able to compare the numbers in a meaningful way.

Here's the question stem again:

> For each of the following statements, select *Would help explain* if the statement would, if true, help explain some of the information in the table. Otherwise, select *Would not help explain*.

The *if true* language in the question stem sends a specific message: You are supposed to accept each statement as true. In other words, your job here is not to decide whether the statement is true. Rather, assuming already that the statement *is* true, does that statement help to explain some portion of the data that you see in the table?

This question is essentially the opposite of what you were asked to do earlier in this chapter. You're not taking the table data and seeing whether you can prove that the statement is true. Rather, you're starting from the given statement and seeing whether it makes the table data make sense.

Here's the first statement:

Would help explain	Would not help explain	
○	○	Consumer purchases of electronics typically drop just after the month of December, but they revive within two to three months after that.

Step 2: Plan your Approach

Just after the month of December would be January, and January is included in the data. The statement is limited to the Electronics division.

Assume that this statement is true. If so, what would you expect to see in the data? First, there would have been a drop from December to January, but December isn't in the table, so ignore that part. Next, from January to February, revenues could have done anything—stayed the same, gone down, or gone up. But starting in March or April (*two or three months after*), Electronics revenues should increase. Check the data to see whether this trend exists.

Ah, but the table doesn't show revenues just for the Electronics division. It shows total revenues and then the percentage of those revenues attributed to each division. So you are going to need to do some calculating to see what's happening with the revenues in this one division. But look for all possible opportunities to eyeball and estimate.

(Note: The revenues are in thousands in the table, but you can ignore that detail when you're just trying to figure out whether revenue increased or decreased.)

Step 3: Solve the Problem

In February, total revenues were about $4,200 and Electronics represented 49.75% of that, or just under 50%. So February revenues were about $2,100 (really, a tiny bit less). Did revenue go up from February to March?

In March, the Electronics percentage was 34.19%, or a little more than $\frac{1}{3}$ of total revenues. Revenues were $6,561, or approximately $6,600, so a third is about $2,200. Electronics was a little more than a third, but revenue was already rounded up a little bit, so $2,200 is a good estimate.

In April, Electronics increased its percentage share *and* total revenues increased, so Electronics revenue also increased in this period.

So, yes, revenue went up from February to March and from March to April.

This statement does explain the relevant part of the data for the Electronics division. The correct answer for statement 1 is *Would help explain*.

Here's the second statement:

Would help explain	Would not help explain	
O	O	Companies that have electronics, housewares, and automotive product lines tend to have higher total sales in housewares than do companies that sell only one or two of these product lines.

Hmm. If a company sells all three lines, then it tends to sell more in housewares than does a company with only one or two of these lines. This prompt is only about one company, though, so how can you tell anything about a different company that sells only one or two of these product lines?

Wait! For the first two months of the period shown in the table, this company *did* sell only two of these product lines. So compare the company to itself, pre- and post-acquisition.

In this case, it isn't necessary to sort the data at all, but you will have to do a little number crunching. Estimate wherever feasible:

Month	Total ($, thousands)	% Electronics	% Housewares	% Automotive
January	3,890	47.09	52.91	0.00
February	4,204	49.75	50.25	0.00
March	6,561	34.19	33.00	32.81
April	6,982	36.44	34.03	29.53
May	6,613	37.97	33.34	28.69
June	7,028	34.58	34.00	31.42

In February, Housewares had about 50% of sales, or about $2,100 (you can continue to ignore the *thousands* designation). It had a slightly higher percentage share in January, but total sales were $300 lower that month, so the dollar amount for Housewares in January was about the same or a little lower than in February.

In March, the automotive business was acquired. Now, Housewares dropped to 33% of total sales, but of a larger base: $6,561. Approximately one-third of the total revenue is about $2,200, so Housewares sales did grow from February to March.

In April, Housewares increased its share of sales and total revenue increased, so housewares was again greater in April than in February. Likewise, in both May and June, Housewares had a greater share than in March and total revenues were greater than in March, so the trend continues.

The correct answer for statement 2 is *Would help explain.*

Here's the third statement:

Would help explain	Would not help explain	
O	O	The Housewares division took a $1.1 million loss in March due to an accounting change.

Don't jump straight to the data and start calculating anything. Understand first. This statement talks about a loss, but the data in the table is entirely about revenues. A loss is a cost; it would be reflected in profits, not in revenues. So the data in the table can't help to explain this cost.

Note: The GMAT doesn't expect you to know about accounting—you'll learn that in grad school!—but it does expect you to know that Profit = Revenue − Cost.

The correct answer for statement 3 is *Would not help explain.*

The answers are:

Would help explain	Would not help explain	
●	○	Consumer purchases of electronics typically drop just after the month of December, but they revive within two to three months after that.
●	○	Companies that have electronics, housewares, and automotive product lines tend to have higher total sales in housewares than do companies that sell only one or two of these product lines.
○	●	The Housewares division took a $1.1 million loss in March due to an accounting change.

If you made a mistake at any step along the way, first try to isolate the error. If you fell into a trap because of the confusing data switch in March, when the Automotive division was acquired, the unusual data there was your clue to pause for a moment to understand what was happening. The two 0.0% entries really stand out; something weird happened. Try to understand what happened and why before you get to the statements.

When a table adds a set of data part way through, you can't compare the data sets as easily, particularly when the percentages have to add up to 100% (as in this case). Pretend that you essentially have two tables, pre- and post- the change. Expect at least one of the statements to hinge on that change, and be prepared to do a little number crunching.

In this case, you had to deal with that change in multiple statements; in fact, that was the main focus of most of the problem. You didn't even have to sort on this table.

Next, don't just review when you make an error. Did you do more work than necessary at any point? Review the problem with SEE on your mind: Where else could you have sorted, eyeballed, or estimated (or done so more aggressively) to save yourself some effort? Don't pull up the calculator or do more precise math when it's not needed.

But when you do need it, don't hesitate to pop up the on-screen calculator on the DI section! Just make sure that you know what you need to calculate before you start punching numbers.

Practice Your Skills

Because you need to be able to sort on Table problems, your practice problems for this chapter are online. Log into the Manhattan Prep platform and navigate to the problem banks or follow the assignments in your course syllabus to practice more Tables.

Digits and Decimals

In This Chapter...

- Digits

- Decimals

- Place Value

- Rounding to the Nearest Place Value

- Powers of 10: Shifting the Decimal

- Decimal Operations

In this chapter, you will learn how digits, decimals, and place value are tested on the GMAT, as well as how to perform the needed computations on numbers in decimal form, including rounding.

CHAPTER 9 Digits and Decimals

Digits

Every number is composed of digits. There are only 10 digits in our number system: 0, 1, 2, 3, 4, 5, 6, 7, 8, 9. The term **digit** refers to one "building block" of a number; it does not refer to the entire number. For example, 356 is a number composed of three digits: 3, 5, and 6.

Integers can be classified by the number of digits they contain. For example:

2, 7, and −8 are each single-digit numbers (they are each composed of one digit).

43, 63, and −14 are each double-digit numbers (composed of two digits).

500,000 and −468,024 are each six-digit numbers (composed of six digits).

789,526,622 is a nine-digit number (composed of nine digits).

Integers such as the above always have a nonzero digit as the first number. For instance, 2 is a single-digit number, but you can't write 02 and call that a two-digit integer. If a problem specifies a two-digit integer, then the first digit has to be some value from 1 to 9.

Non-integers are not generally classified by the number of digits they contain, since you can always add any number of zeros at the end, on the right side of the decimal point:

$$9.1 = 9.10 = 9.100$$

Decimals

Decimals are yet another way to write numbers that fall between integers. For example, the decimal 6.3 falls between the integers 6 and 7:

Some useful groupings of decimals include the following:

Group	Examples
Decimals less than −1:	−3.6, −12.01
Decimals between −1 and 0:	−0.65, −0.5
Decimals between 0 and 1:	0.2, 0.45
Decimals greater than 1:	2.9, 42.42

Note that an integer can be expressed as a decimal by adding the decimal point and the digit 0. For example:

$$8 = 8.0 \qquad -123 = -123.0 \qquad 400 = 400.0$$

Place Value

Every digit in a number has a particular **place value** depending on its location within the number. For example, in the number 452, the digit 2 is in the ones (or units) place, the digit 5 is in the tens place, and the digit 4 is in the hundreds place. The name of each location corresponds to the value of that place. Thus:

The 2 is worth two ones (i.e., $2 \times 1 = 2$).

The 5 is worth five tens (i.e., $5 \times 10 = 50$).

The 4 is worth four hundreds (i.e., $4 \times 100 = 400$).

You can write the number 452 as the *sum* of these products:

$$452 = (4 \times 100) + (5 \times 10) + (2 \times 1)$$

Millions	Hundred Thousands	Ten Thousands	Thousands	Hundreds	Tens	Units Or Ones		Tenths	Hundredths	Thousandths	Ten Thousandths
7	8	9	1	0	2	3	.	8	3	4	7

The chart to the left analyzes the place value of all the digits in the number **7,891,023.8347**.

Notice that all of the place values that end in "ths" are to the right of the decimal; these are all fractional values.

Analyze just the decimal portion of the number **0.8347**:

8 is in the tenths place, giving it a value of 8 tenths, or $\frac{8}{10}$.

3 is in the hundredths place, giving it a value of 3 hundredths, or $\frac{3}{100}$.

4 is in the thousandths place, giving it a value of 4 thousandths, or $\frac{4}{1,000}$.

7 is in the ten-thousandths place, giving it a value of 7 ten thousandths, or $\frac{7}{10,000}$.

To use a concrete example, 0.8 might mean eight tenths of one dollar, which would be 80 cents. Additionally, 0.03 might mean three hundredths of one dollar, or 3 cents.

Rounding to the Nearest Place Value

The GMAT occasionally requires you to round a number to a specific place value. For example:

What is 3.681 rounded to the nearest tenth?

First, find the digit located in the specified place value. The digit 6 is in the tenths place.

Second, look at the right-digit neighbor (the digit immediately to the right) of the digit in question. In this case, 8 is the right-digit neighbor of 6. If the right-digit neighbor is 5 or greater, round the digit in question *up*. Otherwise, leave the digit alone. In this case, the hundredths-digit number, 8, is greater than 5, so you're going to have to round up. Go back to the digit in question, 6, and round up to 7. Thus, 3.681 rounded to the nearest tenth equals 3.7.

One note: All of the digits to the right of the right-digit neighbor are irrelevant when rounding. Ignore them and concentrate only on the digit immediately to the right of the place value to which you were asked to round. For example, if you were asked to round 2.34567 to the tens digit, the correct value would be 2.3 because the digit immediately to the right is a 4, so you round down. The remaining digits to the right are irrelevant.

Rounding appears on the GMAT in the form of questions such as this:

> If *x* is the decimal 8.1*d*5, with *d* as an unknown digit, and *x* rounded to the nearest tenth is equal to 8.1, which digits could NOT be the value of *d*?

In order for *x* to be 8.1 when rounded to the nearest tenth, the right-digit neighbor, *d*, must be less than 5. Therefore, *d* cannot be 5, 6, 7, 8, or 9.

Powers of 10: **Shifting the Decimal**

What are the patterns in this table?

In words	Thousands	Hundreds	Tens	Ones	Tenths	Hundredths	Thousandths
In numbers	1,000	100	10	1	0.1	0.01	0.001
In powers of ten	10^3	10^2	10^1	10^0	10^{-1}	10^{-2}	10^{-3}

The place values continually decrease from left to right by powers of 10. Understanding this can help you understand the following shortcuts for multiplication and division.

When you multiply any number by a positive power of 10, move the decimal to the right the specified number of places. This makes positive numbers larger:

$89.507 \times 10 = 895.07$ — 10 is the same as 10^1, so move the decimal to the right 1 space.

$3.9742 \times 10^3 = 3,974.2$ — The exponent is 3, so move the decimal to the right 3 spaces.

When you divide any number by a positive power of 10, move the decimal to the left the specified number of places. This makes positive numbers smaller:

$89.507 \div 10 = 8.9507$ — Move the decimal to the left 1 space.
$4,169.2 \div 10^2 = 41.692$ — Move the decimal to the left 2 spaces.

Sometimes, you will need to add zeros in order to shift a decimal:

$2.57 \times 10^6 = 2,570,000$ — Add 4 zeros at the end.
$14.29 \div 10^5 = 0.0001429$ — Add 3 zeros at the beginning.

Finally, note that negative powers of 10 reverse the regular process: Move the decimal in the opposite direction that you'd have used for a positive power. Now, multiplication makes the number smaller and division makes the number larger:

$$6{,}782.01 \times 10^{-3} = 6.78201 \qquad 53.0447 \div 10^{-2} = 5{,}304.47$$

You can think about these processes as trading decimal places for powers of 10.

For instance, all of the following numbers equal 110,700:

$$110.7 \times 10^3$$
$$11.07 \times 10^4$$
$$1.107 \times 10^5$$
$$0.1107 \times 10^6$$
$$0.01107 \times 10^7$$

The number in the first column gets smaller by a factor of 10 as you move the decimal one place to the left, but the number in the second column gets bigger by a factor of 10 to compensate, so the overall number still equals 110,700.

Decimal Operations

Addition and Subtraction

To add or subtract decimals, first, check the answers to see whether you can just estimate instead. If not, line up the decimal points. Then, add zeros to make the right sides of the decimals the same length:

4.319 + 221.8

Line up the decimal points and add zeros.

```
   4.319
+ 221.800
 226.119
```

10 − 0.063

Line up the decimal points and add zeros.

```
 10.000
−  0.063
  9.937
```

> **Addition and subtraction:** Line up the decimal points!

Multiplication

To multiply decimals, ignore the decimal point until the end. Just multiply the numbers as you would if they were whole numbers. Then count the total number of digits to the right of the decimal point in the starting numbers. The product should have the same number of digits to the right of the decimal point:

	Count the digits to the right of the decimal:	Multiply normally:	Move the decimal 3 places to the left:
0.02 × 1.4	3	14 × 2 28	28 → 0.028

If the product ends with 0, that 0 still counts as a place value. For example: $0.8 \times 0.5 = 0.40$, since $8 \times 5 = 40$.

> **Multiplication:** Count all the digits to the right of the decimal point—then multiply normally, ignoring the decimals. Finally, put the same number of decimal places in the product.

If you are multiplying a very large number and a very small number, the following trick works to simplify the calculation: Move the decimals the same number of places, but *in the opposite direction*. For example:

$0.0003 \times 40,000 = ?$

Move the decimal point *right* four places on the $0.0003 \rightarrow 3$

Move the decimal point *left* four places on the $40,000 \rightarrow 4$

$0.0003 \times 40,000 = 3 \times 4 = 12$

This technique works because you are multiplying and then dividing by the same power of 10. In other words, you are trading decimal places in one number for decimal places in another number. This is just like trading decimal places for powers of 10, as you saw earlier.

Division

If you ever need to do long division, first...stop. Make sure you can't estimate or do something else that is less annoying. Here's one less annoying way: You can always simplify division problems that involve decimals by shifting the decimal point *in the same direction* in both the divisor and the dividend, even when the division problem is expressed as a fraction:

$$\frac{0.0045}{0.09} = \frac{45}{900}$$ Move the decimal 4 spaces to the right in both the numerator and the denominator to make whole numbers. Always move the same number of places in the top and bottom.

Note that this is essentially the same process as simplifying a fraction. You multiply the numerator and denominator of the fraction by the same number—in this case, 10^4, or 10,000.

> **Division:** Use whole numbers! To dump the decimals, move the decimal the same number of places in the top and the bottom of the fraction.

If you absolutely must do long division with decimals and there is a decimal point in the dividend (the number under the division sign), you can bring the decimal point straight up to the answer and divide normally:

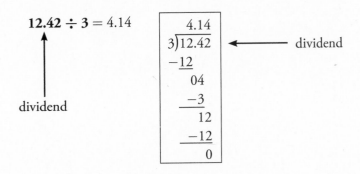

However, if there is a decimal point in the divisor (the outer number), shift the decimal point the same number of times to the right in both the divisor and the dividend to make the *divisor* (the outer number) a whole number. Then, bring the decimal point up and divide:

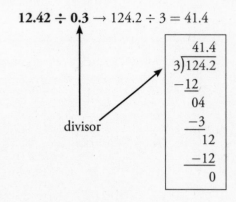

12.42 ÷ 0.3 → 124.2 ÷ 3 = 41.4

divisor

$$\begin{array}{r} 41.4 \\ 3\overline{)124.2} \\ -12 \\ \hline 04 \\ -3 \\ \hline 12 \\ -12 \\ \hline 0 \end{array}$$

Move the decimal 1 space to the right to make 0.3 a whole number. Then, move the decimal 1 space to the right in 12.42 to make it 124.2.

Keep track of the decimal: To simplify multiplication, you can move decimals in *opposite* directions. But to simplify division, move decimals in the *same* direction. Either way, make sure you're moving the decimal the same number of places to trade off equally.

Problem Set

Solve each problem, applying the concepts and rules you learned in this section.

1. In the decimal 2.4*d*7, *d* represents a digit from 0 to 9. If the value of the decimal rounded to the nearest tenth is less than 2.5, what are the possible values of *d* ?

2. Simplify: $\dfrac{0.00081}{0.09}$

3. Which integer values of *b* would give the number $2002 \div 10^b$ a value between 1 and 100 ?

    (A) {−1, −2}
    (B) {−2, −3}
    (C) {1, 2}
    (D) {2, 3}

4. Simplify: $(4 \times 10^{-2}) - (2.5 \times 10^{-3})$

Save the below problem set for review after you finish this entire guide.

5. If *k* is an integer and 0.02468×10^k is greater than 10,000, what is the least possible value of *k* ?

6. What is $4{,}563{,}021 \div 10^5$, rounded to the nearest whole number?

Solutions

1. **{0, 1, 2, 3, 4}:** The rounded decimal is less than 2.5, so it must round to 2.4. This represents rounding down, so the value of d must be 0, 1, 2, 3, or 4.

2. **0.009:** Shift the decimal point five spaces to eliminate the decimal points (note that this means adding zeros to the number in the denominator), then simplify:

    $$\frac{0.00081}{0.09} = \frac{81}{9,000} = \frac{9}{1,000} = 0.009$$

3. **(D) {2, 3}:** Understand before you try to solve (and if you don't understand, guess and move on). Some of the answers contain positive numbers and some contain negative numbers, so should that exponent be positive or negative? The starting value is 2,002, but the ending value is between 1 and 100, so 2,002 needs to get smaller. Specifically, it will have to be either 2.002 or 20.02 in order to fall between 1 and 100.

    If you start from 2,002 and divide by a power of 10 to get to 20.02 or 2.002, you'd want to divide by 10 or 100 or 1,000—in other words, you want that exponent to be positive to make the divisor larger. Eliminate choices (A) and (B).

    Of the two remaining answers, both contain the value 2, so apparently 2 must be one value for b. Is the other value 1 or 3? $2,002 \div 10^1 = 200.2$. Too big! The answer must be 2 and 3.

    If you're not sure of the logic, check. $2,002 \div 10^3 = 2,002 \div 1,000 = 2.002$. Perfect!

    The correct answer is **(D)** {2, 3}.

4. **0.0375:** First, rewrite the numbers in standard notation by shifting the decimal point. Then, add zeros, line up the decimal points, and subtract:

    $$\begin{array}{r} 0.0400 \\ -\ 0.0025 \\ \hline 0.0375 \end{array}$$

5. **6:** Understand and Plan before you Solve. Understand: Multiplying 0.02468 by a positive power of 10 will shift the decimal point to the right. Your goal is to make the number greater than 10,000.

    Plan: Shift the decimal point to the right until the result is greater than 10,000, keeping track of how many times you shift the decimal point.

    Solve: Shifting the decimal point five times results in 2,468. This is still less than 10,000. Shifting one more place yields 24,680, which is greater than 10,000.

6. **46:** To divide by a positive power of 10, shift the decimal point to the left. This yields 45.63021. To round to the nearest whole number, look at the tenths place. The digit in the tenths place, 6, is more than 5. Therefore, round up: The number is closest to 46.

Graphics Interpretation

In This Chapter...

- UPS for Graphs

- Types of Graphs

- Review and Improve on Nonstandard Graphs

- Review and Improve on Standard Graphs

In this chapter, you will learn about the types of standard and not-so-standard graphs that can appear on the GMAT, and you'll learn how to apply the Understand, Plan, Solve (UPS) process to all Graph problems.

CHAPTER 10 Graphics Interpretation

Graphics Interpretation (Graph) problems can be built on a wide variety of graphs, charts, and diagrams, even non-math-based ones. You'll see many examples in this chapter, particularly of the "traditional" types of math graphs.

(Note: In the real world of data analysis, graphs and charts are not quite the same thing. But for the purposes of the GMAT, you can use these two terms interchangeably.)

Graph prompts consist of some sort of graphic with accompanying text. The question always has two parts and always appears below the graph prompt. The example below shows a traditional type of math graph: a scatter plot.

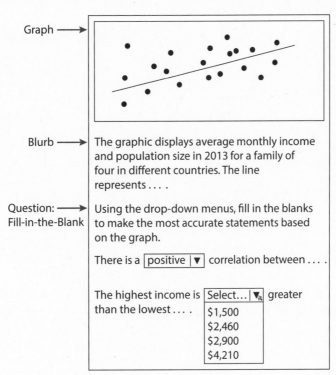

Many graphs are common types that you've seen before: pie charts, bar charts, line graphs, and the like. The test writers will expect you to know how to read these already; you'll learn how in this chapter. Other types could include Venn diagrams, timelines, organizational hierarchies, flowcharts, even things that were just made up for the GMAT. If you are given a graph that doesn't fall into a standard math categorization, don't worry; you'll always be given instructions regarding what it is and how to read it.

The question consists of one or two sentences with two blanks. Your task is to fill in each blank with the best answer, chosen from a drop-down menu sitting right there in the blank. You'll have three to five answer choices for any one blank.

As on some other Data Insights (DI) question types, this is considered a single question, so you have to answer both parts correctly in order to earn credit for the problem.

The two blanks may be related to each other, in which case you'll need to solve both simultaneously. The two blanks may also be completely separate from each other.

UPS for Graphs

Graph questions most often have a quantitative focus. The most commonly tested topics include general Statistics (mean, median, standard deviation, range, correlation), Fractions, Decimals, Percents, and Ratios. Some questions, though, revolve more around your ability to figure out how to read the graph or diagram and think analytically about the information presented.

Step 1: Understand the Prompt and Question

Take a look at this Graph prompt:

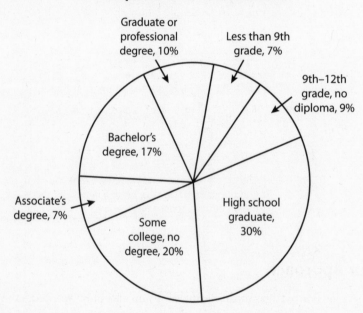

2013 Population 25 Years and Over

In 2013, the percent of the population aged 25 years and over that did NOT have a bachelor's, graduate, or professional degree is Select... ⇅

7%
16%
27%
59%
73%

(Note: Unlike this example, an official question will always have two blanks, each with its own set of options.)

First, understand. This is a pie chart, one of the common types of math graphs. But don't start to look at the detailed data yet. You have one other thing to do first.

As on Table problems, use **SEE**, with one slight change. This time, SEE stands for **Select, Eyeball**, and **Estimate**. On the actual test, you will see a box in each blank with the word *Select* and a little drop-down icon. Click on the word *Select* to glance at the multiple-choice options for that blank.

The form of the answers can completely change how you decide to approach a problem, so click Select and glance at the answers very early in the process. In fact, glance at the answers above right now. Notice anything?

The answers are in percent form, so math is involved. The numbers are also spread pretty far apart. That's a clue that you may be able to estimate to solve. Examine the possibilities for estimation as you orient yourself to the prompt.

Now, go back to the graph. Read the title and any accompanying text in order to understand what the graph is all about. In this case, the title indicates that the chart provides information about a certain population in a certain year.

Next, dive into the graph itself. The wedges are labeled by type of schooling and show a percentage for each, but no real numbers. Since this is a pie chart, the percentages add up to 100%. (You don't need to check this. This is true for all pie charts.)

The answer choices are also in the form of percents, so you might need to add up some of the categories of the pie chart or maybe multiply some things together. The calculations could be tedious, but the answer choices are pretty spread apart, so you can estimate fairly aggressively. With luck, you won't even have to pull up the calculator.

Before you start to read the statement, click on the first drop-down menu so that the multiple-choice options appear. Read the sentence with these options showing. (For a real question, which has two drop-downs, click on the second drop-down menu after you get past the part of the sentence that has the first blank.)

The question asks about certain categories of people: those with a bachelor's, graduate, or professional degree. Take careful note of that capitalized word NOT; the question is actually asking you to find the percentage of all others, *not* those three. You might even jot down that word.

Step 2: Plan Your Approach

Given that there are five pie chart wedges in the "wanted" group and only two wedges in the "not wanted" group, it will be more efficient to add up the two "not wanted" wedges and subtract from 100% in order to find the sum of the remaining five groups. Don't do more math than you have to!

One more thing: The most common error is probably missing the word NOT and therefore solving for the "not wanted" group by accident. Expect to see that trap among the list of answers.

Further, these two groups have to add up to 100%. Glance at the answers. If you have to guess, choose an answer that is part of a pair of numbers that adds to 100%. (In fact, only one pair of numbers fits this pattern: 27% and 73%. If you need to guess, pick one of those.)

Step 3: Solve the Problem

Find the percentage for the two unwanted categories, bachelor's degree and graduate or professional degree:

$$17\% + 10\% = 27\%$$

Bingo! That's the "not wanted" group and that (trap) value is in the answers. Don't pick it. The correct answer is 73%, the other value in the pair that adds to 100%.

In this problem, it's not hard to add up the two numbers, 17 and 10. On another problem, with more cumbersome numbers, you could estimate at this stage, since the answers are pretty far apart.

Types of Graphs

Some types of graphs will be very familiar to you; others may seem unusual. You've probably seen a number of pie charts and bar graphs in your life, and you'll see these on DI questions as well. On the other end of the spectrum, you might see a diagram that was completely made up for this test. In general, charts and graphs typically appear on Graph and Multi-Source Reasoning problems, but they could pop up occasionally on other DI question types, too.

Here are some examples of some standard diagrams, followed by a few not-so-standard diagrams:

Column

Stacked Column

Clustered Column

Bar

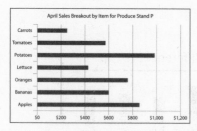

Line

Scatterplot

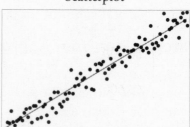

Pie Chart

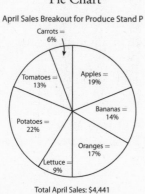

Bubble Chart

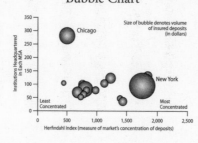

Venn Diagram

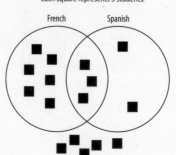

Organizational Chart   Timeline   Others are possible!

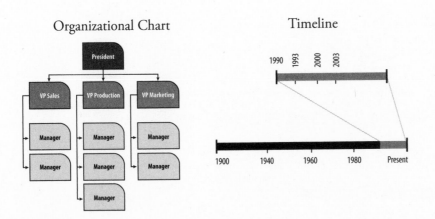

These display formats are commonly used in business and academic settings today—you've likely seen most, if not all, of the math-based ones before. When the GMAT does give a nonstandard visual, it is often the kind of diagram you might see in a company presentation, an annual report, or a business-school case study. You'll be given some kind of context to help you understand it.

The following are the most common types of standard math graphs that you're likely to see on the exam. As you review them, test yourself: See what you notice about a given chart before you read the chapter text explaining how that type of chart works. What kind of information can you glean? And what kind of analyses can you make?

Column and Bar Charts

A column chart shows amounts as heights, so you would scan for changes in the heights as you move from left to right. For example:

Column chart: Scan left to right.

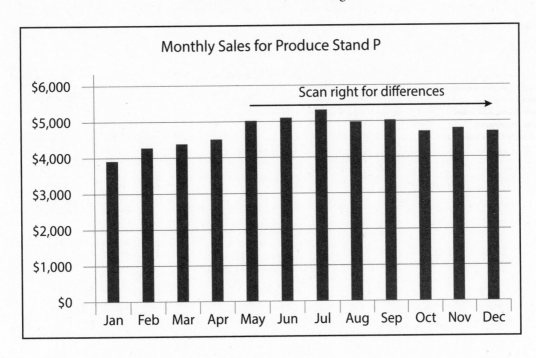

Similarly, bar charts show amounts as lengths, so you would scan for differences in those lengths as you move from top to bottom. For example:

Bar chart: Scan top to bottom.

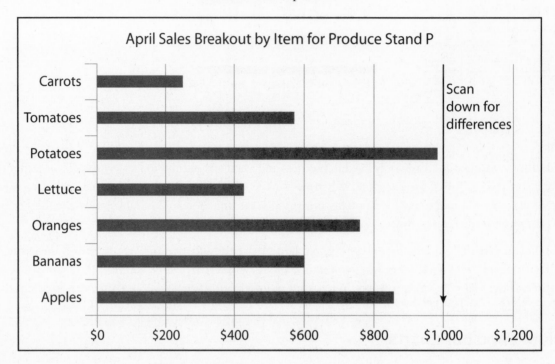

Column charts are often used to show trends over time (e.g., January to December), while bar charts are more frequently used for non-time comparisons (e.g., carrots vs. apples).

It can be difficult to read a value from a column or bar that ends *between* the grid lines. The grid lines are those lighter grey lines that divide the graph into sections—for example, in the column chart, the grid lines show up at $1,000, $2,000, and so on up to $6,000.

If the column or bar does not end exactly on a grid line, you're going to have to estimate a little. Hold your finger, your pen, or even the edge of your scratch paper up to the screen to make a straight line, and take your best guess. (This will be close enough—don't worry!)

A question might ask you to calculate the percent increase or decrease from one time period to the next. Consider the Monthly Sales column graph given earlier, and answer this question:

What was the approximate percent increase in sales from April to May?

April sales were about $4,500 (the column ends about halfway between $4,000 and $5,000). May's column ends right on $5,000. Now, use the percent change formula:

$$\frac{\text{May sales} - \text{April sales}}{\text{April sales}} \approx \frac{5,000 - 4,500}{4,500} = \frac{1}{9} \approx 11\%$$

Variations on Column and Bar Charts

If there is more than one series of numbers, the exam might use a stacked or clustered column chart. The stacked form places the two data points in the same column, one on top of the other, so it emphasizes the *sum* of the two series of numbers. For example:

Stacked column: Emphasizes *sums*.

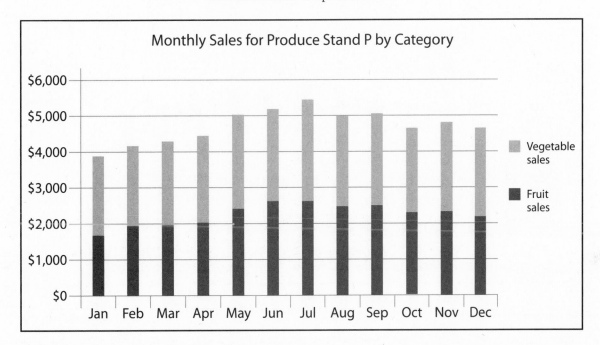

In the stacked column graph, it's easy to find the values for total sales (fruit and vegetable together), and it's also easy to find the sales level for the bottom group (fruit), because the bottom group starts at $0. It's not easy to see the values for the top group (vegetable sales, in this case). You'd need to subtract to find the exact value—for example, in January, vegetable sales were about $3,800 − $1,700 = $2,100.

You could also, though, *eyeball* by using the grid lines. The difference between any one set of grid lines is $1,000; call this difference one "segment" of the graph. Mentally take the entire lighter grey part of the column for January and move it up a little bit so that it starts right on the $2,000 grid line. (You can use your fingers to help eyeball this on the test screen.)

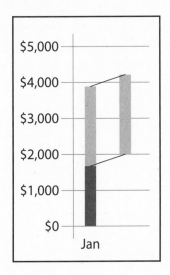

The lighter grey part of the column covers a little bit more than two segments of the graph, so the value is a little more than $2,000, or about $2,200.

The clustered column graph, by contrast, highlights which of the two values is greater at any point along the way. For example:

Clustered column: Emphasizes *differences*.

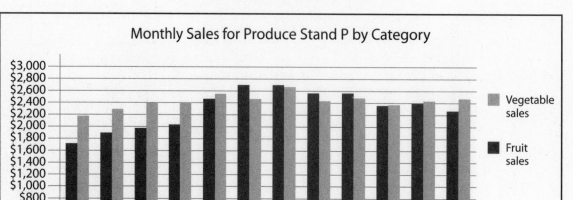

Now, finding the values for each individual category is straightforward, but you would have to add up the two paired columns to find the total sales for that month.

You might think that, if the test wants you to work with the total, it will give you the stacked column, since that shows the total—but not necessarily. And the test writers are not just being deliberately unhelpful to irritate you! The test wants to make sure that you know how to use the kinds of graphs you're likely to need to use in grad school, and you will often want to figure things out that don't fit perfectly with the type of graph given. They really are testing real-world skills with these problems.

Line Charts

Line charts are very similar to column charts. However, each number is shown as a floating dot rather than as a column, and the dots are connected by lines. The *x*-axis almost always represents time, since the lines imply connection. Although lines are continuous, do *not* assume that the data is itself continuous. If it is monthly data, for example, then the chart is showing just that one monthly data point—the line connecting one month to the next does not represent day-by-day data. For example:

Line

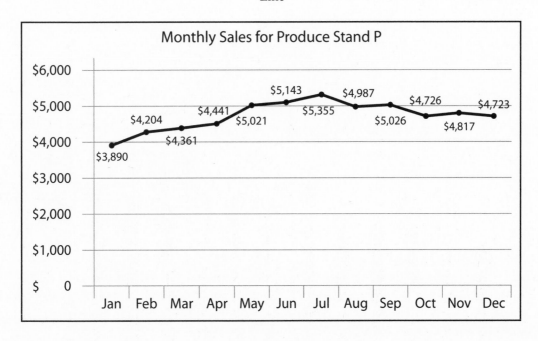

You could also have a line chart that contains multiple lines. Multiple lines are used to show multiple data series changing over time. When the desired emphasis is on the change within each set over time, this graph is more clear than a clustered column graph. For example:

Line (with two data series)

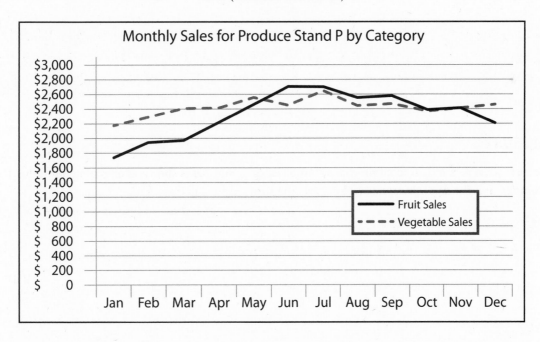

Compare this to the clustered column chart shown earlier. Both charts show how fruit sales compare to vegetable sales in any given month. Here, though, it's easier to see that fruit sales peak in the June–July time frame but are at their lowest in January, while vegetable sales are more steady throughout the year.

Scatter Plots

A scatter plot is a more complex graph. It shows the relationship between two columns of data in a table. Each point on the plot represents a single record (a single row). For example:

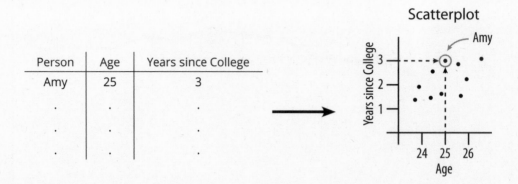

The overall pattern of the dots indicates how the two columns of numbers vary together, if at all. For example, glance back at the very first sample Graph problem shown at the beginning of this chapter. It shows a scatter plot. As you move to the right on the *x*-axis, the dots also tend to move up on the *y*-axis. In other words, as the *x*-value increases, the *y*-value also tends to increase.

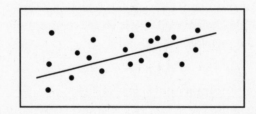

The graph above is showing a correlation between the two sets of data points—in this case, a positive correlation. If you draw a line showing the general trend of the points (as shown in the graphic), the line slopes upward from left to right.

A graph can also show a negative correlation: As one set of data points increases, the other set decreases. If you drew a trend line on such a graph, that line would slope downward from left to right.

If there's no trend—that is, sometimes the points go up and sometimes they go down, with no real connection to each other—then the data in that graph has no correlation at all.

Pie Charts

A pie chart is used to show the relative sizes of "slices" as proportions of a whole, so pie charts are often used when the test writers want to ask you about percents. The size of the angle or wedge of the pie slice is proportional to that item's percent of the whole, and all of the pieces of the pie add up to 100%.

Sometimes the pie chart shows real amounts and sometimes it directly shows percents, but even when there are real numbers, you will probably have to calculate something in terms of a percent. Percents on various slices will always be a percent of the whole.

Take a look at this example:

Pie

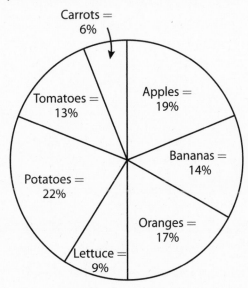

April Sales Breakout for Produce Stand P

Total April Sales: $4,441

Since the total April sales figure is given ($4,441), you can calculate the dollar sales of any item, or any group of items, in the pie.

Try this problem:

What is the total dollar value of lettuce and tomato sales for Produce Stand P in April?

Take a look at the following two sets of answers. How are they different? How might you approach the problem differently, depending on which set of answers you were actually given?

Set 1	Set 2
$103.52	$797.64
$514.91	$895.43
$977.02	$977.02
$1,348.37	$1,120.51

In the first set, the answers are spread quite far apart, so you can estimate aggressively. Lettuce and tomato sales are equal to 9% plus 13%, which sums to 22%, or about 20%.

Find 20% of $4,400 (the approximate April sales). First, take 10% by moving the decimal to the left one place. Then, multiply that number by 2 to get 20%:

$$20\% \times 4,400 = 440 \times 2 = 880$$

Is that close enough? Glance at the first set of answers. The calculation underestimated a bit, so the correct answer must be larger, and the only one that's close enough is $977.02.

That estimation is not quite good enough for the second set of answers, though, so make the calculation a little more precise. You've already found 20%. Use that to find 2% (move the decimal one place to the left) and then add to get 22%:

$$
\begin{array}{ll}
20\% \times 4,400 = 440 \times 2 = & 880 \\
2\% \qquad\qquad\qquad\qquad = & 88 \\
\hline
22\% \qquad\qquad\qquad\qquad = & 968
\end{array}
$$

Alternatively, pull up the calculator and find 22% of $4,400. Lettuce and tomato sales are approximately $968, so the correct answer is $977.02.

Always track whether you under- or overestimated. In this case, the calculation *under*estimated the starting value ($4,400 vs. $4,441). The value you calculate, therefore, will be a little too small but close enough.

Here's a different way to estimate, this time by overestimating a bit: Find 25% of $4,400.

The fastest way to find 25% of a figure is to divide by 4 (or to divide by 2 twice). In this case, $4,400 divided by 4 is $1,100. This is an overestimation, so that last answer choice is too big. Only $977.02 works.

By the way, a pie chart can show only one series of data. If you see two pie charts, they represent two separate series of data.

Other Types of Charts

The test writers can draw any kind of diagram or visual they want. So if you see something you don't recognize, don't panic. Read the title, read the labels, and try to understand how the diagram is laid out visually. If you're stuck, focus on just one small part, such as a single data point. What does that point represent? What do you know about that piece of data? Then, work your way out from there.

Or not! You will want to guess fast on several Data Insights questions overall. If you see a graph that just doesn't make any sense, make this problem one of your guesses.

Bubble charts look intimidating, but they are just scatter plots on steroids. Rather than two pieces of information about each point, you have three. In order to show that third dimension, all the little points are expanded to varying sizes—and those varying sizes give you a relative measure of that third dimension. For example:

Bubble

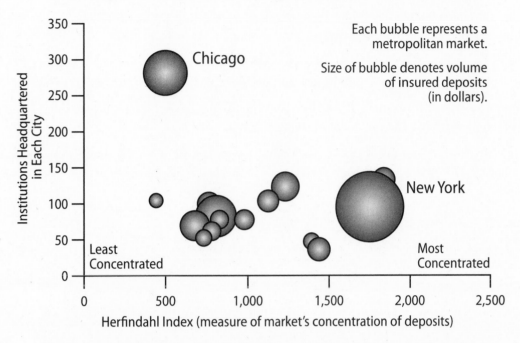

Bank Deposit Concentration in Large Metropolitan Statistical Areas

Sources: Summary of Deposits, June 2002; FDIC's Research and Information System, June 30, 2003.
Note: Fifteen largest markets shown, based on number of institutions headquartered there.

There are two really big bubbles labeled with city names, so compare them. New York has a bigger bubble than Chicago. What does that bubble represent? The *volume of insured deposits*. So more insured deposits are made in New York than in Chicago. (Not sure what insured deposits are? Don't worry about it—right now, it's enough to know that New York has more than Chicago does of whatever this thing is.)

The Chicago bubble is higher up the *y*-axis than the New York bubble. What does that mean? Look at the *y*-axis label: More companies of a certain type (banks in this case) are headquartered in Chicago. That's interesting.

Finally, the New York bubble is farther to the right along the *x*-axis. What does that mean? The *Herfindahl Index* is weird but the chart itself shows the text *Least Concentrated* and *Most Concentrated* at either end of the *x*-axis. So New York is more concentrated than Chicago—whatever *more concentrated* means.

You may only need to understand that New York has this characteristic (*more concentrated*), not what the label truly means, so don't spend any time now trying to "really" understand. Look at the question first and then decide what you need to try to understand more fully.

Speaking of the question, try this:

There is _____ correlation between the value of insured deposits and the Herfindahl Index.

(A) a positive

(B) a negative

(C) no

The question specifies two of the three dimensions: the Herfindahl Index (position along the *x*-axis) and the value of insured deposits (the size of the bubbles). A positive correlation would mean that the bubbles tend to increase in size the farther right you go on the *x*-axis. Is this the case?

Not really. The largest bubble is far to the right, but the next largest one is far to the left, as is the third largest and possibly the fourth or fifth largest.

Is this a negative correlation, then? In this case, the bubbles would be larger to the left and generally decrease as you move to the right—but the placement of New York absolutely kills this possibility.

The correct answer is *no* correlation. There isn't a consistent trend, or connection, between the placement of the bubble along the *x*-axis and the size of the bubble.

Here's another visual the test might toss at you. Venn diagrams consist of two (or three) overlapping circles, showing how two (or three) groups overlap. Here's a two-circle example showing the number of students in certain classes:

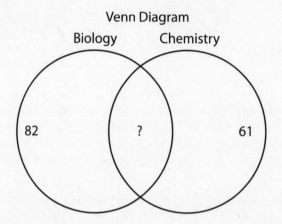

This Venn diagram indicates that there are 82 people in the biology-only group and 61 in the chemistry-only group, as well as an unknown number in the overlap between the two groups. The diagram would be accompanied by a blurb providing additional information, possibly asking you to calculate the number of people in both groups (or in neither group).

The organizational (org) chart and the expanded timeline shown below are good examples of non-math graphs. (Timelines don't have to run horizontally, by the way!)

10

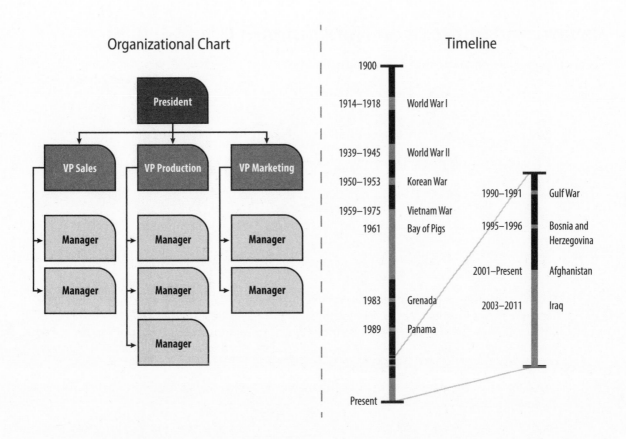

Typical org charts show hierarchical relationships within a business. Expanded timelines give you both a big picture of events in order and a "zoomed in" look at one part of the picture. Note that the scales in the different sections are different; be ready to make comparisons across those different scales.

Here are some other examples of nonstandard graphs, just to give you an idea:

- A diagram showing the workflow or set of steps a company uses to make a certain product
- A genealogy tree or other diagram to show inherited genetic traits or shared characteristics from one generation to the next
- A map showing data tied to different geographical regions
- A project schedule or timeline, possibly showing dependencies across different steps of the project

Anything is possible—which sounds more unsettling than it is. First, most of the nonstandard charts you see will specifically be designed to be read and used intuitively. After all, in the real world, poorly designed charts are rarely adopted for widespread use. Second, you will be given some direction in the blurb as to how to read the visual. Use the blurb to help you interpret the diagram.

Review and Improve on Nonstandard Graphs

Try another problem, this time with a nonstandard graph:

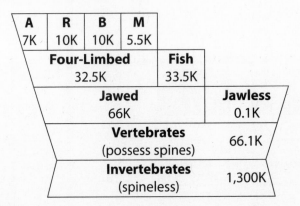

The diagram displays the number of living species represented by two nonoverlapping categories, Vertebrates and Invertebrates, which together comprise all animal species. The diagram also displays the various subcategories of Vertebrates and the approximate number of species in each (the abbreviation K stands for thousands). In the top row, A stands for amphibians, R stands for reptiles, B stands for birds, and M stands for mammals.

Based on the given information, use the drop-down menus to most accurately complete the following statements.

Four-limbed species represent approximately [Select... ▼] of all vertebrate species. Amphibians

Select... ▼
2.5%
15%
35%
50%

and reptiles combined comprise approximately [Select... ▼] of all animal species.

Select... ▼
$\frac{1}{200}$
$\frac{1}{100}$
$\frac{1}{4}$
$\frac{1}{2}$

How did it go? Before reading the explanation below, review your work. Is there anything you want to try calculating a different way? Do you want to double-check anything? Go for it.

Next, check just the correct answer. (Glance ahead. It's listed in the last paragraph of this section, just before Step 1 of the walk-through.) Does knowing that give you any ideas for what to check or do a different way?

Ⓜ

10

If you answered the question incorrectly—or aren't fully confident about something you answered correctly—review each step of the process thoroughly using the official solution. Did you overlook, misunderstand, or fail to comprehend any information in the prompt? Did you answer the question that was asked? Was there a better way to approach the problem? Did you make any mistakes at the solution stage?

If you answered the question correctly and were confident even before you saw the correct answer, then scan the walk-through below for any ideas about how to solve more efficiently. Are there any shortcuts or other methods you can use to make the job easier?

The correct answer for the first blank is fifty percent and the correct answer for the second blank is one one-hundredth. (These are written out in words so that you don't inadvertently spot the correct answers before you're ready to know!)

Step 1: Understand the Prompt and Question

The diagram is not a standard chart, so you will definitely need the blurb to help you understand it. Before doing that, though, take the first step in SEE (select, eyeball, estimate): Click the *Select* drop-downs to see what the answers are. Both are math-focused. The answers for the first part of the question are in percentage form. They are far enough apart that you may be able to estimate at least enough to knock out some of the answers.

The answers for the second part of the question are in fraction form. The first two are clustered together and the final two are clustered together, so you may be able to eyeball enough to narrow down to two answers— that's a valid strategy if it looks like it may take too long to fully solve.

Now, examine the text. The blurb first mentions *two nonoverlapping categories, Vertebrates and Invertebrates*. Glance at the diagram itself: These two categories appear at the bottom.

Nonoverlapping means that no species appears in both categories. Further, the first sentence also states that these two categories *together comprise all animal species*, so all species are either V or Inv. Abbreviate as you jot down this information.

The blurb further explains that the boxes above the V box represent *subcategories* of V and that the numbers represent *the number (in thousands) of species*. Glance at the diagram again.

V's are split into the categories Jawed or Jawless. In total, there are 66K V's, most of which are jawed. Only a very small number are jawless. The jawed vertebrates can then be broken down into the categories Four-Limbed or Fish, and there are roughly equal numbers of each. Finally, the Four-Limbed group can be broken into four subgroups whose names appear only in the blurb: amphibians, reptiles, birds, and mammals. Reptiles and birds are the largest categories and mammals are the smallest category.

The question consists of two separate sentences. The first asks you to find Four-Limbed as a percent of Vertebrate. The second wants to know what fraction A's and R's represent of all species.

The two parts are not related, so solve each individually.

Step 2: Plan Your Approach

In each case, the task is to make sure that you are working with the right categories. (In general, if you see a nonstandard diagram that has a bunch of categories and subcategories, chances are good that at least part of your job will be to make sure you're working with the right categories.) Organize your work carefully and double-check, before calculating, that you have pulled the data from the right groups.

Finally, keep an eye on the answer choices as you go; don't do more math than you have to do.

Step 3: Solve the problem

The first part asks for Four-Limbed as a percent of Vertebrates. The Four-Limbed category has about 32.5K members and the Vertebrate category has about 66K members. Half of 66 is 33, so four-limbed species represent approximately 50% of all vertebrate species. The answer choices are far enough apart that this estimation is close enough.

The second part asks for amphibians and reptiles as a fraction of all animal species. Jot down A + R for the top of the fraction. What about the bottom? Is that all vertebrates? Look back at the prompt.

No, it's not just the vertebrates. The blurb says that vertebrates and invertebrates *together* make up all animal species, so you'll need to add V and Inv. First, double-check the prompt. Does it say the total number of species? Nope, so calculate it:

Total animals = 1,300K + 66K = 1,366K

That's the bottom of the fraction. What goes on top?

A + R = 7K + 10K = 17K

Here's the full fraction:

$$\frac{17}{1,366}$$

Hmm. That's much smaller than $\frac{1}{2}$ or $\frac{1}{4}$, so eliminate those two answers. But which of the other answers is it? One way to find out: Plug that fraction into the calculator. The decimal is 0.0124. The decimal value of $\frac{1}{100}$ is 0.01, and the decimal value of $\frac{1}{200}$ is 0.02. The value 0.0124 is closer to 0.01, so the correct answer is $\frac{1}{100}$.

If you're not a fan of decimals, you can also simplify the fraction. The problem tells you that you can estimate and the two remaining answers are quite far apart, so estimate aggressively:

$$\frac{17}{1,366} = \frac{20}{1,400} = \frac{1}{70}$$

That fraction is closer to $\frac{1}{100}$, so that's the correct answer.

If you prefer fractions, here's one more way! Work backwards from the two remaining answers. If $\frac{1}{100}$ is the correct answer, then that fraction would approximately equal $\frac{17}{1,366}$. Does it? Use your calculator to find out (and do the same for the other remaining answer):

$$\text{Is } \frac{1}{100} \approx \frac{17}{1,366} \text{ ?} \qquad\qquad\qquad \text{Is } \frac{1}{200} \approx \frac{17}{1,366} \text{ ?}$$

Both equations have the number 17 in common, so get all of the other numbers on one side of the equation, away from the 17, then use the calculator to simplify.

$$\text{Is } \frac{1}{100} \approx \frac{17}{1,366} \text{ ?} \qquad\qquad \text{Is } \frac{1}{200} \approx \frac{17}{1,366} \text{ ?}$$
$$\text{Is } 1,366\left(\frac{1}{100}\right) \approx 17 \text{ ?} \qquad\qquad \text{Is } 1,366\left(\frac{1}{200}\right) \approx 17 \text{ ?}$$
$$\text{Is } 14 \approx 17 \text{ ?} \qquad\qquad\qquad \text{Is } 7 \approx 17 \text{ ?}$$

10

The number 14 is closer to 17, so the fraction $\frac{1}{100}$ is a closer match.

Therefore, four-limbed species represent approximately $\boxed{50\%}$ of all vertebrate species. Amphibians and reptiles combined comprise approximately $\boxed{\frac{1}{100}}$ of all animal species.

Review and Improve on Standard Graphs

Try the process one more time:

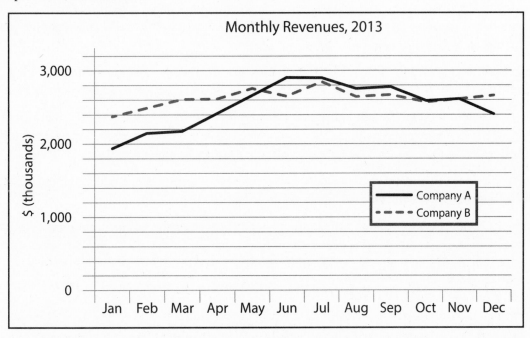

The chart shows 2013 monthly revenues reported by Company A and Company B, which compete in the cellphone market.

Based on the given information, use the drop-down menus to most accurately complete the following statement:

In 2013, Company A's annual revenues were | Select... | ▼ | Company B's annual revenues, and the

>
<
=

positive difference between the two figures was approximately | Select... | ▼ | .

0
250,000
750,000
1,250,000
3,000,000

For your review, first, take stock. How did you feel about the whole thing? Anything you want to try again?

Next, check just the correct answer. (It's at the very end of the explanation.) Does knowing that give you any ideas for what to check or do a different way?

Whether you answered the problem correctly or incorrectly, review each step of the process. Look for ways to do the problem better or faster next time, and look for clues to tell you when to guess and move on.

Step 1: Understand the Prompt and Question

This is a line chart. The first set of answers requires you only to be able to tell whether one thing is greater than, less than, or equal to something else; there's a good chance you'll be able to *eyeball* this. The second blank requires a real value, but the answer choices are far enough apart that you'll likely be able to *estimate*.

Also note that the answers for the second blank seem way too big compared to the *y*-axis given in the graph. The graph is in thousands as shown by the *y*-axis label. The answers show the real number, not the abbreviated numbers shown on the graph.

Use that as your segue into the chart itself. It shows monthly revenues in thousands of dollars during 2013 for two different companies. For example, a point at 2,000 indicates revenues of $2,000,000, or $2 million.

This is a line graph, so you may need to determine differences between points on the line. That's easiest to do by counting segments of the graph, so figure out what each horizontal line segment represents and jot down that figure. In this case, each horizontal segment of the graph represents 200, or $200,000.

In some months, Company A earned higher revenues; in other months, Company B did. Interestingly, Company B started higher and finished higher, while A jumped above B only in the middle of the year.

The two parts of the question ask for related information: which company had higher annual revenues and what that difference was. When this is the case, think about how to save yourself some time and effort by solving the statements simultaneously.

Step 2: Plan Your Approach

The first part asks whether Company A's revenues were greater than, less than, or equal to Company B's, so plan to track the difference in terms of Company A.

The standard math way to solve would be to mark down every monthly figure and add them all up for both companies, then compare the two figures. That involves adding 24 numbers, though—way too much work! There has to be an easier way.

There is! Count only the *differences* between the figures. Further, use the segments to make your calculations easier. Count just by segments, then multiply by 200 (the value of one segment) to convert to the actual figure.

Finally, don't worry about the *thousands of dollars* part of things for now; solve using the *y*-axis scale and add in three zeros later.

Step 3: Solve the Problem

First, just eyeball the graph. For the first five months, Company A is significantly below Company B, enough to create quite a large negative differential. Company B does lose some ground in the middle of the chart, but not enough to offset the initial differential, especially considering that Company B rebounds at the end of the year.

So Company A should end up lower than Company B. You'll have to calculate more precisely to know how much, but the answer to the first blank is *less than*.

10

In January, Company A is about two segments below Company B. For this month, the differential is −2. The February differential is −1.5, so the total differential is now −3.5. Continue counting:

	Jan	Feb	Mar	Apr	May	Jun	Jul	Aug	Sep	Oct	Nov	Dec
Monthly Diff	−2	−1.5	−2	−1	−0.5	1	0	0.5	0.5	0	0	−1
Total Diff	−2	−3.5	−5.5	−6.5	−7	−6	−6	−5.5	−5	−5	−5	−6

Company A finishes the year with a cumulative difference of −6 segments, which translates to a total of $(-6) \times (200) = -1{,}200$ below Company B. Add in three zeros, and Company A's revenue is roughly $1,200,000 below Company B's.

Thus, in 2013, Company A's annual revenues were $\boxed{<}$ Company B's annual revenues, and the positive difference between the two figures was approximately $\boxed{1{,}250{,}000}$.

Counting by segments is a bit strange at first, but it saves a lot of time. Practice until you feel comfortable working with the numbers in this way. You don't actually need to make a table and write everything down. If you feel comfortable counting on screen, you can. Use a finger to point to each month's data as you solve, and consider jotting down just the total at the end of each month so that, if you lose track, you can check your work without having to start from the beginning.

You can also go the long way: Pull up the calculator and plug in each actual value to find the sums for each company. Only do this, though, if you have plenty of time. Don't sacrifice other questions later in the section because you spent too much time adding up 24 numbers at this stage.

If you think the second part will take too long to solve and you're not willing to make that investment, you can invest a small amount of time to increase your odds in making a guess. If you eyeball the data, you can tell that the first part is *less than* without calculating anything. That's also enough information to know that the answer to the second part is not going to be 0. Then, guess from here; you would have at least a 25% chance of guessing correctly.

Practice Your Skills

Because Graph problems come with drop-down menus, your practice problems for this chapter are online. Log into the Manhattan Prep platform and navigate to the problem banks or follow the assignments in your course syllabus to practice more Graphs.

Algebra

In this unit, you will learn how to process all of the algebra found on the GMAT, including exponents, roots, linear and quadratic equations, inequalities, and formulas of various kinds. You'll also learn additional strategies for the Data Sufficiency problem type, as well as for Test Cases and Choose Smart Numbers. Finally, you'll learn how to solve combo and max/min problems.

In This Unit

- Chapter 11: Linear Equations and Combos

- Chapter 12: Exponents

- Chapter 13: Roots

- Chapter 14: Quadratic Equations

- Chapter 15: Formulas

- Chapter 16: Inequalities and Max/Min

Linear Equations and Combos

In This Chapter...

In this chapter, you will learn the difference between expressions and equations, as well as how to simplify and solve linear equations via various methods, including one strategy often used on the GMAT: the combo. You'll also learn how to solve equations containing absolute values.

CHAPTER 11 Linear Equations and Combos

Here's an example of a linear equation: $x - 13y = 24$.

Linear equations are equations in which all variables have an exponent of 1. For example, in the equation above, the variable x can be written as x^1. (This is always true when a variable doesn't have a "visible" exponent: The exponent is in fact 1.)

In addition, in linear equations, no variables are multiplied together.

The term **combo** is short for *combination of variables*. This is a test-taking term referring to questions such as "What is $x + y$?" The expression $x + y$ is a combo.

Expressions vs. Equations

Equations (such as $x + y = 6$) contain an equals sign, while expressions (such as $x + y$) do not.

An expression, even one that contains variables, represents a value. When manipulating or simplifying expressions, you have to follow certain rules to ensure that you don't change the value of the expression.

There are several methods for simplifying expressions. You can:

1. Combine like terms: $\qquad\qquad\quad 6z + 5z \rightarrow 11z$

2. Find a common denominator: $\qquad \frac{1}{12} + \frac{3x^3}{4} \times \left(\frac{3}{3}\right) \rightarrow \frac{1}{12} + \frac{9x^3}{12} = \frac{9x^3 + 1}{12}$

3. Pull out a common factor: $\qquad\quad 2ab + 4b \rightarrow 2b(a + 2)$

4. Cancel common factors: $\qquad$ given $y \neq 0$, simplify $\frac{5y^3}{25y} \rightarrow \frac{y^2}{5}$

These moves are all valid because they do not change the value of the expression. In other words, if you plug numbers into both the original and simplified forms, the value stays the same. For example, plug $z = 3$ into both the original and simplified forms of the first example to see what happens:

Original form	Simplified form
$6z + 5z$	$11z$
$6(3) + 5(3)$	$11(3)$
$18 + 15$	33
33	

Thus, $6z + 5z$ is equivalent to $11z$. When you plug $z = 3$ into either expression, the result is 33.

Since equations contain an equals sign, they behave differently. In order to keep the two sides of the equation equal, any change made to one side must also be made to the other side. Also, the change may alter the values on both sides of the equation—though the two sides will still be equal to each other. For example:

$3 = 3$	This is a valid equation: 3 equals 3.
$(2)3 = 3(2)$	Multiply both sides by 2.
$5 + 6 = 6 + 5$	Add 5 to both sides.
$11 = 11$	The two sides are still equal, but have different values.

In general, there are six operations you can perform to both sides of an equation. Remember to perform the action on the *entire* side of the equation. For example, if you were to square both sides of the equation $\sqrt{x} + 1 = x$, you would have to square the entire expression $(\sqrt{x} + 1)$, as opposed to squaring each term individually.

You can:

1. Add the same thing to both sides:

$$z - 13 = -14$$
$$\underline{+13 \quad +13}$$
$$z \quad\quad = -1$$

2. Subtract the same thing from both sides:

$$x + 8 = 34$$
$$\underline{-8 \quad -8}$$
$$x \quad\quad = 26$$

3. Multiply both sides by the same thing:

$$\frac{4}{a} = a + b$$
$$a \times \left(\frac{4}{a}\right) = (a + b) \times a$$
$$4 = a^2 + ab$$

4. Divide both sides by the same thing:

$$3x = 6y + 12$$
$$\frac{3x}{3} = \frac{6y + 12}{3}$$
$$x = 2y + 4$$

5. Raise both sides to the same power:

$$\sqrt{y} = y + 2$$
$$(\sqrt{y})^2 = (y + 2)^2$$
$$y = (y + 2)^2$$

6. Take the same root of both sides:

$$x^3 = 125$$
$$\sqrt[3]{x^3} = \sqrt[3]{125}$$
$$x = 5$$

Solving One-Variable Equations

In order to solve one-variable equations, isolate the variable on one side of the equation (*isolate* means get the variable by itself). In doing so, make sure you perform identical operations on both sides of the equation.

Also, generally speaking, follow PEMDAS *in reverse*. Where possible, try to make moves that keep values positive, since people usually make fewer math mistakes with positive values versus negative values. Try these examples:

$$3x + 5 = 26 \qquad \text{Subtract 5 from both sides.}$$
$$3x = 21 \qquad \text{Divide both sides by 3.}$$
$$x = 7$$

$$w = 17w - 1 \qquad \text{Subtract } w \text{ from both sides.}$$
$$0 = 16w - 1 \qquad \text{Add 1 to both sides.}$$
$$1 = 16w \qquad \text{Divide both sides by 16.}$$
$$\frac{1}{16} = w$$

$$\frac{p}{9} + 3 = 5 \qquad \text{Subtract 3 from both sides.}$$
$$\frac{p}{9} = 2 \qquad \text{Multiply both sides by 9.}$$
$$p = 18$$

When simplifying an *expression* (not like the examples just given), you'd follow PEMDAS, in which case multiplication and division would come before addition and subtraction. When simplifying an *equation*, by contrast, follow PEMDAS in reverse: Add and subtract first, to get the plain numbers over to the other side of the equation, then multiply or divide to move the numbers that are "attached" to the variable.

Two Variables: Solving by Substitution

Sometimes the GMAT asks you to solve a system of equations with more than one variable. You might be given two equations with two variables, or perhaps three equations with three variables. In either case, there are two primary textbook ways of solving simultaneous equations—substitution or elimination—and a third way that occurs on the GMAT, the combo. This section deals with the first method, substitution. For example:

Use substitution to solve for *y*.

$$x + y = 9$$
$$2x = 5y + 4$$

First, isolate the variable you *don't* want to solve for—in this case, you don't want *x*. Choose the equation in which it is easier to isolate *x*:

$$x + y = 9$$
$$x = 9 - y$$

Next, substitute the right-hand side of that equation into the other equation. In this case, substitute $9 - y$ wherever you see x:

$$2x = 5y + 4$$
$$2(9 - y) = 5y + 4$$

Now you've got an equation with only y, the variable that you want. Solve for y:

$$2(9 - y) = 5y + 4$$
$$18 - 2y = 5y + 4$$
$$14 = 7y$$
$$2 = y$$

You can also substitute your solution for y into either of the original equations in order to solve for x—but first check whether you need to do that. Most of the time, the GMAT will ask for only one variable. Here's how to solve for the second variable, just in case:

$$x + y = 9$$
$$x + 2 = 9$$
$$x = 7$$

If the problem had asked you to solve for x, you would start by isolating y in one of the equations and then substituting into the second equation. You can choose which equation to do first versus second—and if you do have to solve for both variables, you can also choose in which order you solve. But if, as will usually be the case, you're asked to solve only for one variable, first isolate the variable you *don't* want, and then substitute to solve for the variable you do want.

Two Variables: Solving by Elimination

Alternatively, you can solve simultaneous equations by elimination. In this method, you can add or subtract the two equations to eliminate one of the variables—though you'll minimize mistakes if you plan on adding whenever you do this, not subtracting. For example:

Solve the following for y.

$$x + y = 9$$
$$2x = 5y + 4$$

To start, line up the terms of the equations:

$$x + y = 9$$
$$2x - 5y = 4$$

The goal is to get the coefficient (or number) in front of the variable you *don't* want (in this case, x) to be the same *number* but the opposite sign (positive or negative). You accomplish this by multiplying one of the equations by some number. For example, multiply the first equation by -2:

$$-2(x + y = 9) \rightarrow -2x - 2y = -18$$

Now, the x coefficient in both equations is the same number (2) but opposite in sign. Next, add the equations to eliminate the undesired variable:

$$\begin{array}{r} -2x - 2y = -18 \\ +2x - 5y = 4 \\ \hline -7y = -14 \end{array}$$

Finally, solve the resulting equation for the unknown variable:

$$-7y = -14$$
$$y = 2$$

The GMAT will usually ask you to solve for only one of the two variables, but if you do have to find both, then substitute the value for the known variable into either of the starting equations to find the value for the other variable. Use whichever equation looks easier to you:

$$x + y = 9$$
$$x + 2 = 9$$
$$x = 7$$

Two Variables: Solving for the Combo

Combo questions might look, at first glance, much like certain algebra questions or word problems you were asked in school. Try this Data Sufficiency (DS) problem:

> For a certain stock, earnings per share is calculated as total net earnings, e, divided by the number of shares outstanding, n. What are the earnings per share for this stock?
>
> (1) $\dfrac{e + n}{n} = 3$
> (2) $n = 4{,}000{,}000$

It wasn't unusual to be asked, in school, to solve for $\frac{x}{y}$, or $x + y$, or any similar combination of variables. Find x, find y, and voilà! You can calculate any desired combination of the variables, too.

GMAT combo problems, however, have one key difference: Your goal is to solve directly for the *combination* of variables, not for each individual variable. There are two steps in a combo problem: noticing the combo and manipulating to match it.

First: Notice that the question asks for a combo.

When a question asks directly for a combination of variables, you have a combo problem. Many combos on the GMAT are going to be disguised in some way. In the problem above, the combo $\frac{e}{n}$ is described in words only (earnings *per* share); the problem does not explicitly show you $\frac{e}{n}$. (There are other ways to disguise a combo—you'll learn about these later.)

Second: Manipulate any given information to try to match the combo.

In this case, the question itself can be simplified from "what is the earnings per share?" to "what is the value of $\frac{e}{n}$?"

The stem doesn't contain any given information about the values of e or n. The goal will be to try to manipulate any information in the statements to match the desired combo.

Jump into the statements:

(1) $\dfrac{e + n}{n} = 3$

11

If you weren't looking for the combo, you might start to simplify the equation by multiplying both sides by n, getting $e + n = 3n$. However, the combo contains a fraction $\left(\frac{e}{n}\right)$, so keep that denominator right where it is. How else can you manipulate the equation while preserving the fraction? Split the numerator and simplify:

$$\frac{e}{n} + \frac{n}{n} = 3$$

$$\frac{e}{n} + 1 = 3$$

$$\frac{e}{n} = 2$$

Statement (1) is sufficient!

AD
~~BCE~~

Here's statement (2):

(2) $n = 4,000,000$

This statement provides no information about e, so it is not sufficient. The correct answer is (A).

(A)~~D~~
~~BCE~~

When you solve for a combo in DS, your ultimate goal is to try to find a single match for the desired combo. If you can find a match, then the statement is sufficient.

The problem above also contains a C-Trap (first introduced in Chapter 3, Data Sufficiency 101). Problems with this trap appear to work only when both statements are used together—that is, the answer appears to be (C). In actuality, one of the two statements works by itself and (C) is incorrect. Take a look at the two statements again:

(1) $\dfrac{e + n}{n} = 3$

(2) $n = 4,000,000$

If you are trying to solve for both e and n individually, neither statement alone will get you there. Put the two statements together, however, and it is possible to find the individual values of both e and n.

There's just one hitch: The problem didn't ask for the values of e and n. It asked for the value of $\frac{e}{n}$, and statement (1) is sufficient all by itself to find that combo. Since answer (C) specifically says that you have to use both statements together and that *neither one alone is sufficient*, it cannot be correct.

Keep an eye out for the C-Trap on DS problems. If it feels too obvious that the two statements do work together, reexamine each one individually; one might work all by itself. Combo problems are a very common place for C-Traps to occur.

In addition to using words to disguise a combo, as in the problem above, the GMAT can also disguise a combo by asking for it indirectly. Consider this question:

If $a + b = c$, what is the value of c?

The question itself asks for a single variable, but it also provides given information in the form of an equation that contains three variables total. Given that equation, if you are able to find the value of the combo $a + b$, then you could also find the value of c. So the real question is this:

What is c? Or, what is $a + b$?

Try this problem:

If $2x + y = 18$ and $x + 2y = 12$, what is the value of $x + y$?

(A)   2
(B)   6
(C)   8
(D)   10
(E)   12

Since you're given two equations and two variables, you could solve for the individual values of x and y—but when the question asks for a combo, it's usually faster to solve for the combo!

Note two characteristics about the combo: the R & R. First, the desired *relationship* between the two variables is addition ($+$). Second, the desired *ratio* of the coefficients—the values in front of the variables—is 1 : 1 (you have one x and one y).

Take a look at the two equations. Do you see any way to combine them that would give you an addition relationship and a 1 : 1 ratio between the variables?

$$\begin{array}{r} 2x + y = 18 \\ + x + 2y = 12 \\ \hline 3x + 3y = 30 \end{array}$$

Add them up! Divide by 3 to solve for the combo: $x + y = 10$. The correct answer is (D).

You can also solve for x and y individually and then add them up; that will just take longer. A little time investment up front to figure out whether there's a shortcut can often save you more time later on in the problem. (And if you don't see how to solve directly for the combo, you can always go ahead and solve individually.)

Notice that the question asks for a combo.

A question stem may ask for the combo directly or it may try to disguise the combo. You may have to do a little rephrasing in order to find the combo. Start training yourself to look for this feature.

Manipulate any given information to try to match the combo.

Your goal is to try to match the combination of variables (look for the R & R: *relationship* and *ratio*). Most of the time, if you try to solve for each variable individually, it will take longer and, on DS, you risk falling into a trap answer. Go for the combo!

Absolute Value Equations

Absolute value refers to the *positive* value of the expression within the absolute value brackets. For instance, if you know that $|x| = 5$, then x could be either 5 or -5 and the equation would still be true. There's exactly one circumstance in which the value isn't positive: when it's zero. In this case, $|x| = 0$, so $x = 0$.

Unless the answer is zero, equations that involve absolute value generally have two solutions. In other words, there are *two* numbers that the variable could equal in order to make the equation true, because the value of the expression inside the absolute value brackets could be *positive or negative*.

Here's how to solve an absolute value equation:

Solve for w, given that $12 + |w - 4| = 30$.

11

First, isolate the absolute value expression:

$$12 + |w - 4| = 30$$
$$|w - 4| = 18$$

Second, once you have an equation of the form $|\text{variable expression}| = a$ with $a > 0$, you know that the variable expression *without* the absolute value symbols could be $\pm$. Remove the absolute value brackets and solve the equation for two different solutions:

CASE 1: When w is positive, $w = a$.

$$w - 4 = 18$$
$$w = 22$$

CASE 2: When w is negative, $-w = a$.

$$-(w - 4) = 18$$
$$w - 4 = -18$$
$$w = -14$$

Problem Set

Now that you've finished the chapter, try the following problems.

1. Solve for x: $2(2 - 3x) - (4 + x) = 7$

2. Given $z \neq \frac{3}{2}$, solve for z: $\frac{4z - 7}{3 - 2z} = -5$

3. What is the sum of x, y, and z?

    $x + y = 8$
    $x + z = 11$
    $y + z = 7$

    (A) 1
    (B) 13
    (C) 26

4. Solve for y: $22 - |y + 14| = 20$

5. If 37.5% of a equals half of b and $a = 3bc$, then what is the value of c, if $abc \neq 0$?

    (A) $\frac{1}{9}$
    (B) $\frac{1}{4}$
    (C) $\frac{4}{9}$
    (D) 1
    (E) $\frac{9}{4}$

Save the following problems for review after you finish this entire guide.

6. If $A = \dfrac{\frac{x}{3}}{\frac{2}{y}}$ and $y = \frac{18}{x}$, then what is the value of A?

    (A) 27
    (B) 12
    (C) 3
    (D) $\frac{1}{3}$
    (E) $\frac{1}{12}$

11

7. If $y = 2x + 9$ and $7x + 3y = -51$, what is the value of x ?

(A) -6

(B) -3

(C) 0

8. Every attendee at a monster truck rally paid the same admission fee. How many people attended the rally?

   (1) If the admission fee had been raised to $20 and twice as many people had attended, the total admission fees collected would have been three times the amount actually collected.

   (2) If the admission fee had been raised to $30 and two-thirds as many people had attended, the total admission fees collected would have been 150% of the actual admission fees collected.

9. If $x \neq 0$ and $x\left(x - \dfrac{5x + 6}{x}\right) = 0$, what are all of the possible values of x ?

10. At a certain coffee shop, a mocha sells for $3.00 and a cappuccino sells for $2.25. In total, the shop sold $180 worth of mochas and cappuccinos over the course of a day. How many mochas did the shop sell?

    (1) The shop sold 10 more cappuccinos than it did mochas.

    (2) The combined price of all of the cappuccinos sold was equal to the combined price of all of the mochas sold.

Solutions

1. **−1:**

$$2(2 - 3x) - (4 + x) = 7$$
$$4 - 6x - 4 - x = 7$$
$$-7x = 7$$
$$x = -1$$

2. $\frac{4}{3}$:

$$\frac{4z - 7}{3 - 2z} = -5$$
$$4z - 7 = -5(3 - 2z)$$
$$4z - 7 = -15 + 10z$$
$$8 = 6z$$
$$z = \frac{8}{6} = \frac{4}{3}$$

3. **(B) 13:** It is possible to solve for x, y, and z individually, but you can save a significant amount of time by solving for the combo: What is $x + y + z$?

   The equations collectively contain exactly two "copies" of each variable and these variables are always added. Add the three equations together:

$$
\begin{array}{r}
x + y = 8 \\
x + z = 11 \\
+ y + z = 7 \\
\hline
2x + 2y + 2z = 26
\end{array}
$$

   Divide the equation by 2: the combo $x + y + z = 13$.

4. $y = \{-16, -12\}$: First, isolate the expression within the absolute value brackets. Then, solve for two cases, one in which the expression is positive and one in which it is negative:

$$22 - |y + 14| = 20$$
$$2 = |y + 14|$$

   Case 1: $y + 14 = 2$ Case 2: $-(y + 14) = 2$
   $$y = -12$$ $$y + 14 = -2$$
                                       $$y = -16$$

5. **(C)** $\frac{4}{9}$: First, Understand. This Problem Solving question has three unknowns (a, b, and c) and two equations. One is given as an equation, but the other will have to be translated. The question also contains a percent (37.5%) and a fraction (half, or $\frac{1}{2}$). This is one of those times when it's good to have fraction/percent conversions memorized. The fraction equivalent of 37.5% is $\frac{3}{8}$.

   The question asks for a value for c, so there must be a way to eliminate a and b.

11

Make a Plan. Look for an opportunity to simplify one or both equations so that substitution can eliminate a and b. Translate the first statement into math, using the fraction equivalent of 37.5%:

$$\frac{3}{8}a = \frac{1}{2}b$$

Eliminate the fraction by multiplying both sides by the common denominator, which is 8:

$$(8)\left(\frac{3}{8}\right)a = (8)\left(\frac{1}{2}\right)b$$
$$3a = 4b$$

Leave it in this form to avoid having to work with fractions. The second equation has a isolated on the left-hand side. Multiply both sides by 3, so that you can substitute $3a$ from the first equation directly into the second equation:

$$(3)a = (3)(3bc)$$
$$3a = 9bc$$

Plug $4b$ in for $3a$ on the left-hand side, then solve for c:

$$4b = 9bc$$
$$\frac{4\cancel{b}}{9\cancel{b}} = c$$
$$\frac{4}{9} = c$$

6. **(C) 3:** The first step is to Understand. Glance at the problem. There are two equations with fractions, and three total unknowns: A, x, and y. When solving a system of equations, the typical requirement is that there are the same number of linear equations and unknowns. These aren't linear equations, however, and there are only two.

The question asks for A, so first focus on simplifying the equation that contains A.

$$A = \frac{\frac{x}{3}}{\frac{2}{y}} \quad A = \frac{x}{3}\left(\frac{y}{2}\right) \quad A = \frac{xy}{6}$$

The simplified version of the equation has the expression xy in it. Solving for A will require finding the value of the combo xy.

Time to make a Plan. Since the simplified equation for A contains the combo xy, find a way to isolate that combo in the second equation.

Solve by multiplying both sides of the second equation by x.

$$y = \frac{18}{x} \quad xy = 18$$

Now plug the combo $xy = 18$ into the rearranged version of the first equation.

$$A = \frac{18}{6} = 3$$

7. **(A) −6:** The question asks for x, so you need to figure out how to eliminate y. Since the first equation already has y isolated, substitute the first equation into the second equation:

$$y = 2x + 9 \qquad 7x + 3y = -51$$

$$7x + 3(2x + 9) = -51$$
$$7x + 6x + 27 = -51$$
$$13x + 27 = -51$$
$$13x = -78$$
$$x = -6$$

Note that answer (B) is a trap. The value for y is -3, but the question asked for x, not y.

8. **(E):** This question asks how many people attended a monster truck rally. The total amount collected equals the number of attendees times the admission fee, or $T = A \times P$. The question asks for A.

(1) INSUFFICIENT: If the price had been \$20 and twice as many people had attended, the total would be three times greater. Therefore:

$$3T = 2A \times 20$$
$$3T = 40A$$

The value of A depends on the unknown value of T, so more than one answer is possible, and this statement is not sufficient.

(2) INSUFFICIENT: If the price had been \$30 and two-thirds as many people had attended, the total would be 150% of the actual total. Therefore:

$$1.5T = \frac{2}{3}A \times 30$$
$$1.5T = 20A$$

The value of A depends on the unknown value of T, so more than one answer is possible, and this statement is not sufficient.

(1) AND (2) INSUFFICIENT: In order to be able to solve for the value of A, you would need two different equations. The two equations are the same. Combining the two statements is therefore no more sufficient than either statement alone.

The correct answer is **(E):** Using the two statements together is still not sufficient.

9. **{6, −1}:** Distribute the multiplication by x. Note that, when you cancel the x in the denominator, the quantity $5x + 6$ is implicitly enclosed in parentheses:

$$x\left(x - \frac{5x + 6}{x}\right) = 0$$
$$x^2 - (5x + 6) = 0$$
$$x^2 - 5x - 6 = 0$$
$$(x - 6)(x + 1) = 0$$
$$x = 6 \text{ or } -1$$

10. **(D):** Call the number of mochas m and the number of cappuccinos c. The total revenue can be expressed as the equation $3m + 2.25c = 180$. The question asks for the value of m. If you can find the value of c, then you can find the value of m, so the question can be rephrased as this: What is the value of m or c?

(1) SUFFICIENT: This statement can be translated into the equation $m + 10 = c$. This can be substituted into the first equation: $3m + 2.25(m + 10) = 180$. This can be solved for m (though don't actually solve!).

(2) SUFFICIENT: This statement can be translated into the equation $3m = 2.25c$. Again, this can be substituted into the equation given in the question stem: $3m + 3m = 180$. This can be solved for m.

The correct answer is **(D):** Each statement alone is sufficient.

Exponents

In This Chapter...

- All About the Base

- Combining Exponential Terms with Common Bases

- Fractions and Exponents

- Factoring Out a Common Term

- Equations with Exponents

- Same Base or Same Exponent

In this chapter, you will learn all about how to work with exponents—including when dealing with integers, fractions, positives and negatives, and so on. You'll also learn steps to simplify equations with exponents.

CHAPTER 12 **Exponents**

The mathematical expression 4^3 consists of a **base** (4) and an **exponent** (3).

The base (4) is multiplied by itself as many times as the power indicates (3):

$$4^3 = 4 \times 4 \times 4 = 64$$

In other words, exponents are actually shorthand for repeated multiplication.

Two exponents have special names: The exponent 2 is called the square, and the exponent 3 is called the cube:

5^2 can be read as five squared ($5^2 = 5 \times 5 = 25$).

5^3 can be read as five cubed ($5^3 = 5 \times 5 \times 5 = 125$).

All About the Base

A Variable Base

Variables can also be raised to an exponent, and they behave the same as numbers:

$$y^4 = y \times y \times y \times y$$

Base of 0 or 1

0 raised to *any* power equals 0.
1 raised to *any* power equals 1.

For example, $0^3 = 0 \times 0 \times 0 = 0$ and $0^4 = 0 \times 0 \times 0 \times 0 = 0$.

Similarly, $1^3 = 1 \times 1 \times 1 = 1$ and $1^4 = 1 \times 1 \times 1 \times 1 = 1$.

If you are told that $x = x^2$, then x must be either 0 or 1.

A Base of −1

$$(-1)^1 = -1 \qquad (-1)^2 = -1 \times (-1) = 1 \qquad (-1)^3 = -1 \times (-1) \times (-1) = -1$$

This pattern repeats indefinitely. In fact:

$$(-1)^{\text{ODD}} = -1 \qquad (-1)^{\text{EVEN}} = 1$$

A Fractional Base

Squaring a fraction is the equivalent of multiplying the fraction by itself. You can also distribute the exponent before multiplying. For example:

$$\left(\frac{3}{4}\right)^2 = \frac{3}{4} \times \frac{3}{4} = \frac{9}{16} \qquad \left(\frac{3}{4}\right)^2 = \frac{3^2}{4^2} = \frac{9}{16}$$

When a fraction between 0 and 1 is raised to a power, an interesting thing occurs: The value gets smaller, not larger! For example:

$$\left(\frac{3}{4}\right)^1 = \frac{3}{4}$$

$$\left(\frac{3}{4}\right)^2 = \frac{3}{4} \times \frac{3}{4} = \frac{9}{16}$$

$$\left(\frac{3}{4}\right)^3 = \frac{3}{4} \times \frac{3}{4} \times \frac{3}{4} = \frac{27}{64}$$

Notice that $\frac{3}{4} > \frac{9}{16} > \frac{27}{64}$. If the fractional base is positive, as you continue to increase the value of the power, the value of the fraction continues to decrease.

If the base fraction is negative, then raising it to either an even or odd power makes the fraction *larger*, but for slightly different reasons. Raising a negative fraction to an even power turns the fraction positive, and a positive fraction is greater than a negative one:

$$\left(-\frac{3}{4}\right)^2 = -\frac{3}{4} \times -\frac{3}{4} = \frac{9}{16}$$

But when you raise a negative base to an odd power, it actually becomes *less* negative, or closer to 0. Because of that, the new fraction is actually greater than the original:

$$\left(-\frac{3}{4}\right)^3 = -\frac{3}{4} \times \left(-\frac{3}{4}\right) \times \left(-\frac{3}{4}\right) = -\frac{27}{64}$$

In general, remember that raising any proper fraction (fractions between −1 and 1) to any power will result in a new fraction that is *closer* to 0. This is still true for negative fractions raised to even powers. They are still closer to 0; they just happen to be closer on the positive end of the number line.

A Decimal Base

Like proper fractions, decimals between 0 and 1 decrease as their exponent increases, while negative decimals increase as the exponents increase by becoming either positive or less negative:

$$(0.6)^2 = 0.36 \qquad (0.5)^4 = 0.0625 \qquad (0.1)^5 = 0.00001$$

$$(-0.6)^2 = 0.36 \qquad (-0.5)^4 = 0.0625 \qquad (-0.1)^5 = -0.00001$$

A Compound Base

Just as an exponent can be distributed to a fraction, it can also be distributed to a product:

$$10^3 = (2 \times 5)^3 = (2)^3 \times (5)^3 = 8 \times 125 = 1,000$$

This also works if the base includes variables:

$$(3x)^4 = 3^4 \times x^4 = 81\,x^4$$

More on Negative Bases

When dealing with negative bases, pay particular attention to PEMDAS. Unless the negative sign is inside parentheses, the exponent does not distribute. For example:

$$-2^4 \qquad\qquad \neq \qquad\qquad (-2)^4$$

$$-2^4 = -1 \times 2^4 = -16 \qquad\qquad (-2)^4 = (-1)^4 \times (2)^4 = 1 \times 16 = 16$$

As with a base of -1, any negative bases raised to an odd exponent will be negative, and any negative bases raised to an even exponent will be positive.

Combining Exponential Terms with Common Bases

The rules in this section *only* apply when the terms have the *same* base. All of these rules are related to the fact that exponents are shorthand for repeated multiplication.

Multiply Terms: Add Exponents

When *multiplying* two exponential terms with the same base, *add the exponents*. This rule is true no matter what the base is:

$$z^2 \times z^3 = (z \times z) \times (z \times z \times z) = z \times z \times z \times z \times z = z^5$$

$$4 \times 4^2 = (4) \times (4 \times 4) = 4 \times 4 \times 4 = 4^3$$

Fortunately, once you know the rule, you can simplify the computation greatly:

$$z^2 \times z^3 = z^{2+3} = z^5$$

Divide Terms: Subtract Exponents

When *dividing* two exponential terms with the same base, *subtract the exponents*. This rule is true no matter what the base is:

$$\frac{5^6}{5^2} = \frac{5 \times 5 \times 5 \times 5 \times \cancel{5} \times \cancel{5}}{\cancel{5} \times \cancel{5}} = 5 \times 5 \times 5 \times 5 = 5^4$$

Fortunately, once you know the rule, you can simplify the computation greatly:

$$\frac{x^6}{x^2} = x^{6-2} = x^4$$

Anything Raised to the Zero Power is Equal to 1

This rule is an extension of the previous rule. If you divide something by itself, the quotient is 1:

$$\frac{a^3}{a^3} = \frac{\cancel{a} \times \cancel{a} \times \cancel{a}}{\cancel{a} \times \cancel{a} \times \cancel{a}} = 1$$

Look at this division by subtracting exponents:

$$\frac{a^3}{a^3} = a^{3-3} = a^0$$

Therefore, $a^0 = 1$.

Any base raised to the 0 power equals 1. The one exception is a base of 0.

Note that you cannot raise 0 to the 0 power. $0^0 = \frac{0}{0}$, which is *undefined* (but the GMAT does not test undefined numbers, so you don't need to memorize this). Although the GMAT doesn't test undefined numbers directly, you may need to use the knowledge that you cannot divide by 0 when considering values for variables in a denominator.

Negative Exponents

The behavior of negative exponents is also an extension of the rules for dividing exponential terms. For example:

$$\frac{y^2}{y^5} = \frac{\cancel{y} \times \cancel{y}}{y \times y \times y \times \cancel{y} \times \cancel{y}} = \frac{1}{y^3}$$

Look at this division by subtracting exponents:

$$\frac{y^2}{y^5} = y^{2-5} = y^{-3}$$

Therefore, $y^{-3} = \frac{1}{y^3}$.

This is the general rule: *Something with a negative exponent is just "one over" that same thing with a positive exponent.* You can rewrite y^{-3} by taking the reciprocal of y and dropping the negative sign from the exponent:

$$y^{-3} \rightarrow \left(\frac{1}{y}\right)^3 \rightarrow \frac{1}{y^3}$$

Here are some additional examples of how to take the reciprocal and drop the negative sign:

$$\frac{1}{3^{-3}} = 3^3 \qquad \left(\frac{x}{4}\right)^{-2} = \left(\frac{4}{x}\right)^2$$

Note that 0 to a negative power is undefined for the same reason that 0 to the power of 0 is undefined; both result in division by 0:

$$0^{-2} = \frac{1}{(0)^2} = \frac{1}{0} = \text{undefined}$$

Nested Exponents: Multiply Exponents

How can you simplify $(z^2)^3$? Expand this term to show the repeated multiplication:

$$(z^2)^3 = (z^2) \times (z^2) \times (z^2) = z^{2+2+2} = z^6$$

When you raise an exponential term to an exponent, multiply the exponents:

$$(a^2)^3 = a^{2 \times 3} = a^6$$

Fractions and Exponents

There are four broad categories of fractions that all behave differently when raised to a power. The result depends on the size and the sign of the fraction, as well as on the power. While it is not necessary to memorize all of the cases below, it is important to understand how each case works so that you know what numbers to try when testing cases, if necessary.

Divide fractions up into these four categories: less than -1, between -1 and 0, between 0 and 1, and greater than 1:

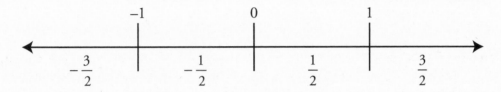

As you examine the math below, think about why the result is what it is.

Even Exponents (such as 2):

Less than -1	Between -1 and 0	Between 0 and 1	Greater than 1
$\left(-\frac{3}{2}\right)^2 = \frac{9}{4}$	$\left(-\frac{1}{2}\right)^2 = \frac{1}{4}$	$\left(\frac{1}{2}\right)^2 = \frac{1}{4}$	$\left(\frac{3}{2}\right)^2 = \frac{9}{4}$
$-\frac{3}{2} < \frac{9}{4}$	$-\frac{1}{2} < \frac{1}{4}$	$\frac{1}{2} > \frac{1}{4}$	$\frac{3}{2} < \frac{9}{4}$
Result is bigger.	Result is bigger.	Result is *smaller*.	Result is bigger.

If the exponent is even, then the fraction will get bigger in all circumstances except for one: when the fraction is between 0 and 1.

Odd Exponents (such as 3):

Less than -1	Between -1 and 0	Between 0 and 1	Greater than 1
$\left(-\frac{3}{2}\right)^3 = -\frac{27}{8}$	$\left(-\frac{1}{2}\right)^3 = -\frac{1}{8}$	$\left(\frac{1}{2}\right)^3 = \frac{1}{8}$	$\left(\frac{3}{2}\right)^3 = \frac{27}{8}$
$-\frac{3}{2} > -\frac{27}{8}$	$-\frac{1}{2} < -\frac{1}{8}$	$\frac{1}{2} > \frac{1}{8}$	$\frac{3}{2} < \frac{27}{8}$
Result is *smaller*.	Result is bigger.	Result is *smaller*.	Result is bigger.

12

If the exponent is odd, on the other hand, then there are two circumstances in which the fraction gets smaller: when the number is between 0 and 1 (as before) *and* when the number is less than -1.

Negative Exponents (such as -2):

To raise a fraction to a negative power, raise the reciprocal to the equivalent positive power:

$$\left(\frac{3}{7}\right)^{-2} = \left(\frac{7}{3}\right)^{2} = \frac{7^2}{3^2} = \frac{49}{9} \qquad \left(\frac{x}{y}\right)^{-w} = \left(\frac{y}{x}\right)^{w} = \frac{y^w}{x^w}$$

Factoring Out a Common Term

In most cases, exponential terms that are added or subtracted cannot be combined; for example, you can't combine these two terms: $2^3 + 3^4$. However, if two terms with the same base are added or subtracted, you can factor out a common term. In the following example, factor out 11^3:

$$11^3 + 11^4$$
$$= 11^3(11^0 + 11^1)$$
$$= 11^3(1 + 11)$$
$$= 11^3(12)$$

For any term that matches what you pulled out, an exponent of 0 is left behind; in this example, factoring 11^3 out of 11^3 leaves 11^0 behind. For all terms, the exponent becomes whatever is left behind. In the example above, 11^3 was pulled to the front, so the 11^4 term has 11^1 left over.

On the GMAT, it generally pays to factor exponential terms that have bases in common, and when doing so, factor out the smallest power. If the exponents are negative, factor out the term with the most negative exponent. Try this example:

If $x = 4^{20} + 4^{21} + 4^{22}$, what is the greatest prime factor of x ?

To find the prime factors of x, express x as a product (terms multiplied together). Factor 4^{20} out of the expression on the right side of the equation:

$$x = 4^{20} + 4^{21} + 4^{22}$$
$$x = 4^{20}(4^0 + 4^1 + 4^2)$$
$$x = 4^{20}(1 + 4 + 16)$$
$$x = 4^{20}(21)$$
$$x = (2^2)^{20}(3 \times 7)$$
$$x = (2^{40})(3)(7)$$

Now that x has been expressed as a product, you can see all of its prime factors: 2, 3, and 7. The greatest prime factor is 7.

If the terms are all identical, you can use a great shortcut. For example:

$$11^4 + 11^4 + 11^4$$

The official math works this way:

$$11^4 + 11^4 + 11^4$$
$$= 11^4(11^0 + 11^0 + 11^0)$$
$$= 11^4(1 + 1 + 1)$$
$$= 11^4(3)$$

Here's the shortcut: Count up the number of terms. In this case, there are three 11^4 terms. Multiply the term, 11^4, by the number of terms, 3: The answer is $11^4(3)$.

Equations with Exponents

Exponents can also appear in equations. In fact, the GMAT often complicates equations by including exponents or roots with unknown variables. Here are a few situations to look out for when equations contain exponents.

Even Exponents Hide the Sign of the Base

Any number raised to an even exponent becomes positive. For example:

$$3^2 = 9 \qquad \text{AND} \qquad (-3)^2 = 9$$

Another way of saying this is that an even exponent hides the sign of its base. Compare the following two equations:

$$x^2 = 25 \qquad\qquad |x| = 5$$

Do you see what they have in common? In both cases, $x = \pm 5$. The equations share the same two solutions. In fact, there is an important relationship: **For any x, $\sqrt{x^2} = |x|$.**

Here is another example:

$a^2 - 5 = 12$ By adding 5 to both sides, you can rewrite this equation as $a^2 = 17$. This equation has two solutions: $\sqrt{17}$ and $-\sqrt{17}$.

You can also say that the equation $a^2 = 17$ has two roots (the word *root* is a synonym for the word *solution*). The GMAT will sometimes use the word *root*, so if this term is new to you, make yourself a flash card to help remember.

Also note that not all equations with even exponents have two solutions. For example:

$x^2 + 3 = 3$ By subtracting 3 from both sides, you can rewrite this equation as $x^2 = 0$, which has only one solution: 0.

Odd Exponents Keep the Sign of the Base

Equations that involve only cube roots or other odd exponents have only one solution:

$x^3 = -125$ Here, x has only one solution, -5, because $(-5)(-5)(-5) = -125$. This will not work with positive 5.

$243 = y^5$ Here, y has only one solution, 3, because $(3)(3)(3)(3)(3) = 243$. This will not work with -3.

If an equation includes some variables with odd exponents and some variables with even exponents, treat it as dangerous, as it is likely to have two solutions. Any even exponents in an equation signal two potential solutions.

Same Base or Same Exponent

In problems that involve exponential expressions on *both* sides of the equation, it is imperative to rewrite the bases so that either the same base or the same exponent appears on both sides of the equation. Once you do this, you can usually eliminate the bases or the exponents and rewrite the rest as an equation. Consider this example:

If $\left(4^w\right)^3 = 32^{w-1}$, what is the value of w?

To start, rewrite the bases so that the same base appears on both sides of the equation. Right now, the left side has a base of 4 and the right side has a base of 32. Both 4 and 32 can be expressed as powers of 2, so you can rewrite 4 as 2^2 and you can rewrite 32 as 2^5.

Next, plug the rewritten bases into the original equation:

$$(4^w)^3 = 32^{w-1}$$

$$\left(\left(2^2\right)^w\right)^3 = \left(2^5\right)^{w-1}$$

Now, simplify the equation using the rules of exponents:

$$\left(\left(2^2\right)^w\right)^3 = \left(2^5\right)^{w-1}$$
$$2^{6w} = 2^{5w-5}$$

When the bases are identical (and no other bases exist), you can drop the bases, rewrite the exponents as an equation, and solve:

$$6w = 5w - 5$$
$$w = -5$$

Be very careful if 0, 1, or -1 is the base (or could be the base), since the outcome of raising those bases to powers is not unique. For instance, $0^2 = 0^3 = 0^{29} = 0$. So if $0^x = 0^y$, you cannot claim that $x = y$.

Likewise, $1^2 = 1^3 = 1^{29} = 1$, and $(-1)^2 = (-1)^4 = (-1)^{\text{even}} = 1$, while $(-1)^3 = (-1)^5 = (-1)^{\text{odd}} = -1$. Fortunately, the GMAT rarely tries to trick you this way.

Problem Set

Now that you've finished the chapter, try the following problems.

For problems 1 and 2, determine whether the inequality is TRUE or FALSE.

1. $\left(-\frac{3}{4}\right)^3 > -\frac{3}{4}$

2. $\left(\frac{x+1}{x}\right)^{-2} > \frac{x+1}{x}$, if $x > 0$.

3. $x^3 < x^2$. Describe the possible values of x.

4. Simplify: $\dfrac{m^8 p^7 r^{12}}{m^3 r^9 p} \times p^2 r^3 m^4$

5. What is the value of p if $\dfrac{-a}{b+c} = -1$ and $p = \dfrac{2^{a-b}}{2^c}$?

   (A) -2
   (B) 0
   (C) 1
   (D) 2
   (E) 4

Save the following problems for review after you finish this entire guide.

6. On a certain assessment, the score on part A is equal to 5^a, where a is the number of questions answered correctly on part A. The score on part B is equal to 5^b, where b is the number of questions answered correctly on part B. The total score is calculated as the product of the score on part A and the score on part B. How many questions did Simon answer correctly on the entire assessment?

   (1) $a = b + 1$
   (2) Simon's total score on the assessment was 125.

7. Which of the following expressions has the greatest value?

   (A) $\left(3^4\right)^{12}$
   (B) $\left[\left(3^{30}\right)^{12}\right]^{\frac{1}{10}}$
   (C) $3^{30} + 3^{30} + 3^{30}$
   (D) $4(3^{47})$
   (E) $\left(3^{90}\right)^{\frac{1}{2}}$

8. Simplify: $(4^y + 4^y + 4^y + 4^y)(3^y + 3^y + 3^y)$

(A) $4^{4y} \times 3^{3y}$

(B) 12^{y+1}

(C) $16^y \times 9^y$

(D) 12^y

(E) $4^y \times 12^y$

9. If m and n are positive integers and $(2^{18})(5^m) = (20^n)$, what is the value of m ?

10. If $B^3 A < 0$ and $A > 0$, which of the following must be negative?

(A) AB

(B) $B^2 A$

(C) B^4

(D) $\dfrac{A}{B^2}$

(E) $-\dfrac{B}{A}$

Solutions

1. **TRUE:** Cubing a negative number will maintain the negative sign, so the left-hand side of the inequality will stay negative. Raising a fraction between 1 and -1 to a power causes that fraction to move closer to 0 on a number line. If the starting number is between 0 and 1, the fraction will get smaller as it moves closer to 0. However, if the starting number is between -1 and 0, as it is in this problem, then the number will get larger as it moves closer to 0.

   The value $\left(-\dfrac{3}{4}\right)^3$, therefore, will be to the right of $-\dfrac{3}{4}$ on the number line, or closer to 0. It is true that $\left(-\dfrac{3}{4}\right)^3$ is greater than $-\dfrac{3}{4}$.

2. **FALSE:** Test a case (a real number!) to understand what the problem is asking. Note that the problem states that x is positive. Any number $\dfrac{x+1}{x}$, where x is positive, will be greater than 1. Therefore, raising that number to a negative exponent will result in a number smaller than 1:

   If $x = 1$, then:

   $$\text{Is } \left(\frac{1+1}{1}\right)^{-2} > \frac{1+1}{1} \text{ ?}$$

   $$\text{Is } (2)^{-2} > 2 \text{ ?}$$

   $$\text{Is } \left(\frac{1}{2}\right)^2 > 2 \text{ ?}$$

   You can solve that last line, but you don't need to if you've learned how numbers work. A fraction between 0 and 1 raised to a positive exponent will always get smaller, so the left side of that inequality cannot be greater than the 2. The statement is false.

3. **Any non-zero number less than 1:** First, consider possible positive values. As positive fractions between 0 and 1 are raised to a power (multiplied together), their value decreases. For example, $\left(\dfrac{1}{2}\right)^3 < \left(\dfrac{1}{2}\right)^2$. So these types of fractions are possible values for x. The number 1 makes the inequality false, though, as does any positive number greater than 1.

   The number 0 does not work in this inequality as 0 raised to any power equals 0 (ignoring the case of 0 raised to the 0 power).

   Now consider negative numbers. A negative number cubed is negative. Any negative number squared is positive. For example, $(-3)^3 < (-3)^2$. By definition, any negative number is smaller than any positive number, so this inequality is true for all negative values.

4. $m^9 p^8 r^6$: First, multiply the term on the right into the numerator of the fraction:

   $$\frac{m^8 p^7 r^{12}}{m^3 r^9 p} \times p^2 r^3 m^4 = \frac{m^{12} p^9 r^{15}}{m^3 r^9 p}$$

   Then, simplify the top and bottom of the fraction:

   $$\frac{m^{12} p^9 r^{15}}{m^3 r^9 p} = m^{(12-3)} p^{(9-1)} r^{(15-9)} = m^9 p^8 r^6$$

5. **(C) 1:** As always, the first step is to Understand. In this algebra problem, some of the variables appear in exponents. This problem will involve simplifying the equation for p using the other equation with a, b, and c in it. Simplify that first equation.

$$\frac{-a}{b+c} = -1$$

$$\frac{a}{b+c} = 1$$

$$a = b + c$$

Time to Plan. This is an algebra problem, with equations in the prompt, so it seems reasonable that doing algebra can solve the problem. What about number testing? The numbers in the answer choices often indicate an opportunity to work backwards, but in this case there are too many unknowns (a, b, and c) left over to work backwards effectively. Furthermore, the values of those unknowns remain forever unknown. That's significant, because it means that the exact values of those variables don't matter, as long as the constraints are obeyed. Sounds like a good problem for using Smart Numbers.

(Both a Smart Numbers approach and an algebraic solution are shown below.)

Finally, Solve. First, try smart numbers. For a, b, and c, pick different small numbers to satisfy the equation $a = b + c$, like $5 = 3 + 2$. Plugging all of those numbers in yields:

$$p = \frac{2^{a-b}}{2^c}$$

$$p = \frac{2^{5-3}}{2^2}$$

$$p = \frac{2^2}{2^2} = \frac{4}{4} = 1$$

Algebra works too. The equation for p has the expression $a - b$ in it, so subtract b from both sides of the reworked version of the first equation to get $a - b = c$. Substitute into the equation for p.

$$p = \frac{2^{a-b}}{2^c}$$

$$p = \frac{2^c}{2^c} = 1$$

Alternatively, the equation for p can be manipulated first. Remember the rule for dividing with exponents.

$$p = \frac{2^{a-b}}{2^c}$$

$$p = 2^{a-b-c}$$

Subtract both b and c from both sides of the equation $a = b + c$ to see that $a - b - c = 0$. The value 2^0 equals 1.

6. **(B):** Understand and Plan first. This value DS question asks for the total number of questions that Simon got right on the assessment. The number correct on part A is a and the number correct on part B is b, so the question is asking for $a + b$.

    But there's more to the story. Simon's total score on the assessment is the product of 5^a and 5^b. Write out that algebraic expression and then simplify.

    $$\text{Total score} = (5^a)(5^b)$$
    $$\text{Total score} = 5^{a+b}$$

    Since the total score is 5 raised to the sum of a and b, knowing the total score would be sufficient to answer the question.

    (1) INSUFFICIENT: This equation cannot be rearranged to isolate the expression $a + b$ on one side.

    (2) SUFFICIENT: If the overall score is 125, then $a + b$ must be equal to whatever power of 5 is equal to 125. More specifically:

    $$5^{a+b} = 125$$
    $$5^{a+b} = 5^3$$
    $$a + b = 3$$

    The correct answer is **(B):** Statement (2) is sufficient, but statement (1) is not.

7. **(D) $4(3^{47})$:** Use the rules of exponents to simplify each expression:

    (A) $\left(3^4\right)^{12} = 3^{48}$

    (B) $\left[\left(3^{30}\right)^{12}\right]^{\frac{1}{10}} = 3^{\left(30 \times 12 \times \frac{1}{10}\right)} = 3^{3 \times 12} = 3^{36}$

    (C) $3^{30} + 3^{30} + 3^{30} = 3(3^{30}) = 3^{31}$ (Since both values have the same base, combine to get 3^{31}.)

    (D) $4(3^{47})$ Cannot be simplified further.

    (E) $\left(3^{90}\right)^{\frac{1}{2}} = 3^{\frac{90}{2}} = 3^{45}$

    Answer choices (A) and (D) are larger than (B), (C), and (E). Compare (A) and (D):

    (A) 3^{48}

    (D) $4(3^{47})$

    The difficult part to compare is the exponent. Is there any way to get the same exponent?

    Factor one 3 out of answer (A): $3(3^{47})$. This is less than $4(3^{47})$, so answer **(D)** is greater.

8. **(B) 12^{y+1}:** Glance at the answers. There are no terms added together, so there must be some way to combine the individual terms in this problem. Factor out common terms from each expression. Use the terms-are-identical shortcut discussed in this chapter:

$$(4^y + 4^y + 4^y + 4^y)(3^y + 3^y + 3^y)$$

$$= (4^y)(4)\,(3^y)(3)$$

$$= (4^{y+1})(3^{y+1})$$

$$= (4 \times 3)^{y+1}$$

$$= 12^{y+1}$$

9. **9:** With exponential equations such as this one, the key is to recognize that as long as the exponents are all integers, each side of the equation must have the same number of each type of prime factor. Break down each base into prime factors and set the exponents equal to each other:

$$(2^{18})(5^m) = (20^n)$$

$$2^{18} \times 5^m = (2 \times 2 \times 5)^n$$

$$2^{18} \times 5^m = 2^{2n} \times 5^n$$

$$18 = 2n;\ m = n$$

$$n = 9;\ m = n = 9$$

Because m and n have to be integers, there must be the **same number of 2's** on either side of the equation and there must be the **same number of 5's** on either side of the equation. Thus, $18 = 2n$ and $m = n$.

10. **(A) AB:** This is a "must be" PS problem! You can Test Cases.

A is positive, so call it $A = 2$. B^3A is negative. If A is positive, then the B^3 term must be negative. Call it $B = -1$.

Double-check that you chose numbers that follow the facts in the problem. A is positive and $B^3A = (-1)^3(2) = -2$. This is negative, which is what the problem states. Good, check the answers. Keep anything that's negative. Cross off anything that's non-negative.

(A) $AB = (2)(-1) = -2$. Keep.

(B) $B^2A = (-1)^2(2) = 2$. Eliminate.

(C) $B^4 = (-1)^4 = 1$. Eliminate.

(D) $\dfrac{A}{B^2} = \dfrac{2}{(-1)^2} = 2$. Eliminate.

(E) $-\dfrac{B}{A} = -\dfrac{-1}{2} = \dfrac{1}{2}$. Eliminate.

Alternatively, you can think it through theoretically, if you feel comfortable with this math. Since A is positive, B^3 must be negative. Therefore, B must be negative. That specific answer isn't among the choices, so keep thinking. If A is positive and B is negative, the product AB must be negative.

12

CHAPTER 13

Roots

In This Chapter...

- Roots and Fractional Exponents

- Simplifying a Root

- Imperfect vs. Perfect Squares

- Memorize: Squares and Square Roots

- Memorize: Cubes and Cube Roots

In this chapter, you will learn how exponents and roots are related, as well as how to manipulate and simplify both square and cube roots. You'll also learn about perfect squares and you'll memorize commonly used squares, cubes, square roots, and cube roots.

CHAPTER 13 **Roots**

Roots are the reverse of exponents. You can square something (multiply a number by itself) or you can take the square root of a number (find what number, multiplied by itself, would give you the starting number). For example, $4^2 = 16$ and $\sqrt{16} = 4$... but there's a little intricacy to the GMAT on that second part.

Compare the following two equations:

$$x^2 = 16 \qquad x = \sqrt{16}$$

Although they may seem very similar, there is an important difference. There are two solutions to the equation on the left: $x = 4$ *or* $x = -4$. There is only *one* solution to the equation on the right: $x = 4$.

If the GMAT itself gives you a square root symbol (e.g., $\sqrt{16}$), *only* use the positive root.

If, on the other hand, the equation contains a squared variable (e.g., x^2), and *you* take the square root, use both the positive and the negative solutions:

$$\text{Given: } x^2 = 16 \qquad x = \sqrt{16}$$

$$\text{Solve: } x = \pm 4 \qquad x = 4$$

This rule applies for any even root (square root, 4th root, 6th root, etc.). For example:

$$\sqrt[4]{81} = 3$$

Odd roots (cube root, 5th root, 7th root, etc.) also have only one solution.

Odd roots, like odd exponents, keep the sign of the base. For example:

$$\text{If } \sqrt[3]{-27} = x, \text{what is } x ?$$

The correct answer is -3, because $(-3)(-3)(-3) = -27$.

By the way, the root symbol is also called a **radical sign**.

Roots and Fractional Exponents

Fractional exponents are the link between roots and exponents. For example:

$$\sqrt{x} = \sqrt[2]{x^1} = x^{\frac{1}{2}}$$

Any number that isn't raised to a power has an implied power of 1, so x can be written x^1. And any root can be written with that little number in the "v" of the radical sign, telling you which root to take (if no number is written there, a square root—or root of 2—is assumed).

Take those two numbers, the 1 and the 2, and write them as a fraction. The exponent of the base x is always the numerator of the fraction. The radical number is always the denominator of the fraction.

Try this problem:

What is $64^{\frac{1}{3}}$?

The numerator of the fraction is 1, so raise the base to the power of 1: 64^1. The denominator is 3, so take the cube root: $\sqrt[3]{64^1}$. In order to determine that root, break 64 down:

$$64 = 4 \times 4 \times 4 = 4^3$$

The value 64 is equal to 4^3, so $64^{\frac{1}{3}} = \sqrt[3]{64} = \sqrt[3]{4^3} = 4^{\left(\frac{3}{3}\right)} = 4^1 = 4$.

As a shortcut, if a number is raised to a certain power and also rooted to that same value, you can cancel out the power and the root. In this case, 4 is raised to the power of 3 but also cube-rooted, so cancel the two operations out to get 4.

Try another one:

What is $\left(\frac{1}{8}\right)^{-\frac{4}{3}}$?

Because the exponent is negative, first take the reciprocal of the base, $\left(\frac{1}{8}\right)$, and change the exponent to its positive equivalent. Next, deal with the root and the power. You can do them in whichever order is easier for you:

$$\left(\frac{1}{8}\right)^{-\frac{4}{3}} = 8^{\frac{4}{3}} = \sqrt[3]{8^4} = \left(\sqrt[3]{8}\right)^4 = (2)^4 = 16$$

Above, it's easier to take the cube first, so move that exponent of 4 to the outside. Take the cube root of 8 (which is 2) and then raise the result to the power of 4.

Try one more:

Express $\sqrt[4]{\sqrt{x}}$ as a fractional exponent.

Transform the individual roots into exponents. The square root is equivalent to an exponent of $\frac{1}{2}$, and the fourth root is equivalent to an exponent of $\frac{1}{4}$:

$$\sqrt[4]{\sqrt{x}} = \sqrt[4]{x^{\frac{1}{2}}} = \left(x^{\frac{1}{2}}\right)^{\frac{1}{4}} = x^{\frac{1}{8}}$$

The value $x^{\frac{1}{8}}$ can also be written as $\sqrt[8]{x}$.

Simplifying a Root

Sometimes there are two numbers inside the radical sign that you'd like to combine, if possible. Other times, you may have two different radical signs to simplify. There are certain rules to follow regarding when you can and cannot simplify.

When Can You Simplify Roots?

You can only simplify roots in the following ways when the roots are connected via multiplication or division. If two roots are added or subtracted, you cannot use this method.

How Can You Simplify Roots?

When multiplying roots, you can split up a larger product into its separate factors, saving you from having to compute large numbers. For example:

$$\sqrt{25 \times 16} = \sqrt{25} \times \sqrt{16} = 5 \times 4 = 20$$

There are two numbers under the same radical sign and each one is a perfect square. Because they are multiplied together, you can take the square root of each first and then multiply them. Here's another example:

$$\sqrt{50} \times \sqrt{18} = \sqrt{50 \times 18} = \sqrt{2 \times 25 \times 2 \times 9} = \sqrt{4 \times 25 \times 9} = 2 \times 5 \times 3 = 30$$

First, the two numbers are not under the same radical, but because they are multiplied, you can combine them under one radical. Next, 50 and 18 are not perfect squares. In this case, break down the numbers into factors and recombine in order to find any perfect squares, then take the square root.

Division of roots works the same way. You can split a larger quotient into two parts. You can also combine two roots that are being divided into a single root. For example:

$$\sqrt{\frac{144}{16}} = \frac{\sqrt{144}}{\sqrt{16}} = \frac{12}{4} = 3$$

$$\frac{\sqrt{72}}{\sqrt{8}} = \sqrt{\frac{72}{8}} = \sqrt{9} = 3$$

However, if the two numbers are added or subtracted, you *cannot* split them apart or put them together. You have to leave them as they are. For example:

$$\sqrt{16 + 9} \nrightarrow \sqrt{16} + \sqrt{9} \quad \text{This move is illegal.}$$
$$\sqrt{25} \qquad 4 + 3$$
$$5 \quad \neq \quad 7$$

$$\sqrt{16} + \sqrt{9} \nrightarrow \sqrt{16 + 9} \quad \text{This move is also illegal.}$$
$$7 \quad \neq \quad 5$$

You may only separate or combine the *product* ($\times$) or *quotient* ($\div$) of two roots. You cannot separate or combine the *sum* or *difference* of two roots.

In this case, first add the numbers together, then take the square root:

$$\sqrt{16 + 9} = \sqrt{25} = 5$$

In this case, first take the square root, then add:

$$\sqrt{16} + \sqrt{9} = 4 + 3 = 7$$

You *can* add two terms together if they have the same value under square root signs. Add only the numbers in front of the roots:

$$2\sqrt{3} + 4\sqrt{3} = 6\sqrt{3}$$

Treat the stuff under the root similar to a variable: $2x + 3x = 5x$. In other words, two x terms plus three x terms gives you five x terms. In the same way, two $\sqrt{3}$ terms plus four $\sqrt{3}$ terms gives you six $\sqrt{3}$ terms.

Imperfect vs. Perfect Squares

Not all square roots yield an integer. For example, $\sqrt{52}$ is the root of an imperfect square. It will not yield an integer answer because no integer multiplied by itself will yield 52.

Simplifying Roots of Imperfect Squares

Some imperfect squares can be simplified into multiples of smaller square roots. For an imperfect square such as $\sqrt{52}$, you can rewrite $\sqrt{52}$ as a product of primes under the radical:

$$\sqrt{52} = \sqrt{2 \times 2 \times 13}$$

Since this is a *square* root, look for *pairs* of numbers under the radical. In this case, there is a pair of 2's. Since $\sqrt{2 \times 2} = \sqrt{4} = 2$, you can rewrite $\sqrt{52}$ as follows:

$$\sqrt{52} = \sqrt{4 \times 13} = 2 \times \sqrt{13} = 2\sqrt{13}$$

Basically, identify a pair. Then, pull one number of the pair out in front of the radical and eliminate the other number in the pair. Leave any unpaired numbers (13, in this case) under the radical.

Look at another example:

Simplify $\sqrt{72}$.

You can rewrite $\sqrt{72}$ as a product of primes:

$$\sqrt{72} = \sqrt{2 \times 2 \times 2 \times 3 \times 3}$$

Since there are a pair of 2's and a pair of 3's inside the radical, you can pull out one of each:

$$\sqrt{72} = 2 \times 3 \times \sqrt{2} = 6\sqrt{2}$$

Memorize: Squares and Square Roots

Memorize the following squares and square roots, as they often appear on the GMAT. If rote memorization is not a strength for you, take the time to learn the squares that are most likely to pop up on the GMAT, which are 1 through 12, as well as 15 and 20.

$1^2 = 1$	$\sqrt{1} = 1$
$1.4^2 \approx 2$	$\sqrt{2} \approx 1.4$
$1.7^2 \approx 3$	$\sqrt{3} \approx 1.7$
$2^2 = 4$	$\sqrt{4} = 2$
$3^2 = 9$	$\sqrt{9} = 3$
$4^2 = 16$	$\sqrt{16} = 4$
$5^2 = 25$	$\sqrt{25} = 5$
$6^2 = 36$	$\sqrt{36} = 6$
$7^2 = 49$	$\sqrt{49} = 7$
$8^2 = 64$	$\sqrt{64} = 8$
$9^2 = 81$	$\sqrt{81} = 9$
$10^2 = 100$	$\sqrt{100} = 10$
$11^2 = 121$	$\sqrt{121} = 11$
$12^2 = 144$	$\sqrt{144} = 12$
$13^2 = 169$	$\sqrt{169} = 13$
$14^2 = 196$	$\sqrt{196} = 14$
$15^2 = 225$	$\sqrt{225} = 15$
$16^2 = 256$	$\sqrt{256} = 16$
$20^2 = 400$	$\sqrt{400} = 20$
$25^2 = 625$	$\sqrt{625} = 25$
$30^2 = 900$	$\sqrt{900} = 30$

Memorize: Cubes and Cube Roots

Memorize the following cubes and cube roots, as they often appear on the GMAT:

$1^3 = 1$	$\sqrt[3]{1} = 1$
$2^3 = 8$	$\sqrt[3]{8} = 2$
$3^3 = 27$	$\sqrt[3]{27} = 3$
$4^3 = 64$	$\sqrt[3]{64} = 4$
$5^3 = 125$	$\sqrt[3]{125} = 5$
$10^3 = 1,000$	$\sqrt[3]{1,000} = 10$

13

Problem Set

Now that you've finished the chapter, try the following problems.

1. For each of these statements, indicate whether the statement is TRUE or FALSE:

    (a) If $x^2 = 11$, then $x = \sqrt{11}$.

    (b) If $x^3 = 11$, then $x = \sqrt[3]{11}$.

    (c) If $x^4 = 16$, then $x = 2$.

    (d) If $x^5 = 32$, then $x = 2$.

Solve or simplify the following problems, using the properties of roots:

2. $\sqrt{18} \div \sqrt{2}$

3. $\left(\dfrac{1}{125}\right)^{-\frac{1}{3}}$

4. $\sqrt{63} + \sqrt{28}$

5. $\sqrt[3]{100 - 36}$

6. Estimate: $\sqrt{60}$

    (A) 6.5

    (B) 7.7

    (C) 8.2

Save the following problems for review after you finish this entire guide.

7. $\sqrt{150} - \sqrt{96}$

8. $10\sqrt{12} \div 2\sqrt{3}$

    (A) 4

    (B) 10

    (C) $10\sqrt{2}$

    (D) $10\sqrt{3}$

9. $\dfrac{\sqrt[4]{64}}{\sqrt[4]{4}}$

10. The formula used by a certain company to estimate the sales, S, in thousands of units, of one of its products is $S = \sqrt{\dfrac{mk}{p}}$, where p equals the price of the product, m equals the price of its competitor's product, and k is a constant. What is the company's estimate of its revenue from sales of this product?

    (1) $kmp = 5{,}184$

    (2) The company charges \$3—half of its competitor's price—for its product.

Solutions

1. (a) **FALSE:** The problem gave you x^2, so you may have two roots, positive and negative. The exponent of 2 is even, so indeed there are both positive and negative roots. If $x^2 = 11$, then $|x| = \sqrt{11}$. Thus, x could be either $\sqrt{11}$ or $-\sqrt{11}$.

   (b) **TRUE:** Odd exponents preserve the sign of the original expression. Therefore, if x^3 is positive, then x must itself be positive. If $x^3 = 11$, then x must be $\sqrt[3]{11}$.

   (c) **FALSE:** Even exponents hide the sign of the original number, so both positive and negative answers are possible. If $x^4 = 16$, then x could be either 2 or −2.

   (d) **TRUE:** Odd exponents preserve the sign of the original expression. Therefore, if x^5 is positive, then x must itself be positive. If $x^5 = 32$, then x must be 2.

2. **3:**
$$\sqrt{18} \div \sqrt{2} = \sqrt{18 \div 2} = \sqrt{9} = 3$$

3. **5:**
$$\left(\frac{1}{125}\right)^{-\frac{1}{3}} = 125^{\frac{1}{3}} = \sqrt[3]{125} = \sqrt[3]{5 \times 5 \times 5} = 5$$

4. $\mathbf{5\sqrt{7}}$: These two roots are added together, so you cannot combine them under one root to start. Simplify separately. At the end, you can combine them because the values under the roots are the same:
$$\sqrt{63} + \sqrt{28} = (\sqrt{9 \times 7}) + (\sqrt{4 \times 7}) = 3\sqrt{7} + 2\sqrt{7} = 5\sqrt{7}$$

5. **4:**
$$\sqrt[3]{100 - 36} = \sqrt[3]{64} = 4$$

6. **(B) 7.7:** The number 60 is in between two perfect squares—49, which is 7^2, and 64, which is 8^2. The answer, then, must be between 7 and 8 and only answer **(B)** qualifies.

   If you did have to estimate the answer more carefully, here's how: The difference between 64 and 49 is 15, so 60 is a little more than $\frac{2}{3}$ of the way toward 64 from 49. A reasonable estimate for $\sqrt{60}$, then, would be about 7.7, which is a little more than $\frac{2}{3}$ toward 8 from 7.

7. $\mathbf{\sqrt{6}}$:
$$\sqrt{150} - \sqrt{96} = (\sqrt{25 \times 6}) - (\sqrt{16 \times 6}) = 5\sqrt{6} - 4\sqrt{6} = \sqrt{6}$$

8. **(B) 10:** You can solve algebraically or estimate. Here's the algebraic solution:
$$10\sqrt{12} \div 2\sqrt{3} = \frac{10\sqrt{4 \times 3}}{2\sqrt{3}} = \frac{20\sqrt{3}}{2\sqrt{3}} = 10$$

   Alternatively, you could approximate the values of the square roots. Since 12 is about halfway between 3^2 and 4^2, use 3.5 as an estimate. Also, the square root of 3 is on the memorization list. It equals about 1.7:
$$\frac{10\sqrt{12}}{2\sqrt{3}} \approx \frac{10 \times 3.5}{2 \times 1.7} \approx \frac{35}{3.4} \approx 10$$

   Answer **(B)** is the same as the estimate.

9. **2:**

$$\frac{\sqrt[4]{64}}{\sqrt[4]{4}} = \sqrt[4]{\frac{64}{4}} = \sqrt[4]{16} = 2$$

Note: Since the problem started you with a square root sign, solve for only the positive value.

10. **(A):** First, Understand and Plan. The question asks for the company's estimate of its revenue. A formula for the expected quantity of sales (S) is given, so expected revenue would be that expected quantity times the product's price (p). Write that out algebraically.

Revenue would be pS, or $p\sqrt{\frac{mk}{p}}$. This expression is complicated because there are some things under the radical and others outside. Specifically, p is in both places. Try to rearrange in order to leave just one p.

Bring the p on the left under the radical as p^2:

$$\text{Revenue} = p\sqrt{\frac{mk}{p}}$$

$$\text{Revenue} = \sqrt{(p^2)\frac{mk}{p}}$$

$$\text{Revenue} = \sqrt{pmk}$$

Statement (1) SUFFICIENT: This statement gives the value of kmp, which is the same product as pmk in the revenue equation above. The revenue can be determined by taking the square root of this product.

Statement (2) INSUFFICIENT: This statement indicates that $p = 3$ and in a roundabout way reveals that $m = 6$, since p is half of m. Plug these values into the rephrased formula for Revenue:

$$\text{Revenue} = \sqrt{(3)(6)k}$$

$$\text{Revenue} = \sqrt{18k}$$

$$\text{Revenue} = 3\sqrt{2k}$$

Without knowing k, it's not possible to figure out what the revenue estimate is.

The correct answer is **(A)**: Statement (1) is sufficient, but statement (2) is not.

CHAPTER 14

Quadratic Equations

In This Chapter...

In this chapter, you will learn how to factor and expand quadratic equations, and you'll memorize three special quadratics (known as the special products) that will save you time and mental energy on the GMAT. You'll also learn some common ways that the GMAT likes to disguise quadratic equations—and how to recognize and strip away those disguises.

CHAPTER 14 Quadratic Equations

One special type of equation is called the **quadratic equation**. Here are some examples of quadratic equations:

$$x^2 + 3x + 8 = 12 \qquad w^2 - 16w + 1 = 0 \qquad 2y^2 - y + 5 = 8$$

The standard form of a quadratic equation is $ax^2 + bx + c = 0$, where a, b, and c are constants and a does not equal 0.

Here are other ways of writing quadratics (in nonstandard form):

$$x^2 = 3x + 4 \qquad a = 5a^2 \qquad 6 - b = 7b^2$$

Like other even-exponent equations, quadratic equations generally have two solutions. That is, there are usually two possible values of x (or whatever the variable is) that make the equation *true*.

Factoring Quadratic Equations

The following example illustrates the process for solving quadratic equations:

If $x^2 + 3x + 8 = 12$, what is x?

To start, move everything to the left side of the equals sign so that the equation is equal to 0. Put the left side in the form $ax^2 + bx + c$ (where a, b, and c are typically integers on the GMAT):

$$x^2 + 3x + 8 = 12 \qquad \text{Subtract 12 from both sides to set the right side to 0.}$$
$$x^2 + 3x - 4 = 0$$

Next, factor the equation. In order to factor, you generally need to think about two terms in the equation. Assuming that $a = 1$ (which is often the case on GMAT quadratic equation problems), focus on the two terms b and c. (If a is not equal to 1, divide everything in the equation by a to make a equal to 1.)

$$x^2 + 3x - 4 = 0$$

Rewrite the equation in the form $(x +)(x +)$, where the blanks represent two spaces you're leaving for numbers that you're about to calculate.

In order to factor this equation, find two integers whose product is equal to c (-4 in this equation) and whose sum is equal to b (3 in this equation).

In the original equation, $a = 1$, $b = 3$, and $c = -4$. To fill in the blanks, find the pair of numbers that will *multiply* to -4 and *add* to $+3$. The GMAT will typically make these integers, so think in those terms. In order for c to be negative, the numbers in the blanks will need to have the opposite signs. Now think of the specific values that are possible:

$$x^2 + 3x - 4 = 0$$
$$(x +)(x -) = 0$$

For example, 2 and -2 multiply to -4, but they do not add to 3, so this is not the correct pairing. The other integer possibility is some combination of 4 and 1. Which one should get the negative sign in order to add to positive 3?

Make the 4 positive and the 1 negative: 4 and -1 multiply to -4 and add to 3. Place these in the spaces in the parentheses:

$$x^2 + 3x - 4 = 0$$
$$(x + 4)(x - 1) = 0$$

The two terms on the left-hand side multiply to 0, so one or both of the terms must be equal to 0. As another example, if you know that $M \times N = 0$, then you know that either $M = 0$ or $N = 0$ (or both M and N are 0).

In this problem, set each factor in parentheses independently to 0 and solve for x:

$$x + 4 = 0 \qquad \text{OR} \qquad x - 1 = 0$$
$$x = -4 \qquad\qquad\qquad x = 1$$

Therefore, the two solutions of the quadratic equation $x^2 + 3x + 8 = 12$ are -4 and 1. The solutions of a quadratic equation are also sometimes called its *roots*. If you see the word *root* in conjunction with a quadratic equation, then this word is a synonym for *solution*.

Disguised Quadratics

The GMAT will often attempt to disguise quadratic equations by putting them in forms that do not quite look like the traditional form of $ax^2 + bx + c = 0$.

Here is a very common "disguised" form for a quadratic:

$$3w^2 = 6w$$

This is a quadratic equation because it contains both a w^2 term and a plain w term. The classic mistake is to try to solve this equation without thinking of it as a quadratic:

$$3w^2 = 6w \qquad \text{Divide both sides by } w.$$
$$3w = 6 \qquad \text{Divide both sides by 3.}$$
$$w = 2$$

The value 2 is one possible solution to this equation—but there's another! If you solve this equation without factoring it like a quadratic, you will miss one of the solutions. Here is how it should be solved:

$$3w^2 = 6w$$
$$3w^2 - 6w = 0$$
$$w(3w - 6) = 0$$

Setting both factors equal to 0 yields the following solutions:

$$w = 0 \quad \text{OR} \quad 3w - 6 = 0$$
$$3w = 6$$
$$w = 2$$

If you recognize that $3w^2 = 6w$ is a disguised quadratic, you will find both solutions instead of accidentally missing one (in this case, the solution $w = 0$).

Here is another example of a disguised quadratic:

Solve for b, given that $\frac{36}{b} = b - 5$.

At first glance, this does not look like a quadratic equation at all. But it's annoying to have a variable on the bottom of a fraction, so try to get rid of that. Watch what happens:

$\frac{36}{b} = b - 5$ Multiply both sides of the equation by b.

$36 = b^2 - 5b$

Now this looks like a quadratic! Solve it by factoring:

$36 = b^2 - 5b$ Subtract 36 from both sides to set the equation equal to 0.

$b^2 - 5b - 36 = 0$

$(b - 9)(b + 4) = 0$ Thus, $b = 9$ or $b = -4$.

Some quadratics are hidden within more difficult equations, such as higher order equations (in which a variable is raised to the power of 3 or more). On the GMAT, these equations can almost always be factored to find the hidden quadratic expression. For example:

Solve for x, given that $x^3 + 2x^2 - 3x = 0$.

$x^3 + 2x^2 - 3x = 0$ Factor out an x from each term.

$x(x^2 + 2x - 3) = 0$

Now, factor the quadratic:

$x(x^2 + 2x - 3) = 0$

$x(x + 3)(x - 1) = 0$

$x = 0$ OR $x + 3 = 0$ OR $x - 1 = 0$

This equation has *three* solutions: 0, −3, and 1.

This example illustrates a general rule:

> If you have a quadratic expression equal to 0, *and* you can factor an x out of the expression, then $x = 0$ is a solution of the equation.

Do not just divide both sides by x. If you do so, you will eliminate the solution $x = 0$. You are only allowed to divide by a variable if you are absolutely sure that the variable does not equal 0.

Taking the Square Root

So far you have seen how to solve quadratic equations by setting one side of the equation equal to 0 and factoring. However, some quadratic problems can be solved without setting one side equal to 0. If the other side of the equation is a perfect square, the problem can be solved by taking the square root of both sides of the equation. For example:

If $(z + 3)^2 = 25$, what is z?

Take the square root of both sides of the equation to solve for z. You just have to consider both the positive and the negative square root:

$$\sqrt{(z+3)^2} = \sqrt{25}$$
$$z + 3 = \pm 5$$
$$z = -3 \pm 5$$
$$z = \{2, -8\}$$

Going in Reverse: Use FOIL

Instead of starting with a quadratic equation and factoring it, you may need to start with factors and rewrite them as a quadratic equation (this is known as *expanding* the quadratic). To do this, use a multiplication process called FOIL: First, Outer, Inner, Last.

To change the expression $(x + 7)(x - 3)$ into a quadratic expression, use FOIL as follows:

First: Multiply the *first term* of each factor together: $(x)(x) = x^2$.

Outer: Multiply the *outer terms* of the expression together: $(x)(-3) = -3x$.

Inner: Multiply the *inner terms* of the expression together: $(7)(x) = 7x$.

Last: Multiply the *last term* of each factor together: $(7)(-3) = -21$.

Now, there are four terms: $x^2 - 3x + 7x - 21$. Combine the two middle terms for the fully simplified quadratic expression: $x^2 + 4x - 21$.

If you encounter a quadratic equation or expression, try factoring it. On the other hand, if you encounter the product of factors such as $(x + 7)(x - 3)$, you may need to use FOIL. Note that if the product of factors equals 0, you should be ready to *interpret* the meaning. For instance, if you are given $(x + k)(x - m) = 0$, then you know that $x = -k$ or $x = m$.

One-Solution Quadratics

Not all quadratic equations have two solutions. Some have only one solution. One-solution quadratics are also called perfect square quadratics, because both roots are the same. Consider the following examples:

$$x^2 + 8x + 16 = 0$$
$$(x + 4)(x + 4) = 0 \qquad \text{Here, the only solution for } x \text{ is } -4.$$
$$(x + 4)^2 = 0$$

$$x^2 - 6x + 9 = 0$$
$$(x - 3)(x - 3) = 0 \qquad \text{Here, the only solution for } x \text{ is } 3.$$
$$(x - 3)^2 = 0$$

When you see a quadratic equation, look for two solutions, but be aware that some circumstances will lead to just one solution. As long as you understand how the math works, you'll know when you should have two solutions and when you should have just one.

Zero in the Denominator: Undefined

When 0 appears in the denominator of an expression, then that expression is called *undefined*. The GMAT (thankfully!) doesn't go into this territory. Consider the following:

What are the solutions to the equation $\dfrac{x^2 + x - 12}{x - 2} = 0$?

For such a question, the GMAT would always first tell you that $x \neq 2$. If x did equal 2, then the bottom of that equation would be 0—and the GMAT won't allow that.

The numerator contains a quadratic equation. Since it is a good idea to start solving quadratic equations by factoring, factor this numerator as follows:

$$\frac{x^2 + x - 12}{x - 2} = 0 \rightarrow \frac{(x - 3)(x + 4)}{x - 2} = 0$$

If either of the factors in the numerator is 0, then the entire expression equals 0. Thus, the solutions (roots) to this equation are $x = 3$ or $x = -4$. (And, for the purposes of finding the roots, you can ignore the denominator, since the test will tell you that it does not equal 0.)

The Three Special Products

Three quadratic expressions called **Special Products** come up so frequently on the GMAT that it pays to memorize them. They are GMAT favorites! Make flash cards and drill them until you immediately recognize these three expressions and know how to factor (or distribute) each one automatically. This will usually put you on the path toward the solution to the problem.

		Memorize these!
Special Product 1:	$x^2 - y^2 = (x + y)(x - y)$	
Special Product 2:	$x^2 + 2xy + y^2 = (x + y)(x + y) = (x + y)^2$	
Special Product 3:	$x^2 - 2xy + y^2 = (x - y)(x - y) = (x - y)^2$	

You may also need to identify these products when they are presented in other forms. For example, $a^2 - 1$ can be factored as $(a + 1)(a - 1)$. Similarly, $(a + b)^2$ can be distributed as $a^2 + 2ab + b^2$.

Within an equation, you may need to recognize these special products in pieces. For instance, if you see $a^2 + b^2 = 9 + 2ab$, move the $2ab$ term to the left, yielding $a^2 - 2ab + b^2 = 9$. This quadratic can then be factored to $(a - b)^2 = 9$, or $a - b = \pm 3$. For example:

Simplify $\dfrac{x^2 + 4x + 4}{x^2 - 4}$, given that x does not equal 2 or -2.

Both the numerator and denominator of this fraction can be factored:

$$\frac{(x + 2)(x + 2)}{(x + 2)(x - 2)}$$

The expression $x + 2$ can be canceled out from the numerator and denominator:

$$\frac{x^2 + 4x + 4}{x^2 - 4} = \frac{x + 2}{x - 2}$$

Problem Set

Now that you've finished the chapter, try the following problems.

1. Simplify: $(3 - \sqrt{7})(3 + \sqrt{7})$

2. If -4 is a root for x in the equation $x^2 + kx + 8 = 0$, what is k?

3. If 8 and -4 are the solutions for x, which of the following could be the equation?

    (A) $x^2 - 4x - 32 = 0$

    (B) $x^2 - 4x + 32 = 0$

    (C) $x^2 + 4x - 12 = 0$

    (D) $x^2 + 4x + 32 = 0$

    (E) $x^2 + 4x + 12 = 0$

4. If $x^2 + k = G$ and x is an integer, which of the following could be the value of $G - k$?

    (A) 7

    (B) 8

    (C) 9

    (D) 10

    (E) 11

Save the following problems for review after you finish this entire guide.

5. If $\dfrac{d}{4} + \dfrac{8}{d} + 3 = 0$, what is d?

6. If $x \neq -3$ and $\dfrac{x^2 + 6x + 9}{x + 3} = 7$, what is x?

7. If $z^2 - 10z + 25 = 9$, what are the possible values for z?

8. If $a \neq 2$ and $ab \neq 0$, which of the following is equal to $\dfrac{b(a^2 - 4)}{ab - 2b}$?

    (A) ab

    (B) a

    (C) $a + 2$

    (D) a^2

    (E) $2b$

Answers and explanations follow on the next page. ▶ ▶ ▶

Solutions

1. **2:** You can use the special product or FOIL to simplify. The special product is faster—but you need to have memorized it.

   The original expression is in the form $(x - y)(x + y)$, which is one of the three special products. Since $(x - y)(x + y) = x^2 - y^2$, the expression in this problem simplifies to this:

   $$3^2 - (\sqrt{7})^2 = 9 - 7 = 2$$

   Alternatively, FOIL to solve:

   $$F: 3 \times 3 = 9$$
   $$O: 3 \times \sqrt{7} = 3\sqrt{7}$$
   $$I: -\sqrt{7} \times 3 = -3\sqrt{7}$$
   $$\underline{L: -\sqrt{7} \times \sqrt{7} = -7}$$
   $$\text{FOIL}: 9 + 3\sqrt{7} - 3\sqrt{7} - 7 = 2$$

2. **6:** The word *root* is a synonym for *solution*. If -4 is a solution, then $(x + 4)$ must be one of the factors of the quadratic equation. The other factor is $(x + ?)$.

   $$x^2 + kx + 8 = 0$$
   $$(x + 4)(x + ?) = 0$$

   The product of 4 and ? must be equal to 8; thus, the other factor is $(x + 2)$. Next, the sum of 4 and 2 must be equal to k. Therefore, $k = 6$.

   Alternatively, if -4 is a solution, then it is a possible value for x. Plug it into the equation for x and solve for k:

   $$x^2 + kx + 8 = 0$$
   $$16 - 4k + 8 = 0$$
   $$24 = 4k$$
   $$k = 6$$

3. **(A)** $x^2 - 4x - 32 = 0$: If the solutions to the equation are 8 and -4, the factored form of the equation is $(x - 8)(x + 4) = 0$.

   Scan the answers. Most of them have a different c term (-32, 32, -12, or 12), so check just that last part first. That's the L in FOIL: $(-8)(4) = -32$. Only answer **(A)** has 32 as the c term, so it must be the answer. (If more than one had that same number, then you would have to do the full FOIL.)

14

4. **(C) 9:** The problem states that x is an integer. It also asks for the combo $G - k$. Rearrange the expression to isolate the combo on one side:

$$x^2 + k = G$$
$$x^2 = G - k$$

Because you know that x is an integer, x^2 is a perfect square (the square of an integer). Therefore, $G - k$ is also a perfect square. The only perfect square among the answer choices is the number 9.

5. **$\{-8, -4\}$:** Multiply the entire equation by $4d$ (to eliminate the fractions) and factor:

$$d^2 + 32 + 12d = 0$$
$$d^2 + 12d + 32 = 0$$
$$(d + 8)(d + 4) = 0$$

$$d + 8 = 0 \quad \text{OR} \quad d + 4 = 0$$
$$d = -8 \qquad\qquad d = -4$$

6. **4:** The problem states that x is not -3, so you can divide out the term on the bottom of the fraction:

$$\frac{x^2 + 6x + 9}{x + 3} = 7$$
$$\frac{(x + 3)(x + 3)}{x + 3} = 7$$
$$\frac{(x + 3)\cancel{(x + 3)}}{\cancel{x + 3}} = 7$$
$$x + 3 = 7$$
$$x = 4$$

7. **$\{2, 8\}$:** The right-hand side is a perfect square (9), so check whether the left-hand side is as well. And it is!

$$z^2 - 10z + 25 = 9$$
$$(z - 5)^2 = 9$$
$$\sqrt{(z - 5)^2} = \sqrt{9}$$
$$z - 5 = \pm 3$$
$$z = 5 \pm 3$$

8. **(C) $a + 2$:** There are variables in the answers and no real values given in the problem, so choose smart numbers. The number 2 is not allowed for a and the number 4 appears in the expression, so try $a = 3$ and $b = 5$, and remember to simplify before you multiply:

$$\frac{b(a^2 - 4)}{ab - 2b} =$$

$$\frac{(5)((3)^2 - 4)}{(3)(5) - 2(5)} =$$

$$\frac{5(9 - 4)}{15 - 10} =$$

$$\frac{5(5)}{5} = 5$$

Now, plug $a = 3$ and $b = 5$ into the answer choices and look for a matching answer of 5:

(A) $ab = (3)(5) =$ too big

(B) $a = (3) = 3$

(C) $a + 2 = (3) + 2 = 5$ Match!

(D) $a^2 = (3)^2 = 9$

(E) $2b = 2(5) =$ too big

Alternatively, you can solve algebraically. Begin by factoring the given expression, then simplify:

$$\frac{b(a + 2)(a - 2)}{b(a - 2)} = a + 2$$

Everything divides out except for the $a + 2$ term. If you spot that quickly, then the algebraic solution is faster. If not, then the algebra can get messy and the Smart Numbers solution may be better.

CHAPTER 15

Formulas

In This Chapter...

In this chapter, you will learn how to simplify and solve standard "plug-in" formulas, functions, and sequences (including both regular and recursive sequences).

CHAPTER 15 **Formulas**

Formulas are another means by which the GMAT tests your ability to work with unknowns. Formulas are specific equations that can involve multiple variables and these problems may be pure math or real-life/story problems. There are four major types of formula problems on the GMAT:

1. Plug-in formulas

2. Functions

3. Sequence formulas

4. Strange symbol formulas

The first three types are covered in this chapter. The final category is fairly rare; if you want to learn about strange symbol formulas, see the supplemental study material for this guide, found online.

Plug-In Formulas

The most basic GMAT formula problems provide you with a formula and ask you to solve for one of the variables in the formula by plugging in given values for the other variables. For example:

> The formula for determining an individual's comedic aptitude, C, on a given day is defined as $\frac{QL}{J}$,
> where J represents the number of jokes told, Q represents the overall joke quality on a scale of 1 to 10, and L represents the number of individual laughs generated. If Niko told 12 jokes, generated 18 laughs, and earned a comedic aptitude of 10.5, what was the overall quality of Niko's jokes?

The first sentence is providing a formula, though it may not look like it. When a variable is *defined as* a combination of some other variables, write a formula:

$$C = \frac{QL}{J}$$

Next, plug the given values into the formula in order to solve for the unknown variable Q:

$$C = \frac{QL}{J}$$

$$10.5 = \frac{18Q}{12}$$

$$Q = \frac{10.5(12)}{18}$$

$$Q = \frac{10.5(2)}{3}$$

$$Q = \frac{21}{3} = 7$$

The quality of Niko's jokes was rated a 7.

Notice that you will typically have to do some rearrangement after plugging in the numbers in order to isolate the desired unknown. The actual computations are typically not very complex (though do remember to simplify before you multiply!). Formula problems are tricky because the given formula is unfamiliar. Do not be intimidated. Figure out how to write down the equation, plug in the numbers carefully, and solve for the required unknown.

Functions

Functions are very much like the "magic boxes" you may have learned about in elementary school. For example:

> You put a 2 into the magic box, and a 7 comes out. You put a 3 into the magic box, and a 9 comes out. You put a 4 into the magic box, and an 11 comes out.

There are many possible ways to describe what the magic box is doing to your number. One possibility is that the magic box is doubling your number and adding 3:

$$2(2) + 3 = 7 \qquad 2(3) + 3 = 9 \qquad 2(4) + 3 = 11$$

Assuming that this is the case, this description would yield the following rule for this magic box: $2x + 3$. This rule can be written in function form as:

$$f(x) = 2x + 3$$

The function f represents the rule that the magic box is using to transform your number. The test might give you the function and say something like "What is $f(3)$?" The direction is telling you to put 3 into the function wherever you see an x, so 3 is the *input*:

$$f(3) = 2x + 3 \rightarrow 2(3) + 3 = 6 + 3 = 9$$

The answer is 9, so 9 is the *output*. By the way, that $f(x)$ form is read "f of x," not fx. It does *not* mean "f times x!" The letter f does not stand for a variable; rather, it stands for the rule that dictates how the input x changes into the output (answer).

Here are some other examples of functions. What do they have in common?

$$f(x) = 4x^2 - 11$$
$$g(t) = t^3 + \sqrt{t} - \frac{2t}{5}$$

They always start with that *letter* (*letter*) format. Most of the time, the first letter will be an f, g, or h. Whenever you see $f(x)$, it's saying "for the function f, follow this rule for any value of x."

The *domain* of a function indicates the possible inputs. The *range* of a function indicates the possible outputs. For instance, the function $f(x) = x^2$ can take any input (x can be anything) but never produces a negative number (because you can't square something and have the result be negative). So the domain is $x =$ all numbers, but the range is $f(x) \geq 0$.

The most basic type of function problem asks you to input a numerical value (say, 5) in place of the independent variable (x) in order to determine the value of the function. For example:

> If $f(x) = x^2 - 2$, what is the value of $f(5)$?

Apply the given rule:

$$f(5) = (5)^2 - 2 = 25 - 2 = 23$$

You could also be told the output and asked to find the input. For example:

> If $f(x) = 3x + 2$ and $f(x) = 5$, what is x ?

The first equation is the function ("given an input x, put it in the form $3x + 2$"). The second equation, though, represents an output: For some particular value of x, the output is 5. What is that value of x? To solve, set the function equal to the output:

$$3x + 2 = 5$$
$$3x = 3$$
$$x = 1$$

When $x = 1$, the output of the function is 5.

Variable Substitution in Functions

This type of function problem is slightly more complicated. Instead of finding the output value for a numerical input, you must find the output when the input is an algebraic expression. For example:

> If $f(z) = z^2 - \frac{z}{3}$, what is the value of $f(w + 6)$?

Input the variable expression $(w + 6)$ in place of the independent variable (z) to determine the value of the function:

$$f(w + 6) = (w + 6)^2 - \frac{w + 6}{3}$$

Compare this equation to the equation for $f(z)$. The expression $(w + 6)$ has taken the place of every z in the original equation. In a sense, you are treating the expression $(w + 6)$ as one thing, as if it were a single letter or variable.

If you needed to simplify the right side, you would do so using standard algebraic simplification.

Sequence Formulas

A **sequence** is a collection of numbers in a set order. For example, {1, 4, 9, 16, 25} is a sequence, as is {1, 1, 2, 3, 5, 8}. Sequences do not necessarily go in increasing order and it's possible to have repeated numbers.

Every sequence is defined by a rule, which you can use to find the values of terms:

$$A_n = 9n + 3$$

Find the first term (A_1) by plugging $n = 1$ into the equation: $A_1 = 12$.

Find the second term (A_2) by plugging $n = 2$ into the equation: $A_2 = 21$.

Find the nth term (A_n) by plugging n into the equation.

Here's another example:

If $S_n = 15n - 7$, what is the value of $S_5 - S_3$?

This question is asking for the difference between the fifth term and the third term of the sequence, or $S_5 - S_3$:

$$S_5 - S_3 = 15(5) - 7 - [15(3) - 7]$$
$$= 75 - 7 - 45 + 7$$
$$= 75 - 45$$
$$= 30$$

Recursive Sequences

Occasionally, a sequence will be defined *recursively*. A **recursive sequence** defines each term relative to other terms in that same sequence, something like "each term is equal to the previous term plus 2."

Take a look at this example:

If $a_n = 2a_{n-1} - 4$ and $a_6 = -4$, what is the value of a_4?

You can recognize that this is recursive because it doesn't have just an a_n term. It also has an a_{n-1} term. That second term refers to a different term in the same sequence; if you see this, you have a recursive sequence.

Solve the problem. If a_n represents the *n*th term, then a_{n-1} is the term right before a_n. You are given the value of the sixth term, and need to figure out the value of the fourth term. Keep track of this on your scrap paper:

$$\underline{\qquad\qquad}\ \ \underline{\qquad\qquad}\ \ \underline{\quad -4 \quad}$$
$$\quad a_4 \qquad\qquad a_5 \qquad\qquad a_6$$

Use the value of the sixth term (a_6) to find the value of the fifth term (a_5):

$$a_6 = 2a_5 - 4$$
$$-4 = 2a_5 - 4$$
$$0 = 2a_5$$
$$0 = a_5$$

The value of the fifth term is 0:

$$\underline{\qquad\qquad}\ \ \underline{\quad 0 \quad}\ \ \underline{\quad -4 \quad}$$
$$\quad a_4 \qquad\qquad a_5 \qquad\qquad a_6$$

Now use the fifth term to find the fourth term:

$$a_5 = 2a_4 - 4$$
$$0 = 2a_4 - 4$$
$$4 = 2a_4$$
$$2 = a_4$$

The value of the fourth term is 2.

When a sequence is defined recursively, the question will have to give you the value of at least one of the terms. Use that value to find the value of the desired term.

Linear Sequence Problems: Alternative Method

For **linear sequences**, in which the same number is added to any term to yield the next term, you can use the following alternative method:

> If each number in a sequence is 3 more than the previous number, and the 6th number is 32, what is the 50th number in the sequence?

Instead of finding the rule for this sequence, consider the following reasoning: From the 6th to the 50th term, there are 44 "jumps" of 3 each. Since $44 \times 3 = 132$, there is an increase of 132 from the 6th term to the 50th term:

$$32 + 132 = 164$$

Problem Set

Now that you've finished the chapter, try the following problems.

1. If $A_n = 3 - 8n$, what is A_1 ?

2. If $A_n = 3 - 8n$, what is $A_{11} - A_9$?

3. If $f(x) = 2x^2 - 12$, what is the value of $f(2\sqrt{3})$?

4. If $a_n = \dfrac{a_{n-1} \times a_{n-2}}{2}$, $a_5 = -6$, and $a_6 = -18$, what is the value of a_3 ?

5. Hugo lies on top of a building, throwing pennies straight down to the street below. The formula for the height, H, that a penny falls is $H = Vt + 5t^2$, where V is the original velocity of the penny (how fast Hugo throws it when it leaves his hand) and t is equal to the time it takes to hit the ground, in seconds. Hugo throws the penny from a height of 60 meters at an initial speed of 20 meters per second. How long does it take, in seconds, for the penny to hit the ground?

    (A)   2
    (B)   20
    (C)   200

Save the following problems for review after you finish this entire guide.

6. Life expectancy is defined by the formula $L = \dfrac{6SB}{G}$, where S = shoe size, B = average monthly electric bill in dollars, and G = GMAT score. If Melvin's GMAT score is twice his monthly electric bill, and his life expectancy is 75, what is his shoe size?

7. The "competitive edge" of a baseball team is defined by the formula $\sqrt{\dfrac{W}{L}}$, where W represents the number of the team's wins and L represents the number of the team's losses. This year, the GMAT All-Stars had 3 times as many wins and one-half as many losses as they had last year. By what factor did their "competitive edge" increase?

8. If $t(x) = 4x^3a$ and $t(3) = 27$, what is $t(2)$?

9. The first term in an arithmetic sequence is -5 and the second term is -3. What is the 50th term? (In an arithmetic sequence, the difference between successive terms is constant.)

10. Challenge problem: If $f(x) = 2x^2 - 4$ and $g(x) = 2x$, for what values of x will $f(x) = g(x)$?

Answers and explanations follow on the next page. ▶ ▶ ▶

Solutions

1. **−5:** Substitute 1 for n and solve:

    $$A_n = 3 - 8_n$$
    $$A_1 = 3 - 8(1)$$
    $$= 3 - 8$$
    $$= -5$$

2. **−16:** Substitute 11 and 9 for n and solve:

    $$A_{11} - A_9 = 3 - 8(11) - [3 - 8(9)]$$
    $$= 3 - 88 - 3 + 72$$
    $$= 0 - 88 + 72$$
    $$= -16$$

3. **12:** Plug in the given value for x and solve:

    $$f(x) = 2(2\sqrt{3})^2 - 12$$
    $$= 2(2)^2(\sqrt{3})^2 - 12$$
    $$= (2 \times 4 \times 3) - 12$$
    $$= 24 - 12$$
    $$= 12$$

4. **−2:** According to the formula, $a_3 = \dfrac{a_2 \times a_1}{2}$. But you aren't given a_1 or a_2. Instead, you're given a_5 and a_6. You have to work backwards from the fifth and sixth terms of the sequence to find the third term. Notice what happens if you plug $n = 6$ into the formula:

    $$a_6 = \frac{a_5 \times a_4}{2}$$

    Plug in the values of a_5 and a_6 to solve for the value of a_4:

    $$-18 = \frac{-6 \times a_4}{2}$$
    $$-36 = -6 \times a_4$$
    $$6 = a_4$$

    Now, use the fourth and fifth terms of the sequence to solve for a_3:

    $$a_5 = \frac{a_4 \times a_3}{2}$$
    $$-6 = \frac{6 \times a_3}{2}$$
    $$-12 = 6 \times a_3$$
    $$-2 = a_3$$

5. **(A) 2 seconds:** If you feel comfortable thinking through the scenario, you can estimate. The penny drops from 60 meters at a speed of 20 meters per second, so it should take no more than 3 seconds to drop. (It will take less than 3 seconds, in fact, since gravity will cause the speed to increase.) Only answer **(A)** is close. Here's how to do the algebra:

$$H = Vt + 5t^2$$
$$60 = 20t + 5t^2$$
$$5t^2 + 20t - 60 = 0$$
$$5(t^2 + 4t - 12) = 0$$
$$5(t + 6)(t - 2) = 0$$

$$t + 6 = 0 \qquad \text{OR} \qquad t - 2 = 0$$
$$t = -6 \qquad\qquad t = 2$$

Since a time must be positive, discard the negative value for t.

6. **Size 25:** The problem states that $G = 2B$, so substitute $2B$ for G in the formula, then simplify:

$$\frac{6SB}{2B} = 75$$
$$3S = 75$$
$$S = 25$$

You could also pick smart numbers for G and B as long as they fit the relationship described in the problem: G is twice B. Try $G = 4$ and $B = 2$. Then, substitute in your smart numbers and solve for S:

$$\frac{6S(2)}{4} = 75$$
$$3S = 75$$
$$S = 25$$

7. $\sqrt{6}$: The question says the competitive edge (call that c) *is defined by* a certain expression, so write a formula:

$$c = \sqrt{\frac{W}{L}}$$

Pick numbers to see what happens to the competitive edge when W is tripled and L is halved. If the original value of W is 4 and the original value of L is 2, the original value of c is $\sqrt{\frac{4}{2}} = \sqrt{2}$. If W triples to 12 and L is halved to 1, the new value of c is $\sqrt{\frac{12}{1}} = \sqrt{12}$. The competitive edge has increased from $\sqrt{2}$ to $\sqrt{12}$. Therefore:

$$\frac{\sqrt{12}}{\sqrt{2}} = \frac{\sqrt{12}}{\sqrt{2}} = \sqrt{6}$$

The competitive edge has increased by a factor of $\sqrt{6}$. (You can also ask yourself: What do I need to multiply $\sqrt{2}$ by to get to $\sqrt{12}$?)

15

8. **8:** The problem contains a function, t, into which you plug values for x. The function also contains a separate variable, a. First, use the given information $t(3) = 27$ to find the value for a:

$$t(x) = 4x^3 a$$

$$t(3) \rightarrow 4(3)^3 a = 27$$

$$4(27)a = 27$$

$$4a = 1$$

$$a = \frac{1}{4}$$

Next, plug that back into the function to find the value of $t(2)$:

$$t(x) = 4x^3 a$$

$$t(2) = 4(2)^3 \left(\frac{1}{4}\right)$$

$$t(2) = 4(8) \left(\frac{1}{4}\right)$$

$$t(2) = 8$$

9. **93:** The first term is -5 and the second term is -3, so you are adding $+2$ to each successive term. How many times do you have to add 2? There are $50 - 1 = 49$ additional "steps" after the first term, so you have to add $+2$ a total of 49 times, beginning with your starting point of -5: $-5 + 2(49) = 93$.

10. **$\{-1, 2\}$:** To find the values for which $f(x) = g(x)$, set the functions equal to each other:

$$2x^2 - 4 = 2x$$

$$2x^2 - 2x - 4 = 0$$

$$2(x^2 - x - 2) = 0$$

$$2(x - 2)(x + 1) = 0$$

$$x - 2 = 0 \quad \text{OR} \quad x + 1 = 0$$

$$x = 2 \qquad\qquad x = -1$$

15

Inequalities and Max/Min

In This Chapter...

- Flip the Sign

- Combining Inequalities: Line 'Em Up!

- Manipulating Compound Inequalities

- Combining Inequalities: Add 'Em Up!

- Maximizing and Minimizing

- Square-Rooting Inequalities

In this chapter, you will learn how to simplify and solve inequalities (almost the same as equations, but not quite!). You'll also learn about a common question feature that shows up on the GMAT: the max/min variation, in which you're asked to find the maximum or minimum possible value of something.

CHAPTER 16 Inequalities and Max/Min

Unlike equations, which relate two equivalent quantities, **inequalities** compare quantities that have different values. Inequalities are used to express four kinds of relationships, illustrated by the following examples:

1. x is less than 4.

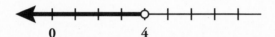

$x < 4$

2. x is less than or equal to 4.

$x \leq 4$

3. x is greater than 4.

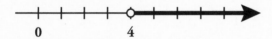

$x > 4$

4. x is greater than or equal to 4.

$x \geq 4$

Number lines, such as those shown above, are an excellent way to visualize exactly what a given inequality means.

When you see inequalities with 0 on one side of the inequality (> 0 or < 0), the problem is likely testing positive and negative characteristics. You'll learn more about this later.

Here are some common inequality statements on the GMAT, as well as what they imply:

Statement	Implication
$xy > 0$	x and y are *both positive* OR *both negative*.
$xy < 0$	x and y have *different signs* (one positive, one negative).
$x^2 - x < 0$ $x^2 < x$	These are two different versions of the same inequality. Both mean that $0 < x < 1$.

Why is that last one true? The inequality to the left is saying that, when you square a number, it gets smaller. Only a very narrow set of circumstances makes this true; most of the time, when you square a number it gets larger.

If you square any negative number, it becomes positive (and, therefore, larger). If you square any positive number greater than 1, it gets larger.

If you square 0, it stays 0. If you square 1, it stays 1. These are the only two numbers that stay the same when you square them.

Finally, if you square a value between 0 and 1, this is the one circumstance in which the value gets smaller.

Flip the Sign

Most operations that can be performed on equations can also be performed on inequalities. For example, in order to simplify an inequality (e.g., $2 + x < 5$), you can add or subtract a constant on both sides:

$$
\begin{array}{c}
2 + x < 5 \\
\underline{-2 \qquad -2} \\
x < 3
\end{array}
\qquad
\begin{array}{c}
x - 5 < 9 \\
\underline{+5 + 5} \\
x \qquad < 14
\end{array}
$$

You can also add or subtract a variable expression on both sides:

$$
\begin{array}{c}
y + x < 5 \\
\underline{-y \qquad\quad -y} \\
x < 5 - y
\end{array}
\qquad
\begin{array}{c}
x - ab < 9 \\
\underline{+ ab \qquad + ab} \\
x \qquad < 9 + ab
\end{array}
$$

You can multiply or divide by a *positive* number on both sides:

$$
\begin{array}{c}
2x < 6 \\
\underline{\div 2 \;\; \div 2} \\
x < 3
\end{array}
\qquad
\begin{array}{c}
0.2x < 1 \\
\underline{\times 5 \quad \times 5} \\
x < 5
\end{array}
$$

One procedure, however, is very different for inequalities: When you multiply or divide an inequality by a negative number, the inequality sign flips! For example:

If $4 - 3x < 10$, what is the range of possible values for x ?

$$
\begin{array}{c}
4 - 3x < 10 \\
\underline{-4 \qquad\quad -4} \\
-3x < \; 6
\end{array}
\qquad \text{First, subtract 4 from both sides.}
$$

$$
\frac{-3x}{-3} < \frac{6}{-3} \qquad \text{Next, divide by } -3.
$$

$$
x > -2 \qquad \text{Because you're dividing by a negative, flip the inequality sign.}
$$

Do not multiply or divide an inequality by a variable unless you know the sign of the number that the variable stands for. If you don't know whether that number is positive or negative, then you don't know whether to flip the inequality sign.

Combining Inequalities: Line 'Em Up!

Some GMAT inequality problems involve more than one inequality. To solve such problems, you may need to convert several inequalities to a compound inequality, which is a series of inequalities strung together, such as $2 < 3 < 4$. To convert multiple inequalities to a compound inequality, line up the variables, then combine. For example:

> If $x > 8$, $x < 17$, and $x + 5 < 19$, what is the range of possible values for x?

First, solve any inequalities that need to be solved. In this example, only the last inequality needs to be solved:

$$x + 5 < 19$$
$$x < 14$$

Second, rearrange the inequalities so that all the inequality symbols point in the same direction, and then line up the common variables in the inequalities:

$$8 < x$$
$$x < 17$$
$$x < 14$$

Finally, put the information together. Notice that $x < 14$ is more limiting than $x < 17$ (in other words, whenever $x < 14$, x will always be less than 17, but not vice versa). The range, then, is $8 < x < 14$ rather than $8 < x < 17$. Discard the less limiting inequality, $x < 17$. Try another example:

> If $u < t$ and $b > r$ and $f < t$ and $r > t$, is $b > u$?

Combine the four given inequalities by simplifying and lining up the common variables.

First, align all inequalities in the same direction: $u < t$, $r < b$, $f < t$, and $t < r$.

Then, line up any like variables . . .   . . . and combine.

$$u < t$$
$$\qquad r < b$$
$$f < t$$
$$\qquad t < r$$

$$u < t < r < b$$
$$f < t < r < b$$

In this problem, it is not possible to combine all the information into a single compound inequality. Both u and f are less than t, but you do not know the relationship between u and f.

The answer to the question is yes, b is greater than u.

Manipulating Compound Inequalities

Sometimes a problem with compound inequalities will require you to manipulate the inequalities in order to solve the problem. You can perform operations on a compound inequality as long as you remember to perform those operations on every term in the inequality, not just the outside terms. For example:

$$x + 3 < y < x + 5 \;\;\nrightarrow\;\; x < y < x + 2$$ **INCORRECT**: You must subtract 3 from *every* term in the inequality.

$$x + 3 < y < x + 5 \;\;\rightarrow\;\; x < y - 3 < x + 2$$ CORRECT

$$\frac{c}{2} \le b - 3 \le \frac{d}{2} \;\;\nrightarrow\;\; c \le b - 3 \le d$$ **INCORRECT**: You must multiply by 2 in *every* term in the inequality.

$$\frac{c}{2} \le b - 3 \le \frac{d}{2} \;\;\rightarrow\;\; c \le 2b - 6 \le d$$ CORRECT

Combining Inequalities: Add 'Em Up!

You can also combine inequalities by adding the inequalities together. In order to add inequalities, the inequality signs must face in the same direction. (Don't subtract inequalities, though—ever.)

For example, if you know that *a* is greater than 3, and *b* is greater than 5, what can you say about the sum of *a* and *b*?

$$
\begin{array}{r}
a > 3 \\
+\, b > 5 \\
\hline
a + b > 8
\end{array}
$$

The sum of *a* and *b* must be greater than 8. This makes sense. Even if *a* is 3.0001 and *b* is 5.0001, the sum will be (a little) bigger than 8.

Note that this does not work with subtraction. We can't say that $b - a > 2$. For instance, if $b = 6$, and $a = 100$, then $b - a = -94$.

You can also multiply inequalities together as long as all possible values of the inequalities are positive, though this doesn't show up a lot on the GMAT.

But remember this: *Never subtract or divide inequalities.*

Maximizing and Minimizing

Some problems ask you to find the maximum or minimum of multiple possible solutions; these are called max/min problems for short.

As you work through the problem, look for the spots where you have flexibility to try multiple possible values. Then, think about what the problem asked you to do. For instance, if the problem asked you to find the maximum value for something, where else in the problem do you need to maximize or minimize values in order to accomplish your overall goal? Try an example:

If $2y + 3 \le 11$ and $1 \le x \le 5$, what is the maximum possible value for *xy*?

Which combinations of extreme values will maximize the value of the product xy? First, simplify whatever you can. The x inequality is already simplified, but the y inequality can be simplified further:

$$2y + 3 \leq 11$$
$$2y \leq 8$$
$$y \leq 4$$

Next, examine the extreme ends of each range. If a range includes 0, it's also a good idea to note that, since 0 can have an unusual effect in problems:

Extreme Values for x	**Extreme Values for y**
The least value for x is 1.	There is no lower limit for y.
The greatest value for x is 5.	The greatest value for y is 4.
	y could be 0.

Now, consider the different scenarios for x and y that could lead to the maximum possible value for xy. The value of y could be positive or negative, but x must be positive. A positive times a negative has to be negative, and that won't be the maximum value, so ignore all negative values for y.

The value of 0 for y also won't help to maximize the value of xy. If you're restricted to positives, then you want to maximize the value of each individual number in order to get the maximum possible product.

In this case, xy is maximized when $x = 5$ and $y = 4$, with the result that $xy = 20$.

How does the situation change if this is the problem:

If $-20 \leq 2y \leq 8$ and $-3 \leq x \leq 5$, what is the maximum possible value for xy?

The first inequality simplifies to $-10 \leq y \leq 4$. Also, this time, both x and y could be negative—and a negative times a negative is positive—so you have to consider the negative scenario this time:

Extreme Values for x	**Extreme Values for y**
The least value for x is -3.	The least value for y is -10.
The greatest value for x is 5.	The greatest value for y is 4.
x could be 0.	y could be 0.

Max scenario 1: Positive $\times$ Positive. Use the greatest possible values for each:

$x = 5$ and $y = 4$, so $xy = 20$

Max scenario 2: Negative $\times$ Negative. Use the least possible values for each:

$x = -3$ and $y = -10$, so $xy = 30$

In this problem, the maximum value for xy is obtained when using the least possible values for x and y. The maximum value is 30.

When you see max/min language in a problem, first jot down whether the problem is asking you to maximize or to minimize. Next, identify the parts of the problem where you have the flexibility to maximize or minimize some values. Finally, consider the different possible scenarios—you may need to test two or three options in order to figure out the correct answer.

Square-Rooting Inequalities

Just like equations involving even exponents, inequality problems involving even exponents require you to consider *two* scenarios. Consider this example:

If $x^2 < 4$, what are the possible values for x?

To solve this problem, recall that when given x^2 and solving for x, you'll have two solutions: the positive version and the negative version. For example, if $x^2 = 4$, then $x = \pm 2$.

Something similar happens when you solve an inequality, with one important difference:

$$x^2 < 4$$
$$x < 2 \text{ and } x > -2$$

If x is positive, then $x < 2$. So far, this is how you would normally solve.

But, if x is negative, then taking the square root is the equivalent of dividing by a negative, so you have to flip the inequality sign: $x > -2$.

Here is another example:

If $10 + x^2 \geq 19$, what is the range of possible values for x?

$$10 + x^2 \geq 19$$
$$x^2 \geq 9$$
$$x \geq 3 \quad \text{AND} \quad x \leq -3$$

If x is positive, then $x \geq 3$, but if x is negative, then $x \leq -3$.

16

Problem Set

Now that you've finished the chapter, try the following problems.

1. Which of the following is equivalent to $-3x + 7 \leq 2x + 32$?

    (A) $x \geq -5$

    (B) $x \geq 5$

    (C) $x \leq 5$

    (D) $x \leq -5$

2. If $G^2 < G$, which of the following could be G ?

    (A) $\frac{23}{7}$

    (B) 1

    (C) $\frac{7}{23}$

    (D) -2

    (E) -4

3. If $5B > 4B + 1$, is $B^2 > 1$?

4. If $|A| > 19$, which of the following could NOT be equal to A ?

    (A) 26

    (B) 22

    (C) 18

    (D) -20

    (E) -24

5. If $-10 \leq a \leq 5$ and $7 \leq b \leq 10$, what is the least possible value of $|a - b|$?

    (A) -2

    (B) 0

    (C) 2

    (D) 3

    (E) 5

Save the following problems for review after you finish this entire guide.

6.   If $0 < ab < ac$ and $b > c$, which of the following must be negative?

    I. a

    II. b

    III. $c - b$

    (A) I only

    (B) II only

    (C) I and II only

    (D) II and III only

    (E) I, II, and III

7.   Sylvie has $65 consisting of bills each worth either $5 or $10. How many bills worth $10 does Sylvie have?

    (1) Sylvie has more bills worth $5 than bills worth $10.

    (2) The total value of Sylvie's $10 bills is greater than the total value of Sylvie's $5 bills.

8.   If $a > 7$, $a + 4 > 13$, and $2a < 30$, which of the following must be true?

    (A) $9 < a < 15$

    (B) $11 < a < 15$

    (C) $15 < a < 20$

    (D) $13 < a < 15$

9.   If $d > a$ and $L < a$, which of the following cannot be true?

    (A) $d + L = 14$

    (B) $d - L = 7$

    (C) $d - L = 1$

    (D) $a - d = 9$

    (E) $a + d = 9$

10. A retailer sells only radios and clocks. If there are currently exactly 42 total items in inventory, how many of them are radios?

    (1) The retailer has more than 26 radios in inventory.

    (2) The retailer has less than twice as many radios as clocks in inventory.

11. If $4x - 12 \geq x + 9$, which of the following must be true?

    (A) $x > 6$

    (B) $x < 7$

    (C) $x > 7$

    (D) $x > 8$

    (E) $x < 8$

16

Solutions

1. **(A)** $x \geq -5$:
$$-3x + 7 \leq 2x + 32$$
$$-5x \leq 25$$
$$x \geq -5$$

2. **(C)** $\dfrac{7}{23}$: If G^2 is less than G, then G must be positive (since G^2 itself has to be 0 or positive). In addition, only values between 0 and 1 get smaller when you square them. Thus, $0 < G < 1$. Only the value in answer **(C)** is between 0 and 1.

3. **Yes:**
$$5B > 4B + 1$$
$$B > 1$$

For any number greater than 1, the square of the number is also greater than 1, so $B^2 > 1$.

4. **(C) 18:** If $|A| > 19$, then $A > 19$ OR $A < -19$. The only answer choice that does not satisfy either of these inequalities is **(C)**, 18.

5. **(C) 2:** The question asks for the least possible value, so this is a max/min problem. Take some time during the Understand and Plan phases to think about what it means to minimize the value of $|a - b|$.

    How low can an absolute value go? It can never be negative. Glance at the answers—choice (A) can't be correct.

    An absolute value can be 0 or positive. Glance at the answers again—0 is in the running. Since the question asks for the least possible value, start there. What would need to happen in order for $|a - b| = 0$ to be true?

    The values for a and b would have to be identical. But this isn't possible, since a is between -10 and 5, inclusive, and b is between 7 and 10 inclusive. Eliminate choice (B) and move on to the next smallest value, 2.

    In order for the absolute value to be 2, the actual difference would have to be either 2 or -2. In other words, a and b would have to be 2 apart (though it doesn't matter which one is larger than the other). Is that a possible outcome? Yes, when $a = 5$ and $b = 7$.

    Alternatively, try each of the four extreme cases:

    Case 1: $|-10 - 7| = 17$

    Case 2: $|-10 - 10| = 20$

    Case 3: $|5 - 7| = 2$

    Case 4: $|5 - 10| = 5$

    The least possible value is 2. Note that answer (A) is a trap. The value of $5 - 7$ is -2, but the value of $|5 - 7|$ is 2, and the question asks about the absolute value.

6. **(E) I, II, and III:** The question asks what must be negative; jot that down. Since ab and ac are both positive, all three variables are non-zero. The variables a and b have the same sign, and the variables a and c also have the same sign, so all three variables must have the same sign (either all three are positive or all three are negative).

   You are also given that $b > c$, but the first inequality says that $ab < ac$. Together, this must mean that a is negative: you can divide $ab < ac$ by a since $a \neq 0$ and if a were positive that would mean $b < c$, but you know that $b > c$, so a must be negative. Statement I must be negative, so eliminate answers (B) and (D).

   Remember that all three variables must have the same sign, so since a is negative, b and c must also be negative. Statement II must be negative, so eliminate answer (A).

   You are down to answers (C) and (E), so you will have to figure out statement III. Since $b > c$ and both are negative, c is a more negative number than b and $c - b$ will still be negative (for example, $-4 - (-3) = -4 + 3 = -1$.

   The correct answer is **(E)**.

7. **(C):** Sylvie has a total of $65, made up of only $5 and $10 bills—what possibilities are there? At one extreme, Sylvie could have thirteen $5 bills and no $10 bills, and at the other Sylvie could have only one $5 bill and six $10 bills. There are only a handful of possibilities, so write them down:

Case:	1	2	3	4	5	6	7
# $5 bills:	13	11	9	7	5	3	1
# $10 bills:	0	1	2	3	4	5	6

   To answer the question, you need enough information to narrow down to just one of these cases.

   (1) INSUFFICIENT: Looking at the table, cases 1 through 5 all fit this statement.

   (2) INSUFFICIENT: In case 4, Sylvie has $35 in $5 bills and $30 in $10 bills, so this case (as well as cases 1 through 3) does not fit this statement. For case 5, though, Sylvie has only $25 in $5 bills and $40 in $10 bills, so cases 5, 6, and 7 all fit.

   (1) AND (2) SUFFICIENT: Only case 5 fits both statements, so Sylvie has four $10 bills.

   The correct answer is **(C)**: Both statements together are sufficient, but neither one alone is sufficient.

8. **(A) $9 < a < 15$:** First, solve the second and third inequalities. The second one, $a + 4 > 13$, becomes $a > 9$. The third one, $2a < 30$, becomes $a < 15$.

   Next, make all of the inequality symbols point in the same direction. Then, line up the inequalities based on the variable a to combine:

   $$9 < a$$
   $$a < 15 \rightarrow 9 < a < 15$$
   $$7 < a$$

   If 7 and 9 are both less than a, the limiting factor is the larger value, 9. (If a is greater than both 7 and 9, then overall a is greater than 9.) Therefore, a is between 9 and 15.

   Notice that, in all of the incorrect answers, the low end is too high. For example, answer (B) indicates that a cannot be 11, but a could in fact be 11. The correct answer will both keep out all the impossible values of a *and* include all the possible values of a.

16

9. **(D)** $a - d = 9$: The *cannot be true* language signals an opportunity to test cases. The wording of the question indicates that the four wrong answers all could be true—so start with answer (A) and see which cases you can create. If you get hung up on a particular answer, maybe that's the one that can't be true. Leave that one aside and keep going with the others.

   The question stem indicates that d is greater than a, but L is less than a. In other words: $L < a < d$. Test cases, making sure to try only numbers that follow this constraint:

   $$L < a$$
   $$a < d \rightarrow L < a < d$$

Answers to test	Given $L < a < d$ Test	Does it work?
(A) $d + L = 14$	$d = 10, L = 4$	Yes
(B) $d - L = 7$	$d = 10, L = 3$	Yes
(C) $d - L = 1$	$d = 10, L = 9$	Yes
(D) $a - d = 9$	$a = 10, d = \text{bigger}...?$	...?
(E) $a + d = 9$	$a = 4, d = 5$	Yes

   For four of the answers, it's possible to choose values that follow the constraint that $L < a < d$. For answer **(D)**, though, this is impossible. The value for a has to be *less* than the value for d, so whatever you try to choose will end up with a negative answer, not positive 9.

10. **(C):** First, assign variables (r = number of radios and c = number of clocks) so that you can jot down the information in the question stem:

    $$r + c = 42$$

    The question asks for r. Note that, if you can find c, then you can find r, so the rephrased question is this: What is r OR What is c?

    (1) INSUFFICIENT: This indicates that $r \geq 27$, so r could equal 27, 28, 29, etc.

    (2) INSUFFICIENT: This statement is tricky to translate. First, pretend that it says that there are twice as many radios as clocks. That translates to $r = 2c$. Then, add in the inequality: There are *less than twice as many radios*: $r < 2c$.

    Combine this information with the original equation $r + c = 42$:

    $$r < 2c$$
    $$r + c = 42$$

    Isolate c in the second equation, then substitute into the inequality:

    $$c = 42 - r$$
    $$r < 2c$$
    $$r < 2(42 - r)$$
    $$r < 84 - 2r$$
    $$3r < 84$$
    $$r < 28$$

This information on its own is insufficient; r could be 27, 26, and so on.

(1) AND (2) SUFFICIENT: Statement (1) tells you $r \geq 27$, and statement (2) tells you $r < 28$. Therefore, r must equal 27.

The correct answer is **(C)**: Both statements together are sufficient, but neither one alone is sufficient.

11.   **(A)** $x > 6$: What must be true? You might want to test some cases. First, though, simplify that annoying inequality:

$$4x - 12 \geq x + 9$$
$$3x \geq 21$$
$$x \geq 7$$

Careful. None of the answers match exactly. So test a couple of cases first before you choose something—make sure you understand what's going on. If $x \geq 7$, then x could be 7 itself.

Answers to test	Test #1: If $x = 7$ Answer true?	Test #2: If $x = 8$ Answer true?
(A) $x > 6$	Yes. Keep.	Yes. Keep.
(B) $x < 7$	No. Eliminate.	(ignore)
(C) $x > 7$	No. Eliminate.	(ignore)
(D) $x > 8$	No. Eliminate.	(ignore)
(E) $x < 8$	Yes. Keep.	No. Eliminate. Done!

The only answer that works every time is answer **(A)**.

16

Stories and Stats

In this unit, you will learn how to translate, organize, and solve all kinds of story-based problems, both math-based and logic-based, with particular emphasis on Problem Solving, Data Sufficiency, Multi-Source Reasoning, and Two-Part problem types. Math topics covered include statistics, rates, work, overlapping sets, and consecutive integers.

In This Unit

Translations

In This Chapter...

- Pay Attention to Units

- Common Relationships

- Draw It Out

- Maximizing and Minimizing

- Write Out the Scenarios

In this chapter, you will learn how to translate stories into solvable setups—including both math-based and visual-based approaches. You'll also learn certain common formulas that the GMAT expects you to know (e.g., Profit = Revenue − Cost), as well as how to convert among different types of units (e.g., meters to kilometers).

CHAPTER 17 **Translations**

Story problems are very common on the GMAT. They can test any math topic (e.g., statistics, fractions, percents, algebra, and so on) and can be found on any Quant or Data Insights (DI) problem type. Tackle story problems using your standard 3-step approach to solving: Understand, Plan, Solve.

Step 1: Understand: What's the Story?

Glance at the problem: The first thing you'll notice is a lot of text. On the DI section, also note what problem type you have. Next, do the answers or statements give you any quick clues about possible approaches? (Example: "Nice" real numbers in the answers on Problem Solving (PS), Multi-Source Reasoning (MSR), or Two-Part problems might lead you to work backwards. An annoying or complicated equation anywhere in the problem or statements signals a chance to rephrase or simplify.)

On story problems, you might read more than usual before you begin to jot down the information. Read far enough to understand the full context of that piece of information; that will help you to figure out the best way to jot it down. (You might even save some of the jotting for the Plan phase.)

Step 2: Plan: Choose an Approach

Your task is two-fold: Get the story on your scratch paper (in math form or visual form) and then decide how you want to approach it. Is algebra the best approach? Can you map out the steps or scenarios and logically analyze your way through? Can you work backwards or choose smart numbers? And so on. One more thing: Choose variables that tell you what they are (more on this below).

Step 3: Solve: Go for It!

When you understand and have a plan, go ahead and solve. If you *don't* understand or have a plan, *don't* try to solve. Guess and move on.

Try this problem:

> A candy company sells premium chocolate candies at $5 per pound and regular chocolate candies at $4 per pound in increments of whole pounds only. If a 7-pound box of chocolate candies costs $31, how many pounds of premium chocolate candies are in the box?
>
> (A) 1
> (B) 2
> (C) 3
> (D) 4
> (E) 5

Ready?

Step 1: **Understand.** The first glance indicates that this is a PS story problem. The answers are small whole numbers, so this might be a candidate for working backwards. Jot down WB on your scratch paper.

Now, read the story and get oriented. There are two different kinds of candies. You have to buy in whole-pound increments. A 7-pound box costs $31, but that box could contain a mix of premium and regular candies. It asks how many pounds were premium candies, specifically. That's a lot of information. Consider pushing the *jot* task to the Plan step.

Step 2: **Plan.** The box probably has both kinds of candies. How can you know? Glance at the answers. The choices are 1 through 5, so there have to be *some* premium candies. But the box weighs 7 pounds, so some are also regular candies as well. Call premium candies *P* and regular candies *R*. (Don't just use *x* and *y* every time. Choose variables that tell you what they are. You don't want to accidentally solve for the wrong thing.)

The question asks specifically for the number of pounds of premium candies. This represents a single variable in the problem (*P*), so working backwards is a good strategy here.

Here's one way to organize this story on paper:

$$P \qquad\qquad R$$
$$\$5/lb \qquad\qquad \$4/lb$$

WHOLE #s ONLY

$$\boxed{P+R}$$

$$P+R = 7 \text{ lbs} = \$31$$

$$\left(P = ?\right)$$

Step 3: **Solve.** Start with either answer (B) or answer (D), whichever you prefer:

	P=	R=	$P 5P	$R 4R	= $31?
(A)					
(B)	2	5	5(2)=10	4(5)=20	No. Too small.
(C)					
(D)					
(E)					

Answer (B) is incorrect. The cost adds up to $30, but it needs to add up to $31. Which direction do you need to go to find the correct answer?

The box should cost a dollar more, so you need more of the more expensive chocolate. Which one is more expensive? The premium brand, so you need more of that type. Cross off answer (A) as well, since that would mean fewer pounds of the premium brand.

Next, if you feel comfortable with this, you can actually think your way through the rest of the math. Answer (B) came to $30, but B spent $31, so you need to add just one more dollar. The difference in price between P and R is also just one dollar. So if you add one pound of P and take away one pound of R, you'll pay one more dollar. The answer must be (C), 3 pounds.

If you're not comfortable thinking that through, that's fine—just go back to the standard process and try answer (D) next. Use the scratch paper setup you already have, and run the new answer choice through the same process.

If P is 4, then R is 3. The cost is $(5)(4) + (4)(3) = 20 + 12 = \$32$. This is too much, so answer (D) is incorrect. Then examine the pattern. Answer (B) was too small at $30 and answer (D) was too large at $32, so answer (C) must be correct.

Either way, the correct answer is (C).

You can also solve algebraically, but fair warning: On this problem, since the answer choice values are such nice numbers, the algebra is probably more annoying than working backwards. It's still a good idea to know how this works, though, because you may need to use algebra on a different problem. For example:

$p =$ pounds of premium chocolate candies
$r =$ pounds of regular chocolate candies

You would also want to write down something similar to this:

$p =$ _____ ?

What else can you write down? The box weighs 7 pounds. Both premium and regular make up that 7 pounds, so you can write an equation:

$p + r = 7$

The other given concerns the total cost of the box, $31. The total cost is equal to the cost of the premium chocolates plus the cost of the regular chocolates.

This is a relationship the GMAT expects you to know: *Total Cost = Unit Price × Quantity*. You can express total cost using information you already have:

Total Cost of Box = $31
Cost of Premiums = (5 \$/pound) × (p pounds) = $5p$
Cost of Regulars = (4 \$/pound) × (r pounds) = $4r$

Note that you can translate "dollars per pound" to "\$/pound." In general, the word *per* is translated as "divided by."

Put that all together to get the second equation:

$31 = 5p + 4r$

Here's your current scratch paper; how can you solve?

$$p = \text{\# prem}$$
$$r = \text{\# reg}$$

$$p + r = 7$$
$$31 = 5p + 4r$$
$$p = \underline{\hspace{2cm}} ?$$

When you have two equations with two variables, the most efficient way to find the desired value is to eliminate the unwanted variable in order to solve for the desired variable.

You're looking for p. To eliminate r, first isolate it in one of the equations. It is easier to isolate r in the first equation:

$$r + p = 7 \rightarrow r = 7 - p$$

Now, replace r with $(7 - p)$ in the second equation and solve for p:

$$31 = 5p + 4(7 - p)$$
$$31 = 5p + 28 - 4p$$
$$3 = p$$

The correct answer is (C).

Story problems typically toss a lot of information at you, which is why it is so important to have a good process. Understand the story first—and possibly hold off on jotting down the math until you start to figure out your Plan. When you understand and have a plan, then you can go ahead and solve.

One last thing: A lot of stories have what's called a *hidden integer constraint*. If the story is talking about people or cars or marbles, there's an assumption that you have only whole numbers of people or cars or marbles. You'll never have 1.2 people or half of a car.

Pay Attention to Units

Unlike problems that test pure algebra, story problems have a context or narrative. Most values in a story problem have *units*—for example, miles or liters or minutes.

Every equation that correctly represents a relationship has units that make sense. Most of these relationships are either additive or multiplicative.

Additive Relationships

Additive relationships are connected by addition or subtraction. In the chocolates problem, there were two additive relationships:

$$\text{pounds } p + \text{pounds } r = 7 \text{ pounds}$$
$$\text{cost of } p + \text{cost of } r = \$31$$

In additive relationships, you have to make sure the units are the same. For example, pounds plus pounds equals pounds. And dollars plus dollars equals dollars. But pounds plus dollars...doesn't really equal anything. Add "same" to "same" and don't change the units label.

Multiplicative Relationships

Multiplicative relationships are connected by multiplication or division. Remember this relationship?

Total Cost = Unit Price × Quantity

In the problem, the cost of p is $5 per pound and the cost of r is $4 per pound. If you're solving algebraically, it works out this way:

$$5\left(\frac{\text{dollars}}{\text{pound}}\right) \times p \text{ (pounds)} = 5p \text{ (dollars)}$$

$$4\left(\frac{\text{dollars}}{\text{pound}}\right) \times r \text{ (pounds)} = 4r \text{ (dollars)}$$

For multiplicative relationships, treat units like numerators and denominators of a fraction. When you multiply these together, the units *do* change.

For example, pounds in the denominator of the first term cancel out pounds in the numerator of the second term, leaving dollars as the final units:

$$5\left(\frac{\text{dollars}}{\cancel{\text{pounds}}}\right) \times p \text{ (}\cancel{\text{pounds}}\text{)} = 5p \text{ (dollars)}$$

Common Relationships

The GMAT will assume that you have mastered the following relationships. For all of these relationships, the units follow the rules laid out in the previous section:

- Total Cost ($) = Unit Price ($/unit) × Quantity Purchased (units)
- Profit ($) = Revenue ($) − Cost ($)
- Total Earnings ($) = Wage Rate ($/hour) × Hours Worked (hours)
- Miles = Miles per Hour × Hours
- Miles = Miles per Gallon × Gallons

Units Conversion

When values with units are multiplied or divided, the units change. This property is the basis of using **conversion factors** to convert units. A conversion factor is a fraction whose numerator and denominator have different units but the same value.

For instance, how many seconds are in 7 minutes? There are 60 seconds in 1 minute. In this case, $\frac{60 \text{ seconds}}{1 \text{ minute}}$ is a conversion factor. Because the numerator and denominator are really the same value, multiplying by a conversion factor is just a sneaky way of multiplying by 1. The multiplication looks like this:

$$7 \cancel{\text{ minutes}} \times \frac{60 \text{ seconds}}{1 \cancel{\text{ minute}}} = 420 \text{ seconds}$$

Because you are multiplying, cancel the minutes, leaving the desired units (seconds).

Questions will occasionally center around your ability to convert units. Try the following problem:

> A certain medicine requires 4 doses per day. If each dose is 150 milligrams, how many milligrams of medicine will a person have taken after the end of the third day, if the medicine is taken as directed?

For any question that involves unit conversion, there will have to be some concrete value given. In this case, the time period is 3 days, there are 4 doses/day, and 1 dose equals 150 milligrams.

The question is asking for the number of milligrams of medicine that will be taken in that time. How can you combine all of those givens so that the only units that remain are milligrams?

Combine the calculations into one big expression, lining up the units so that the ones you *don't* want will cancel out:

$$3 \text{ days} \times \frac{4 \text{ doses}}{1 \text{ day}} \times \frac{150 \text{ milligrams}}{1 \text{ dose}} = 1{,}800 \text{ milligrams}$$

During the GMAT, abbreviate the units for each piece of multiplication—don't write them out completely. Just make sure that your conversion factors are set up properly to cancel out the units you don't want and to leave the units you do want.

Finally, keep an eye out for more of these relationships! For instance, rate and work problems are also built on a common relationship that you're expected to know for the test; you'll learn about that later.

Draw It Out

You don't always have to write algebraic equations when trying to solve story problems. Sometimes, it's faster and more straightforward to draw the solution out.

Try this problem:

> Five identical pieces of wire are joined together end-to-end to form one longer wire, with the pieces overlapping by 4 centimeters at each joint. If the wire thus made is exactly 1 meter long, how long, in centimeters, is each of the identical pieces? (1 meter = 100 centimeters)
>
> (A) 21.2
> (B) 22
> (C) 23.2
> (D) 24
> (E) 25.4

The setup of this problem is unusual, so draw out the story in order to understand what the problem is describing:

How many overlapping areas are there? There's a trap here. Because there are five pieces of wire, many people think that there are also five spots where the wires join. But look at the picture; it turns out that there are only four joints! Sketch out weird scenarios to catch these kinds of details.

Next, you have to figure something out about the total length. What happens when you join the wire together? Consider only the first two segments. Imagine that each one is 10 centimeters long (they aren't—this is just to understand what's going on).

If two 10-centimeter wires were laid end-to-end with no overlap, the length would be 20 centimeters. But since the two wires *do* overlap, you'll lose a portion of that length. How much?

When they're joined together, you don't lose *both* of the overlapping segments—if you did, then there would be a gap in the wire. The two pieces wouldn't actually be connected. Rather, think of it as though the top 4-centimeter segment stays, but the bottom one "disappears" (because it gets melted into the top one). So the length of the combined wire is $10 + 6 = 16$ centimeters. For this one joint, you've lost the length of *one* of the overlapping segments, or 4 centimeters.

Back to the given problem. There are four overlapping segments, or joints. You lose 4 centimeters at each connection, so you'll lose a total of 16 centimeters. The full length *before* all four wires are joined together is $100 + 16 = 116$ centimeters.

Because there are five wires, the length of each individual wire is $\frac{116}{5} = \ldots$ wait! That's a little annoying without a calculator (this is a PS problem). Break it into pieces that are more easily divisible by 5:

$$\frac{100 + 15 + 1}{5}$$

$$\frac{100}{5} = 20 \qquad \frac{15}{5} = 3 \qquad \frac{1}{5} = 0.2$$

The length is 23.2. Keep an eye on the answer choices as you do this math. Once you realize that the answer is 23-point-*something*, you can stop.

The correct answer is (C).

This problem can also be done algebraically; the relevant equation is $5x - 4(4) = 100$, where x is the length of each wire. Those who don't draw it out, though, are much more likely to fall into the trap of thinking that there are five joints. If so, you'll mistakenly write the equation as $5x - 5(4) = 100$, which leads to trap answer (D) 24.

Whenever you find a problem that could actually be happening to someone in the real world, ask yourself: If I were in this situation right now, how would I try to figure out the answer?

You almost certainly wouldn't start writing equations. Instead, you'd sketch out the situation using a combination of logic, math, and just trying out numbers or scenarios.

17

How could you sketch out this problem?

> A train travels at a constant rate of 90 kilometers/hour. How many hours does it take the train to travel 450,000 meters? (1 kilometer = 1,000 meters)

First, 450,000 meters is a really annoying number—but the problem gives you a conversion metric. And the rate is in kilometers per hour, so definitely convert the ugly meters figure to kilometers. Divide by 1,000 to convert this distance: It turns out to be 450 kilometers.

You're driving the train and you're going a steady 90 kilometers/hour. How long is it going to take you to go 450 kilometers? After an hour, you've gone 90 kilometers. After two hours, you've gone 180. What's the pattern?

It's all in multiples of 90. It's going to take you five multiples, or 5 hours, to get to 450. (By the way, if you like, you can make the numbers easier to look at by chopping a 0 off of each one. You're driving 9 kilometers every hour and want to go 45 kilometers total. That will take 5 hours.)

A problem could also ask something like this:

> A train leaves a station at 1 p.m. and travels at a constant rate of 90 kilometers/hour. At what time does the train reach the next station, a distance of 450,000 meters? (1 kilometer = 1,000 meters)

It still takes the train 5 hours to travel that distance, but the answer is now 1 p.m. + 5 hours = 6 p.m. As on any problem, take note of what the question wants you to find; a good (and very annoying!) trap answer on this problem would be 5 p.m.

Most of the time, the GMAT will ask for the "stopwatch" time—the actual time that something takes (e.g., 5 hours). Occasionally, the GMAT will ask you to solve in terms of clock times (e.g., 6 p.m.).

There are usually multiple ways to draw out the problem to get to the answer. Using this approach can often help you to avoid math traps and to better understand how the story works. Put yourself in the situation and ask yourself how this would play out in the real world. You'd almost never start writing a bunch of equations; rather, you'd use logic and estimation to get to a close-enough answer.

Rate and work problems, in particular, often lend themselves well to a draw-it-out approach. You'll see more of these later.

17

Maximizing and Minimizing

As you learned a little earlier in this guide, a story problem might ask you to find the minimum or maximum possible value of something.

For example:

> There are enough available spaces on a school team to select at most $\frac{1}{3}$ of the 50 students trying out for the team. What is the greatest number of students that could be rejected, while still filling all available spaces for the team?
>
> (A) 16
> (B) 17
> (C) 33
> (D) 34
> (E) 35

You're asked to maximize the number of *rejected* students. What else might you need to minimize or maximize in the problem in order to maximize the number of rejected students?

In order to maximize the rejected students, minimize the accepted students. First, the problem requires you to fill all available spaces on the team. If at most $\frac{1}{3}$ of the students can be selected, then at most $\frac{50}{3}$, or $16\frac{2}{3}$, students can be selected. It's impossible to select $\frac{2}{3}$ of a person, though! Is the maximum possible 16 or 17 ?

If the *maximum* is 16 and a bit, then you can't go up to 17, since that's greater than the maximum. Round down to 16. (Note that both of these values are in the answers; they're traps!)

The maximum number of rejected students, then, is $50 - 16 = 34$. The correct answer is (D).

This problem has a hidden *integer constraint*. They didn't explicitly say that the number of people has to be an integer, but they do expect you to follow that constraint. Next, you have to be careful to round in the right direction—not up, but down. If the maximum number of available spaces is $16\frac{2}{3}$, then 17 students is more than that max, so round down to 16.

Try another. How would you logic this problem out?

> Orange Computers is breaking up its conference attendees into groups. Each group must have exactly 1 person from Division A, 2 people from Division B, and 3 people from Division C. There are 20 people from Division A, 30 people from Division B, and 40 people from Division C at the conference. What is the least number of people who will NOT be able to be assigned to a group?
>
> (A) 12
> (B) 5
> (C) 2
> (D) 1
> (E) 0

You're in charge of the conference and you have to figure this out. First, you need to **understand** what the parameters are. Jot down the given information on your scratch paper:

Div.	Total People	Per Group
A	20	1
B	30	2
C	40	3

Plan. The goal is to place as many people as possible in groups. Consider Division A. There are 20 of these people and you need 1 per group, so that's 20 groups. . . .

Hmm. If there were 20 groups, you'd need 40 people from B and there are only 30 in this division, so that won't work. There have to be fewer than 20 groups. (And, incidentally, this proves that at least 1 person will be without a group, so the answer can't be 0.) What else? If starting with Division B, you'd have 15 groups…but that would require 45 people from Division C and there are only 40 in that division.

The most constrained or limited group is Division C because you need 3 in each group and you only have 40 people overall, for a maximum of 13 groups. So start there.

Solve. Division C can make 13 groups of 3, using a total of 39 people. One person from C is left without a group. Glance at the answers. Answer (E) can't be correct (if you didn't already notice this earlier), since at least 1 person is already without a group.

Next, Division B will use $13 \times 2 = 26$ people in these 13 groups. There are 4 Division B people left without a group. So there are at least 5 total without a group now; eliminate answers (C) and (D).

You'll also need 13 people from Division A, leaving 7 more without a group. Look at the answers. Don't even bother to add up the numbers—the answer must be more than 5, so answer (A) must be correct.

Some max/min problems will be more like the first one, where the path of the math is fairly straightforward, but you have to make decisions along the way about maximizing or minimizing other pieces in order to get to your desired answer.

In others, the situation will be more logic-based. As with the second problem, you'll try a couple of scenarios until you find the limiting factor, and then you'll follow the math from there.

In both cases, make sure to pay attention to any constraints, especially those not explicitly stated. People and saxophones and llamas cannot be split into fractional parts.

Write Out the Scenarios

Try this one:

> During a week-long sale at a car dealership, the greatest number of cars sold on any one day was 12. If at least 2 cars were sold each day, was the average (arithmetic mean) daily number of cars sold during that week greater than 6 ?
>
> (1) During that week, the second fewest number of cars sold on any one day was 4.
>
> (2) During that week, the median number of cars sold was 10.

Note: The average is found by taking the sum of a set of numbers and dividing by the number of terms. The median is the middle number in a set of numbers arranged in increasing order. You'll learn more about statistics a bit later in this book—but you can solve this problem even though you haven't gotten to the Statistics chapter yet.

Pretend you're the manager of the car dealership and the owner has asked you to figure this out. Your manager knows you're not a mathematician...and you don't need to be one to do this.

The best sales day was 12, but you don't know which day of the week that was. And at least 2 cars were sold each day, but more cars *could* have been sold. The problem allows multiple possible scenarios, so how could you draw something that shows what you know but allows for flexibility?

Glance at the statements. They provide information about the fewest number of sales and the median number of sales.

Since it's asking about median, try organizing the number of sales from least to greatest.

Draw out seven slots (one for each day) and add the information given in the question stem:

$$\geq 2 \ \underline{\quad} \ \underline{\quad} \ \underline{\quad} \ \underline{\quad} \ \underline{\quad} \ 12$$

The problem indicates that at least 2 cars were sold on each day, so the smallest number has to be at least 2 (though it could be greater). The greatest number sold on any one day was 12. The other days have to be somewhere in this range from 2 to 12, *inclusive*. You are allowed to have two or more days on which the same number of cars were sold.

The question asks whether the average number of daily sales for the week is more than 6. Because this is a Yes/No Data Sufficiency question, test each statement to see whether it can give you both a "Yes, the average is more than 6" answer and a "No, the average is not more than 6" answer. If so, then you'll know the statement is insufficient.

> (1) During that week, the second smallest number of cars sold on any one day was 4.

Draw out a version of the scenario that includes statement (1):

$$\geq 2 \ \ 4 \ \ \underline{\quad} \ \underline{\quad} \ \underline{\quad} \ \underline{\quad} \ 12$$

Can you find a way to make the average less than 6 ? Keep the first day at 2 and make the other days as small as possible. You can use the same number more than once:

$$\geq 2 \ \ 4 \ \ 4 \ \ 4 \ \ 4 \ \ 4 \ \ 12$$

If the first day is 2, the sum of the numbers is 34. The average is $\frac{34}{7}$, which is a little less than 5. So the answer to the question for this one case is No, the average is not greater than 6.

Can you also make the average greater than 6 ? Try making the numbers as big as you can:

$$4 \ \ 4 \ \ 12 \ \ 12 \ \ 12 \ \ 12 \ \ 12$$

You may be able to eyeball that and tell it will be greater than 6. If not, calculate: The sum is $8 + 5(12) = 68$, so the average is $\frac{68}{7}$, which is a bit less than 10. So, in this one case, the answer to the question is Yes.

Statement (1) is not sufficient because the average might be greater than 6 or less than 6.

Cross off answers (A) and (D) and move to statement (2):

(2)   During that week, the median number of cars sold was 10.

Again, draw out the scenario (using *only* the second statement this time!). The median is the middle number or slot in the list:

$$\underline{\geq 2} \quad \underline{} \quad \underline{} \quad \underline{10} \quad \underline{} \quad \underline{} \quad \underline{12}$$

Can you make the average less than 6 ? The three lowest days could each be 2. Then, the next three days could each be 10.

$$\underline{2} \quad \underline{2} \quad \underline{2} \quad \underline{10} \quad \underline{10} \quad \underline{10} \quad \underline{12}$$

The sum is $6 + 30 + 12 = 48$. The average is $\frac{48}{7}$, or just less than 7, but greater than 6. The numbers cannot be made any smaller. First, you have to have a minimum of 2 a day. Once you hit the median of 10 in the middle slot, you have to have something greater than or equal to the median for the remaining slots to the right.

The smallest possible average is greater than 6, so this statement is sufficient to answer the question. Yes, the average must be greater than 6 in all cases. The correct answer is (B).

The slot method is a really valuable way to solve certain kinds of math-based problems as well as logic-based problems. If a problem talks about a set of numbers but doesn't give you the value of all of those numbers, try drawing out slots to represent each number in the set and stepping through the allowed scenarios. If it's a max/min problem, test the extreme scenarios (make everything as small as possible or as large as possible) to see the range of possible outcomes. If a problem includes information about the median, order the numbers from least to greatest.

You'll learn more strategies for the slot method later in this book.

17

Problem Set

Now that you've finished the chapter, try the following problems.

1. United Telephone charges a base rate of $10.00 for service, plus an additional charge of $0.25 per minute. Atlantic Call charges a base rate of $12.00 for service, plus an additional charge of $0.20 per minute. For what number of minutes would the bills for each telephone company be the same?

2. Caleb spends $72.50 on 50 hamburgers for the marching band. If single burgers cost $1.00 each and double burgers cost $1.50 each, how many double burgers did he buy?

3. Carina has 100 ounces of coffee divided into packages of 5 or 10 ounces. If she has 2 more 5-ounce packages than 10-ounce packages, how many 10-ounce packages does she have?

    (A)   2
    (B)   4
    (C)   6
    (D)   8
    (E)   10

4. A circus earned $150,000 in ticket revenue by selling a total of 1,800 VIP and Standard tickets. They sold 25% more Standard tickets than VIP tickets. If the revenue from Standard tickets represents one-third of the total ticket revenue, what is the price of a VIP ticket?

5. A full bookshelf holds both paperback and hardcover books. The ratio of paperback books to hardcover books is 8 to 5. Each paperback book is half as wide as each hardcover book. What is the maximum fraction of the length of the shelf that can be freed up by replacing hardcover books with paperback editions of the same book?

    (A) $\frac{5}{18}$
    (B) $\frac{4}{13}$
    (C) $\frac{1}{3}$
    (D) $\frac{4}{9}$
    (E) $\frac{13}{18}$

6. Velma has exactly one week to learn all 71 Japanese hiragana characters. If she can learn at most a dozen hiragana on any one day and will only have time to learn four on Friday, what is the least number of hiragana that Velma will have to learn on Saturday?

7. A casino uses chips in $5 and $7 denominations only. Which of the following amounts CANNOT be paid out using these chips?

    (A) $31

    (B) $29

    (C) $26

    (D) $23

    (E) $21

8. The integers a and b are in the set $\{a, 73, b, 71, 75\}$, and $b > a > 70$. If all of the numbers in the set are distinct, which of the following cannot be the median of the set?

    (A) 73

    (B) 74

    (C) 75

    (D) a

    (E) b

17

Solutions

1. **40 minutes:** Let $x =$ the number of minutes.

    A call made by United Telephone costs \$10.00 plus \$0.25 per minute: $10 + 0.25x$.

    A call made by Atlantic Call costs \$12.00 plus \$0.20 per minute: $12 + 0.20x$.

    Set the expressions equal to each other and solve for x:

    $$10 + 0.25x = 12 + 0.20x$$
    $$0.05x = 2$$
    $$x = 40$$

    For that last math step, you can multiply both sides by 100 to get rid of the decimal ($5x = 200$), then solve. You could also recognize that 0.05 is the same as 5% and use percent benchmarks to solve. If 5% of a number equals 2, then 10% of the number equals 4, and 100% of the number equals 40.

2. **45 double burgers:** Let $s =$ the number of single burgers purchased and $d =$ the number of double burgers purchased:

    Caleb bought 50 burgers: Caleb spent \$72.50 in all:

    $$s + d = 50 \qquad\qquad\qquad s + 1.5d = 72.5$$

    Combine the two equations by subtracting equation 1 from equation 2:

    $$s + 1.5d = 72.50$$
    $$\underline{-(s + d = 50)}$$
    $$0.5d = 22.5$$
    $$d = 45$$

3. **(C) 6:** The answers are small integers and represent a single variable in the problem, so work backwards to solve. Set up a table to keep your work organized as you test the answer choices. Start with answer (B) or (D).

    Let T equal the number of 10-ounce packages and F equal the number of 5-ounce packages. *Last* refers to the value in the previous column.

$T =$	Amt in 10 oz $(T \times 10)$	Amt in 5 oz $(100 - \text{last})$	$F = (\text{last}/5)$	$F - T = 2$?
(B) 4	40 oz	60 oz	12	$12 - 4 = 8$ No
(D) 8	80 oz	20 oz	4	$4 - 8 = -4$ No

    Answer (B) is too large and answer (D) is too small; the correct answer must be in between the two.

Alternatively, solve via algebra. Let F equal the number of 5-ounce packages and T equal the number of 10-ounce packages:

Carina has 100 ounces of coffee: She has 2 more 5-ounce packages than 10-ounce packages:

$$5F + 10T = 100 \qquad\qquad F = T + 2$$

Combine the equations by substituting the value of F from equation 2 into equation 1:

$$5(T + 2) + 10T = 100$$
$$5T + 10 + 10T = 100$$
$$15T + 10 = 100$$
$$15T = 90$$
$$T = 6$$

4. **$125:** To answer this question correctly, make sure to differentiate between the *price* of tickets and the *quantity* of tickets sold. Let V equal the number of VIP tickets sold and S equal the number of Standard tickets sold.

The question indicates that the circus sold a total of 1,800 tickets, and that the circus sold 25% more Standard tickets than VIP tickets. Create two equations:

$$V + S = 1,800 \qquad 1.25V = S$$

Use these equations to figure out how many VIP tickets were sold:

$$V + S = 1,800$$
$$V + (1.25V) = 1,800$$
$$2.25V = 1,800$$
$$\frac{9}{4}V = 1,800$$
$$V = 1,800\left(\frac{4}{9}\right)$$
$$V = 800$$

Now, find the cost per VIP ticket. The circus earned $150,000 in ticket revenue, and Standard tickets represented one-third of that revenue. Therefore, Standard tickets accounted for $\frac{1}{3} \times \$150,000 = \$50,000$. VIP tickets then accounted for the other $100,000 in revenue.

Thus, $\frac{100,000}{800} = \frac{1,000}{8} = \$125$ per VIP ticket.

5. **(A)** $\frac{5}{18}$**:** First things first: Understand the problem. This problem has givens that deal with ratios and fractions, and it asks for a fraction. Notice that there are no actual numbers anywhere in the problem; nowhere does it give or ask for a number of books or an exact shelf length.

The gist of the problem is that a shelf has two types of books, hardcover and paperback. The proportion of each type is given along with their relative widths. Some of the hardcovers will be replaced by paperbacks, and the question asks for the *maximum* length of the shelf that could be freed up.

17

Make a Plan. Since there are no actual numbers, use **Smart Numbers**. The simplest way to apply the ratio of 8 to 5 is to assume there are 8 paperbacks and 5 hardcovers. Next, choose values for the width of each book. Say a paperback is 1 inch wide and a hardcover is 2 inches wide.

Finally, Solve. Drawing this out may help to make sense of the problem:

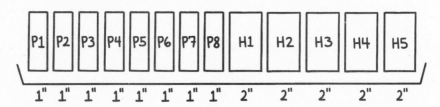

The shelf is full, so the total length of the shelf is the sum of all of these widths: $8(1) + 5(2) = 18$. The fact that the shelf is 18 inches long means the fraction should have a factor of 18 in the denominator, so answer (B) can't be correct.

How can the space saved by converting hardcover books into paperback books be maximized? By replacing *all* of the hardcover books! There are no constraints in the problem that prevent this. If all five hardcover books are replaced with paperbacks, there will be 13 paperbacks and 0 hardcovers. The shelf space occupied by 13 paperback books is 13 inches. Be careful; the question asks for the fraction of the shelf that is freed up. The shelf is 18 inches long, so it must be that 5 inches, out of the original 18, have been freed up. The answer is $\frac{5}{18}$.

6.   **7:** Draw it out! Draw seven slots and label them for the days of the week. The problem states that Velma will learn 4 hiragana on Friday and at most 12 on any other day. Finally, it asked for the least possible number that she will need to learn on Saturday:

$$\frac{\leq 12}{\text{Sun}} \quad \frac{\leq 12}{\text{M}} \quad \frac{\leq 12}{\text{Tu}} \quad \frac{\leq 12}{\text{W}} \quad \frac{\leq 12}{\text{Th}} \quad \frac{4}{\text{F}} \quad \frac{\text{least?}}{\text{Sat}}$$

Since she'll learn 4 on Friday, she has 67 more to learn. To minimize the number of hiragana that she will have to learn on Saturday, *maximize* the number that she learns on the other days. If Velma learns the maximum of 12 hiragana from Sunday to Thursday, then she will have $67 - 5(12) = 7$ left for Saturday:

$$\frac{12}{\text{Sun}} \quad \frac{12}{\text{M}} \quad \frac{12}{\text{Tu}} \quad \frac{12}{\text{W}} \quad \frac{12}{\text{Th}} \quad \frac{4}{\text{F}} \quad \frac{7}{\text{Sat}}$$

7.   **(D) \$23:** The payouts will have to be in the sum of some integer number of \$5 chips and some integer number of \$7 chips. Which of the answer choices *cannot* be the sum? First, check the answers for any multiples of 7 and/or 5; this eliminates answer (E).

Glance at the answers. The numbers are not that large, so you could try to re-create them. Write out some multiples of 5 and 7 and try to combine them to create the remaining four answers:

Multiples of 5	Multiples of 7
5	7
10	14
15	21
20	

You don't need to go higher than 20 for the multiples of 5, because $25 + 7$ is greater than the greatest number in the answers. Ditto, if you went up to 28 for the multiples of 7, then added 5 more, you'd be beyond the range of answers.

Now, pair up the numbers systematically and see which answer choices you can match. $5 + 7$? $5 + 14$? $5 + 21$? Bingo, that last one equals 26. Eliminate answer (C).

Next, $10 + 7$? $10 + 14$? $10 + 21$? Bingo again, the last one equals 31. Eliminate answer (A).

Keep going; $15 + 14 = 29$, so eliminate answer (B). The only remaining value is 23; by process of elimination, it must be the sum that cannot be paid out in these chips, so **(D)** is the correct answer.

8. **(E) b:** The first job is to Understand. The answer choices look odd in this question in that some are numbers and some are variables. There is a set of numbers given that contains a mix of numbers and variables, so this problem will likely involve trying to logic out as much about this set as possible.

The problem states that all of the numbers are unique integers, so a and b cannot be equal to each other, and they can't be equal to any of the numbers already in the set. There is an additional constraint that is really two constraints: b has to be greater than a, and a has to be greater than 70. Since all of the numbers are integers, "greater than 70" means "at least 71." But a can't be 71 because that number is already in the set. Therefore, 71 must be the least number in the set, and the least that a can be is 72. Using the same logic, the least possible value of b is 74.

Next, Plan. Since the first number is 71, and there are lots of constraints on the others, it is probably possible to methodically list out possible sets and check their medians.

Also, when the question asks "which of the following…," it is usually possible to answer the question by testing cases. In this case, try to create a set of numbers for each answer choice in which the answer choice is the median and then eliminate any that can work.

Okay, time to Solve. When making a list of possibilities, it is important to keep track of the constraints and be methodical. The constraints are: The first number is 71, all of the numbers are unique, all of the numbers are integers, and b is greater than a. To be methodical, first try to make a as low as possible and work from there.

The least that a can be is 72. In that case, the set contains 71, 72, 73, and 75. The two possibilities for b are 74 or some number greater than 75:

$$71, \ a = 72, \ \textcircled{73}, \ b = 74, \ 75$$
$$71, \ a = 72, \ \textcircled{73}, \ 75, \ b > 75$$

It looks like 73 can be the median. Eliminate (A). The next lowest possibility for a is 74, since it can't be 73.

This leaves only one possibility for b, that it is greater than 75:

$$71, \ 73, \ \boxed{a = 74}, \ 75, \ b > 75$$

This set eliminates two answer choices: (B) and (D), since the median is both a and 74. The only possibility left is that a and b are both numbers greater than 75:

$$71, \ 73, \ \textcircled{75}, \ a > 75, \ b > a$$

This eliminates choice (C). The only answer choice that cannot be the median is choice **(E)**.

Multi-Source Reasoning

In This Chapter...

- UPS for MSR

- Review and Improve on MSR

In this chapter, you will learn how to process and map the information from Multi-Source Reasoning (MSR) problems, as well as how to use UPS (Understand, Plan, Solve) to approach the two types of questions that come with this problem type.

CHAPTER 18 Multi-Source Reasoning

Multi-Source Reasoning (MSR) problems are similar to Reading Comprehension (RC) passages, with two key differences: MSR can include mathematical data, graphics, and tables along with the text, and the information provided will be split across two or three separate tabs.

You will only be able to view one tab at a time. Also, if you see a table in an MSR tab, you will *not* be able to sort the table as you can on Table problems.

Much like RC passages, the MSR prompts appear on the left side of the screen and the (typically) three accompanying questions appear on the right side of the screen, one at a time. These questions are of two different types: standard multiple-choice and either-or.

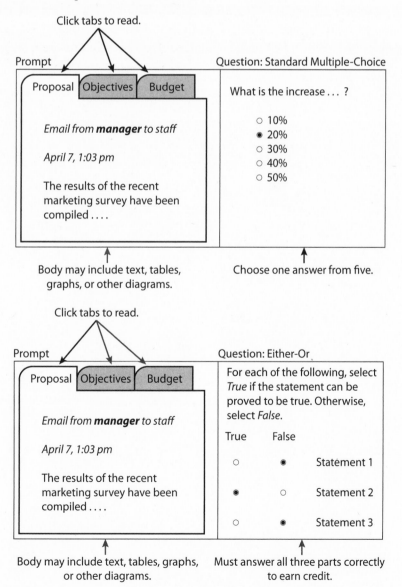

The standard multiple-choice problems are in the same format as Problem Solving problems. The either-or problems look just like the ones you've seen on Table problems. You can use all of the same strategies you've been learning for these other problem types on MSR problems as well.

For example, on a math-focused problem, you may be able to use smart numbers or work backwards. On a verbal-focused problem, you may be able to predict an answer (as on RC) or eliminate answers based on common traps that you've learned about for RC or Critical Reasoning. And, in a few chapters, you'll learn more about how to tackle logic-based problems; those strategies can also be used on MSR logic problems.

The most typical configuration for the three MSRs problems is one standard multiple-choice question and two separate either-or questions. Occasionally, you might be given two or four total questions, but this is pretty rare. (We've mostly seen this only in official practice problem sets.)

As the word *multi-source* implies, the vast majority of questions will require you to integrate information from two or even all three of the tabs. MSR prompts are going to try to overwhelm you with data (much like the real world!). Your task will be to pick out the pieces needed to solve the problem that's on the screen right now.

UPS for MSR

Since there's quite a lot of information in MSR tabs, the Understand step is going to take some time. Because you will usually see three separate questions associated with the same MSR tabs, though, you can afford to invest a couple of minutes at the beginning to understand the information in the tabs.

18

Step 1: Understand the Prompt and Question

Take a look at the two-tab MSR prompt below. Here's the first tab:

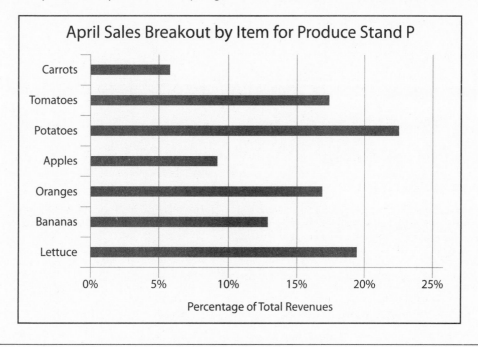

| Sales Breakout | Vitamin Content |

E-mail from Purchasing Supervisor to Sales Manager:

Total April sales for your produce stand were $4,441; the itemized data is below.

We already know that customers base their purchasing decisions on whether something is in season and how much it costs. Management believes that customers also care about the health factor, such as how high the vitamin content is for different types of produce. Do you have any data that could help us to evaluate this question?

We also need to think about pricing strategies in light of the fact that some items have a far longer shelf life. Potatoes will last weeks in cold storage, while the tomatoes won't last more than a few days without suffering a reduction in quality. Please send me any information you have about spoilage rates or other factors we should consider when setting prices.

April Sales Breakout by Item for Produce Stand P

Glance first at the labels on the two tabs: *Sales Breakout* and *Vitamin Content*. Also, click briefly on the second tab just to see whether it's pure text or whether it also contains a graph, table, or other non-text information. Don't read anything; just glance and see what it is. (In this case, you'd see some text and a table on the second tab—more on this in a bit.)

Now, go back to the first tab and start reading to understand the overall story. As on Reading Comprehension (RC), don't get too deep into the detail; you'll come back to that later when answering questions.

The blurb first sets some context and provides overall sales figures for a produce stand. The first big paragraph then talks about the factors that customers consider when buying produce and asks an explicit question about vitamin content. The second tab's title is actually *Vitamin Content*, so presumably that tab will address this question.

The second big paragraph raises the issue of shelf life for their pricing strategy. Perhaps the supervisor is thinking that they will have to reduce prices on certain items with a shorter shelf life in order to make sure

18

they sell before they spoil? (She doesn't actually say this, but go ahead and speculate a little. Put yourself in the story.) The text also mentions spoilage rates, so perhaps the second tab will address this as well.

Finally, the bar graph provides the percentage of sales by item; there may be some calculations to do.

As you understand what's going on, jot down information on your scrap paper, but as with RC, don't take very detailed notes. The test is open book; the source information will be in front of you the whole time. Rather, you are going to create a **Tab Map** that will help you figure out where to go in order to answer the various questions.

The entire first tab might condense down into this map:

> #1   Sales
>
> Apr $4,441
>
> Buy in season. Cost. Care about V?
>
> Pricing strat → spoilage
>
> Ⓖ % sales by item

Use some kind of visual designation as a signal when you have a graph, a table, or some other visual or set of data. That way, you'll know at a glance which tab to click back to when you need that data.

Try it again with the second tab:

Sales Breakout	**Vitamin Content**

E-mail from Sales Manager to Purchasing Supervisor:

Carrots, apples, and potatoes last a very long time in cold storage. I am a bit concerned about the lettuce, though; our farmers generally produce a higher volume of lettuce than of any other single item. The other items generally sell within acceptable time frames, even the tomatoes and bananas.

Customers do sometimes ask about the vitamin and nutrient content of various items. Maybe I should post the data on the pricing signs? Here's some data on the vitamin A and vitamin C content of our produce:

Vitamin Content of Produce Items Sold at Produce Stand P in April		
	Vitamin C content	*Vitamin A content*
Apples	low	low
Bananas	medium	low
Carrots	low	high
Lettuce	high	low
Oranges	high	medium
Potatoes	medium	low
Tomatoes	high	high

I also have research indicating that organic produce has a higher vitamin content than non-organic counterparts. I think that could be a very valuable marketing point.

18

In contrast to Table problems, MSR problems have static tables—you can't sort them. A map for the second tab might look like this:

> #2 Vit
>
>> Spoil: maybe lettuce
>>
>> (T) Vit A + C
>>
>> Org = more Vit, +

It sounds like lettuce might have spoilage or shelf-life issues, though the sales manager doesn't explicitly say so. Then there's a bunch of data on vitamin content; note that this data exists and just notice that it's in the form high-medium-low (not numbers), but ignore the details until you get a question about it. Finally, the last couple of sentences introduce the idea that organic produce could be a positive selling point.

Take a moment to think about how the two tabs connect; feel free to click back and forth to glance at the info again. The supervisor asks some questions and the manager responds to those questions. The two visuals contain the same list of fruits and vegetables (though not in the same order—be careful). It isn't clear at this point how the sales data and the vitamin content data might otherwise connect, so wait to see what questions you're asked.

Here is the first question:

> For each of the following, select *Justified* if it is a justified inference on the basis of the information provided. Otherwise, select *Not justified*.

Justified	Not justified	
O	O	Some of Produce Stand P's lettuce may spoil or be in danger of spoiling before it is all sold.
O	O	More bananas than apples are sold at Produce Stand P.
O	O	Produce high in vitamin A, vitamin C, or both accounted for more than half of April revenues at Produce Stand P.

This is an either-or question, the exact same format as is used on Table questions. These questions always present answers in the form *either X or Y*, such as true/false, yes/no, or, as in this case, justified/not justified. Three statements will accompany the question; your task is to choose a single answer for each statement. In order to earn credit for this question, you have to answer all three statements correctly.

This question specifically asks whether the statement is a *justified inference*. These statements will not be found directly in the tabs; rather, you will have to determine whether something is reasonably justified, or able to be proven, based upon related information from the prompt.

Next, scan through the three statements. On some problems, the statements are very similar and can be solved simultaneously or very similarly. On others, the statements are independent and must be solved separately.

In this case, the statements each address different aspects of the information provided, so work through them individually. Here's the first statement:

Justified	Not justified	
○	○	Some of Produce Stand P's lettuce may spoil or be in danger of spoiling before it is all sold.

This statement talks about lettuce spoilage. Where do you need to go to find this information? Glance at your map. Spoilage was mentioned in both tabs.

Step 2: Plan Your Approach

Sales Breakout | **Vitamin Content**

E-mail from Purchasing Supervisor to Sales Manager:

Total April sales for your produce stand were $4,441; the itemized data is below.

We already know that customers base their purchasing decisions on whether something is in season and how much it costs. Management believes that customers also care about the health factor, such as how high the vitamin content is for different types of produce. Do you have any data that could help us to evaluate this question?

We also need to think about pricing strategies in light of the fact that some items have a far longer shelf life. Potatoes will last weeks in cold storage, while the tomatoes won't last more than a few days without suffering a reduction in quality. Please send me any information you have about spoilage rates or other factors we should consider when setting prices.

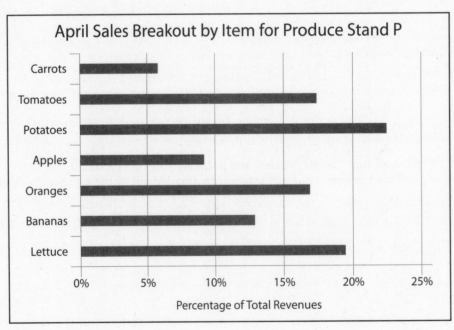

Sales Breakout	Vitamin Content

E-mail from Sales Manager to Purchasing Supervisor:

Carrots, apples, and potatoes last a very long time in cold storage. I am a bit concerned about the lettuce, though; our farmers generally produce a higher volume of lettuce than of any other single item. The other items generally sell within acceptable time frames, even the tomatoes and bananas.

Customers do sometimes ask about the vitamin and nutrient content of various items. Maybe I should post the data on the pricing signs? Here's some data on the vitamin A and vitamin C content of our produce:

Vitamin Content of Produce Items Sold at Produce Stand P in April		
	Vitamin C content	*Vitamin A content*
Apples	low	low
Bananas	medium	low
Carrots	low	high
Lettuce	high	low
Oranges	high	medium
Potatoes	medium	low
Tomatoes	high	high

I also have research indicating that organic produce has a higher vitamin content than non-organic counterparts. I think that could be a very valuable marketing point.

The *Sales Breakout* tab mentioned spoilage and the *Vitamin Content* tab specifically mentioned lettuce, so you'll need both tabs to answer the question. Scan to find the relevant text:

> (Sales Breakout Tab): We also need to think about pricing strategies in light of the fact that some items have a far longer shelf life. Potatoes will last weeks in cold storage, while the tomatoes won't last more than a few days without suffering a reduction in quality. Please send me any information you have about spoilage rates or other factors we should consider when setting prices.

> (Vitamin Content Tab) Carrots, apples, and potatoes last a very long time in cold storage. I am a bit concerned about the lettuce, though; our farmers generally produce a higher volume of lettuce than of any other single item. The other items generally sell within acceptable time frames, even the tomatoes and bananas.

Step 3: Solve the Problem

The supervisor points out that some items will last much longer than others, then asks about spoilage rates, implying that some items may spoil or be in danger of spoiling. The sales manager indicates that certain items do last a long time, but he is *concerned about the lettuce*. He also indicates that the *other items generally sell within acceptable time frames*, implying that the lettuce might *not* sell within an acceptable time frame. So the lettuce might spoil before it can be sold. The first statement, then, is *Justified*.

Evaluate the second and third statements in the same manner:

Justified	Not justified	
O	O	More bananas than apples are sold at Produce Stand P.

Careful! The bar graph in the *Sales Breakout* tab shows information about sales *revenues*, not sales *volume*. While it is true that banana sales revenues were higher than apple sales revenues, the prompt does not indicate the relative number of items sold. Maybe bananas cost $10 each and apples are $0.10 each. The second statement is *Not justified*. Here's the third statement:

Justified	Not justified	
O	O	Produce high in vitamin A, vitamin C, or both accounted for more than half of April revenues at Produce Stand P.

Note first that the question asks whether this group accounted for *more than half* of revenues. You will not have to calculate the exact figure; it will be enough to tell whether it is more or less than half. The *Vitamin Content* tab has the vitamin data; the *Sales Breakout* tab has the sales data. Combine the two tabs to answer.

First, go to *Vitamin Content* and look for the items that are high in either or both of the vitamins: carrots, lettuce, oranges, and tomatoes. The remaining items—apples, bananas, and potatoes—are not high in either vitamin. Jot the items in two clearly labeled lists: high-V and not-high-V. Since you are comparing to 50%, it's only necessary to estimate the sum for one group.

Next, click on *Sales Breakout* and find the percentage of revenue for each item. It is easier to sum three categories than four, so eyeball the bars for the not-high-vitamin items: Do they sum to less than 50%?

$$A < 10\%$$
$$B < 15\%$$
$$\underline{P < 25\%}$$
$$\text{sum} < 50\%$$

The not-high-vitamin items account for less than half of revenues, so the high-vitamin items do account for more than half of revenues.

Alternatively, eyeball the bars for the high-vitamin items. If you approximate or round down and the sum is still greater than 50%, the statement must be true.

$$C > 5\%$$
$$L > 15\%$$
$$O > 15\%$$
$$\underline{T > 15\%}$$
$$\text{sum} > 50\%$$

Even if you round each bar down to the closest grid line, the sum is still 50%. The longest bar is actually closer to 20%, so this sum will definitely cross the 50% threshold. Therefore, the third statement is *Justified*.

The answers are as follows:

Justified	Not justified	
◉	○	Some of Produce Stand P's lettuce may spoil or be in danger of spoiling before it is all sold.
○	◉	More bananas than apples are sold at Produce Stand P.
◉	○	Produce high in vitamin A, vitamin C, or both accounted for more than half of April revenues at Produce Stand P.

Try the second question:

In the month of April, Produce Stand P generated approximately how much revenue, in dollars, from items that were high in both vitamin A and vitamin C?

(A) $775

(B) $1,280

(C) $1,575

(D) $2,080

(E) $2,875

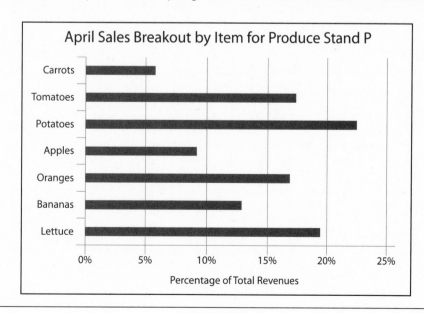

Sales Breakout | Vitamin Content

E-mail from Purchasing Supervisor to Sales Manager:

Total April sales for your produce stand were $4,441; the itemized data is below.

We already know that customers base their purchasing decisions on whether something is in season and how much it costs. Management believes that customers also care about the health factor, such as how high the vitamin content is for different types of produce. Do you have any data that could help us to evaluate this question?

We also need to think about pricing strategies in light of the fact that some items have a far longer shelf life. Potatoes will last weeks in cold storage, while the tomatoes won't last more than a few days without suffering a reduction in quality. Please send me any information you have about spoilage rates or other factors we should consider when setting prices.

April Sales Breakout by Item for Produce Stand P

Sales Breakout	Vitamin Content

E-mail from Sales Manager to Purchasing Supervisor:

Carrots, apples, and potatoes last a very long time in cold storage. I am a bit concerned about the lettuce, though; our farmers generally produce a higher volume of lettuce than of any other single item. The other items generally sell within acceptable time frames, even the tomatoes and bananas.

Customers do sometimes ask about the vitamin and nutrient content of various items. Maybe I should post the data on the pricing signs? Here's some data on the vitamin A and vitamin C content of our produce:

Vitamin Content of Produce Items Sold at Produce Stand P in April		
	Vitamin C content	*Vitamin A content*
Apples	low	low
Bananas	medium	low
Carrots	low	high
Lettuce	high	low
Oranges	high	medium
Potatoes	medium	low
Tomatoes	high	high

I also have research indicating that organic produce has a higher vitamin content than non-organic counterparts. I think that could be a very valuable marketing point.

First, make sure you understand the question. You'll need to find items that are high in *both* vitamins A and C (*not* items high in just one or the other).

Second, what's the plan? You'll need to use *Vitamin Content* to find those items high in both vitamin A and C. To calculate the revenue, add up the percentages of sales for the relevant items and then multiply by the dollar figure given for total sales in the first paragraph of the *Sales Breakout* tab. Lay these steps out on your scratch paper.

Finally, go ahead and solve. Only tomatoes are high in *both* vitamins A and C. Tomatoes accounted for approximately 17% to 18% of total revenues (glance at those answers; you don't need to be very precise), so pull up the calculator and plug in this calculation: $0.17 \times 4{,}400 = 748$.

The closest match in the answers is $775. The correct answer is (A).

If you feel comfortable working by hand, the answers are far enough apart to estimate pretty roughly. For example, 10% of $4,441 is about $444, so 20% is about $888. The answer has to be close to but less than $888; only answer (A) matches.

Review and Improve on MSR

If you answer a question incorrectly, aren't fully confident about a correct answer, or just think it took longer than it could have, review each step of the UPS process.

Understand: Did you overlook, misunderstand, or fail to comprehend any information in the prompt? How was your map—should you have included something that you didn't write down, or did you get too far into the detail? Did you miss any connections between different tabs or pieces of information? Did you answer the question that was asked?

What about your plan? Was there an easier or more efficient way to approach the problem? And did you make any mistakes at the solution stage, or just do more work than you really needed to do?

Try another MSR problem set to test your skills. This time, you'll do all three questions first. A word of warning: The prompt is extremely technical. Often, when this happens, the questions themselves *don't* require you to dive very deeply into the technical details. Use that knowledge to your advantage as you work through this problem set.

Ready? Set a timer for 8 minutes and go!

| Proposal | Purpose | Budget |

The government of Storinia has proposed to conduct three particle physics experiments in Antarctica, as described below.

The *ultra-high-energy cosmic ray detector* (UHECR-D) will track a variety of subatomic particles with exceptionally high kinetic energy traveling from outer space by recording secondary showers of particles created by these UHECRs as they collide with the upper atmosphere of Earth.

The *polyethylene naphthalate neutrino observatory* (PEN-NO) will search for neutrinos, extremely light and fast subatomic particles that interact only weakly with normal matter. To prevent false-positive results from cosmic rays, PEN-NO will be buried deep below the ice.

The *magnetic monopole detector* (MaMoD) will attempt to verify the existence of magnetic monopoles, hypothetical subatomic particles that some physical theories postulate are left over from the creation of the universe.

| Proposal | Purpose | Budget |

The purpose of UHECR-D is to ascertain the identity, composition, and extraterrestrial origin of ultra-high-energy cosmic rays, which are much less prevalent and well-understood than lower-energy cosmic rays. PEN-NO will measure the mass and speed of neutrinos produced in particle accelerators and nuclear reactors, both to reduce uncertainty in the known mass of a neutrino and to contribute to the resolution of a recent challenge to Einstein's theory of relativity posed by the observation of neutrinos supposedly traveling slightly faster than light. PEN-NO will also measure the passage of solar and other neutrinos of astronomical origin. Finally, if MaMoD is successful in its search, it will provide experimental proof for Dirac's explanation of charge quantization and fix an asymmetry in Maxwell's equations of electromagnetism.

| Proposal | Purpose | Budget |

The government of Storinia projects that it will cost $42 million in total and take 2 years to construct UHECR-D, PEN-NO, and MaMoD. The government also projects that once construction is finished, the annual operating budget for each experiment will be $3.6 million for UHECR-D, $4.3 million for PEN-NO, and $2.7 million for MaMoD. All these figures are in real 2015 dollars (removing the effect of predicted inflation).

1. For each of the following statements, select *Yes* if the statement is supported by the evidence provided. Otherwise, select *No*.

Yes	No	
O	O	With a construction budget of $30 million, the Storinian government will be able to search for proof of an explanation of charge quantization and help resolve a controversy by measuring the speed of neutrinos produced in nuclear reactors.
O	O	In its Antarctic experiments, the Storinian government will attempt to ascertain the mass and speed of cosmic rays.
O	O	If the PEN-NO experiment operates on the surface of the ice in Antarctica, its findings will be considered more valid than those produced by the experiment as currently envisioned.

2. According to the information provided, the proposed measurement of which of the following kinds of particles is intended to improve the estimate of the mass of these particles?

   (A) Ultra-high-energy cosmic rays
   (B) Particles created by UHECRs above the Earth
   (C) Neutrinos produced in nuclear reactors
   (D) Neutrinos that originate in the Sun
   (E) Magnetic monopoles

3. For each of the following particle types, select *Can conclude* if you can conclude from the information provided that the particles in question have a negligible effect on ordinary matter. Otherwise, select *Cannot conclude*.

Can conclude	Cannot conclude	
O	O	Ultra-high-energy cosmic rays
O	O	Neutrinos produced in particle accelerators
O	O	Magnetic monopoles

How did it go? Before reading the following explanations, review your work yourself.

Where are you confident and where are you unsure? What felt cumbersome to analyze or process, and can you think of any way to make that cumbersome part easier? Do you want to re-try any of the problems? Go ahead. This time, you don't even need to time yourself. Take as much time as you want.

Next, check the correct answers but nothing else. (You'll have to scroll down a bit—we didn't want to give away the answers too soon.) Does knowing the answers give you any ideas about what else to try—or what might have gone wrong—on any part of any problem? If so, dig in to see whether you can figure things out on your own. Whenever you can do this, you'll remember the lesson a lot more easily.

Finally, start to read through the explanation, but stop as soon as you read something that gives you an idea. Try to push that idea as far as you can before you go back to the explanation for more. Again, the more you can figure out for yourself, the easier it will be for you to remember and reuse what you're learning in future.

Step 1: Understand the Prompt and Question

The long-hand text below summarizes what someone might *think* while reading each tab—but don't write all this down. A sample map is shown at the end.

Proposal tab:

> Storinia is planning 3 experiments in Antarctica.
>
> I don't understand a lot of these words. That's okay—ignore them.
>
> (Glancing down.) One paragraph per experiment. Right now, I just need a basic understanding. Hopefully I won't ever need to really understand this detail.
>
> #1 is something about outer space coming to Earth.
>
> #2 will be buried in ice.
>
> #3 is something about magnetic something that has to do with the creation of the universe.

Purpose tab:

> The name of the tab is Purpose, so presumably they're going to tell me the purpose of at least some of these experiments.
>
> (Glancing down.) All three acronyms are listed in this paragraph.
>
> The details here are really hard. Big picture only.
>
> #1 is something about a certain type of cosmic ray that isn't well understood—what is it, what's it made of, where it comes from.
>
> #2 involves learning more about neutrinos and something about Einstein's theory of relativity.
>
> #3 is searching for something; if successful, it will prove one theory and fix another.

Budget tab:

> What the experiments will cost and how long they'll take to start.
>
> Also provides annual operating costs for each one.

Here is one version of a map for this prompt. The first line of the first tab indicates that it will discuss three experiments, so consider using a table to organize the information by experiment and by tab.

Exp	T1 Prop	T2 Purp	T3 Budg
UHECR-D	space to Earth	made of? come from? high-energy cosmic ray	$3.6m annual
PEN-NO	neutrinos below ice	mass and speed Einstein relativity	$4.3m ann
MaMoD	exist? creation of universe	prove D's theory (CQ) fix M's eqns	$2.7m ann
All			$42m initial 2 yrs

When numbers are presented in a table or graph, don't jot them down. Just go back and look at the data as needed. But where there are a few numbers scattered throughout the written text, as in tab 3, consider jotting those down.

At this stage, you *maybe* feel comfortable with about half of what you read. That's actually what you want! Don't get too bogged down in possibly-never-to-be-used details right now. You'll figure out the details you need as you work through the questions.

For instance, part of *UHECR-D* does stand for *high-energy cosmic ray*, but the significance of these words doesn't really become apparent until the *Purpose* tab—so you might not write them down until you get to that point. Or you might not even notice unless or until you get asked a question about that.

Here are all of the correct answers to this question set:

> Question 1: No, No, No
>
> Question 2: (C)
>
> Question 3: Cannot, Can, Cannot

Ideas about how to improve? Test them out yourself before you continue on with the explanations.

1. For each of the following statements, select *Yes* if the statement is supported by the evidence provided. Otherwise, select *No*.

The question asks whether, using information from the tabs, you can support, or prove true, the given statements.

Glance through them to see whether the statements are related in any way. They are not, so solve each one individually.

This kind of question is basically a "search and match" exercise. Read the statement first, then use your map to figure out where to look in the tabs to try to prove the statement. Here is the first statement:

Yes	No	
○	○	With a construction budget of $30 million, the Storinian government will be able to search for proof of an explanation of charge quantization and help resolve a controversy by measuring the speed of neutrinos produced in nuclear reactors.

The overall construction budget was $42m, so $30m is a subset of this budget. The question is asking whether this subset will be sufficient to accomplish only a certain part of the job. Which part?

Step 2: Plan Your Approach

Wait! Before you get into the annoying technical details of that part of the job, review the monetary information you were given. Tab 3 provides the *annual* budget to operate each separate experiment, but the initial *construction* budget was never split up by experiment—it's $42m for all three together. No information is given to allow you to assume, for example, that each will cost roughly the same to construct or, alternatively, that the ratio of construction costs will mirror the ratio of operating costs. The facilities for any one experiment could cost more or less than $30m to construct.

Step 3: Solve the Problem

That's it! The answer to the first statement is *No*: This is not supported by the given evidence.

If you messed anything up, pinpoint the specific mistake(s) and figure out what you could do differently to avoid that mistake in the future.

Alternatively, maybe you answered this correctly but realize in hindsight that you spent more time than necessary to do so. How could you save time next time? For instance, if you spent time digging into the detail on the experiments before realizing that you didn't need any of that to address the statement, then remind yourself next time to slow down and apply the process. Understand and plan before you try to solve.

Repeat your review of all three steps as you work through the second statement:

Yes	No	
○	○	In its Antarctic experiments, the Storinian government will attempt to ascertain the mass and speed of cosmic rays.

Hmm. All three experiments take place in the Antarctic. This question is asking whether one certain thing is planned for one of these experiments.

This time you do have to get a bit more into the details. You've got two different sets of key words you could go with: either *mass and speed* or *cosmic rays*. Glance at your map.

And here's where your first big clue comes in! *Cosmic rays* are the first experiment, but *mass and speed* go with the second experiment. It looks like this choice might be a **Mix-Up** trap: It mixes up text from two different parts of the prompt, creating a statement that the passage didn't actually say.

Here's the sentence on cosmic rays:

> *The purpose of UHECR-D is to ascertain the identity, composition, and extraterrestrial origin of ultra-high-energy cosmic rays, which are much less prevalent and well-understood than lower-energy cosmic rays.*

This sentence says nothing about either *mass* or *speed*.

It's enough to check only the part that discusses cosmic rays, since the statement does specify this type of particle. But you can also check the part that describes the second experiment:

> *PEN-NO will measure the mass and speed of neutrinos produced in particle accelerators and nuclear reactors, both to reduce uncertainty in the known mass of a neutrino and to contribute to the resolution of a recent challenge to Einstein's theory of relativity posed by the observation of neutrinos supposedly traveling slightly faster than light. PEN-NO will also measure the passage of solar and other neutrinos of astronomical origin.*

Mass and speed are mentioned, but not *cosmic rays*. This part is all about something called a neutrino.

Indeed, this is a mix-up trap! They jammed together information about two different types of particles, hoping that people would remember reading about both *cosmic rays* and *mass and speed* and just assume that this meant the statement could be supported. If you fell for this trap, this is a good reminder to make sure that you check the proof in the source material—every time! Don't just rely on your memory; the test writers know people do this and they set traps accordingly.

The correct answer for the second statement is *No*: The statement is not supported by the given information.

Here's the third statement:

Yes	No	
○	○	If the PEN-NO experiment operates on the surface of the ice in Antarctica, its findings will be considered more valid than those produced by the experiment as currently envisioned.

This problem explicitly mentions the second experiment—great. The statement asks whether changing a certain condition (operating *on the surface of the ice*) would lead to a better outcome. Glance at your map. The first tab mentioned something about being *below the ice*. Go back and scan for that text.

> *To prevent false-positive results from cosmic rays, PEN-NO will be buried deep below the ice.*

It was a conscious choice, then, to conduct the experiment below the ice: Doing so will prevent a certain bad outcome. If that is the case, then moving the experiment to the surface of the ice might allow that bad outcome to occur, so the results would *not* be better.

The correct answer for the third statement is *No*: This is not supported by the information given in the prompt.

The third statement was similar to an Inference question. The passage doesn't say outright that conducting the experiment on the surface wouldn't be as beneficial. Rather, you have to infer from the stated information to arrive at that conclusion.

18

Here are the correct answers for the first question:

1. For each of the following statements, select *Yes* if the statement is supported by the evidence provided. Otherwise, select *No*.

Yes	No	
○	◉	With a construction budget of $30 million, the Storinian government will be able to search for proof of an explanation of charge quantization and help resolve a controversy by measuring the speed of neutrinos produced in nuclear reactors.
○	◉	In its Antarctic experiments, the Storinian government will attempt to ascertain the mass and speed of cosmic rays.
○	◉	If the PEN-NO experiment operates on the surface of the ice in Antarctica, its findings will be considered more valid than those produced by the experiment as currently envisioned.

UPS Redux

Repeat the process with the second question. This one is a standard multiple-choice problem:

2. According to the information provided, the proposed measurement of which of the following kinds of particles is intended to improve the estimate of the mass of these particles?

    (A) Ultra-high-energy cosmic rays

    (B) Particles created by UHECRs above the Earth

    (C) Neutrinos produced in nuclear reactors

    (D) Neutrinos that originate in the Sun

    (E) Magnetic monopoles

This problem asks for a certain kind of particle that fits the question information. Glance at the answers—the first two are cosmic rays, the next two are neutrinos, and the last is magnetic monopoles. So the first thing to figure out is this: Which experiment is the question referring to?

The particles are going to be measured and that measurement is going to *improve the estimate of the mass.* That is, measure the particles and get a better idea of the mass of those particles.

Glance at your map. The second experiment, PEN-NO, talked about the mass of particles, so start there. The particles for this experiment are neutrinos, so it looks like the answer will probably be (C) or (D), but dive into the text to confirm this.

> *PEN-NO will measure the mass and speed of neutrinos produced in particle accelerators and nuclear reactors, both to reduce uncertainty in the known mass of a neutrino and to . . .*
> *PEN-NO will also measure the passage of solar and other neutrinos of astronomical origin.*

First, it is the neutrinos: *Reduce uncertainty in the known mass* is a synonym for *improve the estimate of the mass.* Eliminate answers (A), (B), and (E) for talking about the wrong type of particle. The next sentence does mention solar neutrinos but says only that the experiment will measure the *passage* of these neutrinos, not their mass.

The correct answer is (C): neutrinos produced in nuclear reactors.

While the answer choices for this question appear to imply that you have to get into all of the technical detail, you really don't have to go very far. The key word *mass* allows you to narrow down to two answers pretty quickly. And choosing between just two answers is not nearly as hard as evaluating all five.

Back to either-or for the third problem:

> 3. For each of the following particle types, select *Can conclude* if you can conclude from the information provided that the particles in question have a negligible effect on ordinary matter. Otherwise, select *Cannot conclude*.

Each of the statements accompanying the question stem is one of the three types of particles discussed in the prompt: Ultra-high-energy cosmic rays, neutrinos produced in particle accelerators, and magnetic monopoles. This question asks whether the information given in the prompt allows you to conclude that each type of particle has *a negligible effect on ordinary matter*.

What does *a negligible effect on ordinary matter* even mean? In general, if you don't really understand the question, don't move to plan or solve. Just guess and move on.

If you do want to tackle this problem, a *negligible* effect means an unimportant or minor effect. Next, where could that information be? The third tab was all about budget, so it won't be there. The first tab describes the particles themselves and the second describes the experiments. The desired information could be in either tab, so start with the first tab.

The first tab discusses cosmic rays but says nothing about ordinary matter. Flip over to the second tab. The first sentence provides more information about cosmic rays but still says nothing about ordinary matter, so you *cannot conclude* anything about the effect cosmic rays have on ordinary matter.

Go back to the first tab to see what it says about *neutrinos produced in particle accelerators*. This tab says that neutrinos in general *interact only weakly with normal matter*. That almost matches what the question stem says—it's not a very important effect. In this case, you *can conclude* that *neutrinos produced in particle accelerators* have a *negligible effect on ordinary matter*.

Finally, check what the text says about *magnetic monopoles*. The first tab doesn't mention ordinary matter in connection with these particles, nor does the second tab. As a result, you *cannot conclude* anything about the effect magnetic monopoles have on ordinary matter. Here are the correct answers for the third question:

> 3. For each of the following particle types, select *Can conclude* if you can conclude from the information provided that the particles in question have a negligible effect on ordinary matter. Otherwise, select *Cannot conclude*.

Can conclude	Cannot conclude	
○	●	Ultra-high-energy cosmic rays
●	○	Neutrinos produced in particle accelerators
○	●	Magnetic monopoles

That was a very challenging MSR prompt. Here are some things that might help you with something similar next time.

18

First, while the tabs did have extremely detailed scientific information, you didn't have to become an expert in particle physics in order to answer all of the questions. The technical language was often just window dressing. For instance, in problem 1, the first statement mentions all kinds of details (*charge quantization*??), but all you needed to know was that the prompt didn't provide any information regarding how much each of the three experiments would cost separately to build. Likewise, you can get through the second and third statements of the first question without having to understand all of the details.

The third question was pretty challenging—even the question stem itself was hard to parse. When you realize that you don't understand what the question is saying or asking, that's an excellent clue to get out. Guess randomly and move on! You'll need to do this multiple times in each section in order to get through the GMAT on time.

If you do feel okay with this subject matter, great! Even then, it's possible to answer the questions correctly without understanding every last detail. In the third question, the one statement that did match used close synonyms (e.g., *ordinary matter* in the question and *normal matter* in the prompt). The descriptions for the other two particles don't mention any kind of interactions with any matter at all. The test writers want to see whether you can read around the scary technical language and still process the high-level information.

This fits a lot of what happens in the real world, too. You run up against some really technical detail at work, and you may have to understand it well enough to make a high-level business call about something—but you don't suddenly have to become an expert about this technical thing. Expect that to happen on MSR as well.

Finally, when you're done answering any question, your learning has just begun. Take the time to pick apart the prompt, the question, and your own reasoning in order to get better the next time you tackle an intricate MSR question.

And remember: Getting better also involves knowing what *not* to do so that you can guess and move on quickly. Use that precious time to better advantage elsewhere in the section!

Practice Your Skills

Log into your Manhattan Prep online account for additional MSR practice problems. Give yourself a block of time to do an entire MSR prompt plus three problems—review after you're done with the whole question set for that prompt, not after each problem.

Statistics

In This Chapter...

- Averages

- Using the Average Formula

- Median: The Middle Number

- Standard Deviation

In this chapter, you will learn how to calculate averages in a variety of situations, as well as how to lay out median problems and how to logic your way through standard deviation problems.

CHAPTER 19 **Statistics**

The most common statistics, or stats, you'll need to deal with on the GMAT are averages and median, both of which you'll learn about in this chapter, and weighted average, which is covered in the next chapter.

You may also see questions about standard deviation, range, or mode on the exam, although these are somewhat less common. You'll learn about standard deviation in this chapter.

The **range** of a set is equal to the difference in value between the greatest and least numbers in that set. For example, in the set {1, 2, 5, 6, 11}, the range is $11 - 1 = 10$.

The **mode** of a set is the number that appears most frequently. For example, in the set {1, 3, 3, 6, 8}, the mode is 3 because it appears twice in the set while the other values each appear just once.

Averages

The **average** (or the **arithmetic mean**) of a set is given by the following formula:

$$\text{Average} = \frac{\text{Sum}}{\text{\# of terms}}, \text{ which is abbreviated as } A = \frac{S}{n}.$$

The sum, S, refers to the sum of all the terms in the set.

The number, n, refers to the number of terms that are in the set.

The average, A, refers to the average value (arithmetic mean) of the terms in the set.

The language in an average problem will often refer to an arithmetic mean. However, occasionally, the concept is implied. "The cost per employee, if equally shared, is \$20" means that the *average* cost per employee is \$20. Likewise, the "per capita income" is the average income per person in an area.

Here's a commonly used variation of the average formula:

$$\text{Average} \times \text{Number of terms} = \text{Sum, or } A \times n = S$$

Using the Average Formula

Every GMAT problem dealing with averages can be solved using some form of the average formula. In general, if the average is unknown, the first formula, $A = \frac{S}{n}$, will solve the problem more directly. If the average is known, the second formula, $A \times n = S$, is better.

When you see any GMAT average problem, write down the average formula. Then, fill in any of the three variables (S, n, and A) that are given in the problem. Try an example:

> The sum of 6 numbers is 90. What is the average of the numbers?

$A = \frac{S}{n}$ The sum, S, is given as 90. The number of terms, n, is given as 6.

By plugging in, you can solve for the average: $\frac{90}{6} = 15$.

Notice that you do *not* need to know each term in the set to find the average!

Sometimes, using the average formula will be more involved. For example:

> If the average of the set {2, 5, 5, 7, 8, 9, x} is 6.1, what is the value of x?

Plug the given information into the average formula, and solve for x:

$$A \times n = S \qquad (6.1)(7 \text{ terms}) = 2 + 5 + 5 + 7 + 8 + 9 + x$$

$$42.7 = 36 + x$$

$$6.7 = x$$

More complex average problems involve setting up two average formulas. For example:

> Sam earned a $2,000 commission on a big sale, raising his average commission by $100. If Sam's new average commission is $900, how many sales has he made?

To keep track of two average formulas in the same problem, you can set up a table. Sam's new average commission is $900, and this is $100 higher than his old average, so his old average was $800.

Note that the Number and Sum columns add up to give the new cumulative values, but the values in the Average column do *not* add up:

	Average	×	Number	=	Sum
Old total	800	×	n	=	$800n$
This sale	2,000	×	1	=	2,000
New total	900	×	$n + 1$	=	$900(n + 1)$
	DON'T add vertically		add vertically		add vertically

The right-hand (Sum) column gives the equation you need:

$$800n + 2,000 = 900(n + 1)$$

$$800n + 2,000 = 900n + 900$$

$$1,100 = 100n$$

$$11 = n$$

Since you are looking for the new number of sales, which is $n + 1$, Sam has made a total of 12 sales.

19

Median: The Middle Number

Some GMAT problems feature another stats concept: The **median**, or middle value in a list of values placed in increasing order. The median is calculated in one of two ways, depending on the number of data points in the set:

1. For sets containing an *odd* number of values, the median is the *unique middle value* when the data are arranged in increasing (or decreasing) order. For example, the median of the set {5, 17, 24, 25, 28} is the unique middle number, 24.

2. For sets containing an *even* number of values, the median is the *average (arithmetic mean) of the two middle values* when the data are arranged in increasing (or decreasing) order. For example, the median of the set {3, 4, 9, 9} is the mean of the two middle values (4 and 9), or 6.5.

Notice that the median of a set containing an *odd* number of values must be an actual value in the set. However, the median of a set containing an *even* number of values does not have to be in the set—and indeed will not be, unless the two middle values are equal.

Medians of Sets Containing Unknown Values

Unlike the arithmetic mean, the median of a set depends only on the one or two values in the middle of the ordered set. Therefore, you may be able to determine a specific value for the median of a set *even if one or more unknowns are present*.

For example, consider the unordered set {x, 2, 5, 11, 11, 12, 33}. No matter whether x is less than 11, equal to 11, or greater than 11, the median of the resulting set will be 11. (Try substituting different values of x to see why the median does not change.)

By contrast, the median of the unordered set {x, 2, 5, 11, 12, 12, 33} depends on x. If x is 11 or less, the median is 11. If x is between 11 and 12, the median is x. Finally, if x is 12 or more, the median is 12.

Standard Deviation

The mean and median both give *average* or *representative* values for a set, but they do not tell the whole story. It is possible for two sets to have the same average but to differ widely in how spread out their values are. For example, both of these sets have an average and median of 5: {2, 4, 6, 8} and {0, 0, 10, 10}.

To describe the spread, or variation, of the data in a set, use a different measure: the **Standard Deviation** (SD).

Standard deviation indicates how far from the average (mean) the data points typically fall. Therefore:

- A small SD indicates that a set is clustered closely around the average (arithmetic mean) value. In the two sets given earlier, the set {2, 4, 6, 8} has the smaller SD.

- A large SD indicates that the set is spread out widely, with some points appearing far from the mean. In the two sets given earlier, the set {0, 0, 10, 10} has the larger SD.

What about the set {5, 5, 5, 5}? When a set contains all the same value, the numbers are not spread out at all, so the SD is 0.

For most sets, even if you know both the average and the SD of a set, you cannot tell what the numbers are in that set. Multiple possible combinations of numbers can result in the same average and the same SD. The exception is any set with an SD of 0. For example, if the SD is 0 and the average is 13, then all of the members of that set must equal 13. (You still don't know, though, how many instances of 13 are in the set; there might be 1 or 1,000.)

	Set 1	Set 2	Set 3
Mean = 5 Median = 5	{5, 5, 5, 5}	{2, 4, 6, 8}	{0, 0, 10, 10}
Difference from the mean of 5 (in absolute terms)	{0, 0, 0, 0} SD = 0 An SD of 0 means that all the numbers in the set are equal.	{3, 1, 1, 3} moderately spread out SD = moderate (technically, SD = $\sqrt{5} \approx 2.24$ but you won't have to calculate this!)	{5, 5, 5, 5} more spread out (technically, SD = 5) If every absolute difference from the mean is equal, then the SD equals that difference.

You might be asking how to calculate the $\sqrt{5}$ shown as the SD for the second set. The good news is that you do not need to know—the GMAT will not ask you to calculate a specific SD unless a shortcut exists, such as knowing that the SD is 0 if all of the numbers in the set are identical. If you just pay attention to what the *average spread* is doing, you'll be able to answer all GMAT standard deviation problems, which involve either (1) *changes* in the SD when a set is transformed or (2) *comparisons* of the SDs of two or more sets. Just remember that the more spread out the numbers, the larger the SD.

If you see a problem focusing on changes in the SD, ask yourself whether the changes move the data closer to the mean, farther from the mean, or neither. If you see a problem requiring comparisons, ask yourself which set is more spread out from its mean.

Following are some sample problems to help illustrate SD properties:

1. Which set has the greater standard deviation: {1, 2, 3, 4, 6} or {441, 442, 443, 444, 445}?

2. If each data point in a set is increased by 7, does the set's standard deviation increase, decrease, or remain constant?

3. If each data point in a set is increased by a factor of 7, does the set's standard deviation increase, decrease, or remain constant? (Assume that the set consists of different numbers.)

Answers and explanations follow on the next page. ▶ ▶ ▶

Answer Key

1. **The first set has the greater SD.** One way to understand this is to observe that the gaps between its numbers are, on average, slightly bigger than the gaps in the second set (because the last two numbers in the first set are 2 units apart, while the numbers in the second set are all only one unit apart, including the final two values in the set). Another way to resolve the issue is to observe that the set {441, 442, 443, 444, 445} would have the same standard deviation as {1, 2, 3, 4, 5}. Replacing 5 with 6, which is farther from the mean, will increase the SD of that set.

2. **The SD will not change.** "Increased by 7" means that the number 7 is *added* to each data point in the set. This transformation will not affect any of the gaps between the data points, and thus it will not affect how far the data points are from the mean. If the set were plotted on a number line, this transformation would merely slide the points 7 units to the right, taking all the gaps and the mean along with them.

3. **The SD will increase.** "Increased by a *factor* of 7" means that each data point is *multiplied* by 7. This transformation will make all the gaps between points 7 times as big as they originally were. Thus, each point will fall 7 times as far from the mean. The SD will increase by a factor of 7. Why did the problem specify that the set consists of different numbers? If each data point in the set was the same, then the SD would be 0. Multiplying each data point by 7 would still result in a set of identical numbers and an identical SD of 0.

19

Problem Set

Now that you've finished the chapter, try the following problems.

1. The average (arithmetic mean) of 11 numbers is 10. When one number is eliminated, the average of the remaining numbers is 9.3. What is the eliminated number?

2. Given the set of numbers {4, 5, 5, 6, 7, 8, 21}, how much higher is the mean than the median?

3. For an entire class of students, the mean score on a test was 60, and the standard deviation was 15. If Eike's score was within 2 standard deviations of the mean, what is the lowest score Eike could have received?

4. Matt earned a $1,000 commission on a big sale, raising his average commission by $150. If Matt's new average commission is $400, how many sales has he made?

Save the following problems for review after you finish this entire guide.

5. If the average of x and y is 50, and the average of y and z is 80, what is the value of $z - x$?
   (A) 20
   (B) 30
   (C) 50
   (D) 60
   (E) 80

6. The median price of all houses sold in the Seaside Hills neighborhood last year was $450,000. Was the average (arithmetic mean) price of the houses sold last year greater than $400,000?
   (1) The most expensive house sold in Seaside Hills last year was sold for $800,000.
   (2) Exactly three houses were sold in Seaside Hills last year.

Solutions

1. **17:** If the average of 11 numbers is 10, their sum is $11 \times 10 = 110$. After one number is eliminated, the average is 9.3, so the sum of the 10 remaining numbers is $10 \times 9.3 = 93$. The number eliminated is the difference between these sums: $110 - 93 = 17$.

2. **2:** The mean of the set is the sum of the numbers divided by the number of terms. First, group numbers to make it easier to add them up. For example, $4 + 6 = 10$, $5 + 5 = 10$ and $7 + 8 = 15$. The mean is $56 \div 7 = 8$. The median is the middle number in the set, which is 6. The difference between the two numbers is 2.

3. **30:** Eike's score was within 2 standard deviations of the mean. Since 1 standard deviation is 15, her score is no more than $15 \times 2 = 30$ points from the mean. The lowest possible score she could have received, then, is $60 - 30$, which is equal to 30.

4. **5:** For this kind of problem, you can do your calculations just in terms of the "extra" money that Matt made, over his prior average.

    Before the big sale, Matt's average commission was $250. For the big sale, he got a commission of $1,000. Count the first $250 toward his original average and the other $750 as his "extra" money. If he hadn't made any extra money, then his average would have stayed at $250. But he did make $750 extra, so how does that impact the average?

    Imagine that, prior to the big sale, Matt had made exactly one other sale. Then, the big sale with an extra $750 would increase his average across two sales by $\frac{750}{2} = 375$. His average actually increased by only $150, so he must have made more than two sales. If he had had two prior sales with an average of $250, then adding the extra $750 from the third sale would increase the average by $\frac{750}{3} = 250$. In short, you can calculate the increase in the average using this shortcut:

    $$\frac{\text{Extra Amount}}{\text{\# of Sales}} = \text{Increase in Average}$$

    In this problem, $\frac{750}{\text{\# of sales}} = 150$, so Matt had 5 total sales.

    Alternatively, you can solve algebraically. Before the big sale, Matt's average commission was $250, so the sum of the previous sales was $S = 250n$. After the sale, three things happened: The sum of Matt's commissions increased by $1,000, the number of sales he made increased by 1, and his average commission was $400. Express this algebraically with the following equation:

    $$S + 1,000 = 400(n + 1)$$
    $$250n + 1,000 = 400(n + 1)$$
    $$250n + 1,000 = 400n + 400$$
    $$150n = 600$$
    $$n = 4$$

    Before the big commission, Matt had made 4 sales. Including the big commission, Matt made 5 sales.

5. **(D) 60:** This is an interesting hybrid problem. At first glance, it may seem like a candidate for working backwards, since the answers are real numbers. However, it asks for a relative value: the difference between z and x. In this case, you can choose smart numbers for the values of the individual variables, as long as those numbers make the given facts true.

    Let $x = 40$ and $y = 60$ (the average must be equal to 50). Next, the average of y and z must be 80. If $y = 60$, then z has to be 100. Therefore, $z - x = 100 - 40 = 60$.

    You can also solve algebraically, though that is more cumbersome on this problem. First, translate the given information:

    $$\frac{x + y}{2} = 50 \qquad \frac{y + z}{2} = 80$$

    The first equation can be rearranged to give $x = 100 - y$. The second equation can be rearranged to give $z = 160 - y$. Plug the information into $z - x$ and solve:

    $$\begin{aligned} z - x &= (160 - y) - (100 - y) \\ &= 160 - y - 100 + y \\ &= 160 - 100 \\ &= 60 \end{aligned}$$

6. **(C):** The question stem provides information about a median for a data set and asks whether the average of the same data set was greater than $400,000, which can be abbreviated $400K. When you're given a median, it's often a good idea to draw out dashes for each item in the set (e.g., for a three-item set: __ __ __), but this question stem doesn't indicate how many items are in the set. And that's your first clue as to how to think about this information.

    If the set contains exactly one item, then that item is $450K and the average is also $450K. If the set contains two items, then the two items must again average to $450K, since the median of a two-item set is found by averaging the two items. So if you know that the set has one or two items, then the average matches the median ($450K).

    If the set contains exactly three items, then the middle item is $450K, but the least expensive item could be anything between 0 and $450K and the most-expensive item could be anything from $450K to infinity. That flexibility would allow an average below or above $400K. The same will be true for a four-item set, a five-item set, and so on. If the set has three or more items, then you'd have to be given more information in order to be able to find the average.

    Glance at the statements. Begin with statement (2) on this one.

    (2) INSUFFICIENT: Three houses were sold, but no additional information is given. It's not possible, therefore, to calculate anything about the average price for all three houses.

    (1) INSUFFICIENT: The most expensive house was $800K, but how many houses were sold? It could have been two, in which case the average equals the median, $450K. In this case, the answer to the question is Yes, the average is greater than $400K.

But there could also have been more houses sold. Imagine that five houses were sold for the following prices: $1, $1, $450K, $450K, and $800K. The average would be approximately $\frac{\$1,700K}{5}$. That value is less than $400K, so the answer is No. (For the average to be $400K, the numerator would have to be $2,000K.)

(1) AND (2) SUFFICIENT: If three houses (an odd number) were sold, then the median must be the price of one of the houses, so two of the three houses were sold for $450K and $800K, respectively. If the third house sold for $1 (almost the minimum, which is actually $0), the average would be $\frac{\$1 + \$450K + \$800K}{3}$. Is that value going to be greater than $400K or less than $400K? The sum of the prices is greater than $1,200K, so the average of the three prices is greater than $400K. This is the minimum average possible, so the answer is Always Yes.

The correct answer is **(C)**: The two statements are sufficient when used together, but neither one works alone.

Weighted Averages

In This Chapter...

- The Algebraic Method

- The Teeter-Totter Method

- Mixtures, Percents, and Ratios

In this chapter, you will learn how to recognize weighted average and mixture problems, and how to use both logical and algebraic approaches to solve.

CHAPTER 20 Weighted Averages

The concept of **weighted averages** will come up all the time in graduate school—and in the general business world. It's worth spending some extra time digging in to understand this topic. If you can get to the point that you can think logically about weighted averages, as this chapter shows, you'll be in a strong position to talk about similar quant topics in grad school and beyond.

The regular formula for averages, $A = \frac{S}{n}$, applies only to sets of data consisting of individual values that are equally weighted—that is, all of the values "count" equally toward the average. For example, if you earn 100 on one exam and 80 on another exam, an equally weighted average of your scores is 90.

Some averages, however, are weighted more heavily toward certain data points. For example, imagine that your teacher tells you that your midterm exam will count for 40% of your grade and your final exam will count for 60% of your grade. If you can score a perfect 100 on only one of those components, which one would you want it to be?

Your final exam, of course! It counts more heavily toward your final grade. Next, imagine that you score 100 on your final exam but only 80 on your midterm exam. What is the weighted average of those two scores?

Any average has to be between the two starting points, in this case 100 and 80. The *regular* average would be 90. Is the weighted average higher or lower than the regular average of 90?

The final exam counts for more than 50% of your final score, so the weighted average must be closer to the final exam score of 100 than to 80. The weighted average must be between 90 and 100.

That knowledge is usually enough to get you to the right answer on a Data Insights problem and it can often be enough to get to the right answer even on a Problem Solving problem. If you do need to calculate further, there are two ways to calculate the exact value: *algebraically* or via the *Teeter-Totter*.

The Algebraic Method

The **algebraic method** can be time-consuming with or without a calculator. It's usually only worth using if you have two data points and relatively easy numbers. It is worth *understanding*, though, because this will allow you to understand and remember the faster method introduced in the next section.

First, think about how a regular (nonweighted) average works. In a regular average, each item has exactly equal weight. For example, if there are two items, both are weighted $\frac{1}{2}$. If your teacher weighted your two exams equally, then this would be the calculation:

$$100\left(\frac{1}{2}\right) + 80\left(\frac{1}{2}\right) = 50 + 40 = 90$$

That is, the average is 90, exactly halfway between 80 and 100. The initial equation could be rearranged in this way:

$$100\left(\frac{1}{2}\right) + 80\left(\frac{1}{2}\right) = \frac{1}{2}(100 + 80) = \frac{100 + 80}{2}$$

Is that starting to look familiar? That's the average formula: Find the sum of the two numbers and divide by 2. Technically, regular averages all have these equal weightings, so you can always write the equation in the simplified form: $\dfrac{\text{Sum}}{\text{\# of terms}}$.

Weighted averages are solved using the same initial formula, but the weightings are not $\dfrac{1}{2}$ for each of the two terms.

You scored 100 on your final exam and it has a 60%, or $\dfrac{3}{5}$, weighting. You scored 80 on your midterm and it has a 40%, or $\dfrac{2}{5}$, weighting. Here's what that looks like:

$$100\left(\dfrac{3}{5}\right) + 80\left(\dfrac{2}{5}\right) = ?$$
$$60 + 32 = 92$$

The weighted average is 92.

If you're going to solve algebraically for a weighted average, you always have to use the "long" form of the average equation. You'll always have a component multiplied by its weighting, and then the next component multiplied by its weighting, and so on:

Weighted Average = (Component1)(Weighting1) + (Component2)(Weighting2)

You can have more than two components. The GMAT typically sticks to two or three.

The Teeter-Totter Method

The **Teeter-Totter method** is very efficient as long as you understand what a weighted average is and how the concept works in general. If you struggle with the concept, then you may want to stick with the algebraic method—and just guess if you get a complicated problem that's too annoying to solve algebraically.

The problem is the same: You scored 100 on your final exam and it has a $\dfrac{3}{5}$ weighting. You scored 80 on your midterm and it has a $\dfrac{2}{5}$ weighting. What is your final grade?

As with the algebraic method, begin by thinking about what would happen if you had two evenly weighted scores:

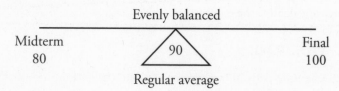

If you had a "regular" average, then the teeter-totter would be perfectly balanced and you would have an average of 90, halfway between 80 and 100.

In this case, though, you have a weighted average. Which way does the teeter-totter tilt?

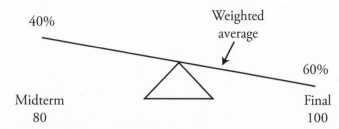

The final exam is weighted more heavily. The weighted average "slips" down toward the heavier end of the teeter-totter, so you know that the weighted average must be between 90 and 100. On problems that don't need you to actually calculate the average, for example, on Data Sufficiency (DS) questions, this could be enough!

On other math-based problems, you might have a mix of answers such as the following: 82, 90, 92, 98, 105. You can knock out 82, 90, and 105 immediately, since they aren't between 90 and 100.

The two remaining answers, 92 and 98, are at opposite ends of the possible spectrum. Look at the weightings you were given: Are they pretty close to the regular weighting of $\frac{1}{2}$ or 50/50? If so, then the answer should be closer to the regular average (90 in this case).

Or are the given weightings really far from the 50/50 regular average calculation? If so, then the answer should be farther away from the regular average.

In this problem, the weightings are $\frac{3}{5}$ and $\frac{2}{5}$, or 60/40. This is pretty close to the 50/50 case, so the answer should be closer to 90—and, indeed, 92 is the correct answer.

If you do have to calculate the exact weighted average, here's what you do: The two ends of the teeter-totter are 80 and 100, and the difference between them is 20. Write that down. The final exam has a weighting of 60%, so it is responsible for 60% of that length of 20. Find 60% of 20: It is equal to 12. The average will weigh down the 100 end of the teeter totter more:

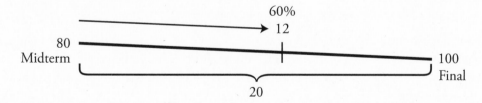

Therefore, the average is $80 + 12$, which sums to 92 (and this makes logical sense; the value is between 90 and 100).

You don't need to draw out a full teeter-totter, but do draw at least the sloped line. Use logic to know which side is heavier. Calculate the "length" of the line (the difference between the two ends) and use it to calculate the value of the heavier weighting (in this case, 12); then, add that weight to the lighter side to see how far it tilts the teeter-totter down to the heavier side.

20

Imagine the situation were reversed: The score of 80 had the 60% weighting and the score of 100 had only a 40% weighting. In this case, you would start from the lighter end of the teeter-totter (the 100 end) and subtract instead:

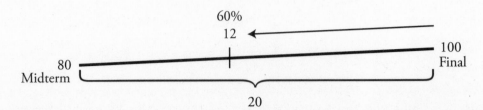

In this case, the average needs to be closer to the midterm end, so start from the higher (lighter) end, 100. Subtract from that end: $100 - 12 = 88$. Again, this makes logical sense: This time, the answer should be between 80 and 90.

In both cases, draw the sloped line and place the final number in roughly the appropriate position. That step will tell you which end is the lighter end and whether you'll need to add from the smaller end ($80 + 12$) or subtract from the larger end ($100 - 12$).

What if the problem changed the given information? Try this:

> You score 80 on your midterm exam and 100 on your final exam. Only these two exams make up your final grade of 92. How heavily did your teacher weight the final exam?

First, draw your teeter-totter:

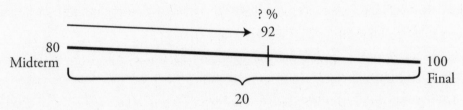

In this case, you still know the two end points (and the length), but now you're given the final average of 92 and you have to figure out the weighting that results in that average.

Because the weighted average is closer to 100 than to 80, you know that 100 is the heavier weight, so your final exam should be weighted more than 50%. But it shouldn't be a lot more, because 92 is not that much higher than the regular/unweighted average of 90. Depending on the answer choices, this might be enough to find the correct answer.

If you do need to calculate more precisely, find the longer of the two distances. In this case, that's between 80 and 92:

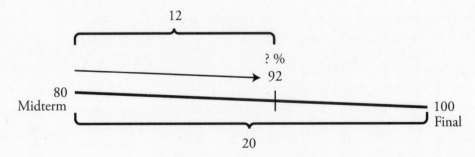

The weighting of the heavier (final exam) side is the fractional part 12 over the total length 20: $\frac{12}{20} = \frac{3}{5}$, which is equal to 60%.

If the problem had asked you to calculate the weighting of the *less*-heavily weighted value, the midterm exam, then you would find the *shorter* of the two distances, 8, and divide by the total distance, 20: $\frac{8}{20} = \frac{2}{5}$, which is equal to 40%.

Try this DS problem:

> The average number of students per class at School X is 25 and the average number of students per class at School Y is 33. Is the average number of students per class for both schools combined less than 29?
>
> (1) There are 12 classes in School X.
>
> (2) There are more classes in School X than in School Y.

Because this is a DS problem, there's a very good chance that you will not have to complete the calculations. In this case, try the teeter-totter method.

First, the question stem provides this information:

$$X \underset{25}{\overset{\text{(weight?)}}{\rule{8cm}{0.4pt}}} \underset{33}{\overset{\text{(weight?)}}{}} Y$$

You don't know how to tilt the teeter-totter, because you don't know enough information yet. The question itself, though, implies something very intriguing.

If the two schools are equally weighted, then the regular average would be 29. What would have to be true to make the average *less* than 29?

The teeter-totter would have to be tilted down toward School X; this school would be weighted more heavily. Keep this in mind as you examine the statements:

> (1) There are 12 classes in School X.

This statement doesn't provide any information about School Y, so it's impossible to tell whether one school is weighted more heavily. Statement (1) is not sufficient. Eliminate answers (A) and (D).

> (2) There are more classes in School X than in School Y.

If there are more classes over at School X, then the weighted average has to tilt down toward this school:

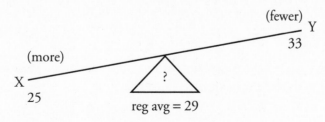

As a result, the weighted average has to be less than the regular average of 29.

Statement (2) is sufficient; the correct answer is (B).

On weighted average problems, you can choose whether to use the algebraic method or the teeter-totter method. The teeter-totter method is generally faster—*if* you really understand how weighted averages work. Try both methods out on some *GMAT Official Guide* problems and decide when you want to use each approach.

Mixtures, Percents, and Ratios

Percents and ratios can also show up in weighted average problems, particularly in the form of mixtures.

First, try this regular mixtures problem (you don't need to calculate a weighted average for this one):

> A 400 milliliter solution is 20% alcohol by volume. If 100 milliliters of water is added, what is the new concentration of alcohol, as a percent of volume?
>
> (A)   5%
> (B)   10%
> (C)   12%
> (D)   12.5%
> (E)   16%

To start, you have two liquid solutions: a 400 milliliter solution that is 20% alcohol and 80% something else and a 100 milliliter solution that is 100% water (and therefore 0% alcohol).

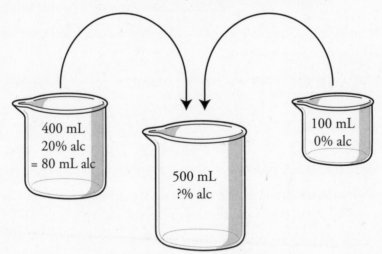

You can actually calculate the milliliters of alcohol in the 400 milliliter beaker: 20% of 400 is 80 milliliters. The 100 milliliter beaker doesn't contribute any alcohol at all, so the 500 milliliter beaker contains a total of 80 milliliters of alcohol. The big beaker, then, is $\frac{80}{500} = \frac{8}{50} = \frac{16}{100} = 16\%$ alcohol. The correct answer is (E).

In this case, only one of the two beakers contributed alcohol to the mixture. What happens when both parts of the problem contribute to the desired mixture?

Try this example:

> Kris-P cereal is 10% sugar by weight, whereas healthier but less delicious Bran-O cereal is 2% sugar by weight. To make a delicious and healthy mixture that is 4% sugar, what should be the ratio of Kris-P cereal to Bran-O cereal, by weight?
>
> (A) 1 : 2
>
> (B) 1 : 3
>
> (C) 1 : 4
>
> (D) 3 : 1
>
> (E) 4 : 1

You can use the algebraic method or the teeter-totter—your choice. Both solutions are shown below.

The question asks for a ratio. Note that you don't necessarily need to know the real values of something in order to find a ratio. Call the weight of Kris-P cereal, K, and the weight of Bran-O cereal, B.

To solve algebraically, set up an equation:

$$0.1K + 0.02B = 0.04(K + B)$$

Kris-P is weighted 10% and Bran-O is weighted 2%. The final mixture (the sum of the two components K and B) is weighted 4%.

Because the question asks for the ratio of K to B, manipulate the equation to solve for $\frac{K}{B}$. First, multiply the whole equation by 100 to get rid of the decimals. Then, simplify from there:

$$10K + 2B = 4(K + B)$$
$$10K + 2B = 4K + 4B$$
$$6K = 2B$$
$$\frac{K}{B} = \frac{2}{6} = \frac{1}{3}$$

The ratio of Kris-P to Bran-O is 1 : 3. The correct answer is (B).

To use your teeter-totter, start drawing:

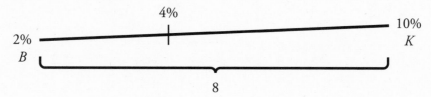

20

Because 4% is closer to 2%, the Bran-O side is heavier. Calculate the distance between the two ends: $10 - 2 = 8$. Finally, find the distances of the two subparts of the line:

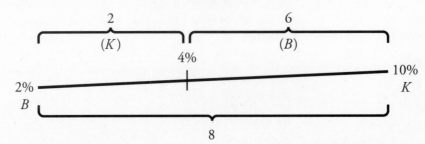

The smaller number, 2, is associated with the less-heavily weighted end (Kris-P, 10%). Note that the 10% K figure is on the other end of the teeter-totter; it will always be the case that the subpart is associated with the opposite end of the teeter-totter.

The larger number, 6, is associated with the more heavily weighted end (Bran-O, 2%). Again, it will always be the case that the subpart is associated with the opposite end of the teeter-totter.

Therefore, the ratio of Kris-P to Bran-O is 2 : 6, or 1 : 3, which is answer (B).

Try out both methods to see which works best for you in various circumstances.

20

Problem Set

Now that you've finished the chapter, try these problems.

1. Imani has won 40% of the first 25 poker games she played this week. If she wins 80% of the remaining games she plays this week, how many additional games must Imani play in order to win 60% of all games for the week?

2. Hot dog vendors sold an average of 66 hot dogs per stand. Trainee vendors averaged 70 hot dogs sold. The ratio of non-trainee vendors to trainee vendors was 1 : 2. What was the average number of hot dogs sold by the non-trainee vendors?

3. Tickets to a play cost $10 for children and $25 for adults. If 100 tickets were sold, were more adult tickets sold than children's tickets?

    (1) The average revenue per ticket was $18.25.
    (2) The revenue from ticket sales exceeded $1,800.

Save the following problems for review after you finish this entire guide.

4. A feed store sells two varieties of birdseed: Brand A, which is 40% millet and 60% sunflower, and Brand B, which is 65% millet and 35% safflower. If a customer purchases a mix of the two types of birdseed that is 50% millet, what percent of the mix is Brand A?

    (A) 15%
    (B) 40%
    (C) 50%
    (D) 60%
    (E) 85%

5. On a particular exam, the seniors in a history class averaged 86 points and the juniors in the class averaged 80 points. If the overall class average was 82 points, what was the ratio of seniors to juniors in the class?

6. A mixture of lean ground beef (10% fat) and super-lean ground beef (3% fat) has a total fat content of 8%. What is the ratio of lean ground beef to super-lean ground beef?

Solutions

1. **25 additional games:** This is a weighted averages problem. You can calculate this algebraically, but sketch it out first to understand the moving parts:

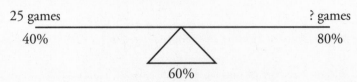

Which way should the teeter-totter tilt, to the right or to the left?

Actually, it doesn't tilt at all. Since 60% is exactly halfway between 40% and 80%, this isn't a weighted average at all; it's a regular average, where the two sides are equally weighted.

Since that's the case, the number of games at each end should match. Since Imani played 25 games for the 40%-win-rate group, she must also have played 25 games for the 80%-win-rate group. No algebra needed!

2. **58 hot dogs:** You can save yourself some calculation time by using smart numbers for part of this problem. The overall average of hot dogs sold is 66; trainees sold an average of 70. The ratio of non-trainees to trainees is 1 : 2, so just assume there was one actual non-trainee and two actual trainees (these are your smart numbers):

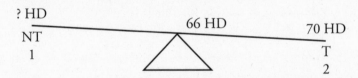

The teeter-totter is tilted toward the trainees. If those two trainees sold 70 hot dogs each, then those two people sold 140 hot dogs together. The overall average is 66 hot dogs and there were three people selling hot dogs, so there was an overall total of $(66)(3) = 198$ hot dogs sold. The one non-trainee, then, must have sold $198 - 140 = 58$ hot dogs.

But this can be solved in an even more streamlined way. The overall sum of $(66)(3)$ hot dogs sold must stay constant. If the two trainees sold 70 hot dogs each, then each one sold 4 hot dogs above the average, for a total of 8 extra hot dogs above the average of 66. In order for the overall average to be 66, those 8 extra hot dogs have to be taken away from the other group—in this case, the one non-trainee. The non-trainee, therefore, must have sold $66 - 8 = 58$ hot dogs.

3. **(D):** First things first: How would you recognize that this question is about weighted averages? The two different prices for tickets are like two different data points, and the number of tickets sold will act as the weight. If more adult tickets were sold, then the average ticket price will be closer to $25. If more children's tickets were sold, then the average ticket price will be closer to $10.

(1) SUFFICIENT: $18.25 is closer to $25 than to $10, so there must have been more adult tickets sold than children's tickets. Statement (1) is sufficient.

(2) SUFFICIENT: The total revenue from ticket sales exceeded $1,800. How are ticket sales calculated?

To figure that out, look at the information in the question stem again. One hundred tickets were sold. Consider two extreme scenarios:

100 children's tickets sold = 100 × $10 = $1,000 revenue

100 adult tickets sold = 100 × $25 = $2,500 revenue

If there were an equal number of adult and children's tickets sold, the revenue would be an average of $1,000 and $2,500, or $1,750. That's the connection to weighted averages. If the revenue is greater than $1,800, it is closer to $2,500 than to $1,000, which means more adult tickets must have been sold. Statement (2) is also sufficient.

The correct answer is **(D)**: Each statement works alone.

4. **(D) 60%:** The mixtures contain various things, but the question is only about the percent of millet, so ignore the other ingredients. Brand A is 40% millet and Brand B is 65% millet. The mixture is 50% millet, so this is a weighted averages problem. Sketch it out:

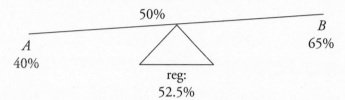

The regular average of 40% and 65% is halfway between, or 52.5%. If there were 50% of each brand in the mix, then the percentage of millet would be 52.5%.

The actual weighted average is 50%; this is closer to 40%, so there's more of Brand A in the mix. The correct answer has to be more than 50%, so eliminate answers (A), (B), and (C).

Compare the diagram to the two remaining answers. Is the given average of 50% closer to the regular average in the middle or closer to the extreme end of 40%? Since it's closer to the regular average (which represents a 50/50 mixture), the correct answer must be 60%, not 85%.

5. **1 : 2:** The seniors in the class scored 4 points higher on average than the entire class. Similarly, the juniors scored 2 points lower on average than the class. Draw a teeter-totter to solve:

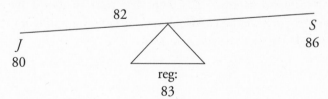

There are more juniors because the weighted average is closer to the 80 side of the teeter-totter. What's the ratio of the two parts?

The total distance of the line is 6, broken down into two portions of 2 and 4. Which is which?

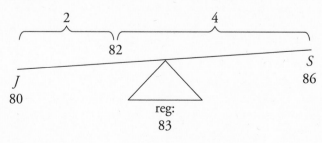

Think logically: There are fewer seniors than juniors, so the ratio of seniors to juniors must be 2 : 4, or 1 : 2. (You might also remember that these parts are always associated with the opposite end of the teeter-totter, so the 2 portion is associated with seniors and the 4 portion is associated with juniors.)

6. **5 : 2:** The question asks for the ratio of the two types of beef, so you don't need to worry about the actual amount of beef.

To set up this problem algebraically, first set up an equation, letting L be lean beef and S be super-lean beef:

$$1L + 0.03S = 0.08(L + S)$$

The question asks for the ratio of L to S, or $\frac{L}{S}$. First, multiply the equation by 100 to get rid of the decimals, then solve:

$$10L + 3S = 8(L + S)$$
$$10L + 3S = 8L + 8S$$
$$2L = 5S$$
$$\frac{L}{S} = \frac{5}{2}$$

Alternatively, draw a teeter-totter:

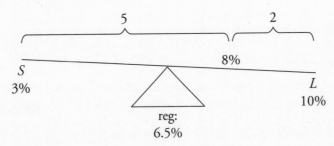

There's more lean ground beef, because 8% is closer to 10%. What's the ratio?

The "length" of the line is $10 - 3 = 7$. The lean (L) side is associated with the larger number, 5, and the super-lean (S) side is associated with the smaller number, 2. The ratio of $L : S = 5 : 2$.

Two-Part Analysis

In This Chapter...

- UPS for Quant Two-Parts

- UPS for Verbal Two-Parts

- UPS for Logic Two-Parts

In this chapter, you will learn how to UPS (Understand, Plan, Solve) your way to the answer for all three types of Two-Part problems: quant-, verbal-, and logic-based.

CHAPTER 21 Two-Part Analysis

Two-Part Analysis problems closely resemble regular multiple-choice questions on the Quant and Verbal sections of the exam—but with one twist. As the name implies, the question will have two parts to answer, not just one.

The prompt will appear at the top of the screen, followed by the question. The multiple-choice answers will appear in a table below that, as shown here:

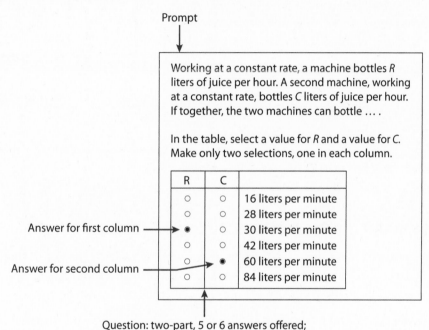

The prompt will likely contain more information than the typical quant or verbal problem, so Two-Parts are more likely to need 2 to 2.5 minutes to solve. In addition, you will choose from the same set of answers for each part of the question, so the two parts of the question are often closely related in some way. For example, you might be asked to strengthen *and* weaken an argument.

It's also possible for the questions to be quite different, as long as the set of answers logically follows both questions. For example, a set of numerical answers in units of *boxes per hour* might accompany two dissimilar rate questions, such as the rate at which machine X operated *and* the rate at which the night crew fell short of a production goal.

The correct answer for each part could actually be the same answer (though this doesn't happen often). And, at times, you may be asked to solve for the answers simultaneously. For example, they may ask you to find the speed for Truck A and for Truck B—but only give you enough information to tell that Truck A's rate was 5 kilometers per hour less than Truck B's rate, not what the actual rates are. In this case, only two of the answer choices would be 5 kilometers per hour apart, so those two values would be the only possible answers.

Two-Parts typically fall fairly cleanly into one of three categories: quant-, verbal-, or logic-based. Sometimes, problems incorporate elements from two categories, but that's less common.

UPS for Quant Two-Parts

Try this quant-based Two-Part problem:

> Two water storage tanks, Tank Alpha and Tank Bravo, can each hold more than 20,000 liters of water. Currently, Alpha contains 5,000 liters of water and Bravo contains 8,000 liters. Alpha will be filled at a constant rate of A liters per hour and Bravo will be filled at a constant rate of B liters per hour. If both tanks begin to be filled at the same time, after 15 hours, the two tanks will contain the same amount of water, though neither will be full.
>
> In the table below, identify a value for A and a value for B that together are consistent with the given information. Make only one selection in each column.

A	B	
O	O	30
O	O	90
O	O	150
O	O	220
O	O	290

Ready? Let's go!

Step 1: Understand the Prompt and Question

Before you start to read a Two-Part prompt, glance at the answers. What form are they in? In this case, they're numbers. Glance also at the question stem; it asks for the value of A and the value of B. This quick glance will give you an early clue that you've got a quant-based problem.

Treat this as you would a standard math story problem and translate the information carefully on your scratch paper. A quick sketch can help keep the information straight:

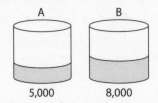

The two tanks are filling at different rates. In 15 hours, they'll have the same amount of water. What does that tell you about the rate for each tank?

Because Alpha has less water than Bravo to start, it must be filling at a faster rate—otherwise, Tank A couldn't catch up to Tank B. Jot a note on your scrap paper that $A > B$. If your answers don't match that idea, then you'll know you made a mistake somewhere. (And, if you have to guess, pick a greater value for A and a lesser value for B.)

The question stem contains an important clue: It specifically tells you to find values that *together are consistent* with the details given in the problem. As you move forward, look for opportunities to solve for the two values in tandem.

Step 2: Plan Your Approach

This is a work problem, so consider the RTW formula: Rate × Time = Work.

How are you going to go from a starting point of 5,000 and 8,000 liters to an ending point of the same number of liters?

Alpha has 5,000 liters now and will be filled at a rate of A liters per hour for 15 hours...hmm. If you ignore Bravo, that's not enough to solve for A. It is the case that you're going to need to solve for the two variables simultaneously.

There are two possible approaches. First, you could do algebra. Use the given variables to set up a mathematical representation for the final number of liters for Tank Alpha, at a rate of A, and the final number of liters for Tank Bravo, at a rate of B. Then, set those two numbers equal.

Second, you could try the answer choices. Rate A must be greater than rate B, so it's possible for the value of B to be one of four answer choices (everything but 290). Try one of the two middle answer choices and work from there.

Step 3: Solve the Problem

Here's the algebraic solution. Tank Alpha is filling at the rate of A liters per hour. Over 15 hours, it will add $15A$ liters. It started with 5,000 liters, so Alpha's final amount of water is equal to $5{,}000 + 15A$.

Since Tank Bravo is filling at the rate of B liters per hour, it will wind up with $8{,}000 + 15B$ liters. Now, set the equations equal to each other:

$$5{,}000 + 15A = 8{,}000 + 15B$$

That equation can't be solved for A and B individually—this is why you have to solve simultaneously. There are multiple possible solutions, but there is a consistent relationship between the two rates. Your task is to figure out what that relationship is. Only one *pair* of answer choices will fit that relationship.

$5{,}000 + 15A = 8{,}000 + 15B$	
$15A = 3{,}000 + 15B$	Subtract 5,000 from each side.
$15A - 15B = 3{,}000$	Subtract $15B$ from each side.
$A - B = 200$	Divide both sides by 15.

This is the relationship between the two rates: They have to differ by 200, and A must be greater than B. Look at the answers. The only pairing that works is $A = 290$ and $B = 90$:

A	B	
○	○	30
○	◉	90
○	○	150
○	○	220
◉	○	290

Double-check that you filled in the right columns with the appropriate numbers! Alpha has to fill faster, so A has to be the greater rate.

Here's the working backwards solution. Start with either 90 or 150 for B, your choice. Use the calculator when needed.

If Bravo's rate is 90 liters per hour, and it runs for 15 hours, it will add $(90)(15) = 1,350$ liters. It already had 8,000 liters, so it will finish with 9,350 liters.

Alpha also has to finish at 9,350 and it started at 5,000, so it added 4,350 liters during the 15 hours. Calculate the rate: $\frac{4,350}{15} = 290$. Check the answers—is 290 there? It is, so the correct pair of answers is $A = 290$ and $B = 90$.

What if you'd chosen to start with $B = 150$ instead? In 15 hours, Bravo would have added 2,250 liters, for a total of 10,250 liters. Since Alpha would also have had to finish with the same number of liters, Alpha would have had to add 5,250 liters in the 15 hours, or 350 liters per hour.

First, 350 is not in the answer choices, so this can't be the correct pair of answers. Second, 350 is too big—all of the answers are less than that. So not only is B not equal to 150, B also can't be 220, as that's even bigger. Therefore, B has to be either 30 or 90.

From here, go ahead and try another answer (your choice which value to try next!) until you get to the correct answer (which is still $A = 290$ and $B = 90$).

UPS for Verbal Two-Parts

Verbal Two-Parts most often feel similar to Critical Reasoning (CR) problems from the Verbal section, though they can also resemble mini-Reading Comprehension (RC) passages.

Try this problem:

> Software Company M accused Company S of intellectual property theft, citing as evidence similar user interface designs for the company's new operating system products, both of which launched this year, and the fact that Company M's chief designer defected to Company S nine months ago. Company S countered that the product was 90% completed by the time the former chief designer joined Company S and that the designer was not allowed to work on that product in order to avoid any potential conflicts of interest.

Select the additional information that, if true, would provide the strongest evidence *For* Company S's claim that it did not illegally obtain information about Company M's products, and select the additional information that, if true, would provide the strongest evidence *Against* that claim.

For	Against	
○	○	A comparison with a third operating system company's user interface design shows overlap with Company M only in features that have been in industry-wide use for years.
○	○	Company S's former chief designer quit after a dispute over creative control.
○	○	Last year, another company released software that incorporates some of the same user interface designs at issue in the dispute.
○	○	Several key parts of the software code in Company S's product are nearly identical to code that Company M's former chief designer wrote for Company M.
○	○	It is quite common for software companies to accuse other companies of intellectual property theft.

How did it go? Before reading the explanations below, review your work yourself. Then, use the walk-through below to help you past any sticking points or to help you brainstorm more efficient approaches to your solution process.

Step 1: Understand the Prompt and Question

Glance at the answers: The fact that there are sentences indicate that this is likely either a verbal- or logic-based problem. Complete sentences usually indicate verbal problems. Logic problems tend to have short words or phrases in the answers.

The next clue: The question asks for evidence *For* something and evidence *Against* something. This is similar to a Critical Reasoning problem from the Verbal section, so tackle this in the same way that you tackle CR.

Read the argument and make a map:

M: S stole our design

1. Similar design

2. M's designer → S

S: 90% done; designer not allowed to work on it

The first part of the question asks you to strengthen Company S's claim that it did *not* steal anything from Company M; in other words, the question is oriented from S's point of view, not M's. The second part asks you to weaken Company S's claim.

Step 2: Plan your Approach

Use the same strategies you use for CR problems. A correct strengthen answer makes the conclusion at least a little more likely to be valid, so the first column will validate (at least a little) the claim that Company S did *not* steal from Company M. Look through the answers now, concentrating just on this part of the question.

Step 3: Solve the Problem

If you're very good at CR, you can try to find the strengthen and weaken answers at the same time. If, on the other hand, you have ever accidentally picked a strengthen answer when you were supposed to weaken, or vice versa, then concentrate on finding the *For* answer first. Then, go through again for the *Against* answer.

The answer choices are labeled (A) through (E) for clarity. As you read each one, ask yourself whether it makes Company S's case any better:

> (A) *A comparison with a third operating system company's user interface design shows overlap with Company M only in features that have been in industry-wide use for years.*

A third company's system doesn't overlap much with Company M's system. A *lack* of overlap doesn't strengthen Company S's case. If a third company's system were super similar to M's system, that might help S's case—but that's not what this choice says. Eliminate this answer.

> (B) *Company S's former chief designer quit after a dispute over creative control.*

Careful! The argument is about Company M's designer, the one who moved over to Company S. The reason Company S's former designer (a different person) quit has no bearing on what happened when Company M's designer joined. Eliminate this choice.

> (C) *Last year, another company released software that incorporates some of the same user interface designs at issue in the dispute.*

A third company released software *last* year that contains some of the designs that are in dispute. The argument states that Company M released its own software *this* year, so this certainly bolsters Company S's claim that it did not steal anything from Company M (though maybe they both stole ideas from the third company!). This one looks good but check the final two answers.

> (D) *Several key parts of the software code in Company S's product are nearly identical to code that Company M's former chief designer wrote for Company M.*

If some parts of the software code are identical to code written by Company M's former chief designer while working for that company, this definitely does not help Company S's claim that it didn't steal any ideas. This might even *weaken* S's claim. Note that down. Also, eliminate this choice.

> (E) *It is quite common for software companies to accuse other companies of intellectual property theft.*

This may be true in general, but it does not provide any evidence as to what happened in the specific case discussed in the argument.

The correct answer for the first part, *For*, is answer (C).

Now, reuse your initial analysis to help narrow down the answers faster for the second part. Which choice goes *against* S's claim that it didn't steal any ideas?

Start with answer (D), the one that you already thought might be a weaken. If parts of the code written by the employee who switched companies are *nearly identical* in the two products, this definitely weakens S's claim that it did not steal anything from M. It would be pretty unlikely for someone else to have written code that is *nearly identical* in *several key parts*.

Do review the other answers, just to be sure. For answer (A), this third company's design overlaps with M only on commonly used features. What impact does that have on the claim that S stole some of M's features? It's not clear what features M is claiming S stole, so this information about a third company is not relevant to the argument.

Answers (B) and (E) are irrelevant one way or the other, so they can't be the *Against* answer. If answer (C) is the *For* answer, then it can't also be the *Against* answer; these two classifications are opposites. So answer (D) must be correct for *Against*.

The answers are:

For	Against	
○	○	A comparison with a third operating system company's user interface design shows overlap with Company M only in features that have been in industry-wide use for years.
○	○	Company S's former chief designer quit after a dispute over creative control.
●	○	Last year, another company released software that incorporates some of the same user interface designs at issue in the dispute.
○	●	Several key parts of the software code in Company S's product are nearly identical to code that Company M's former chief designer wrote for that company.
○	○	It is quite common for software companies to accuse other companies of intellectual property theft.

When the two parts of the question are not connected, as in the first verbal example above, you could save time by thinking about the two parts simultaneously—but you are taking a risk. If you ever make mistakes with this (e.g., if you swapped the two answers on the last problem), then tackle the two questions separately in the future.

Some Two-Part questions will ask for two connected answers, as you saw in the quant-based question earlier, and this can happen on a verbal-based problem, too. For example, you might be asked to find a specific *Cause* and *Effect* sequence or a certain *Circumstance* that would lead to a specific *Prediction*. In these cases, you must think about the two parts of the question simultaneously.

Try another one:

The Golden Age of Radio—the period of time during which radio broadcasting in the United States reached its widest audience—came to an end in the 1950s as radio was supplanted by television. World War II, which had caused widespread shortages of the technology used in television sets, ended in 1945. As a result of a greatly reduced cost of materials as well as a sudden influx of workers seeking employment after the war, television-manufacturing companies multiplied. Competition kept the price of television sets modest, compared to the relatively high income of many U.S. households during the post-war years; by the end of the decade, the number of households with a television had increased more than a hundredfold.

Identify in the table one *Cause* and one *Effect* of that cause that together, according to the author, likely contributed to the end of the Golden Age of Radio. Make only two selections, one in each column.

21

Cause	Effect	
○	○	An increase in competition among television manufacturers
○	○	A decrease in the number of U.S. homes with a radio
○	○	A widespread shortage of television-manufacturing technology
○	○	A reduction in the number of available manufacturing workers during World War II
○	○	A decrease in the cost of television-manufacturing materials
○	○	The relatively high income of post-war U.S. households

Step 1: Understand the Prompt and Question

The sentences signal a verbal- or logic-based problem. The fact that the question asks for a *Cause* and an *Effect* signals a CR-type verbal problem. Further, a cause-effect setup will usually need to be solved simultaneously.

The prompt first makes a general claim: The Golden Age of Radio ended in the 1950s when television took over.

Then it provides a series of events that led to this outcome. After World War II ended in 1945, raw costs for making TVs went down a lot, and a lot of people were looking for work. In addition, household income was relatively high. These facts meant that companies could make a lot of TVs and sell them cheaply, allowing the number of households with TVs to greatly increase.

The blurb basically explains why TV was able to overtake radio as the entertainment medium of choice in the 1950s. The question asks what *Cause* led to what *Effect* that together contributed to the rise of TV.

Step 2: Plan Your Approach

The various facts in the argument are a bit jumbled together. Since the question asks specifically about a cause and an effect, it's worth the effort to map the information logically:

> WWII ends → workers avail + material costs decr.
>
> → more comp make more TVs
>
> → cheaper TVs
>
> Also: more inc to buy

There is one big chain of information: the business reasons that led to more cheap TVs on the market. Anything in the chain except for the last piece of information could be the cause, and anything in that chain except for the first piece of information could be the effect.

Separately, household income also increased, but the blurb doesn't provide any information as to why or how that happened. As a result, this fact can't be part of any cause-effect chain in the answers.

21

Step 3: Solve the Problem

Examine the answers, looking for a cause that falls earlier in the chain of events and an effect that both falls later in the chain of events and can reasonably be called a result of the earlier cause. Take a look at answer choice (A):

(A) *An increase in competition among television manufacturers*

This is in the chain, so it is one of the potential pieces of the puzzle, though it's not possible to say whether it's the cause or the effect without reviewing the rest of the answers. Put a star next to this information in your map. Now, move to choice (B):

(B) *A decrease in the number of U.S. homes with a radio*

This one is tricky. Technically, the blurb says only that *radio was supplanted by television*; it does not specify what this means. It could be that people who already had radios kept those radios but also bought TVs and spent more time watching TV. So the *number* of radios didn't necessarily have to decrease. Here is choice (C):

(C) *A widespread shortage of television-manufacturing technology*

The shortage existed during the war; once the war ended in 1945, these shortages no longer existed, and that fact contributed to the greater number of TVs built. This choice is the opposite of one cause of the growth of the TV market. Move on to choice (D):

(D) *A reduction in the number of available manufacturing workers during World War II*

It is true that fewer workers were available during the war but, as with the last choice, this changed after the war. The fact that more workers were available after the war helped the TV market to thrive. This choice is the opposite of one cause of the growth of the TV market. Here is choice (E):

(E) *A decrease in the cost of television-manufacturing materials*

This is part of the argument given in the blurb. First, the cost of these materials decreased. That allowed more companies to make TVs, and that in turn increased competition in the market, which is what the first answer choice said. This choice is the *cause* and the first answer is the *effect*. And finally, look at choice (F):

(F) *The relatively high income of post-war U.S. households*

This was also mentioned, but it is not connected to any other pieces of information in the blurb, so it cannot be either the cause or the effect.

The answers are:

Cause	Effect	
○	◉	An increase in competition among television manufacturers
○	○	A decrease in the number of U.S. homes with a radio
○	○	A widespread shortage of television-manufacturing technology
○	○	A reduction in the number of available manufacturing workers during World War II
◉	○	A decrease in the cost of television-manufacturing materials
○	○	The relatively high income of post-war U.S. households

UPS for Logic Two-Parts

21

Try this logic-based problem:

A chemical plant operating continuously has two 12-hour shifts, a day shift and a night shift, during each of which as many as five chemicals can be produced. Equipment limitations and safety regulations impose constraints on the types of chemicals that can be produced during the same shift. No more than two oxidizers can be produced per shift; the same limit holds true for monomers. On either shift, the sum of the safety rating for all chemicals should be no greater than 13 for health risk and 9 for reactivity.

Four chemicals have already been chosen for each shift, as shown below:

Day Shift

Acrylonitrile	(health = 4, reactivity = 2, oxidizer = no, monomer = yes)
Chloroprene	(health = 2, reactivity = 0, oxidizer = no, monomer = yes)
Hydrogen peroxide	(health = 3, reactivity = 2, oxidizer = yes, monomer = no)
Titanium dioxide	(health = 1, reactivity = 0, oxidizer = no, monomer = no)

Night Shift

Ammonium nitrate	(health = 2, reactivity = 3, oxidizer = yes, monomer = no)
Phosphine	(health = 4, reactivity = 2, oxidizer = no, monomer = no)
Potassium perchlorate	(health = 1, reactivity = 1, oxidizer = yes, monomer = no)
Propylene	(health = 1, reactivity = 1, oxidizer = no, monomer = yes)

Select a chemical that *Could* be added to either shift. Then, select a chemical that *Cannot* be added to either shift. Make only two selections, one in each column.

Could be added to either shift	Cannot be added to either shift	
O	O	Chlorine (health = 3, reactivity = 0, oxidizer = yes, monomer = no)
O	O	Ethylene (health = 3, reactivity = 2, oxidizer = no, monomer = yes)
O	O	Nickel carbonyl (health = 4, reactivity = 3, oxidizer = no, monomer = no)
O	O	Phenol (health = 3, reactivity = 0, oxidizer = no, monomer = no)
O	O	Sulfuric acid (health = 3, reactivity = 2, oxidizer = yes, monomer = no)
O	O	Vinyl chloride (health = 2, reactivity = 2, oxidizer = no, monomer = yes)

Step 1: Understand the Prompt and Question

Glance at the answers: text *and* numbers. The complexity of the information in the answers (not pure numbers or sentences), coupled with the tables of information in the question stem, indicate that this is likely a logic problem.

This is also a really technical problem. Don't get caught up in the language. You don't need to know what a *monomer* is or what *reactivity* means. You just need to be able to classify things.

Whenever you have a logic problem, list out the details in a clear and organized way:

> 2 shifts: D and N
> Max 5 chem per shift

Four of the five slots on each shift are already filled, so you're looking to fill the fifth slot. Map the constraints:

> Slot constraints:
> – No more than 2 O's per shift
> – No more than 2 M's per shift
> – H ≤ 13
> – R ≤ 9

You have to identify a single chemical that *Could* fit either shift (there's only one) and another chemical that *Cannot* fit either shift (again, there's only one). The characteristics of the chemicals you are to choose from are in the answer choices.

Since you are going to have to work with the information from the answers in order to solve, jot down a little table on your scratch paper, something like this:

COULD	CANNOT	Chemical
		Chl
		Eth
		NC
		Ph
		SA
		VC

Use this to keep track of your eliminations as you go.

Step 2: Plan Your Approach

Since this problem is about following a chain of logic, first figure out what *must* and *must not* be true about the fifth chemical, based on the given constraints and the four chemicals that are already set for each shift. Then, armed with these more refined constraints about the fifth possibility for each shift, go through the list of chemicals in the answer choices to figure out whether the chemical in question could be added to the shift.

Step 3: Solve the Problem

First, lay out what each shift already has:

Day Has:	Night Has:
H = 10	H = 8
R = 4	R = 7
1 O	2 O's
2 M's	1 M

You're only allowed 2 M's total, which the day shift has, and 2 O's total, which the night shift has. So the fifth chemical can't be an M or an O. Glance through the answers. In the COULD column, write NO for chlorine, ethylene, sulfuric acid, and vinyl chloride. Four down, two to go!

You're also allowed only 13 H total, and the day shift already has an H of 10, so the H rating of the final chemical has to be ≤ 3. Likewise, R can't be more than 9 total, and the night shift already has an R of 7, so the R rating of the final chemical has to be ≤ 2.

Scan the two remaining answers. Nickel carbonyl fails on both counts—it has an H rating of 4 and an R rating of 3.

The only chemical that *could* be added to either shift is phenol.

Use the work you've already done to figure out which chemical cannot go on either shift. Of the rejected answers, start with nickel carbonyl, since you've looked most carefully at that one so far and it has the highest health and reactivity safety ratings. As noted above, nickel carbonyl can't go on the day shift because it has an H rating of 4. And it can't go on the night shift because it has an R rating of 3. This is the one that cannot be added to either shift!

Here are the answers:

Could be added to either shift	Cannot be added to either shift	Chemical
○	○	Chlorine (health = 3, reactivity = 0, oxidizer = yes, monomer = no)
○	○	Ethylene (health = 3, reactivity = 2, oxidizer = no, monomer = yes)
○	●	Nickel carbonyl (health = 4, reactivity = 3, oxidizer = no, monomer = no)
●	○	Phenol (health = 3, reactivity = 0, oxidizer = no, monomer = no)
○	○	Sulfuric acid (health = 3, reactivity = 2, oxidizer = yes, monomer = no)
○	○	Vinyl chloride (health = 2, reactivity = 2, oxidizer = no, monomer = yes)

When you see a quant- or verbal-based Two-Part, it will usually resemble the questions in the Quant and Verbal sections of the exam, and you can use the same strategies you're learning for those sections. Logic problems are a bit different. Take a little time to understand the story and make an organized map of the given constraints. Use that map to make any logical inferences you can to narrow down the possibilities further. In a few chapters, you'll learn some additional strategies for more advanced logic problems.

Practice Your Skills

Log into your Manhattan Prep online account for additional Two-Part practice problems. Also: You've now learned about all five types of Data Insights (DI) problems on the GMAT! Start doing mixed practice sets, combining at least three different problem types from this section of the exam.

Rates and Work

In This Chapter...

- Basic Motion: RTD Chart or Draw It Out

- Matching Units in the RTD Chart

- Multiple Rates

- Relative Rates

- Average Rate: Find the Total Time

- Basic Work Problems

- Working Together: Add the Rates

In this chapter, you will learn how to set up and solve a variety of rate and work problems, both algebraically and by using logic. (The latter approach is often the easier one!) You'll also learn what to do with more complicated scenarios such as relative rates, average rates, and working together.

CHAPTER 22 **Rates and Work**

Rate problems come in a variety of forms on the GMAT, but all are marked by three primary components: *rate*, *time*, and either *distance* or *work*.

These three elements are related by the following equations:

Rate × Time = Distance

Rate × Time = Work

These equations can be abbreviated as $RT = D$ or as $RT = W$.

This chapter will discuss the ways in which the GMAT makes rate situations more complicated. Often, $RT = D$ problems, also known as RTD problems, will involve more than one person or vehicle traveling. Similarly, many $RT = W$ problems will involve more than one worker.

Let's get started with a review of some fundamental properties of rate problems.

Basic Motion: RTD Chart or Draw It Out

All basic motion problems involve three elements: rate, time, and distance.

Rate is expressed as a ratio of distance and time, with two corresponding units. Some examples of rates include 30 miles per hour, 10 meters/second, and 15 kilometers/day.

Time is expressed using a unit of time. Some examples of times include 6 hours, 23 seconds, and 5 months.

Distance is expressed using a unit of distance. Some examples of distances include 18 miles, 20 meters, and 100 kilometers.

You can make an RTD chart to organize the information for a basic motion problem. Read the problem and fill in two of the variables. Then, use the $RT = D$ formula to find the missing variable. For example:

> If a car is traveling at 30 miles per hour, how long does it take to travel 75 miles?

Fill in your RTD chart with the given information. Then, solve for the time:

	Rate (miles/hour)	×	Time (hours)	=	Distance (miles)
Car	30	×		=	75

$30t = 75$, or $t = 2.5$ hours

Up next is a much more complicated problem. Rather than use the RTD chart approach, try drawing this out as described in Chapter 17, the Translations chapter, earlier in this unit.

Annika hikes at a constant rate of 12 minutes per kilometer. She has hiked 2.75 kilometers east from the start of a hiking trail when she realizes that she has to be back at the start of the trail in 45 minutes. If Annika continues east, then turns around and retraces her path to reach the start of the trail in exactly 45 minutes, for how many kilometers total did she hike east?

(A) 2.25
(B) 2.75
(C) 3.25
(D) 3.75
(E) 4.25

22

This is a pretty nasty problem. You could use an RTD chart to solve algebraically. But to set that up correctly, you've got to understand the weird scenario, so start by drawing it out.

Here's Annika partway down her hiking trail, suddenly realizing that she's got 45 minutes till she needs to get back:

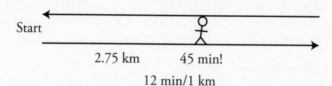

Pretend that isn't Annika at all—now, it's you. Are you going to whip out paper and pencil to start doing some algebra to figure out when to turn around? No way. You're going to use real-world logic to figure out what to do.

What do you want to figure out? The question asks how far you will have traveled east. The first part of the distance is 2.75 kilometers, but you don't know how much *farther* east you can go before turning around. Glance at the answers. Hey, the answer can't be (A) because you've already gone more than 2.25 kilometers. And the answer can only be (B) if you have to turn around right now. Do you?

First, if you didn't go a step farther, how long would it take to get back?

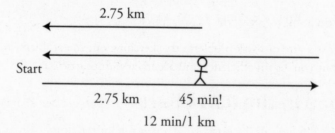

You're going to need 2.75 kilometers to get back. How long is that going to take if you're going 1 kilometer every 12 minutes? Let's see, you can go 3 kilometers in (count it out) 12, 24, 36 minutes. So if you turn around right now (at 2.75 kilometers), you'll be back in less than 36 minutes. But you still have 45 minutes to go, so answer (B) isn't correct.

The next possible answer is 3.25 kilometers. If you go that far east in total, you'd have to go another half a kilometer right now, then turn around and hike 3.25 kilometers back. How long does it take you to go 0.5 kilometer? If it takes 12 minutes to go 1 kilometer, then you'll need 6 minutes to go 0.5 kilometer.

So, first, you'd continue east for another 6 minutes. Then you'd turn around and hike back 3.25 kilometers. You can go 3 kilometers in 36 minutes, and you'd need another 3 minutes to go that last 0.25 kilometer, for a total of 39 minutes hiking west.

Therefore, 6 minutes east + 39 minutes west = 45 minutes total and you're back at your car. The correct answer is (C).

Here's another way to draw it out:

Go back to the beginning.

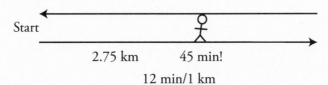

2.75 km   45 min!

12 min/1 km

Step back from the problem for a second—forget that you want 2.75 kilometers plus some unknown distance. Look at your diagram. You're asking yourself how far you can travel east before you turn around and go back; that is, you want to know how far *half* of the trip is. If you can calculate the total distance, you can find the halfway mark.

To start, you travel 2.75 kilometers. Then, you travel another 45 minutes at 12 minutes per kilometer. You can count it out again or do the straight math—$12 \times 4 = 48$—so it takes 48 minutes to go 4 kilometers. How can you find the distance for 45 minutes?

If you hike 1 kilometer in 12 minutes, then you hike 0.25 kilometer in 3 minutes. Subtract: You hike $4 - 0.25 = 3.75$ kilometers in $48 - 3 = 45$ minutes.

Therefore, you travel $2.75 + 3.75 = 6.5$ kilometers total. Half of that, 3.25 kilometers, is spent hiking east. The correct answer is (C).

There are usually multiple ways to logic out the problem to get to the answer; you can do whatever feels easiest to you. Put yourself in the situation and ask yourself how you would go about this in the real world. You'd almost never start writing a bunch of equations; rather, you'd start just sketching out scenarios, using real-world logic and estimation to get to the answer (or close enough!).

Whenever you run across a rate or work problem, try sketching out the problem to gain practice. At first, you'll likely feel slow, but you'll gain efficiency and accuracy with practice!

Matching Units in the RTD Chart

When you do use an RTD chart, all the units in your chart must match up with one another. The two units in the rate should match up with the unit of time and the unit of distance. For example:

> An elevator operates at a constant rate of 4 seconds to rise one floor. How many floors will the elevator rise in 2 minutes?

The elevator moves 1 floor every 4 seconds: $\dfrac{1 \text{ floor}}{4 \text{ seconds}} = \dfrac{1}{4}$ floor/second.

There are two common potential mistakes people make. First, always express the rate as per *one* unit of time: one second, one minute, one hour. In the case above, the rate is the fraction $\dfrac{1}{4}$ of a floor per one second, not 1 floor per 4 seconds.

Second, the rate is *not* $\frac{4 \text{ seconds}}{1 \text{ floor}}$. Always express rates as *distance over time*, not as *time over distance*.

Given the rate of $\frac{1}{4}$ floor per second, how many floors will the elevator rise in 2 minutes?

Watch out! There is a problem with the RTD chart below. The rate is expressed in floors per second, but the time is expressed in minutes. This will yield an incorrect answer.

	R (floors/second)	×	T (minutes)	=	D (floors)
Elevator	0.25	×	2	=	?

To correct this table, change the time into seconds. To convert minutes to seconds, multiply 2 minutes by 60 seconds per minute, yielding 120 seconds, as shown in the chart below:

	R (floors/second)	×	T (seconds)	=	D (floors)
Elevator	0.25	×	120	=	?

Once the time has been converted from 2 minutes to 120 seconds, the time unit will match the rate unit, and you can solve for the distance using the $RT = D$ equation:

$$0.25(120) = d$$
$$d = 30 \text{ floors}$$

Thus, the elevator will go up 30 floors in 2 minutes.

You can also try to logic it out. Sketch out the answer as though it's happening in the real world.

You're on the elevator. Every 4 seconds, you're going to go up one floor, and you'll be on the elevator for 2 minutes. After 8 seconds, you're at floor 2. After 12 seconds, you're at floor 3. It's annoying to keep going up by increments of 4; what would be easier?

After 40 seconds, you're at floor 10. After 80 seconds, you're at floor 20. And after 120 seconds (or 2 minutes), you're at floor 30.

The RTD chart or the sketch-it-out approach may seem like overkill for problems in which you need to set up just one equation ($RT = D$ or $RT = W$) and then substitute. However, these two methods will help you to address more complicated scenarios, as you'll see in the next section.

Multiple Rates

Some rate problems on the GMAT will involve *more than one trip or traveler*. To deal with this, you will need to deal with multiple $RT = D$ relationships. Try this example:

> Amal runs a 30-mile course at a constant rate of 6 miles per hour. If Cahaya runs the same course at a constant rate and completes the course in 60 fewer minutes, how fast did Cahaya run, in miles per hour?

Draw the scenario. This is a good idea whether you plan to continue with a logic-it-out approach or whether you plan to use an RTD chart; sketching the scenario will help you to keep the moving parts straight:

C: ?? mph, but 60 min <u>faster</u>

A: 6 mph ⟶

30 mi

Start thinking logically. What's the connection between A and C? The time: C was 60 minutes faster than A. What can you figure out around this connection? You can figure out how fast A went. If A ran 6 miles every hour and had to cover 30 miles, then A took 5 hours to go the whole 30 miles.

Therefore, C took $5 - 1 = 4$ hours to run the 30 miles. If C covered 30 miles in 4 hours, then C ran $\frac{30}{4} = 7.5$ miles in 1 hour, or 7.5 miles per hour.

Alternatively, create an RTD chart. A chart for this question has two rows, one for Amal and one for Cahaya, as shown below:

	R (miles/hour)	×	T (hours)	=	D (miles)
A					
C					

Pay attention to the relationships between these two equations. Try to use the minimum necessary number of variables.

For example, Cahaya ran for 60 fewer minutes, so use t and $t - 60$ minutes for the two times. To make units match, convert 60 minutes to 1 hour. If Amal ran t hours, then Cahaya ran $(t - 1)$ hours. The distance they both ran was 30 miles. Fill in this information on your chart:

	R (miles/hour)	×	T (hours)	=	D (miles)
A	6	×	t	=	30
C	?	×	$t - 1$	=	30

Now, solve for t:

$$6t = 30$$
$$t = 5$$

If $t = 5$, then Cahaya ran for $5 - 1 = 4$ hours. Now, solve for Cahaya's rate:

$$r \times 4 = 30$$
$$r = 7.5$$

For questions that involve multiple rates, start by sketching the situation. From there, decide whether you would rather logic it out or whether you would rather set up the $RT = D$ equations. Either way, look for connections, or relationships, between the different parts of the problem. These relationships will help you to be able to solve efficiently.

Relative Rates

Relative rate problems are a subset of multiple rate problems. The defining aspect of relative rate problems is that two bodies are traveling *at the same time*. There are three possible scenarios:

1. The bodies move *toward* each other.

2. The bodies move *away* from each other.

3. The bodies move in the *same direction* on the same path.

These questions can be dangerous because they can take a long time to solve using the conventional multiple rates strategy (discussed in the last section). You can save valuable time and energy by considering the *combined* rate at which the distance between the bodies changes:

Toward each other:

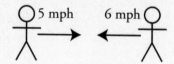

Away from each other:

Same direction:

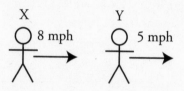

Two people decrease the distance between themselves at a rate of $5 + 6 = 11$ mph.

Two cars increase the distance between themselves at a rate of $30 + 45 = 75$ mph.

Persons X and Y decrease the distance between themselves at a rate of $8 - 5 = 3$ mph.

Try an example:

> Two people are 14 miles apart and begin walking toward each other. Person A walks 3 miles per hour, and Person B walks 4 miles per hour. How many hours will it take them to reach each other?

What is the combined rate of the two people? Since they are walking toward each other, they are both contributing to getting closer together at a rate of $3 + 4 = 7$ miles per hour. For every hour that they both walk, they get 7 miles closer together.

How long will it take to cover the 14-mile distance between them? Walking 7 miles an hour for 2 hours will bring them together, so the answer is 2 hours. You can literally sketch out all of the movement:

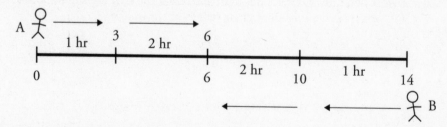

Some people might prefer an RTD chart (though the logical approach used above works on a surprising number of GMAT problems, even harder ones). Create an $RT = D$ equation for the combined rate: $3 + 4 = 7$ miles per hour.

	R (miles/hour)	×	T (hours)	=	D (miles)
A + B	7	×	t	=	14

$$7t = 14$$

$$t = 2$$

Note that the draw-it-out technique will still work even when the answer isn't an integer. Let's say that Person B is walking at a rate of 5 miles per hour:

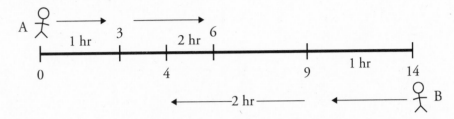

They haven't passed at 1 hour, but they have at 2 hours. You would typically be able to eliminate two or three multiple-choice answers at this stage. Next, try 1.5 hours:

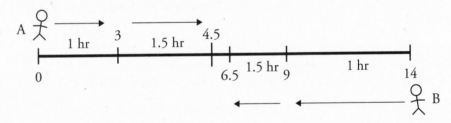

They haven't passed yet. This is usually enough for you to narrow the choices down to a single answer, though it depends on the exact mix of answer choices.

Average Rate: Find the Total Time

Consider the following problem:

> If Lior walks to work at a rate of 4 miles per hour and walks home by the same route at a rate of 6 miles per hour, what is Lior's average walking rate for the round trip?

It is very tempting to find an average rate as you would find any other average: that is, to add and then divide. Thus, you might say that Lior's average rate is 5 miles per hour ($4 + 6 = 10$ and $10 \div 2 = 5$). However, this is incorrect!

If an object moves over the same distance twice, but at different rates each time, then *the average rate will NEVER be the "straight" average of the two rates given for the two legs of the journey*. Instead, because the object spends more time traveling at the slower rate, *the average rate will ALWAYS be closer to the slower of the two rates than to the faster*. Basically, the slower trip is weighted more heavily in the calculations (this is a type of weighted average, discussed in an earlier chapter).

In order to find the average rate, first find the *total* combined distance for the trips and the *total* combined time for the trips. Use this formula:

$$\text{Average Speed} = \frac{\text{Total Distance}}{\text{Total Time}}$$

The problem above never establishes a specific distance. Because Lior walks the *same* route to work and back home, the average does not depend upon the specific distance. Whether the person or vehicle in the question goes 1 mile or 15, the *average* will be the same, so pick your own smart number for the distance.

Since 12 is a multiple of the two rates in the problem, 4 and 6, 12 is a good number to use.

Set up an RTD chart or draw out the scenario, your choice. Both approaches are shown here:

$$\frac{\text{Dist}}{\text{Time}} = \frac{24}{5} = 4.8$$

The calculations are shown in the chart, but you would typically perform these outside of the chart and then enter the information into your chart:

	Rate (miles/hour)	×	Time (hours)	=	Distance (miles)
Going	4	×	$\frac{12}{4} = 3$	=	12
Return	6	×	$\frac{12}{6} = 2$	=	12
Total	$\frac{24}{5} = 4.8$	×	$3 + 2 = 5$	=	$12 + 12 = 24$

If you like, test different numbers for the distance (try 24 or 36) to prove that you will get the same answer, regardless of the number you choose for the distance.

Basic Work Problems

Work problems are just another type of rate problem. These questions are concerned with the amount of work of some type performed rather than the distance traveled.

Work: Work takes the place of distance. Instead of $RT = D$, use the equation $RT = W$. The amount of work done is often a number of jobs completed or a number of items produced.

Time: This is the time spent working.

Rate: In work problems, the rate expresses the amount of work done in a given amount of time.

$$R = \frac{W}{T}$$

As with rate problems, always express a rate as work per unit time $\left(\frac{W}{T}\right)$. For example, if a machine produces pencils at a constant rate of 120 pencils every 30 seconds, the rate at which the machine works is $\frac{120 \text{ pencils}}{30 \text{ seconds}} = 4$ pencils/second.

Many work problems will require you to calculate a rate. Try the following problem:

> Malak can paint $\frac{2}{9}$ of a room in 40 minutes. At this rate, how long will it take Malak to paint the entire room?
>
> (A) 2 hours
>
> (B) 3 hours
>
> (C) 4 hours

You can use an RTW chart or logic it out, your choice. Both approaches are shown here.

The question asks how long it takes Malak to paint the whole room. In terms of the fraction given in the question stem, the whole job is $\frac{9}{9}$.

If Malak takes 40 minutes to paint $\frac{2}{9}$ of a room, how long would is take to paint $\frac{1}{9}$ of the room? Since $\frac{1}{9}$ is half as much as $\frac{2}{9}$, it would take half as long, or 20 minutes.

If it takes 20 minutes to paint $\frac{1}{9}$ of the room, then it takes 9 times as long to paint the whole room: $(20)(9) = 180$ minutes, or 3 hours. The correct answer is (B).

Alternatively, set up an RTW chart with your known information to find Malak's rate; note that the given information is in minutes but the question asks for hours, so at some point you'll need to convert from minutes to hours:

	R (rooms/hour)	×	T (hours)	=	W (rooms)
Malak	r	×	$\frac{2}{3}$	=	$\frac{2}{9}$

Now, solve for the rate:

$$r \times \frac{2}{3} = \frac{2}{9}$$
$$r = \frac{2}{9} \times \frac{3}{2} = \frac{1}{3}$$

Malak paints $\frac{1}{3}$ of the room every hour. Painting the whole room is the same as doing $\frac{3}{3}$ of the job, so it will take a total of 3 hours to complete. The correct answer is (B).

One interesting item. Malak's rate is $\frac{1}{3}$ and the time to complete the whole job is 3. These two numbers, $\frac{1}{3}$ and 3, are reciprocals. It will always be the case that the rate and the time it takes to do one job are reciprocals—that knowledge may save you some calculation time on some problems.

Working Together: Add the Rates

More often than not, work problems will involve more than one worker. When two or more workers are performing the same task, their rates can be added together. For instance, if Machine A can make 5 boxes in an hour, and Machine B can make 12 boxes in an hour, then working together the two machines can make $5 + 12 = 17$ boxes per hour.

Likewise, if Ren can complete $\frac{1}{3}$ of a task in an hour and Serena can complete $\frac{1}{2}$ of that task in an hour, then working together they can complete $\frac{1}{3} + \frac{1}{2} = \frac{5}{6}$ of the task every hour.

If, on the other hand, one worker is undoing the work of the other, subtract the rates. For example, if one hose is filling a pool at a rate of 3 gallons per minute, but another hose is draining the pool at a rate of 1 gallon per minute, the pool is being filled at a rate of $3 - 1 = 2$ gallons per minute.

Try the following problem:

> Machine A fills soda bottles at a constant rate of 60 bottles every 12 minutes, and Machine B fills soda bottles at a constant rate of 120 bottles every 8 minutes. How many bottles can both machines working together at their respective rates fill in 25 minutes?

First, check the given rate information against the question. It's asking about a 25-minute time frame. It would be easy to take the given information and "scale it up" for a 24-minute time frame (Machine A fills 120 bottles every 24 minutes, and Machine B fills 360 bottles every 24 minutes). If this problem had multiple-choice answers, you would want to glance at them at this point to see whether you can get away with rounding from here.

That's not the case on this problem, though. Instead, begin by putting the rates in proper form (per 1 unit of time):

$$\text{Rate}_{\text{Machine A}} = \frac{60 \text{ bottles}}{12 \text{ minutes}} = 5 \text{ bottles/minute}$$

$$\text{Rate}_{\text{Machine B}} = \frac{120 \text{ bottles}}{8 \text{ minutes}} = 15 \text{ bottles/minute}$$

Working together, they fill $5 + 15 = 20$ bottles every minute. In 25 minutes, then, they would fill $(20)(25) = 500$ bottles.

If you're not sure about that final calculation, you can fill out an RTW chart. Let b be the number of bottles filled:

	R (bottles/minute)	×	T (minutes)	=	W (bottles)
A + B	20	×	25	=	b

$b = 20 \times 25 = 500$ bottles

Even as work problems become more complex, there are still only a few relevant relationships:

- $RT = W$
- When two machines (or similar) are both contributing to the same job, add the rates.
- If one machine is undermining or taking away from a job, subtract the rate of that machine.

Try another example:

> Alejandro, working alone, can build a doghouse in 4 hours. Betty can build the same doghouse in 3 hours. If Betty and Carey, working together, can build the doghouse twice as fast as Alejandro can alone, how long would it take Carey, working alone, to build the doghouse?

22

Begin by solving for the rate that each person works. Let c represent the number of hours it takes Carey to build the doghouse.

Alejandro can build $\frac{1}{4}$ of the doghouse every hour, Betty can build $\frac{1}{3}$ of the doghouse every hour, and Carey can build $\frac{1}{c}$ of the doghouse every hour.

The problem states that Betty and Carey, working together, can build the doghouse twice as fast as Alejandro. In other words, their rate is twice Alejandro's rate:

$$\text{Rate}_B + \text{Rate}_C = 2(\text{Rate}_A)$$
$$\frac{1}{3} + \frac{1}{c} = 2\left(\frac{1}{4}\right)$$
$$\frac{1}{c} = \frac{1}{2} - \frac{1}{3} = \frac{1}{6}$$
$$c = 6$$

It takes Carey 6 hours to build the doghouse alone.

You can also logic it out. Alejandro takes 4 hours to build the doghouse, and Betty takes 3 hours.

Betty and Carey together can build the doghouse twice as fast as Alejandro. It takes Alejandro 4 hours, so Betty and Carey together take 2 hours.

What portion of the doghouse will Betty do in that 2 hours? Since she can do the whole thing in 3 hours, she'll have $\frac{2}{3}$ of it done in 2 hours. Therefore, Carey will have to do the other $\frac{1}{3}$ of the doghouse in 2 hours.

That's Carey's rate; use it to figure out how long Carey will take to do the whole job alone:

$$2 \text{ hours} \rightarrow \frac{1}{3} \text{ of job}$$
$$6 \text{ hours} \rightarrow \frac{3}{3} \text{ of job}$$

When dealing with multiple rates, be sure to express rates as work completed per unit of time. When the work involves completing a task, treat completing the task as doing 100% of the work. Once you know the rates of every worker, add the rates of workers who work together to complete the same task.

Problem Set

Now that you've finished the chapter, try the following problems.

1. An empty bucket is filled with paint at a constant rate, and after 6 minutes, the bucket is filled to $\frac{3}{10}$ of its capacity. How much more time will it take to fill the bucket to full capacity?

2. Two hoses are pouring water into an empty pool. Hose 1 alone would fill up the pool in 6 hours. Hose 2 alone would fill up the pool in 4 hours. How long would it take for both hoses to fill up two-thirds of the pool?

   (A) 1 hour 36 minutes
   (B) 2 hours 24 minutes
   (C) 5 hours

3. A certain ship traveled 9 kilometers in 3 hours. If the ship's speed was 70 meters per minute for the first hour, what was its average speed, in meters per minute, in the last 2 hours?
   (1 kilometer = 1,000 meters)

   (A) 30
   (B) 32.5
   (C) 40
   (D) 47.5
   (E) 50

4. Twelve identical machines, running continuously at the same constant rate, take 8 days to complete a shipment. How many additional machines, each running at the same constant rate, would be needed to reduce the time required to complete a shipment by 2 days?

   (A) 2
   (B) 3
   (C) 4
   (D) 6
   (E) 9

Save the following problems for review after you finish this entire guide.

5. Mary, working at a steady rate, can perform a task in m hours. Nadir, working at a steady rate, can perform the same task in n hours. Mary can perform the task in four-fifths the time it takes Nadir. How many hours will it take the two of them to perform the task if they work together at their respective steady rates, in terms of m ?

(A) $\dfrac{2m}{5}$

(B) $\dfrac{4m}{9}$

(C) $\dfrac{5m}{9}$

(D) $\dfrac{4m}{5}$

(E) $\dfrac{9m}{5}$

6. Train A departs the depot at 1:00 p.m., heading east toward Station Z at an average speed of 45 miles per hour. At 3:00 pm, it speeds up to an average speed of 50 miles per hour. Train B departs the depot at 3:00 pm, heading east toward Station Z. If Train A and Train B both arrive at Station Z at 9:00 p.m., at what average speed, in miles per hour, does Train B travel?

(A) 47.5

(B) 55

(C) 60

(D) 65

(E) 72.5

7. Al and Barb shared the driving on a certain trip. What fraction of the total distance did Al drive?

(1) Al drove for $\dfrac{3}{4}$ as much time as Barb did.

(2) Al's average driving speed for the entire trip was $\dfrac{4}{5}$ of Barb's average driving speed for the trip.

8. Nicky and Chadi begin running a race at the same time, though Nicky starts the race 36 meters ahead of Chadi. If Chadi runs at a pace of 5 meters per second and Nicky runs at a pace of only 3 meters per second, how many seconds will Nicky have run by the time Chadi passes him?

(A) 15 seconds

(B) 18 seconds

(C) 25 seconds

(D) 30 seconds

(E) 45 seconds

Solutions

1. **14 minutes:** The question asks how much more time it will take to finish filling the bucket. You would need another $\frac{7}{10}$ to fill the bucket. One way to go from $\frac{3}{10}$ to $\frac{7}{10}$ is this:

$$\frac{3}{10} \text{ capacity} \rightarrow 6 \text{ minutes}$$
$$\frac{1}{10} \text{ capacity} \rightarrow 2 \text{ minutes}$$

To get to $\frac{7}{10}$ capacity, multiply by 7: It will take (2 minutes)(7) = 14 minutes.

Alternatively, assign a smart number for the capacity of the bucket. The logic is the same, but this approach allows you to work with more whole numbers and fewer fractions. The bucket is initially filled to $\frac{3}{10}$ of its capacity, so pick a multiple of 10.

If the capacity is 20 (call it gallons), then the bucket is currently $\frac{3}{10} \times 20 = 6$ gallons full. It took 6 minutes for the bucket to get this full, so the bucket is filling at a rate of 1 gallon per minute.

There are $20 - 6 = 14$ more gallons to go until the bucket is full, so it will take another 14 minutes to fill.

2. **(A) 1 hour 36 minutes:** The question is a bit unusual. It doesn't ask how long it will take to fill the pool to capacity but how long it will take to fill the pool to *two-thirds* of capacity. Ideally, try to solve directly for this value.

To start, glance at the answers. First, they're fairly far apart, so you may be able to estimate. Second, if the second hose alone can fill the pool completely in 4 hours, then it can't take more time than that for the two hoses together to fill the pool to two-thirds of capacity. Eliminate answer (C). There are only two answers left; take the math as far as you need to in order to tell whether it will take more or less than 2 hours.

If Hose 1 can fill the pool in 6 hours, its rate is $\frac{1}{6}$ "pool per hour," or the fraction of the job it can do in 1 hour. Likewise, if Hose 2 can fill the pool in 4 hours, its rate is $\frac{1}{4}$ pool per hour. Therefore, the combined rate is $\frac{5}{12}$ pool per hour $\left(\frac{1}{4} + \frac{1}{6} = \frac{5}{12}\right)$.

Convert $\frac{2}{3}$ of capacity to have the same denominator: $\frac{2}{3} \rightarrow \frac{8}{12}$.

After 1 hour, the pool is $\frac{5}{12}$ full. After 2 hours, the pool is $\frac{10}{12}$ full. This is too much! It takes less than 2 hours to get to $\frac{8}{12}$ full. The only possible answer is **(A)**.

3. **(C) 40:** First, Understand. This story problem involves rates as well as unit conversions. The problem gives information about the whole trip and then some information about one part of the trip. The problem then asks for information about the *other* part of the trip.

Come up with a Plan. First convert the information about the whole journey into meters, since the answer is in meters per minute. Then, subtract the distance traveled in the first hour from the total. The remaining distance was covered in 2 hours (converted to minutes); use that fact to calculate the average speed.

Solve. Since 1 km = 1,000 m, the 9 km in this journey equals 9,000 m. In the first hour (60 minutes), the ship's speed was 70 meters per minute. Since $D = RT$, the ship traveled $70 \times 60 = 4,200$ meters in the first hour. That leaves $9,000 - 4,200 = 4,800$ meters to be covered in the last two hours. Two hours is $2 \times 60 = 120$ minutes. Divide the distance by the time to find the rate. $4,800 \div 120 = 40$ meters per minute. The answer is choice **(C)**.

4. **(C) 4:** This is a complicated story. Lay it out carefully before you figure out how to solve. All the machines run at the same rate, so you can ignore that potential aspect of things. There are 12 machines to start and they take 8 days to do the job.

   The problem states that the time required will be reduced *by* 2 days—so that's a total of 6 days. (Note the trap: The test writer is hoping you'll think the time was reduced *to* 2 days.)

   If you feel really comfortable with work problems, there's a neat shortcut you can use. Twelve machines complete the job in 8 days, or $(12r)(8) = 1$ job. An unknown number of machines (call it n) completes the job in 6 days, or $(nr)(6) = 1$ job. The left sides of those two equations equal the same thing, so you can set them equal to each other and solve:

   $$(12r)(8) = (nr)(6)$$

   $$\frac{(12)(8)}{6} = \frac{nr}{r}$$

   $$(2)(8) = n$$

   $$n = 16$$

   The *new* number of machines is 16. The *added* number of machines is $16 - 12 = 4$.

   If that doesn't work for you, use the standard RTW approach. Let the work rate of 1 machine be r. Then the work rate of 12 machines is $12r$, and you can set up an RTW chart:

	R	×	T	=	W
Original	12r	×	8	=	96r

   The shipment work is then $96r$. To figure out how many machines are needed to complete this work in $8 - 2 = 6$ days, set up another row and solve for the unknown rate:

	R	×	T	=	W
Original	12r	×	8	=	96r
New		×	6	=	96r

   Therefore, there are $\frac{96r}{6} = 16r$ machines in total, or $16 - 12 = 4$ additional machines.

5. **(C)** $\frac{5m}{9}$**:** First, Understand what's going on in the problem. This is a story problem about rates and work, but it uses variables. The variables show up in the answer choices. This is a clue that Smart Numbers could work. Though less obvious, the fact that the answer choices are all fractions of m, which is how long it takes Mary working alone, means that it might be possible to estimate—at least enough to eliminate some answer choices.

If they were both as fast as Mary, the answer would be $\frac{m}{2}$; they'd be able to do the job in half the time working together. But Nadir is not as fast as Mary, so he slows her down. So the answer should be greater than $\frac{m}{2}$, but less than m. That leaves only (C) and (D).

Choice (D) seems like a bad guess, since $\frac{4}{5}$ is in the problem. Also, choice (C)'s reciprocal shows up as another answer choice, choice (E). This makes (C) the best bet.

To be absolutely sure it's (C) and not (D), make an RTW chart and plug in smart numbers. The rates are unknown (for now). Since Mary can do the job in four-fifths the time it takes Nadir, assign the variables accordingly, say $m = 4$ and $n = 5$. Last, fill in the amount of work. For each row of the table, the number in the work column will be the same, because it is the same amount of work each time. Pick a number for the amount of work that will make the math easy. In this case, a multiple of 4 and 5 works well. Make the work 20:

	Rate (tasks/hour)	×	Time (hours)	=	Work (tasks)
Mary	?	×	4	=	20
Nadir	?	×	5	=	20
Together	?	×	⬭	=	20

Now solve for the rates of Mary and Nadir. Then, their rates can be added to calculate the combined rate.

	Rate (tasks/hour)	×	Time (hours)	=	Work (tasks)
Mary	5	×	4	=	20
Nadir	4	×	5	=	20
Together	$5 + 4 = 9$	×	⬭	=	20

Divide the work by the rate to find the time they take, working together: $\frac{20}{9}$ hours. Plug $m = 4$ into the answer choices to see which one yields $\frac{20}{9}$. It's **(C)**, since $\frac{5 \times 4}{9} = \frac{20}{9}$.

6. **(D) 65:** First, make sure to understand the story. One train leaves first and travels two legs of the trip at different speeds, and another train leaves later, traveling at a constant speed. The question asks for the average speed of the second train. Average speed equals total distance divided by total time, so finding those two values will be the key to this problem.

Draw this problem out to make it easier to understand. Both trains A and B travel east from the depot to Station Z. Train A's journey has two parts: the first part when it is traveling at 45 mph and the second part when it is traveling at 50 mph. Train B has one average speed for its whole journey. Draw it out and use the clock times given in the prompt to figure out the stopwatch times.

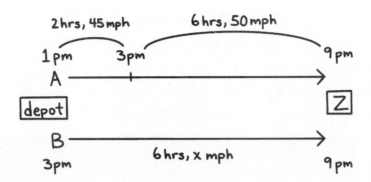

Finally, Solve. The total time for Train B is 6 hours. Now, all that is needed is the total distance. There's not enough information about Train B to figure that out directly, so use the information about Train A. Since $D = RT$, the distance of the first leg of A's journey is 45 mph × 2 hours = 90 miles. The second leg is 50 mph × 6 hours = 300 miles. The total distance is 90 + 300 = 390 miles.

So the total distance traveled by both trains is 390 miles, and Train B covers the distance in 6 hours. Do the math: 390 miles ÷ 6 hours = 65 miles per hour.

The answer is **(D)**.

7. **(C):** The problem asks for a relative value, not the actual value. Rephrase the question as follows: What is the ratio of Al's driving distance to the entire distance driven? Alternatively, since the entire distance is the sum of only Al's distance and Barb's distance, you can find the ratio of Al's distance to Barb's distance:

(1) INSUFFICIENT: Knowing only the relative amount of time each drove indicates nothing about distance driven.

(2) INSUFFICIENT: Knowing only the relative rates at which each drove indicates nothing about distance driven.

(1) AND (2) SUFFICIENT: Set up an RTD chart to combine the information:

	R	×	T	=	D
Al	$\left(\frac{4}{5}\right)r$	×	$\left(\frac{3}{4}\right)t$	=	$\left(\frac{3}{5}\right)rt$
Barb	r	×	t	=	rt
Total					$\left(\frac{8}{5}\right)rt$

Call the distance measurement *miles*. The total trip distance was $\frac{8}{5}$ miles or 1.6 miles (ignore the *rt*, since that's identical for all three entries for distance). Bob drove 0.6 miles of the total distance, so he drove $\frac{0.6}{1.6}$ of the distance.

The correct answer is **(C)**: The two statements work together, but neither one works alone.

8. **(B) 18 seconds:** Save time on this problem by considering the rate at which Chadi closes the gap with Nicky. If Nicky runs at a rate of 3 meters per second and Chadi runs at a rate of 5 meters per second, then Chadi catches up at a rate of 5 − 3 = 2 meters per second.

Since Nicky starts off 36 meters ahead of Chadi, Chadi needs to make up 36 meters to catch up to Nicky. If Chadi closes the gap by 2 meters per second, then it will take Chadi $\frac{36}{2} = 18$ seconds to catch up to Nicky.

Alternatively, use a single $RT = D$ equation. The rate at which Chadi catches up to Nicky is 2 meters per second, and the distance is 36 meters (because that's how far apart Nicky and Chadi are):

R (meters/second)	×	T (seconds)	=	D (meters)
2	×	t	=	36

$$2t = 36$$

$$t = 18$$

A third way to solve this problem is to draw it out. Draw Nicky and Chadi's starting points:

Next, map out how their positions will change over time. It will take a while for Chadi to catch up to Nicky; Chadi runs 5 meters per second and needs to make up 36 meters. Map out their progress in increments of 10 seconds rather than 1 second (looking at the answer choices is another way to get this hint; the smallest answer is 15):

Seconds	Nicky's Position = 36 + 3 meters/second	Chadi's position = 5 meters/second
0	36	0
10	36 + 3(10) = 66	5(10) = 50
20	36 + 3(20) = 96	5(20) = 100

After 20 seconds, Chadi has just passed Nicky, so Chadi overtook Nicky at some time between 10 and 20 seconds. Only answers (A) and (B) are in this range. Logic it out from here. The two runners are much closer together after 20 seconds ($100 - 96 = 4$ meters) than they are after 10 seconds ($66 - 50 = 16$ meters). Thus, the exact time Chadi passed Nicki must be closer to 20 seconds than 10 seconds, so answer (**B**), 18 seconds, makes more sense.

CHAPTER 23

Overlapping Sets

In This Chapter...

- The Double-Set Matrix

- Overlapping Sets and Percents

- Overlapping Sets and Algebraic Representation

In this chapter, you will learn how to organize and solve overlapping set stories in both percent and algebraic form.

CHAPTER 23 Overlapping Sets

Stories that involve two (or more) given sets of data that partially intersect with each other are termed **overlapping sets**. For example:

> Of 30 integers, 15 are in set A, 22 are in set B, and 8 are in both sets A and B. How many of the integers are in NEITHER set A nor set B ?

This problem involves two sets, *A* and *B*. The two sets overlap because some of the numbers are in both sets. Thus, these two sets can actually be divided into four categories:

1. Numbers in set *A*

2. Numbers in set *B*

3. Numbers in both *A* and *B*

4. Numbers in neither *A* nor *B*

Solving double-set GMAT problems, such as in the example above, involves finding values for one of these four categories.

The Double-Set Matrix

For GMAT problems involving only *two* sets of data, the most efficient tool is the **double-set matrix**. Here's how to set one up, using the previous example:

> Of 30 integers, 15 are in set A, 22 are in set B, and 8 are in both set A and B. How many of the integers are in NEITHER set A nor set B ?

First, set up a table:

	A	Not *A*	Total
B			
Not *B*			
Total			

For two data sets, you'll always have four columns and four rows. The final column and the final row will always be labeled Total. Next, ask yourself what are the two data sets. In this case, the sets are *A* and *B*. A particular value can be either in set *A* or not in set *A*. These are called *mutually exclusive*, a term you'll hear in graduate school. Label the columns so that the mutually exclusive options *A* and not *A* are side by side. Likewise, a particular value can be either in set *B* or not in set *B*.

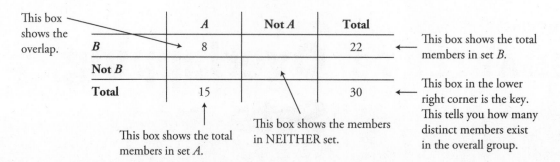

This box shows the overlap.

This box shows the total members in set *B*.

This box shows the total members in set *A*.

This box shows the members in NEITHER set.

This box in the lower right corner is the key. This tells you how many distinct members exist in the overall group.

23

Once the information given in the problem has been filled in, as in the chart below, complete the rest of the chart. Each row and each column sum to a total value as shown here:

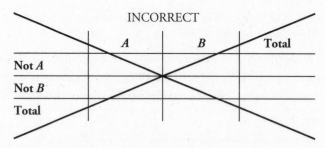

		A	Not A	Total
+	B	8	14	22
=	Not B	7	1	8
	Total	15	15	30

The question asks for the number of integers that are in *neither* set. Look at the chart to find the number of integers that are Not *A* and Not *B*; the answer is 1.

There are two important points to remember. First, you likely will not need to fill in the entire chart; you only have to fill in enough to get the particular value that the question asked you to find. To that end, before you start solving, put a circle in the box that you want to find.

Second, when you construct a double-set matrix, the rows must correspond to the *mutually exclusive options* for one decision: You have *A* or you don't have *A*. Likewise, the columns should correspond to the mutually exclusive options for the other decision: You have *B* or you don't have *B*. Do *not* draw the table this way:

INCORRECT

	A	B	Total
Not A			
Not B			
Total			

Once you've set up the matrix, take a moment to check the logic of a couple of the boxes. In the incorrect example, the first open box shows the intersection of *A* and Not *A*. How many items can be both in *A* and not in *A* at the same time? Zero. The same is true of *B* and Not *B*. It's also the case that you could have some items in both *A* and *B*, but the matrix doesn't contain any box that allows that combination. Logically, then, this cannot be the correct setup for the matrix.

One final note: Venn diagrams (overlapping circles) can also be used for these problems, but the double-set matrix is strongly recommended for problems with only two sets of data points. The double-set matrix conveniently displays *all* possible combinations of options, including the totals, whereas the Venn diagram displays only a subset of the combinations.

Overlapping Sets and Percents

Many overlapping sets problems involve *percents* or *fractions*. The double-set matrix is still effective on these problems, especially if you choose a smart number for the grand total. For problems involving percents, choose a total of 100. For problems involving fractions, choose a common denominator for the total. For example, choose 15 if the problem mentions categories that are $\frac{1}{3}$ and $\frac{2}{5}$ of the total. Try this problem:

> The books on a bookshelf are either hardcover or paperback. Sixty percent of the books are paperback and half of the hardcover books are fiction. If 40% of the paperback books are fiction, what percent of the books are nonfiction?

(A) 30

(B) 40

(C) 44

(D) 56

(E) 60

First, set up your chart. The two groups are fiction/nonfiction and hardcover/paperback. Because the problem uses only percentages, no real numbers, choose 100 for the total number of books. The problem asks for the percentage that are nonfiction; put a circle in that box.

Then, begin to fill in the other information given in the problem. The second sentence indicates that 60% of the books are paperback. That allows you to figure out the portion that are hardcover, since the two have to add up to 100. You also know that half of the hardcover books are fiction; therefore, half of the hardcover books are nonfiction. Fill in the table:

	F	NF	Total
HC	50% Tot HC = 20	50% Tot HC = 20	100 − 60 = 40
PB	40% Tot PB = 24		60
Total		⬯	100

Next, add the information from the third sentence and solve for the desired box. Of the paperbacks, 40% are fiction; there are 60 paperbacks, so 40% is 24. (Take 10%, then multiply by 4: $(6)(4) = 24$.) Now, you have a choice. You can solve to the right or solve down in order to get to the circle. Here's how to solve down:

	F	NF	Total
HC	50% Tot HC = 20	50% Tot HC = 20	$x = 40$
PB	40% Tot PB = 24		60
Total	20 + 24 = 44	100 − 44 = 56	100

You don't need to complete the entire chart, since you have already answered the question asked in the problem. If you want to check your work—and you have the time!—you can complete the matrix. The last box you fill in must work both vertically and horizontally.

The correct answer is (D), 56. There are some traps built into the answer choices. The last number before the answer, 44, is in the answer choices; this number represents an adjacent category, fiction, rather than the desired category, nonfiction. Someone choosing (C) solved for the wrong box.

Note one important thing about this pair of answers, 44 and 56: They add up to 100%! Trap answer (C) has a name: It's an Evil Twin. One of the most common careless mistakes people make is to solve for the wrong thing. In this case, you would do everything correctly, right up to the end, and then just choose the wrong answer.

Evil Twins pop up on all kinds of story problems, not just ones that involve percents. When you see that a story problem contains two adjacent things you could have solved for (nonfiction *or* fiction, in this case, or the number of cats vs. the number of dogs), and the answers contain real numbers, glance at those answers first to see whether Evil Twins are present. In this case, there are *two* pairs of Evil Twins adding up to 100: the pair 44/56 and the pair 40/60. Answer choice (A), 30, is the odd one out, so if you have to guess, don't guess that one.

The other pairing, 40/60, is the result of a calculation error along the way. The problem states that 40% of the paperbacks are fiction. If someone mistakenly reads that as 40% of *all* of the books are fiction, then she would put 40 in the fiction total box and calculate the final answer as 60. Alternatively, if someone did place the 40% properly in the paperback fiction box but mistakenly took 40% of 100 rather than 40% of 60, then she would put 60 in the fiction total box and calculate the final answer as 40.

As with any problem, only use smart numbers if the problem contains only relative values (such as fractions and/or percents), but no actual *numbers* of items or people. In that case, go ahead and pick a total of 100 (for percent problems) or a common denominator (for fraction problems). If actual quantities appear anywhere in the problem, though, then all the totals are already determined. In that case, you cannot assign numbers, but must solve for them instead.

Overlapping Sets and Algebraic Representation

When solving overlapping sets problems, pay close attention to the wording of the problem. For example, consider this problem:

> A researcher estimates that 10% of the children in the world are between the ages of 8 and 18 and dislike soccer, and that 50% of the children who like soccer are between the ages of 8 and 18. If 40% of the children in the world are between the ages of 8 and 18, what percentage of children in the world are under age 8 and dislike the game of soccer? (Assume all children are between the ages of 0 and 18.)

It is tempting to fill in the number 50 to represent the percent of children aged 8 to 18 who like soccer. However, this approach is incorrect:

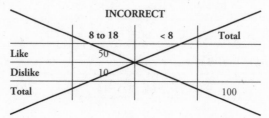

You'll need some grammar skills here. The sentence says that 50% of the children *who like soccer* are between the ages of 8 and 18. This is different from saying that 50% of the children *in the world* are between the ages of 8 and 18. The children *who like soccer* are a subset—a smaller number—of *all* of the children in the world.

You do not yet know how many children like soccer, so you can't actually find the 50% figure (yet!). Instead, represent the unknown total number of children who like soccer with the variable x. Then, represent the number of children aged 8 to 18 who like soccer with the expression $0.5x$:

	8 to 18	< 8	Total
Like	0.5x		x
Dislike	10		
Total	40		100

The "8 to 18 + Like" box must equal $40 - 10 = 30$; set up an equation to solve for x:

$$0.5x = 30$$
$$x = 60$$

Fill in whatever you need to get to the desired cell. Here's one possible path:

	8 to 18	< 8	Total
Like	0.5x = 30		x = 60
Dislike	10	30	40
Total	40		100

Therefore, 30% of the children are under age 8 and dislike soccer.

Problem Set

Now that you've finished the chapter, try the following problems.

1. Set *A* contains 16 even integers, and set *B* contains 22 integers that are all multiples of 3. If 7 of the integers fall into both sets *A* and *B*, how many integers are in exactly one of the two sets?

2. Of the 28 people in a park, 12 are children and the rest are adults. Eight people have to leave the park at 3 p.m.; the rest will stay. If, after 3 p.m., there are 6 children still in the park, how many adults are still in the park?

    (A)   2

    (B)   8

    (C)   11

    (D)   14

    (E)   20

3. Of the students at a certain high school, 40% take physics. Of those students who don't take physics, 20% do take calculus. What percentage of students take neither physics nor calculus?

Save the following problems for review after you finish this entire guide.

4. Of 30 snakes at the reptile house, 10 have stripes, 21 are poisonous, and 5 have no stripes and are not poisonous. How many of the snakes both have stripes and are poisonous?

5. At a car dealership, 10% of all cars are red and have heated seats, and 75% of cars without heated seats are red. If 40% of all of the cars are red, what percent of the cars have heated seats?

    (A)   25%

    (B)   40%

    (C)   60%

    (D)   75%

    (E)   85%

Answers and explanations follow on the next page. ▶ ▶ ▶

Solutions

1. **24 integers:** Use a double-set matrix to solve this problem. First, fill in the numbers given in the problem: 16 integers total in set *A* and 22 integers total in set *B*. There are 7 integers in the overlap of sets *A* and *B*. Next, use subtraction to solve for the number of integers in set *A* but not in set *B* (9) and the number of integers in set *B* but not in set *A* (15). Finally, add those two numbers: $9 + 15 = 24$.

	A	Not A	Total
B	7	15	22
Not B	9		
Total	16		

2. **(D) 14:** Use a double-set matrix to solve this problem. First, fill in the numbers given in the problem: There are 28 people total; 12 are children, and the rest ($28 - 12 = 16$) are adults; 8 leave at 3 p.m. and the rest ($28 - 8 = 20$) stay. Next, 6 children stay in the park after 3 p.m. Since there are a total of 20 people in the park after 3 p.m., the remaining 14 people who stay must be adults. Here is the table:

	C	A	Total
Leave			8
Stay	6	14	20
Total	12	16	28

    Notice that there are two pairs of Evil Twins in the answers choices. Answers (A) and (D) sum to 16, the total number of adults. If you thought the question asked how many adults left the park, rather than stayed, you would come up with answer (A).

    Answers (B) and (E) sum to 28, the total number of people in the park. If you thought the question asked for the total number of people who stayed in the park, rather than just the adults who stayed, you might choose answer (E).

3. **48%:** Since all the numbers in this problem are given in percentages, assign a grand total of 100 students. The problem indicates that 40% of all high school students take physics, so fill in 40 for this total. The number who don't take physics must be $100 - 40 = 60$.

    Next, 20% of those students who do not take physics do take calculus. (It does not say that 20% of *all* students take calculus!) According to the table, 60 students do not take physics, so 20% of those, or 12, do take calculus. Therefore, fill in 12 for the students who take calculus but not physics. Finally, subtract: $60 - 12 = 48$ students who take neither physics nor calculus.

	P	No P	Total
C		12	
No C		48	
Total	40	60	100

4. **6:** Use a double-set matrix to solve this problem. First, fill in the numbers given in the problem: 30 snakes total, 10 with stripes (and therefore 20 without), 21 that are poisonous (and therefore 9 that are not), and 5 that are neither striped nor poisonous. Use subtraction to fill in enough of the chart to answer the question (one way is shown below). A total of 6 snakes have stripes and are poisonous.

	S	Not S	Total
P	6		21
Not P	4	5	9
Total	10	20	30

5. **(C) 60%:** Use a double-set matrix to solve this problem. Since all the numbers in this problem are given in percentages, assign a grand total of 100 cars. The problem indicates that 10% of all cars are red and have heated seats, so enter 10 in the R + HS cell. It also indicates that 75% *of cars without heated seats* are red. At this point, you don't know how many cars don't have heated seats, so assign the variable x to represent the Total Not HS. Of these cars, 75% are red, so enter $0.75x$ in the R + Not HS cell.

Next, 40% of all cars are red, so enter 40 in the Total R cell. Column R has to add up $(10 + 0.75x = 40)$, so the R + Not HS cell $(0.75x)$ must equal 30. Solve the equation to find that $x = 40$. If 40 cars do not have heated seats, then 60 have heated seats. Therefore, 60% of all of the cars have heated seats as shown in the table below:

	R	Not R	Total
HS	10		60
Not HS	$0.75x = 30$		$x = 40$
Total	40		100

Did you notice the two pairs of Evil Twins that add to 100 in this problem? Answers (A) and (D) are one pair, and answers (B) and (C) are the other. You might get answer (B) if you solved for the cars without, rather than with, heated seats. You could get answers (A) or (D) if you focused on red cars as opposed to all cars.

Strategy: Arithmetic vs. Algebra 201

In This Chapter...

- Choosing Numbers for Smart Numbers

- Pick for Any Unknown on Smart Numbers

- Smart Numbers Disguised as Working Backwards

- Draw It Out and Work Backwards

In this chapter, you will learn more advanced approaches for the Choose Smart Numbers, Work Backwards, and Draw It Out strategies, including when to choose certain kinds of numbers, how to work more flexibly with smart numbers, and how to both draw out and work backwards on the same problem.

CHAPTER 24 Strategy: Arithmetic vs. Algebra 201

This chapter focuses on more advanced techniques for handling harder Smart Numbers, Work Backwards, and Draw It Out problems.

Try this problem:

> Cost is expressed by the formula tb^4. If b is doubled and t remains the same, the new cost is how many times greater than the original cost?
>
> (A)   1.2
> (B)   2
> (C)   6
> (D)   8
> (E)   16

You can use an algebraic approach on this problem—and the algebraic approach is really streamlined *if* you know exactly how to set it up. Here's how:

$$\text{Original} = tb^4$$
$$\text{New} = t(2b)^4 = 16tb^4$$
$$\frac{\text{New}}{\text{Old}} = \frac{16tb^4}{tb^4} = 16$$

The correct answer is (E). If you feel comfortable with this algebraic approach, go for it. More people, though, will be unsure about that approach or setup. Instead, use real numbers to solve.

At first glance, the problem might seem like a candidate for working backwards—there are real numbers in the answer choices. In fact, though, those numbers are *relative* values, not actual ones: They represent the multiplier to go from the original cost to the new cost. If the multiplier were 5, then it wouldn't matter whether your original cost was $10 or $10 million—you'd still multiply the original cost by 5 to get the new one.

Further, there are never any real values given for the cost. This is actually a Smart Numbers problem!

The original cost is defined as tb^4. Choose something for b that isn't very large, since you're going to have to raise it to a power of 4. Try $b = 2$ and $t = 3$:

$$\text{Original cost} = tb^4 = 3(2^4)$$

The numbers are a little annoying, so don't multiply it out yet. Just leave it for now; later, you may be able to simplify before you multiply. Keep in mind that you're looking for opportunities to divide out either the 3 or the 2^4 or both.

Next, figure out the new cost. The value of b doubles, but t stays the same:

$$\begin{aligned} \text{New cost} &= t(2b)^4 \\ &= 3(2 \times 2)^4 \\ &= (3)(2^4)(2^4) \end{aligned}$$

Since you're looking for opportunities to divide out a 3 or a 2^4, in the second step, distribute the exponent to each 2 and keep them separate. Now you have two 2^4 elements that you might be able to divide out later.

The question asks how many times greater the new cost is than the old one, or New = y(Old). In other words, divide the new by the old to find the multiplier:

$$\frac{\text{New}}{\text{Old}} = \frac{(\cancel{3})(2^4)(2^4)}{(\cancel{3})(2^4)} = 2^4 = 16$$

The math with real numbers is the same math as the algebra—in both cases, everything cancels out except for the 16. Using real numbers can just help you to see how the math works and to set it up correctly.

Choosing Numbers for Smart Numbers

Earlier in this book, you learned how to choose good numbers for certain strategies. This section summarizes the earlier guidelines for the Smart Numbers strategy and adds some new ones.

First, you always have to follow any constraints given in a problem. For example, if the problem says that x is a positive integer, then you can only try positive integers for x.

When using the Smart Numbers strategy on Problem Solving (PS) problems, the general guidelines are to avoid 0, 1, and numbers that appear in the problem. If you have to choose for more than one variable, choose different numbers for each variable.

In addition to the above, try to choose numbers that will work well in the problem. Here are some of the most common ways in which you'll choose numbers on the exam.

Choosing Smart Numbers	
When I see...	*I'll choose...*
Percents	100 or 50
Fractions (part to whole)	A common denominator for all of the fractions
Ratios (even if in fraction form)	The parts of the ratio e.g., The number of dogs is $\frac{3}{4}$ the number of cats. e.g., The ratio of dogs to cats is 3 : 4. Use 3 dogs to 4 cats.
Numbers that I'll need to divide	A multiple of the divisor e.g., Someone bought 8 pens for x dollars. Use a multiple of 8; if $x = 16$, then the pens were $2 each.

Choosing Smart Numbers	
Variation of dividing:	Values that will give integers when calculating a rate
Rate or work problems	Rate = Distance (or Work) divided by Time
A lot of multiplication or exponents	Smaller numbers (e.g., 2)
A variable under a square root sign	A perfect square, such as 4
A variable under a cube root sign	A perfect cube, such as 8
2 or more variables; choosing for one will determine the value of the other(s)	*Don't* default to choosing for the first variable mentioned. Think it through. What's the easiest starting point? e.g., If $x + y = a$ and $x - y = b$, it's easier to choose x and y than a and b. e.g., If Pool A's capacity is twice Pool B's capacity, choose for the smaller capacity first, then multiply by 2 to get the larger capacity.

On more advanced problems, you may see two such clues and have to decide which one to use first. This is what your Plan phase is for—to figure out which characteristic you should prioritize.

As you study, continue adding to the list above as you come across more examples of smart numbers and find your own ways to decide how to choose specific numbers.

Pick for Any Unknown on Smart Numbers

On a Smart Numbers problem, it's often easiest to pick for the actual variables in the problem. Sometimes, though, it's easier to pick for a different unknown, *not* the variable that shows up in the problem and answer choices.

Here's an example:

> A truck is filled to $\frac{1}{4}$ of its maximum weight capacity. An additional y pounds are added such that the truck is now filled to $\frac{7}{8}$ of its capacity. In terms of y, what is the maximum weight capacity of the truck, in pounds?
>
> (A) $\frac{5}{8}y$
>
> (B) $\frac{5}{4}y$
>
> (C) $\frac{8}{5}y$

Understand. This is a PS problem with variable expressions in the answers and no real value ever given for the weight. You can choose smart numbers. The question asks for the maximum capacity. The variable y represents the additional weight added to the truck to go from $\frac{1}{4}$ to $\frac{7}{8}$ of capacity.

Plan. What kind of value for y would be a "good" number, given that y covers the gap between $\frac{1}{4}$ and $\frac{7}{8}$ of the truck's capacity? That's an annoying question. This problem would be a lot easier if it *gave* the maximum capacity and *asked* you to find y.

Guess what? You're actually allowed to choose for the maximum capacity, if you think that's easier!

The two fractions have denominators of 4 and 8, so choose a value for the total capacity that works nicely with both: 8.

Solve. If the total capacity of the truck is 8 pounds (it's a *really* small truck!), then at first it contains 2 pounds of material. Later, it contains 7 pounds, so $y = 5$ pounds were added. Plug this value into the answers and look for the answer that equals the total capacity of 8:

(A) $\dfrac{5}{8}y = \dfrac{5}{8}(5) \neq 8$ Eliminate

(B) $\dfrac{5}{4}y = \dfrac{5}{4}(5) \neq 8$ Eliminate

(C) $\dfrac{8}{5}y = \dfrac{8}{5}(5) = 8$ Match!

The correct answer is (C).

When using smart numbers, you can always choose where to start. A lot of the time, it will be easier to choose for the variable that shows up in the answers, but if you ever find yourself thinking that the math would be easier if they had given you some other value in the problem, go ahead and reverse the process. Choose your own value for that unknown and work your way to the variable that shows up in the answers.

By the way, one of the answer choices in the truck problem doesn't make logical sense—though most people don't stop to consider the problem in this way. The variable y represents a *subset* of the truck's capacity, since it's the amount of capacity that allows the truck to go from $\dfrac{1}{4}$ to $\dfrac{7}{8}$ full. The answer choices represent the total capacity of the truck. Logically, the total capacity must be greater than a subset of the capacity, so the correct answer must be y times a number greater than 1. In answer (A), the fraction is less than 1. That would make the truck's total capacity less than y, which is a subset of the truck's total capacity—illogical!

You don't absolutely have to learn to spot those kinds of traps—but if you do, that can help you to narrow down answers when you need to guess. It can also help you to avoid careless mistakes—if you know logically that the fraction should be greater than 1, but you end up getting answer (A), you'll know to check your work.

Smart Numbers Disguised as Working Backwards

Some problems do have real numbers in the answer choices, but can still be solved via smart numbers anyway.

Try this problem:

> A company pays the same hourly rate to all of its employees. Four people work for 8 hours each and earn a total of y dollars collectively. How many people need to work for 20 hours each in order to earn a total of $1.25y$ dollars collectively?
>
> (A) 1
> (B) 2
> (C) 3

Understand. This problem fits all of the hallmarks of a Working Backwards problem—"nice" real numbers in the answers, and those answers represent a single variable in the problem, the number of people—but there's a hitch. What do you do with that variable y in the story?

The *y* represents the dollars earned for a certain number of hours worked. Later, the problem uses 1.25*y* to represent the dollars earned for a different number of hours worked. The problem also states that the hourly pay rate is the same for everyone—but it *never* gives a real number for rate of pay or for dollars anywhere in the problem.

That's a characteristic of Smart Numbers! If the problem keeps talking about something but never gives you a real number for that something, you're allowed to choose your own number, even when other parts of the problem do give real numbers for other things.

Plan. Choose your own pay rate and work through the problem accordingly. How about $10/hour? (You may be tempted to go with something like $15. Don't think real world. Make your task as easy as you can.)

Solve. The pay rate is $10 per hour. In the first scenario, four people work for 8 hours each, or a total of 32 hours. Collectively, they are paid $(32)(10) = \$320$. This is *y*.

The problem asks about a second scenario in which the workers earn 1.25*y*. This is 25% greater than *y* itself, so take 25%, or $\frac{1}{4}$, of *y* and add to *y*: $320 + 80 = \$400$.

Aside: You can also benchmark to find this percentage: $25\% = 10\% + 10\% + 5\% = 32 + 32 + 16 = 80$.

Alternatively, to find $\frac{1}{4}$, divide by 2 twice: $\frac{320}{2} = \frac{160}{2} = 80$.

In order to earn a total of $400 at a pay rate of $10 per hour, the workers must have collectively worked a total of 40 hours. For the second scenario, the problem states that the workers worked 20 hours each, so there must have been 2 workers to work a total of 40 hours.

The correct answer is (B).

You can also solve this problem by choosing a value for the variable *y* and then calculating the hourly pay rate. You'd need to divide *y* by both 4 (people) and 8 (hours each) to find the hourly rate, so $y = 32$ might be a good fit. (This would work out to a pay rate of $1/hour.) As on any Smart Numbers problem, start with whatever seems easiest or most natural to you.

Whenever a problem talks about some variable and never gives you a real value for that variable, you can choose your own number for that thing—even if the problem gives you real numbers for other items in the problem.

Draw It Out and Work Backwards

Try this problem:

> Train X is traveling at a constant speed of 30 miles per hour, and Train Y is traveling at a constant speed of 40 miles per hour. If the two trains are traveling in the same direction along the same route, but Train X is 25 miles ahead of Train Y, how many hours will pass before Train Y is 10 miles ahead of Train X?
>
> (A) 1.5
> (B) 2.0
> (C) 2.5
> (D) 3.0
> (E) 3.5

Understand. Glance at the answers before reading the problem. They're all small numbers—so when you read the problem, check whether you can work backwards. The problem itself involves two trains moving in certain ways, so sketch out the story. The question does ask for a single variable (the number of hours it will take for a certain scenario to happen), so you can work backwards. Sketch out the story to make sure you know all of the moving parts:

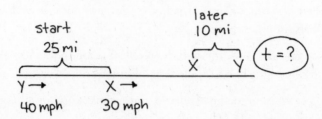

Plan. How can you use the sketch to work backwards? The answer choices represent the amount of time that both trains move. You know the rates of both trains, so for each answer choice that you try, you could sketch another line below and map out how the trains move each hour (or half hour) of the trip.

Solve. Try answer (B) first:

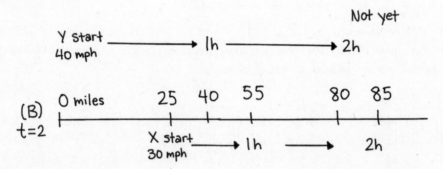

Train Y hasn't passed Train X yet at the 2-hour mark, so answer (B) is incorrect, and answer (A) must be wrong, too. Cross off both.

Glance at the answers. Answer (D) is 3 hours, so just extend the line a little farther to find where the trains are after 1 more hour:

Close! But not quite. Train Y has passed Train X, but it is not yet 10 miles ahead of Train X. So (D) isn't enough time either.

Only answer (E) represents a longer time, so it must be the correct answer.

You can also solve algebraically. The most efficient algebraic method is shown below.

Because the problem focuses on the difference in movement between the two trains, find the difference in distance and the difference in rate, then plug into the Rate-Time-Distance (RTD) formula.

The two trains are currently 25 miles apart, with X ahead of Y. The problem asks you to solve for the time at which Y has moved 10 miles ahead of X. Therefore, Y has to catch up to X to erase that initial 25-mile deficit and then move an additional 10 miles beyond X. In other words, Y has to travel an additional $25 + 10 = 35$ miles farther than X travels. Use 35 as the distance in the RTD formula.

For every hour that the two trains travel, Y goes 10 miles per hour faster (since it travels 40 miles per hour to X's 30 miles per hour). Use 10 miles per hour as the rate in the RTD formula:

$$\frac{35 \text{ miles}}{10 \text{ miles per hour}} = 3.5 \text{ hours}$$

When the algebra for a particular problem feels easier for you, that solution can be quite efficient—but on a problem that you find complex, it's *very* easy to mess up one or more parts of the equation. As you study, think about when you would want to use an algebraic approach (usually when the problem feels straightforward to you) and when you would want to draw it out and work backwards (usually when the problem feels more complex). If you study how to make the best choice for your own brain, then you can react quickly on test day.

Problem Set

Pop quiz! The problems in this set may cover any strategies from the entire guide up to this point.

1. In a college class, each student's overall grade is calculated by averaging the student's grades on *t* different exams. Up until the last exam, Wei had earned an average exam grade of 0.75*g*. After earning a grade of *g* on the last exam, Wei's overall grade in the class was 0.8*g*. What is the value of *t* ?

    (A) 2
    (B) 3
    (C) 4
    (D) 5
    (E) 6

2. The Crandall's hot tub has a capacity of *x* liters and is half full. Their swimming pool, which has a capacity of *y* liters, is filled to four-fifths of its capacity. If enough water is drained from the swimming pool to fill the hot tub to capacity, the pool is now how many liters short of full capacity, in terms of *x* and *y* ?

    (A) $0.8y - 0.5x$
    (B) $0.8y + 0.5x$
    (C) $0.2y + 0.5x$
    (D) $0.3(y - x)$
    (E) $0.3(y + x)$

3. Four brothers split a sum of money between them. The first brother received 50% of the total, the second received 25% of the total, the third received 20% of the total, and the fourth received the remaining $4. The first brother received how much more money than the third brother received?

    (A) $4
    (B) $16
    (C) $20
    (D) $24
    (E) $36

4. If *x* is a positive integer and $3x + 2$ is divisible by 5, then which of the following must be true?

    (A) *x* is divisible by 3.
    (B) 3*x* is divisible by 10.
    (C) $x - 1$ is divisible by 5.
    (D) *x* is odd.
    (E) 3*x* is even.

Save the following problems for review after you finish this entire guide.

5. A rental car agency owns a total of $5x$ cars and $2x$ trucks, where x is a positive integer. If the agency purchases c new cars, will the new ratio of cars to trucks be at least 3 to 1 ?

    (1) $c = x + 5$
    (2) $x = 11$

6. Teachers and students at a school are solving problems. There are twice as many students as teachers, and each student solves 3 more problems than each teacher. If teachers solve 24 of the 90 total problems solved, how many problems does each teacher solve?

    (A) 3
    (B) 4
    (C) 5
    (D) 6
    (E) 8

7. Vimbai spends $\frac{3}{8}$ of her monthly paycheck on rent and $\frac{1}{4}$ on food. Her roommate, Carrie, who earns twice as much as Vimbai, spends $\frac{1}{4}$ of her monthly paycheck on rent and $\frac{1}{2}$ on food. If the two roommates decide to donate the remainder of their money to charity each month, what fraction of their combined monthly income will they donate?

    (A) $\frac{5}{24}$
    (B) $\frac{7}{24}$
    (C) $\frac{11}{24}$
    (D) $\frac{17}{24}$
    (E) $\frac{19}{24}$

8. Can the students at Ridgecrest Elementary School be divided evenly into 6 classrooms?

    (1) Cascade Elementary School has a total of 240 students.
    (2) Ridgecrest Elementary School has 20% more students than Cascade Elementary School.

Solutions

1. **(D) 5:** The answer choices contain real numbers, represented by t in the problem, but the problem also contains an unspecified value, g. No real value is ever given for g, so choose your own. You'll need to take both 0.75 and 0.8 of g, so choose a value that will work well in both calculations.

    Let $g = 100$. Wei's average for all but the last exam (or $t - 1$ exams) was 75. The last exam grade was 100. The sum of all of the grades is $75(t - 1) + 100$. The total number of tests is t. Plug these values and variables into the average formula and solve for t:

    $$\text{Average} = \frac{\text{Sum}}{\text{\# of terms}}$$

    $$80 = \frac{75(t - 1) + 100}{t}$$

    $$80t = 75(t - 1) + 100$$

    $$80t = 75t - 75 + 100$$

    $$5t = 25$$

    $$t = 5$$

    Wei took a total of 5 exams.

2. **(C) $0.2y + 0.5x$:** The answers contain the variables x and y; the question stem never offers real values for these variables, so you can choose your own smart numbers.

    The problem contains two fractions: The hot tub is *half* full and the pool is filled to *four-fifths* of its capacity. The two capacities are not related (that is, once you pick for one variable, the other variable is not automatically determined), so you'll have to pick two numbers. Pick something divisible by 2 for x and divisible by 5 for y. Try $x = 4$ and $y = 10$:

Hot Tub	Pool
$x = $ H cap $= 4$	$y = $ P cap $= 10$
Half full $= 2$	$\frac{4}{5}$ full $= 8$

    The hot tub, with a capacity of 4, is half full, so there are 2 liters of water in the hot tub. The pool, with a capacity of 10, is four-fifths full, so there are 8 liters in the pool.

    Next, the problem says that water is siphoned off from the pool and put into the hot tub. How much? The hot tub needs 2 more liters to be full, so subtract 2 from the pool. The pool now has only 6 liters, so it is 4 liters short of its capacity of 10.

    Plug $x = 4$ and $y = 10$ into the answer choices and look for an answer that matches: 4 liters short.

    (A) $0.8y - 0.5x = (0.8)(10) - (0.5)(4) = 8 - 2 = 6$

    (B) $0.8y + 0.5x = (0.8)(10) + (0.5)(4) = $ too big, since (A) was too big.

    (C) $0.2y + 0.5x = (0.2)(10) + (0.5)(4) = 2 + 2 = 4$ Match!

    (D) $0.3(y - x) = 0.3(10 - 4) = 0.3(6) = $ not an integer

    (E) $0.3(y + x) = 0.3(10 + 4) = 0.3(14) = $ not an integer

3. **(D) $24:** The answer choices are "nice" integers; check the question stem to see whether you can work backwards.

The question asks for the difference between the first brother and the third brother. If you started with answer (B), 16, what values would you choose for each brother? They can be anything, as long as the difference is 16.

Don't work backwards on this problem. (This is why the Work Backwards strategy specifies that the question should ask for a single variable in the problem.) Do the actual math to solve.

The first three brothers got 50% + 25% + 20% = 95% of the money. The fourth brother, then, got the remaining 5%, and that 5% is equal to $4.

If 5% = $4, then 10% = $8, and 100% = $80. The total amount of money is $80. The first brother got 50%, or $40, and the third brother got 20%, or $16. The difference is $40 − $16 = $24.

4. **(C) $x − 1$ is divisible by 5:** The question stem is asking a *must be* question, so test cases on this problem. Use positive integers for x that make the following equation true:

$$\frac{3x + 2}{5} = \text{integer}$$

If $x = 1$, then $3(1) + 2 = 5$, which is divisible by 5. So this is a valid case to test. Check $x = 1$ against the answer choices. Answers (A), (B), and (E) are all false for this case, so eliminate them.

Try another case. If $x = 2$, then $3(2) + 2 = 8$, which is not divisible by 5. This is an invalid case; discard it. What about $x = 3$? In this case, $3(3) + 2 = 11$. Still invalid. You can continue to try increasing integers or take a moment to think about what's happening with the math to help you find the next case. Rearrange that starting equation a little:

$$\frac{3x + 2}{5} = \text{int}$$
$$3x + 2 = (5)(\text{int})$$
$$3x = (5)(\text{int}) - 2$$

In other words, $3x$ must equal a multiple of 5 minus 2. Multiples of 5 are 5, 10, 15, 20, 25, and so on. Subtract 2 from these multiples of 5 to find the potential values of $3x$, which are 3, 8, 13, 18, 23, and so on.

Because x itself must be an integer, $3x$ must be a multiple of 3. This narrows down the list of potential values of $3x$ to 3, 18, and so on, and the corresponding x-values are 1, 6, and so on. The first case, $x = 1$, has already been tested, so the next one to try is $x = 6$.

Case 2: $x = 6$. Verify that this is valid: $(3)(6) + 2 = 20$. This is divisible by 5, so proceed. Answers (A), (B), and (E) have already been eliminated, so test only answers (C) and (D). In this case, answer (D) is false, so eliminate it. The only remaining answer is **(C)**.

5. **(A):** This is a Yes/No question and it asks an *at least* question, so expect to use an inequality to translate into math. The story problem discusses ratios using the variables c and x. Glance at the statements. The second statement provides a value for the unknown x. The first statement would allow you to find c if you know x. So is the answer (C)?

That's probably too good to be true. Be suspicious—this might be a C-Trap. Jot down the information from the question stem. The current number of cars to trucks is $5x$ to $2x$, or a ratio of 5 : 2.

If there are c more cars, then there are a total of $5x + c$ cars. The question asks whether this new situation has a car-to-truck ratio of *at least* 3 : 1. Use this information to set up a proportion for the question: Is the ratio of the new number of cars to the number of trucks at least 3 to 1 ?

$$\text{Is } \frac{\text{Cars}}{\text{Trucks}} = \frac{5x + c}{2x} \geq \frac{3}{1} \text{ ?}$$

The left-hand side shows the real-number representation for cars and trucks after c cars are added. The right-hand side shows the ratio for the same scenario. The question asks whether that ratio is *at least* 3 : 1, so use the greater-than-or-equal-to symbol.

Fractions are annoying; can you cross-multiply to simplify the equation? Yes, the problem indicates that x is positive, so don't switch the direction of the inequality sign when you cross-multiply:

Is $5x + c \geq 6x$?
Is $c \geq x$?

This is the rephrased question. Statement (2) is easier, so start there.

(2) INSUFFICIENT: This statement provides no information about c, so it's not possible to tell whether $c \geq x$.

(1) SUFFICIENT: The question stem states that x is a positive integer. Take any positive integer and add 5; what happens? The number gets larger, so c does have to be greater than x. (In fact, this would work with any number, positive or negative, integer or fraction.) This information is sufficient to answer the question Always Yes.

The correct answer is **(A)**: Statement (1) is sufficient alone, but statement (2) is not.

6. **(E) 8:** The answers contain easy integers, so check whether you can work backwards. The question does ask for a single variable, so you can. (Note: The problem might seem pretty straightforward at first glance, but there are three variables: number of teachers, number of students, and number of problems solved. This will make for a very messy algebraic solution. Even if you really like algebra, consider working backwards on this problem.)

The problem gives enough information to solve for the total number of problems solved by students. If teachers solve 24 out of the 90 problems, then the students must solve $90 - 24 = 66$ problems.

The answers represent the number of problems solved by each teacher. Each student solves 3 more than each teacher, so start by adding 3 to each answer choice:

	Prob per T:	$\rightarrow$	Prob per S:
(A)	3	$\rightarrow$	6
(B)	4	$\rightarrow$	7
(C)	5	$\rightarrow$	8
(D)	6	$\rightarrow$	9
(E)	8	$\rightarrow$	11

(# of students)(# problems solved per student) = 66

The students solve a total of 66 problems, and there must be an integer-number of students (no partial people!), so the number of problems solved per student must be a factor of 66. Only answers (A) and (E) qualify; eliminate the other three.

Try either remaining answer. If the one you try is incorrect, then the correct answer has to be the other one.

Prob per T	Prob per S (Prob per T + 3)	# S (66 ÷ prior)	# S = twice # T
(A) 3	6	$\frac{66}{6} = 11$	5.5 teachers…

There are supposed to be twice as many students as teachers, so that would be 5.5 teachers…no good! The only remaining answer is **(E)**. (If you try it: problems per teacher = 8, problems per student = 11, # of students = 6, # of teachers = 3. The teachers solve (8)(3) = 24 problems, which is what the problem said, so this answer is correct.)

7. **(B)** $\frac{17}{24}$: The answer choices represent a relative amount, so use smart numbers to solve. The question asks what fraction of their total income Vimbai and Carrie will donate, or $\frac{\text{combined donation}}{\text{combined total}}$.

Since the denominators in the problem are 8, 4, and 2, assign Vimbai a monthly paycheck of $8. Assign Carrie, who earns twice as much, a monthly paycheck of $16. Total income is $8 + $16 = $24. The roommates' monthly expenses break down as follows:

	Rent	Food	Left over/to donate
V	$\frac{3}{8}$ of 8 = 3	$\frac{1}{4}$ of 8 = 2	8 − (3 + 2) = 3
C	$\frac{1}{4}$ of 16 = 4	$\frac{1}{2}$ of 16 = 8	16 − (4 + 8) = 4

Vimbai and Carrie will donate a total of $3 + $4 = $7 out of their combined monthly income of $24.

Notice the two pairs of Evil Twins: Answers (A) and (E) sum to 1, as do answers (B) and (D).

Answer (D) represents the fraction of total income that Vimbai and Carrie *spend*, rather than donate, a classic GMAT trap on this kind of question. Answer (A) results from using the same income for Vimbai and Carrie (but doing everything else correctly). And answer (E) makes both of those mistakes. Avoid guessing (C) on this problem, since it does not have an Evil Twin at all.

8. **(B):** The question stem doesn't have any explicit givens, but it does have a hidden integer constraint: if R is the number of students at Ridgecrest Elementary School, then R must be a positive integer. Jot that down. It's a Yes/No question; either Yes, R is divisible by 6, or No, R is not divisible by 6.

(1) INSUFFICIENT: The statement tells you nothing about R. Eliminate answers (A) and (D).

(2) SUFFICIENT: Let C be the number of students at Cascade Elementary School and translate this statement into the equation $R = 1.2C$. This may not look sufficient on its own, but it does tell you something about R, and there is a hidden integer constraint on both R and C. Test some cases before assuming anything about statement (2) in this situation.

If $C = 5$, then $R = 6$. Because 6 is divisible by 6, the answer is Yes. Can you get a valid case for which the answer is No? If $C = 10$, then $R = 12$, another Yes case. It turns out that, if you try a value for C that is not a multiple of 5, you will get a non-integer value for R, resulting in an invalid case because it violates the hidden integer constraint. This occurs because 20% as a fraction is $\frac{1}{5}$. It is impossible to get a valid No case, so this statement is sufficient.

If you do not take the time to test cases, you may think that this statement is not enough to answer the question. This is a C-Trap: The statements together are definitely enough, but the answer cannot be (C) because one of the statements works by itself.

The correct answer is **(B):** Statement (2) is sufficient alone, but statement (1) is not.

Consecutive Integers

In This Chapter...

In this chapter, you will learn how to recognize and solve problems involving consecutive integers and other evenly spaced sets, as well as how to determine the number of integers in a large set and the sum of the integers in a set.

CHAPTER 25 Consecutive Integers

Consecutive integers are integers that follow one after another from a given starting point, without skipping any integers. For example, 4, 5, 6, and 7 are consecutive integers, but 4, 6, 7, and 9 are not. There are many other types of consecutive patterns. For example:

Consecutive even integers: 8, 10, 12, 14   **Consecutive primes:** 11, 13, 17, 19

(8, 10, 14, and 16 is incorrect, as it skips 12)   (11, 13, 15, and 17 is incorrect, as 15 is not prime)

Evenly Spaced Sets

In **evenly spaced sets**, the values of the numbers in the set go up or down by the same amount (or **increment**) from one item in the sequence to the next. For example, the set {4, 7, 10, 13, 16} is evenly spaced because each value increases by 3 over the previous value. Think of this as the broadest grouping—the biggest circle in the diagram shown below:

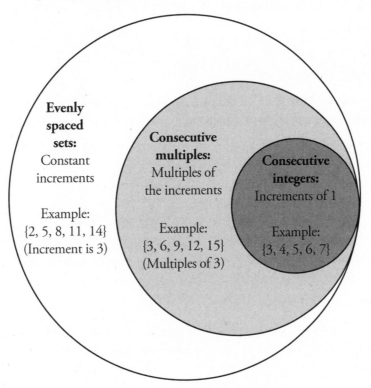

Within that circle is the subset **consecutive multiples**. These are special cases of evenly spaced sets in which all of the values in the set are multiples of the increment. For example, in the set {12, 16, 20, 24}, the values increase from one to the next by 4, and each element is a multiple of 4. Sets of consecutive multiples must be composed of integers.

The inner circle, **consecutive integers**, holds special cases of consecutive multiples: All of the values in the set increase by 1, and all integers are multiples of 1. For example, {12, 13, 14, 15, 16} is a set of consecutive integers.

Counting Integers: Add 1 Before You Are Done

How many integers are there from 6 to 10, inclusive? Four, right? No! There are actually *five* integers from 6 to 10. Count them: 6, 7, 8, 9, 10.

How did that happen? When you subtract $(10 - 6 = 4)$, you are actually subtracting out the lower extreme, 6; that number is not included in the count. If you *do* want to include it in the count, then add 1 before you're done. For example:

How many integers are there from 14 to 765, inclusive?

The word *inclusive* indicates that you need to include both numbers at the ends of the range in your count. The formula is **(Last − First + 1)**: $765 - 14 + 1 = 752$.

This is straightforward when you are dealing with consecutive integers. Sometimes, however, the question will ask about consecutive multiples.

In this case, if you subtract the greatest number from the least and add 1, you will be overcounting. For example, "All of the even integers between 12 and 24, inclusive" yields seven integers: 12, 14, 16, 18, 20, 22, and 24. However, (Last − First + 1) would yield $(24 - 12 + 1) = 13$, which is too big. How do you amend this? Since the items in the list are going up by increments of 2 (you are counting only the even numbers), divide (Last − First) by 2. Then, add the 1 before you're done:

$$\frac{(\text{Last} - \text{First})}{\text{Increment}} + 1 = \frac{(24 - 12)}{2} + 1 = 6 + 1 = 7$$

For consecutive multiples, the formula is $\dfrac{(\textbf{Last} - \textbf{First})}{\textbf{Increment}} + \textbf{1}$.

The bigger the increment, the lower that fraction will go. This makes logical sense, since a bigger increment between numbers in the range means that there are fewer numbers to be counted in that range.

Sometimes, it is easier to list the terms of a consecutive pattern and count them, especially if the list is short or if one or both of the extremes are omitted. For example:

How many multiples of 7 are there between 10 and 40 ?

First, note that the question says *between* 10 and 40 but does not include the word *inclusive*. So don't include 10 or 40 in this count. (Also, don't include them because neither one is a multiple of 7!)

Second, there aren't that many multiples of 7 in such a short range, so it may be fastest to just write them down: 14, 21, 28, 35. There are four multiples of 7 in the given range. Try another example:

How many multiples of 7 are there between 10 and 80 ?

This time, it would be more annoying to write out the possibilities. Instead, find the least multiple of 7 and the greatest multiple of 7 in that range and use those as your First and Last numbers. The least one is 14 and the greatest is 77. Now use the formula:

$$\frac{(\text{Last} - \text{First})}{\text{Increment}} + 1 = \frac{(77 - 14)}{7} + 1 = \frac{63}{7} + 1 = 9 + 1 = 10$$

Properties of Evenly Spaced Sets

The following properties apply to all **evenly spaced sets**:

1. The average (arithmetic mean) and median are equal to each other. For example:

    What is the arithmetic mean of 4, 8, 12, 16, and 20 ?

    In this example, the median is 12. Since this is an evenly spaced set, the arithmetic mean (average) is also 12. Now, try another example:

    What is the arithmetic mean of 4, 8, 12, 16, 20, and 24 ?

    In this example, the median is the average (arithmetic mean) of the two middle numbers, or the average of 12 and 16. Thus, the median is 14. Since this is an evenly spaced set, the average of the set is also 14.

    In a set with an odd number of evenly spaced integers, such as the first example above, the median/average will always be a member of the set (and, therefore, an integer).

    In a set with an even number of evenly spaced integers, such as the second example above, the median/average will *not* be a member of the set, since you'll always have to average the two middle numbers of the set in order to find the median.

2. The mean and median of the set are equal to the average of the First and Last terms. For example:

    What is the arithmetic mean of 4, 8, 12, 16, and 20 ?

    In this example, the arithmetic mean and median are both equal to $\frac{(4 + 20)}{2} = 12$. Now, try another example:

    What is the arithmetic mean of 4, 8, 12, 16, 20, and 24 ?

    In this example, the arithmetic mean and median are both equal to $\frac{(4 + 24)}{2} = 14$.

    For all evenly spaced sets, the average equals $\frac{\textbf{First} + \textbf{Last}}{2}$.

The Sum of Consecutive Integers

Consider this problem:

What is the sum of all the integers from 20 to 50, inclusive?

(A) 990

(B) 1,085

(C) 1,167

Adding all those integers would take much more time than you have for a GMAT problem. Since the set is evenly spaced, though, there's a way to calculate the sum:

Sum of Evenly Spaced Set = Average × Number of Terms

First, use the first and last terms of the set to find the average:

$\frac{20 + 50}{2} = 35$

Find the number of terms: $50 - 20 + 1 = 31$. Then, plug these values into the formula to find the sum:

$$\text{Sum} = (35)(31)$$

Glance at the answer choices to see how far you have to go with the calculation. The answers are fairly close together, so standard estimation doesn't seem like a great bet.

But the math you have to do is multiplication, so check the units digits of the answers. All three are different, so you can find just the units digits of $(35)(31)$ and you're done. In multiplication, the units digit of the answer depends only on the units digits of the starting numbers. In this case, $(5)(1) = 5$, so choose the answer with a units digit of 5.

The correct answer is (B).

25

Problem Set

Now that you've finished the chapter, try these problems.

1. How many terms are there in the set of consecutive integers from −18 to 33, inclusive?

2. What is the sum of all the positive integers up to 100, inclusive?

3. In a sequence of eight consecutive integers, how much greater is the sum of the last four integers than the sum of the first four integers?

Save the following problems for review after you finish this entire guide.

4. If the sum of the last three integers in a set of six consecutive integers is 624, what is the sum of the first three integers of the set?

5. The operation $x \Rightarrow y$ is defined as the sum of all integers from x to y, inclusive. For example, $3 \Rightarrow 7 = 3 + 4 + 5 + 6 + 7$. What is the value of $(100 \Rightarrow 150) - (125 \Rightarrow 150)$?

Solutions

1. **52:** Number of terms = First − Last + 1:

$$33 - (-18) + 1 = 52$$

2. **5,050:** Sum = (Average)(Number of Terms). To find the average, take the average of the first and last terms in the set: $\frac{1 + 100}{2} = 50.5$. To find the sum, find the difference between the last and the first and then add 1 before you're done: $(100 - 1) + 1$. Finally, multiply 100 by 50.5 to find the sum of all the integers in the set: $100 \times 50.5 = 5,050$.

3. **16:** The problem never specifies a set of numbers, so it must be the case that you get the same outcome no matter what numbers you use. In that case, choose your own set of numbers!

   For example, try 1, 2, 3, 4, 5, 6, 7, and 8. The sum of the first four integers is 10. The sum of the last four integers is 26. The difference is $26 - 10 = 16$.

   If you want to get extra fancy, line up those eight numbers in two rows as follows:

   $$1 \quad 2 \quad 3 \quad 4$$
   $$5 \quad 6 \quad 7 \quad 8$$

   What is the problem asking you? Find the difference between the sum of the top row and the sum of the bottom row. Make this easier by first finding the *differences*, not the sums. For instance, the difference between 1 and 5 is $+4$. Likewise, the difference between 2 and 6 is $+4$. The same is true for all numbers in the set (since they're all consecutive!), so the total difference is $4 + 4 + 4 + 4 = (4)(4) = 16$.

   Here's how to solve algebraically. The numbers can be represented as follows: n, $(n + 1)$, $(n + 2)$, $(n + 3)$, $(n + 4)$, $(n + 5)$, $(n + 6)$, and $(n + 7)$.

   First, find the sum of the first four integers:

   $$n + (n + 1) + (n + 2) + (n + 3) = 4n + 6$$

   Then, find the sum of the next four integers:

   $$(n + 4) + (n + 5) + (n + 6) + (n + 7) = 4n + 22$$

   The difference between these two partial sums is:

   $$(4n + 22) - (4n + 6) = 22 - 6 = 16$$

4. **615:** Think of the set of integers as n, $(n + 1)$, $(n + 2)$, $(n + 3)$, $(n + 4)$, and $(n + 5)$. Thus, $(n + 3) + (n + 4) + (n + 5) = 3n + 12 = 624$. Don't solve that quite yet, though—it's a little annoying. What does the problem want you to find?

   It asks for $n + (n + 1) + (n + 2) = 3n + 3$. Look back at the other equation.

   If $3n + 12 = 624$, then $3n + 3$ is 9 less than 624, or $624 - 9 = 615$.

Alternatively, another way you could solve this algebraically is to line up the algebraic expressions for each number so that you can subtract one from the other directly:

Sum of the last three integers	$(n + 3) + (n + 4) + (n + 5)$
Less the sum of the first three integers	$- \quad [n \; + (n + 1) + (n + 2)]$
	$\overline{3 + \quad 3 \quad + \quad 3 \quad = 9}$

Thus, the sum of the last three numbers is 9 greater than the sum of the first three numbers, so the sum of the first three numbers is $624 - 9 = 615$.

5. **2,800:** Definitely take your time to understand what's going on. This problem contains two components: the sum of all the numbers from 100 to 150 and the sum of all the numbers from 125 to 150. Since the problem asks for the *difference* between these components, you are essentially finding just the sum of all the numbers from 100 to 124 (because you will subtract out the value of the numbers from 125 to 150). You can think of this logically by visualizing a simpler problem: Find the difference $(1 \Rightarrow 5) - (3 \Rightarrow 5)$. Set up an equation:

$$
\begin{array}{r}
1 + 2 + 3 + 4 + 5 \\
- \qquad\quad 3 + 4 + 5 \\
\hline
1 + 2 \qquad\qquad\quad
\end{array}
$$

Back to the given problem. Find the sum of the integers from 100 to 124. Use the Sum = Average × Number of Terms formula.

There are 25 numbers from 100 to 124 ($124 - 100 + 1$). To find the sum of these numbers, multiply by the average term:

Average: $\dfrac{100 + 124}{2} = 112$

Sum: $25 \times 112 = 25 \times 100 + 25 \times 12 = 2{,}500 + 300 = 2{,}800$

25

Logic Problems

In This Chapter...

- Conditional Logic

- Creating Conditional Logic Chains

- Compound Conditionals

- Spatial Logic

In this chapter, you will learn how to build diagrams to more precisely analyze questions that rely on two types of logic: conditional logic and spatial logic.

CHAPTER 26 Logic Problems

Certain harder Data Insights questions test two styles of formal logic: conditional logic and linear logic. (Linear logic is a specialized application of the slot method that you learned earlier in this book.) How do you recognize when a problem will rely on one or both of these styles of logic?

There are a few clues that signal a formal logic problem:

Clue	Example
If-then statements	*If the bouquet contains roses, then it will also contain tulips.*
Statements that can be rephrased to if-then statements	Original: *Yolanda will not go to the party without Javier.* Rephrased: *If Yolanda is at the party, then Javier is also at the party.*
Defined lists of characters or options	*Adelaine, Bhavin, and Chao will choose from items K, L, M, and N.*
Rules about the ordering or placement of something	*Any digits in the code precede any letters.* *The third house cannot be red.*

You have seen less complicated examples of some of these types of logic problems earlier in this guide; this chapter covers strategies for handling more complicated scenarios. If you'd like a refresher on this topic before diving into the more advanced material in this chapter, review Chapter 3 (Data Sufficiency 101) and the logic-problem portion of Chapter 21 (Two-Part Analysis).

Conditional Logic

Conditional logic is, at its core, reflected by *if-then* statements. However, there are myriad ways the English language can be used to disguise this core relationship. Certain words and phrases, such as *the only way, unless, without,* or *every,* can all be used to create conditional relationships without explicitly using an if-then structure.

Every conditional logic statement includes at least one of two things: a sufficient condition or a necessary condition. For example:

Condition	Example	Interpretation
Sufficient	All cats are mammals.	If a certain animal is a cat, that's *sufficient* to know that you also have a mammal. If you know one thing, that's sufficient to determine another thing.
Necessary	In order to mail a letter successfully, you must put a delivery address on the envelope.	It's *necessary* to include a delivery address on a letter in order to mail it. But the address alone may *not* be *sufficient* to mail the letter successfully. For example, it's probably also necessary to put a stamp on the letter.

The first example, *all cats are mammals*, is an example of a sufficient condition. If you know the first condition (this animal is a cat), then that information is *sufficient* to conclude that this animal is also a mammal.

For sufficient conditions, construct the if-then statement this way:

Original Statement	If-Then Construction	Rephrased Statement
All cats are mammals.	If a *certain condition* is true, then *another condition* is *also* true.	If the animal is a cat, then the animal is also a mammal.

If you can figure out that the animal is a cat, then you have *sufficient* information to conclude that this animal is also a mammal.

One way to check your work is to try to reverse the statement: If you know you have a mammal, do you definitely have a cat? No, that's not logical, so this is not the correct if-then construction.

It would take too long to write all of that down during the test, of course. Think through the setup mentally, then abbreviate the information on your scratch paper:

Example	If-Then	Shorthand	Read It Back
All cats are mammals.	If this is a cat, then it is also a mammal.	c $\longrightarrow$ m	If cat, then mammal

Write c $\rightarrow$ m on your scratch paper. When you *re-read* your abbreviation, think "If cat, then mammal."

One more question: What can you conclude if you're told that a certain animal is a mammal?

Nothing (at least, not from the statement *All cats are mammals*). If you know the animal is a mammal, there's no way to tell whether it is or is not a cat. Expect the test to try to trip you up on this. The arrow goes from *c* to *m*, so you can only conclude in that direction, not the other way around.

The second example, *in order to mail a letter successfully, you must put a delivery address on the envelope*, can also be rephrased as an if-then statement, but it's a little more complicated.

In order to mail the letter successfully, it's *necessary* to put an address on the letter, but it may *not* be *sufficient*. You might also need to do something else, like put a stamp on the letter. In contrast, the cat example was *sufficient* all by itself: If you know you have a cat, you don't need to know anything else in order to conclude that you have a mammal.

If you have a *necessary* statement, first articulate the desired outcome (in this case, to mail a letter). Then, ask yourself what is necessary to achieve that outcome (in this case, you have to include an address). Construct the if-then statement in this way:

Original Statement	If-Then Construction	Rephrased Statement
In order to mail a letter successfully, you must put a delivery address on the envelope.	If the *outcome is achieved*, then the *needed component* was present.	If the letter was successfully mailed, then the letter did have a delivery address.

If you successfully mailed the letter, then the letter did have a delivery address. If you achieved the successful outcome, then the *necessary* component was present.

Again, check your work by trying to reverse the statement: If the letter did have a delivery address, then was it successfully mailed? Maybe, maybe not. There may also be other necessary components—a stamp, for example—in order to mail the letter. Or maybe you forgot to take it to the mailbox. Knowing that you did remember to put the address on the letter is *necessary* to mail the letter, but not necessarily *sufficient* to mail the letter.

Once you've mentally figured out the if-then statement, here's how to shorthand it on your scratch paper:

Example	If-Then	Shorthand	Read It Back
In order to mail a letter successfully, you must put a delivery address on the envelope.	If the letter was successfully mailed, then the letter did have a delivery address.	$\ell \longrightarrow a$	If letter mailed successfully, then had address

The shorthand will help to remind you of the full *if . . . then* statements. You can literally read them back to yourself without having to go back to the original (and likely more confusingly-worded) question prompt.

The if-then statements created so far actually have more to tell you. Every time you create an if-then statement, you can also infer a second statement, called a **contrapositive**. You won't see this actual term on the test. You just have to know what it is and how to infer it.

Here's how:

Original If-Then	How to Infer	Contrapositive
If this is a cat, then it is also a mammal. $c \longrightarrow m$	1. Reverse the order of the two items 2. Negate them both	If this is *not* a mammal, then it is *not* a cat. $\cancel{m} \longrightarrow \cancel{c}$

If an animal is a *cat*, then it must be a *mammal*. Therefore, if you know that the animal is *not* a mammal, then that animal also *can't* be a cat.

You can always use this mechanical method to infer the contrapositive of any if-then statement:

1. Start from your first jotting: $c \rightarrow m$

2. Reverse and negate: $\cancel{m} \rightarrow \cancel{c}$

That's it! Every time you are given or create an if-then statement, jot down *two* different pieces of useful information: first, the original statement, and then, its contrapositive. Here's what it looks like for the example about mailing a letter:

Original If-Then	Original Shorthand	Contrapositive Shorthand	Contrapositive Read It Back
If the letter was successfully mailed, then the letter did have a delivery address	$\ell \longrightarrow a$	$\cancel{a} \longrightarrow \cancel{\ell}$	If no address, then letter not mailed successfully

26

To form the contrapositive, you literally do not need to think through the logic mentally. Just create your shorthand for the original statement, then reverse and negate, every time.

What if the statement is already negative? In that case, "negating" turns the resulting statement positive. For example:

Original If-Then	Original Shorthand	Contrapositive Shorthand	Contrapositive Read It Back
If you don't eat your main meal, you can't have dessert.	m̸ → d̸	d → m	If you do eat dessert, then you must have eaten your main meal.

Common Language Clues

The following are some of the most common words and phrases that signal that a statement contains conditional logic. (This is not an exhaustive list! Keep an eye out for additional phrasings as you continue your studies. If any trip you up, put them on a flash card.)

Condition	Common words	Example
Sufficient	• If • When • Whenever • Every • Any • All	Whenever the forecast calls for rain, I carry an umbrella.
Necessary	• Only • Only if • Must • Require • Depends • Unless • Without	To create a high-quality meal, you must have high-quality ingredients.

Here's how to shorthand each example and create its contrapositive:

Example	Shorthand	Contrapositive Shorthand	Contrapositive
Whenever the forecast calls for rain, I carry an umbrella.	FR → U	U̸ → F̸R	If no umbrella, forecast didn't call for rain
To create a high-quality meal, you must have high-quality ingredients.	HQM → HQI	H̸Q̸I̸ → H̸Q̸M̸	If no HQI, can't make HQM

For the second example, why can't you rephrase it as, "If you have high-quality ingredients, then you can make a high-quality meal?" Try to answer that question in your own words before you keep reading.

This statement is an example of a *necessary* condition. In order to create a high-quality meal, it is necessary to have high-quality ingredients. But it is not sufficient *just* to have high-quality ingredients. You also need proper cooking equipment and a chef who knows how to cook, for example! So it's not possible to claim that, if you have high-quality ingredients, someone can definitely make a high-quality meal. There are other factors that also need to be present to achieve that outcome.

These signal words and phrases are especially helpful when the English-language ordering is not the same as the diagram ordering. For example:

Original Example	Equivalent Example	If-Then
Whenever the forecast calls for rain, I carry an umbrella.	I carry an umbrella whenever the forecast calls for rain.	If the forecast calls for rain, then I carry an umbrella.
To create a high-quality meal, you must have high-quality ingredients.	You must have high-quality ingredients to create a high-quality meal.	If a high-quality meal was made, then high-quality ingredients must have been used.

Each pair of example sentences ultimately presents the same information, even though the examples are written in reverse order of each other. The pair of examples about the weather forecast both resolve to the same sufficient condition: If a certain condition is true (the forecast calls for rain), then another condition is also true (I'm definitely going to carry an umbrella).

And the second pair also both resolve to the same necessary condition: If a certain outcome was achieved (we cooked a high-quality meal), then a certain necessary condition was present (we used high-quality ingredients).

Most of the common signal words on the list are pretty straightforward, but the necessary-condition signal words *unless* and *without* have a substantial twist. Take a look at this example:

> You cannot drive legally *unless* you have a valid driver's license.

This is a *necessary*-type condition. The desired outcome is to drive legally; the necessary factor is to have a valid license. If you can drive legally, you have to have a valid driver's license.

Here's the twist: When you create the if-then statement, you have to switch the desired outcome from negative (*You cannot drive legally . . .*) to positive (*If you can drive legally . . .*). As a rule, when you see the words *unless* or *without*, negate the phrasing of the desired outcome (switch from negative to positive or from positive to negative). Also, the *unless* component is always going to be the necessary component, which comes after the arrow:

Original Statement	Negate Desired Outcome	Shorthand	Read It Back
You cannot drive legally *unless* you have a valid driver's license.	Cannot drive legally becomes *Can* drive legally	D leg → val L	If can drive legally, have valid driver's license

The word *without* operates similarly to the word *unless*, but the language might make it more confusing. You cannot drive legally *without* a valid driver's license. The first element is *you cannot drive legally*. The second element is *a valid driver's license*. When parsing that second element, don't include the word *without*—when that word is removed or ignored, the meaning is that you do have a valid driver's license:

Original Statement	Negate Desired Outcome	Shorthand	Read It Back
You cannot drive legally *without* a valid driver's license.	Cannot drive legally becomes *Can* drive legally	D leg → val L	If can drive legally, *do* have valid driver's license

Try It Out!

Create the shorthand for the following generic conditional statements. Also, shorthand their contrapositives.

1. All *A*s are *B*s.

2. *G* can occur only if *H* also occurs.

3. *E* happens whenever *F* happens.

4. If *not C* then *D*.

5. *K* happens unless *L* happens.

6. *N* cannot happen without *M*.

Ready to check your answers?

① A → B   B̸ → A̸
② G → H   H̸ → G̸
③ F → E   E̸ → F̸
④ C̸ → D   D̸ → C
⑤ K → L   L̸ → K
⑥ N → M   M̸ → N̸

Statement 1: All *A*s are *B*s.

$$A \rightarrow B \qquad B̸ \rightarrow A̸$$

This is the same construction used in the statement *all cats are mammals*. If you know you have *A* (a cat), then you definitely have *B* (a mammal). Conversely, if you don't have *B* (a mammal), then you can't have *A* (a cat).

Statement 2: *G* can occur only if *H* also occurs.

$$G \rightarrow H \qquad H̸ \rightarrow G̸$$

This sentence is a real-world example of this statement: *I can go to the concert* [*G*] only if *I can get tickets* [*H*]. The desired outcome is to go to the concert. It's necessary to get tickets in order to achieve that desired outcome. So *G* goes first in the shorthand and then *H*. The contrapositive is this: If I can't get tickets [no *H*], then I can't go to the concert [no *G*].

When you see an abstract statement, try to come up with a real-world example; it can help you to understand the abstract statement. Take a moment now to look at the remaining statements above and try to come up with your own real-world example before you keep reading.

Statement 3: *E* happens whenever *F* happens.

$$F \rightarrow E \qquad \cancel{E} \rightarrow \cancel{F}$$

Did you get *E* → *F* instead? This is one of the most common traps in conditional logic. Consider this real-word scenario that mimics the original statement: *The dog gets a bath*[E] whenever *it plays in the mud* [F]. What's the logic?

If the dog plays in the mud, then it's going to get a bath. Therefore, the right order is *F* → *E*. If the reverse were true, you'd be saying that if the dog gets a bath, then it will go play in the mud! Many dogs would probably love this, but that's likely not the human's motivation when giving the dog a bath.

You can also use mechanics to help diagram this one correctly. The word "whenever" is the sufficient condition word. Whatever action is written right after the signal word *whenever* is always the first element in the logic.

Statement 4: If *not C* then *D*.

$$\cancel{C} \rightarrow D \qquad \cancel{D} \rightarrow C$$

Here's an example real-world scenario: If *I don't order dessert* [C], then *I'll order coffee* [D]. This is another *sufficient* setup. Once I decide not to do one thing, I'll definitely do another thing. The only twist on this one is that the *C* gets a slash through it for the original statement, since you're *not* doing it. And since everything is negated in the contrapositive, *C* becomes positive and loses its slash in the contrapositive shorthand.

Statement 5: *K* happens unless *L* happens.

$$\cancel{K} \rightarrow L \qquad \cancel{L} \rightarrow K$$

Another especially tricky one. Here's a real-world example: *The endangered species will become extinct* [K] unless *its habitat is preserved* [L]. If you struggled with this one or got it wrong, review the section earlier on how to diagram *unless / without* statements.

Find the desired outcome: the endangered species will become extinct (well … that's not truly *desired*, of course, but it is the outcome). Negate that part for the if-then statement: If the endangered species does *not* become extinct, then the habitat must have been preserved.

In the original if-then shorthand, negate the *K* (in this case, switch it from positive to negative) but leave the *L* positive. For the contrapositive, reverse and negate both elements: The *K* becomes positive, the *L* becomes negative and they switch places.

Sometimes, the "desired" outcome is actually an *undesired* outcome. The key word is really that it is an outcome, regardless of whether it's desired or undesired.

The most common incorrect diagram for #5 is "K → L". Translate that using the real-world scenario: If the species does go extinct, then its habitat is preserved. Wait, what?! That's the exact opposite of the logical meaning.

Statement 6: *N* cannot happen without *M*.

$$N \longrightarrow M \qquad \cancel{M} \longrightarrow \cancel{N}$$

Here's a real-world example for this statement: *The computer won't work properly* [*N*] without *a power source* [*M*]. The literal translation (which is a trap!) would be $\cancel{N} \rightarrow \cancel{M}$. If the computer isn't working, then it doesn't have any power? No, that's only one reason why your computer might not be working; there are lots of other possible reasons.

First, this is a *without* statement—one of the two (along with *unless*) that has that weird twist. The undesired outcome is a non-functioning computer; negate that component. And when addressing the power-source component, ignore the negative word *without*. If the computer *is* working, then you *do* have a functioning power source—a power cord, a charged battery, something.

Creating Conditional Logic Chains

In math, you can sometimes combine two statements into one longer statement. For example:

If $a > b$ and $b > c$, then $a > b > c$.

In certain instances, conditional logic statements can also be chained together to create a multi-step conditional relationship.

Consider the following expansion of the cats and mammals example:

- All cats are mammals.
- All mammals are warm-blooded.

And here are the corresponding shorthand abbreviations for the two statements:

$$c \longrightarrow m$$
$$m \longrightarrow w$$

Since these two statements connect through the symbol *m*, you can combine them into one big statement:

$$c \longrightarrow m \longrightarrow w$$

This diagram can be phrased as *if cat then mammal then warm-blooded*.

You can also take the contrapositive of this multi-part statement. As before, reverse the order of the symbols *and* negate all the symbols:

$$\cancel{w} \longrightarrow \cancel{m} \longrightarrow \cancel{c}$$

This diagram can be phrased as *if not warm-blooded then not mammal then not cat*.

Beware of reversing the chain unless you also negate it! If a cat is a mammal, it's not necessarily the case that a mammal is a cat. If you reverse without negating, the logic will be wrong; the only valid inference is the one shown above—reverse *and* negate.

Compound Conditionals

There is one last aspect of conditional logic to address: compound conditionals. These exist when multiple conditions affect an outcome. Consider airplane travel: Multiple conditions must be fulfilled before you can board a plane at the airport. You must purchase a ticket, obtain a boarding pass, and go through security, at a minimum. Here's an example of a two-part conditional:

> One cannot board a plane at the airport without purchasing a ticket and going through security.

If the above phrasing seems stilted or overly formal, that is intentional. You may have already noticed that the GMAT often words things this way! Translate the statement into an *if . . . then* relationship: *If someone boards a plane, then that person has purchased a ticket and gone through security.* Take a look at the shorthand for that statement:

$$ bp \longrightarrow \begin{matrix} pt \\ and \\ s \end{matrix} $$

The arrow in the diagram points to the word *and* because you have to fulfill *both* of these conditions (purchase a ticket, go through security) in order to board the plane.

How can you build the contrapositive of that statement? First, consider the mechanics of the contrapositive: You reverse and negate the components. So what happens if someone does not purchase a ticket? That *alone* proves that they cannot board a plane. Likewise, what if someone does not go through security? Again, that *alone* proves that they cannot board a plane. So if someone *either* does not have a ticket *or* does not go through security, they cannot board the plane. The correct contrapositive is the following diagram.

$$ \begin{matrix} \cancel{pt} \\ or \\ \cancel{s} \end{matrix} \longrightarrow \cancel{bp} $$

You are still going to reverse and negate, just as you do for a more straightforward contrapositive. But also replace the word *and* with the word *or*.

One more thing: If the original statement had used the word *or*, then you'd replace it with the word *and*. Think through the logic to prove why.

(Here's an example to prove why. Aud wants to eat at her favorite restaurant tonight. If she can get a reservation *or* if she can arrive before 6 p.m., then she will eat at the restaurant. It's enough to do just one of those things (either make a reservation or arrive early) in order to eat at that restaurant. Here's the contrapositive: If Aud did *not* go out to dinner tonight, then you know she wasn't able to get a reservation *and* she wasn't able to arrive early.)

Now, with these diagramming tools in hand, revisit this problem from Chapter 3:

> A concession stand sells chips, dip, pretzels, and soda. If Vikram buys either chips or a pretzel, he will buy a soda. If he does not buy chips, then he will not buy dip. Does Vikram buy chips?
>
> (1) Vikram buys exactly three different items from the concession stand.
>
> (2) Vikram buys at least a pretzel and a soda from the concession stand.

Begin by diagramming the constraints just in the question stem. Use *c* for chips, *p* for pretzel, *s* for soda, and *d* for dip:

$$\begin{matrix} c \\ \text{or} \\ p \end{matrix} \longrightarrow s \qquad \cancel{c} \longrightarrow \cancel{d}$$

In the compound conditional, the arrow stems from the *or*, indicating that either chips or pretzel (or both) guarantee that Vikram also buys a soda. Since both shorthand representations reference *chips*, can you combine them? Not at the moment; in one case, the *c* is "positive" and in one *c* is "negative."

Is there anything you can do to change that? Take the contrapositive of the second statement and that negative *c* will turn into a positive *c*:

$$\begin{matrix} c \\ \text{or} \\ p \end{matrix} \longrightarrow s \qquad \begin{matrix} \cancel{c} \longrightarrow \cancel{d} \\ d \longrightarrow c \end{matrix}$$

Now these two statements can be linked to form a chain:

$$d \longrightarrow \begin{matrix} c \\ \text{or} \\ p \end{matrix} \longrightarrow s$$

The arrow from *d* targets only *c*, acknowledging that *d* has no relationship to *p*. This chain now shows all the possible relationships among the four things Vikram could buy. That should help make the problem easier to process.

> (2)   Vikram buys at least a pretzel and a soda from the concession stand.

The diagram shows that, if Vikram buys a pretzel, then he buys a soda. Soda doesn't lead anywhere in the diagram. Finally, the phrase *at least* indicates that Vikram could have bought other items. So, Vikram could have bought just a pretzel and soda and nothing else, in which case, no, he did not buy chips. Alternatively, Vikram could have bought a pretzel, a soda, and chips, in which case, yes, he did buy chips. Statement (2) is not sufficient to answer the question.

The first statement is trickier because it gives only numerical restrictions; it does not name specific items. Start at the beginning of the diagram. If Vikram buys dip, he must buy chips and soda; since he's restricted to three items total, he cannot buy pretzels. In this case, yes, Vikram did buy chips.

But that is not the only way that Vikram can buy three unique items. He could also buy chips, a pretzel, and a soda—but in this case, too, he buys chips.

The only way to avoid buying chips would be to buy the other three items: a pretzel, a soda, and dip. But if he buys dip, then he has to buy chips. So there's no way for Vikram to buy three different items and yet *not* buy chips.

Statement (1) is sufficient to answer the question: Yes, Vikram does buy chips.

Here's one way to draw out all of this work on your scratch paper:

$$d \rightarrow c$$
$$\text{or} \rightarrow s$$
$$P$$

?c?

B̶D̶
Ⓐ C̶ E̶

---

(1) $d \rightarrow \boxed{c} \rightarrow s$

or

$\boxed{c}, p + s$

Ⓢ

(2) $p + s$

$p \rightarrow s$ ✓

c?   (NS)

Now, apply your conditional logic skills to a new problem!

> There are 22 items on a restaurant menu. A menu item cannot contain nut products unless it also has an allergy warning on the menu. All items with an allergy warning, and only those items, must be prepared at a specially-designated kitchen station. How many items on the menu have an allergy warning?
>
> (1)   Exactly 8 menu items are prepared at the specially-designated kitchen station.
> (2)   Exactly 14 menu items do not contain nut products.

Of the 22 items on the menu, how many have an allergy warning? Start by rephrasing the constraints into if-then statements. First, the second sentence indicates that any item that contains nut products needs an allergy warning, so *if nuts, then allergy warning* is an effective rephrase.

The third sentence contains two similar but separate conditional logic statements. All allergy-warning items are prepared at the specially-designated kitchen station, so *if allergy warning, then special station* is an effective rephrase. Additionally, this sentence indicates that *only* allergy-warning items can be prepared at the special station.

So, *if* an item is prepared at the special station, *then* that item must have an allergy warning. Here's the shorthand for each statement, using *n* for nuts, *aw* for allergy warning, and *sks* for special kitchen station:

$$n \longrightarrow aw$$
$$aw \longrightarrow sks$$
$$sks \longrightarrow aw$$

The top and middle diagram can be chained together. But because the third statement is the exact reverse of the second statement, leave it on its own.

$$n \longrightarrow aw \longrightarrow sks$$
$$sks \longrightarrow aw$$

Statement (1) asserts that *exactly* 8 items are prepared at a special station. Use the second shorthand statement to infer: If exactly 8 items are prepared at the special statement, then exactly 8 items have an allergy warning. Statement (1) is sufficient to answer the question.

Statement (2) talks about items that do *not* contain nut products, but the current shorthand is about having nut products. Find the contrapositive of the chain that contains *n* to figure out what must be true when *not* having nut products. Reverse and negate:

$$s̶k̶s̶ \longrightarrow a̶w̶ \longrightarrow n̶$$

26

In the contrapositive chain, *not n* is at the end of the chain rather than at the beginning. So knowing something about *not n* will not lead to knowing anything about the other elements in the chain. Statement (2) is not sufficient to answer the question.

Alternatively, think it through logically: An item without nut products could still contain other allergens—maybe it contains gluten or shellfish. So, it is possible that some of the 14 no-nut-product items could still have other allergens that require an allergy warning. Statement (2) is (still) not sufficient to answer the question.

The correct answer is (A): The first statement is sufficient but the second statement is not.

On easier problems, you may not need to convert to if-then statements or find contrapositives. But on harder ones, be prepared for anything. And these techniques will also help you to process the information more efficiently—a great benefit on a timed test!

Spatial Logic

Multiple problems—both math-based and problem-based—in prior chapters have used the slot method to organize scratch work. Drawing out slots is especially useful on spatial-logic problems. (If you want to refresh your memory, take a look at the final problem in the Testing Cases section of Chapter 3—it's the problem about the three siblings choosing different kinds of candy.)

How do you recognize when a problem is testing spatial logic rather than math? The first clue is absence: an absence of mathematical language. The second clue is also language-based. You may see constraints that deal with who can and cannot be near each other or in the same group. Or you may have constraints that deal with ordered placement, for example, which brand of coffee is placed on a higher or lower shelf. These types of constraints indicate a spatial logic problem.

There are two core themes to efficient diagramming of spatial logic problems:

	Theme	Example
#1	**Draw enough slots to encapsulate the story.** Make sure you have enough slots to track all the elements of the story. This could mean breaking the slots into sub-groups. A story that has, for example, a first half + second half, or a team 1 + team 2, would need some sub-grouping of the slots.	5 items: — — — — — T_1: T_2: — — — — — — —
#2	**Differentiate absolute constraints from flexible constraints.** For example, the diagram for *A must come immediately before B* would be different from the diagram for *A is before B*, because these two constraints convey different information. The first constraint is absolute: Not only is *A* before *B*, but they must be immediately next to each other. The second constraint is more flexible: *A* is before *B*, but *A* could be anywhere before *B*.	absolute: [AB] flexible: A … B

Let's try this out. You've got 10 variables to place in an ordered list, from first to last: A, B, C, D, E, F, G, K, L, and X. And you've got 6 constraints to follow, listed below.

Draw 10 horizontal slots. Below those slots, leave some blank space, and then start figuring out shorthand notations for each constraint. After you finish each shorthand notation, consider whether that piece of information allows you to infer anything else about what must be true or what can't be true. Jot down any inferences immediately below the 10 horizontal slots.

You can try just one constraint at a time, then check the solution below, or try all six first and then keep reading—your choice. Here's the full list of constraints.

1. A is before B.

2. C is immediately after D.

3. F and G cannot be next to each other.

4. E is not third.

5. X cannot be before any vowel.

6. There must be at least one space between K and L, regardless of whether K comes before or after L.

Ready to see the "solution"? That word is in quotes because shorthand notation is personal—you don't have to use exactly the same shorthand as everyone else. You just have to make sure that your own shorthand is consistent and clear to you. So, feel free to adapt the suggestions below or use any shorthand you like, as long as the shorthand you use consistently conveys the correct meaning.

Here's one way to write the notation for the six statements:

Statement	Considerations	Shorthand
A is before B.	A, then B, but not necessarily right next to each other.	A...B
C is immediately after D.	D, then C, and must be next to each other.	DC
F and G cannot be next to each other.	Not next to each other. Nothing about order.	(FG)
E is not third.	E is not third.	E₃
X cannot be before any vowel.	The vowels are A and E; they have to be before X. Nothing else about order.	A E ... X
There must be at least one space between K and L, regardless of whether K comes before or after L.	K and L are not right next to each other. Nothing about order.	(KL)

The ellipses (...) shown in 1 and 5 indicate flexibility: These things must come in this order, but they can be as near or as far apart as needed. In notation 2, the box indicates an absolute: D and C must be *both* in this exact order *and* right next to each other. A box locks everything in. What if you're told that D and C are next to each other but you're not given the order? In that case, use parentheses rather than a box. The parentheses signal flexibility on the order of the letters.

Constraints 3 and 6 both have parentheses, indicating that you weren't told anything about the order of these letters. And the slash marks indicate that this information is *not* true. F and G are *not* right next to each other; likewise, K and L are *not* right next to each other.

Like notation 2, notation 4 is an absolute: E cannot be third. Use subscripts to denote specific positions (in this case, 3 for third) and a slash mark to indicate that this is not true.

Go back and look over your notations. Any ideas for how you'd like to write certain kinds of information differently in the future? (You may not know yet. Just think about this and refine your notation style as you continue to practice.)

Okay, that addresses the first instruction you were given (to shorthand all of the constraints). Now, let's talk about the second instruction: What else can you infer from each of these constraints?

Statement	Shorthand	Inference
A is before B.	A...B	A can't be in slot 10. B can't be in slot 1.
C is immediately after D.	DC	D can't be in slot 10. C can't be in slot 1.
F and G cannot be next to each other.	(FG)	Nothing
E is not third.	E̸₃	Nothing—but add to diagram.
X cannot be before any vowel.	A E ∴ X	A can't be in slot 10. E can't be in slot 10. X can't be in slots 1 or 2.
There must be at least one space between K and L, regardless of whether K comes before or after L.	(KL)	Nothing

Here's the full diagram, including the original constraints and the inferences:

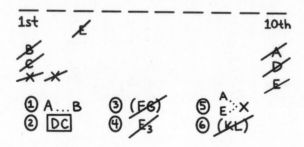

There are a few good practices for building diagrams and pictures:

- Make your spatial logic notations distinct from your mathematics notations. Avoid using inequality signs, equals signs, or other math-style symbols as part of your spatial logic notations.

- Reuse your Critical Reasoning notations wherever appropriate. Arrows can indicate causality, for example.

- Make spatial logic diagrams consistent with the picture you've built for the problem. For example, if you've arranged slots horizontally from left to right, also maintain a left-to-right orientation in your shorthand notations, as opposed to up and down.

- Clearly identify the endpoints of your diagram or picture. For example, if a problem is ordering packages from heaviest to lightest, clearly note which end of the slots is the heaviest and which end is the lightest.

- Make notations for things that are not possible. Sometimes, inferring what cannot happen is as valuable as inferring what *could* happen.

Try the following Two-Part problem:

Management assessed the working styles of the 9 employees in one department in order to create two teams, one with 4 employees and one with 5 employees. Each employee's working style is identified by a unique code: A, B, C, D, E, F, G, H, and I. In order to create the most effective teams, management will keep the following in mind. Neither worker A nor worker C works effectively with worker D. Neither worker B nor worker D works effectively with worker G. Worker F does not work effectively with worker E. Worker H does not work effectively with worker I.

Based on the information provided, and assuming management creates the most effective teams possible, in the first column select a working style that must be represented on the four-person team, and in the second column select a working style that must be represented on the five-person team.

Must be on the four-person team	Must be on the five-person team	
○	○	B
○	○	E
○	○	F
○	○	G
○	○	H
○	○	I

If that problem felt overwhelming, that's okay! The goal of this section is to give you tools to take overwhelming text and efficiently incorporate the constraints into a more manageable diagram.

Nine people will be split into two teams: one team of four, one team of five. Each person has a unique designation for their working style (A, B, C, D, E, F, G, H, or I). So, just use those nine letters to represent the nine workers.

Draw out two levels of slots, one of four and one of five (representing each team). Then, map out the constraints. Here's one way to draw it all out:

$$T_1: \underline{}\ \underline{}\ \underline{}\ \underline{} \qquad \cancel{AD}\ \cancel{BG}\ \cancel{FE}$$
$$T_2: \underline{}\ \underline{}\ \underline{}\ \underline{}\ \underline{} \qquad \cancel{CD}\ \cancel{DG}\ \cancel{HI}$$

In this problem, it's not necessary to use either ellipses or parentheses to indicate ordering or placement of the people, since the information given indicates that each pair of people is not on the same team. Since they're not on the same team, you won't have to worry about placing them relative to each other.

If you ever do see a problem that places people in teams *and* orders them within the team, you would need to build your notation to show both the team and the ordering within the team. In that instance, ellipses, boxes, parentheses, and the like would be required.

Scan the constraints to find the letter that shows up the most. This is the person with the most constraints; always start with the most-constrained person or item. In this case, D is the most constrained, so test out your first possible case. Put D on team 1 and then see what else you can figure out:

$$T_1: \underline{D}\ \underline{}\ \underline{}\ \underline{} \qquad \cancel{AD}\ \cancel{BG}\ \cancel{FE}$$
$$T_2: \underline{A}\ \underline{C}\ \underline{G}\ \underline{}\ \underline{} \qquad \cancel{CD}\ \cancel{DG}\ \cancel{HI}$$

If D is in *T1*, that forces A, C, and G into *T2*, since those three workers can't be on the same team as D.

Map the remaining constraints:

$$T_1: \underline{D}\ \underline{B}\ \underline{F/E}\ \underline{H/I} \qquad \cancel{AD}\ \cancel{BG}\ \cancel{FE}$$
$$T_2: \underline{A}\ \underline{C}\ \underline{G}\ \underline{E/F}\ \underline{I/H} \qquad \cancel{CD}\ \cancel{DG}\ \cancel{HI}$$

G can't be on the same team as B, so B will go into *T1*. This leaves F, E, H, and I. These four could be on either team, as long as F is not on the same team as E and H is not on the same team as I. The notation shows either F or E in *T1* and then the reverse (E or F) for *T2*; in other words, if F is on team 1, then E is on team 2, and vice versa. The pair H and I work the same way.

Now, use this case to answer the question. Since the question asks who *must* go on a certain team, eliminate F, E, H, and I. All four could be on either team.

The two remaining possibilities are B and G. In the case mapped out, B is on the four-person team, so it's not the case that B must be on the five-person team. Therefore, the only person still in the running for the five-person team is G; this person must be on the five-person team.

Similarly, in this case, G is on the five-person team, so it's not the case that G must be on the four-person team. The only possibility still remaining for the four-person team is B.

The correct answer is B for the first column (four-person team) and G for the second column (five-person team).

When you see a long list of constraints on a logic problem, first map them out. Then use your shorthand notation to make any possible inferences. If that's not enough to be able to answer the question, test a case, just like you do on Data Sufficiency. Often, testing one case will be enough on a complicated problem like this one.

26

Problem Set

Now that you've finished the chapter, try the following problems. You'll get additional chances to practice these techniques later in this guide.

1. Adelaine will complete five exercises during today's workout: incline bench press, overhead press, lat pulldowns, rows, and squats. Incline bench press and overhead press work the chest and shoulder muscles. Lat pulldowns and rows work the back muscles. Squats work the leg muscles. Adelaine organizes her exercise routine so that consecutive exercises do not work the same muscle groups. Will Adelaine end her routine with an exercise that works her back muscles?

    (1) Adelaine does all of the chest and shoulder exercises before she does squats.

    (2) Adelaine does not do a back exercise earlier than third in the workout routine.

2. Janelle and Vik are meeting for dinner at a restaurant that offers a variety of appetizers, main courses, and desserts. In deciding what to order, Vik will order dessert unless he orders both an appetizer and a main course. Janelle may order an appetizer, but only if Vik doesn't order one. If Vik does order one, Janelle will share his instead. In either case, Janelle will order a main course. Does Vik order dessert?

    (1) Janelle orders an appetizer for herself.

    (2) Vik orders a main course.

3. On Fridays in July, the Schick family goes to the pool; however, if it rains or the temperature forecast is higher than 95 degrees Fahrenheit, they do not go to the pool. If they do not go to the pool, they either visit the museum or go to the movie theater. When choosing between the museum or a movie, if there are no new movie releases on a particular weekend, they go to the museum. Where did they go on the last Friday in July?

    (1) It rained on the last Friday in July.

    (2) On the last Friday in July, the forecasted temperature was 96 degrees Fahrenheit, and there was a new movie released that weekend.

4. Zhaleh is throwing a party and has invited 8 of her friends: Antoinette, Betsy, Cecile, Dvora, Esperanza, Fausta, Gwen, and Hedda. Due to the complicated interpersonal relationships in Zhaleh's friend group, the following is known about attendance at the party: Antoinette will attend only if Dvora and Esperanza both attend. Hedda will not attend unless Antoinette does not attend, in which case Hedda will attend. Betsy will attend if there will be fewer than 6 total people in attendance, including herself and Zhaleh. Cecile and Gwen will both attend, Fausta will not.

Based on the information provided, in the table below, select in the first column the minimum number of people who will attend the party, including Zhaleh, and select in the second column the maximum number of people who will attend the party, including Zhaleh.

Minimum	Maximum	
O	O	3
O	O	4
O	O	5
O	O	6
O	O	7
O	O	8

Solutions

1. **(B):** The paragraph provides no numbers or math notation, indicating that this is a Logic problem. Since the question stem provides a spatial constraint (*consecutive exercises do not work the same muscle groups*) and the question is about ordering (*Will Adelaine end her routine with an exercise that works her back muscles?*), this is a spatial logic question. The prompt describes five exercises spread across three categories.

1. Chest and shoulder exercises: incline bench press (*IBP*) and overhead press (*OP*)

2. Back exercises: lat pulldowns (*LP*) and rows (*R*)

3. Leg exercises: squats (*S*)

The question asks whether Adelaine's fifth workout will be either *LP* or *R*. The only potential rephrase is to categorize the exercises by muscle groups instead of by name: *B* for back exercises, *C* for chest and shoulder exercises, and *L* for the leg exercise. The question can now be rephrased as "Is *B* fifth?"

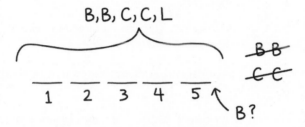

(1) INSUFFICIENT: The two *C* exercises occur before *L*. The two *C*s cannot occur consecutively, so the earliest they could happen is first and third. Therefore, the earliest possible position for *L* is fourth. This leaves two options: *L* could occur fifth, with the back exercises second and fourth, or *L* could occur fourth, with the back exercises second and fifth.

$$\text{(1)} \quad C, C \ldots L$$

$$\underline{C} \quad \underline{B} \quad \underline{C} \quad \underline{B} \quad \underline{L} \;=\; NO$$

$$\underline{C} \quad \underline{B} \quad \underline{C} \quad \underline{L} \quad \underline{B} \;=\; YES$$

(2) SUFFICIENT: Adelaine does not do a back exercise earlier than third. In this case, the two *B* exercises must occur third and fifth, since consecutive exercises cannot be from the same muscle group. Therefore, Adelaine will definitely end with a back exercise.

$$\text{(2)} \quad B, B = 3^{\text{rd}} \text{ or later}$$

$$\underline{\;\;} \quad \underline{\;\;} \quad \underline{B} \quad \underline{\;\;} \quad \underline{B} \quad YES$$

The correct answer is **(B):** Statement (2) is sufficient, but statement (1) is not.

26

2. **(A):** The lack of mathematical language and the presence of *unless, only if,* and *if* statements indicate that this is a conditional logic problem. It lays out several conditions governing how Vik and Janelle will order from among three courses—appetizer (A), main (M), and dessert (D)—at a restaurant. The first constraint establishes that Vik's default is to order dessert. He will order dessert, unless he orders both an appetizer and a main course. Following the rules laid out for *unless* rule notations, place the *A* for appetizer and the *M* for main on the necessary (right) side of the arrow. Negate the sufficient side, so *dessert* becomes *not dessert*. Janelle's appetizer order is dependent on whether Vik orders an appetizer; if she does order an appetizer, then Vik did not. Janelle's default is to order a main course: This will occur regardless of any other constraints.

The question asks whether Vik orders dessert. This can rephrased as "Did Vik not order an appetizer or not order a main course?"

(1) SUFFICIENT: If Janelle ordered an appetizer, then Vik did not. If Vik did not order an appetizer, then he did order dessert.

(2) INSUFFICIENT: Vik does order a main course, but this does not prove whether Vik ordered dessert. Vik may or may not have ordered an appetizer.

The correct answer is **(A):** Statement (1) is sufficient, but statement (2) is not.

3. **(E):** Glancing at the problem, there are no apparent mathematical relationships. Skimming the question stem, the prevalence of conditional language (*if, when*) indicates that this is a conditional logic problem.

Reading the problem, the rules can be rephrased into if-then statements.

1. If it rains or if the temperature forecast is higher than 95 degrees, they do not go to the pool.

2. If they do not go to the pool, they go to either the museum or the movie theater.

3. If there are no new movies that weekend, they will go to the museum. (This rule only applies if the Schick family is not going to the pool!)

The question itself is direct and allows no productive rephrase: Where did they go on the last Friday in July?

(1) INSUFFICIENT. If it rained on the Friday in question, the Schick family did not go to the pool. However, this does not indicate whether they went to the museum or to the movie theater.

(2) INSUFFICIENT: The high temperature forecast means that they did not go to the pool, so they must have gone to either the movie theater or the museum. It is tempting to assume that if there is a new movie release on a weekend, then the Schick family would go to the movie theater. However, this is a trap! The rule only applies to weekends when there is not a new movie release; there is no rule given for what they do if there is a new movie release. This statement does not actually indicate whether the Schick family will go to the museum or to the movie theater.

(1) and (2) INSUFFICIENT: Each statement alone indicates that the Schick family will go to either the museum or the movie theater. However, neither statement, even combined, gives information to determine which of those two options they would choose.

The correct answer is **(E)**: Statements (1) and (2) together are not sufficient.

4. **The answer for the first column is 5. The answer for the second column is 7:** The lack of mathematics language, combined with the prevalence of conditional logic language, indicates that this is a conditional logic problem. Create a diagram that can incorporate nine slots (eight friends plus Zhaleh herself) into two groups: a *yes* group and a *no* group. One immediate challenge is that you do not know how many slots will be in each group. Build rule notations for the individual rules, similar to the following diagram.

Some of the rules already help place slots in the two groups. *Z*, *C*, and *G* are all in the *yes* group, and *F* is in the *no* group.

- If Antoinette will attend only if Dvora and Esperanza attend, then if *A* is a yes, both *D* and *E* are a *yes*. This is rule notation 1 in the diagram.

- Hedda will not attend unless Antoinette does not attend … apparently, Hedda and Antoinette do not like each other! If you see one of them at the party, then the other will not be there. This is rule notation 2 in the diagram.

- Antoinette does not attend, in which case Hedda will attend. If *A* is a no, then *H* is a yes. This is rule notation 3.

- Betsy will attend if there will be fewer than 6 total people in attendance, including herself and Zhaleh. So if there are fewer than six total people, Betsy will be one of those six. This is rule notation 4. (Be careful! It is easy to assume that if there are more than six people, then Betsy will not attend. The rule does not state this! You only know what happens if there are **fewer** than six people, not more! If there are six or more people, Betsy can do whatever she wants!)

Rule notations 2 and 3 combine for a deduction that can be placed in the diagram. *A* and *H* are opposites: One of them will be at the party, and one of them will not. This allows the placement of one more slot in each of the groups, and places *A* and *H* in opposite positions in those slots. Now three slots remain, for *B*, *D*, and *E*. See the diagram below.

$$A, B, C, D, E, F, G, H + Z$$

$$A \rightarrow \begin{matrix} D \\ \text{and} \\ E \end{matrix} \qquad \begin{matrix} \text{if} \\ \text{total} < 6 \end{matrix} \rightarrow B$$

$$H \rightarrow \cancel{A} \qquad C, G : \text{Yes}$$
$$\qquad\qquad\qquad F : \text{No}$$

$$\cancel{A} \rightarrow H$$

					B?
yes:	Z	C	G	A/H	D?
no:	F	H/A			E?

Could four be the minimum? No, because if there are fewer than six total people, Betsy will attend. *D* and *E*, however, could both be *no*. Since *A* does not have to attend, *D* and *E* similarly may not attend. The minimum that could attend is five (see below for the diagram).

$$A, B, C, D, E, F, G, H + Z$$

$$A \rightarrow \begin{matrix} D \\ \text{and} \\ E \end{matrix} \qquad \begin{matrix} \text{if} \\ \text{total} < 6 \end{matrix} \rightarrow B$$

$$H \rightarrow \cancel{A} \qquad C, G : \text{Yes}$$
$$\qquad\qquad\qquad F : \text{No}$$

$$\cancel{A} \rightarrow H$$

yes:	Z	C	G	A/H	B
no:	F	H/A	D	E	

Could there be more than five people? Certainly. *D* and *E* could still go to the party, and *B* is always an option. (Remember, if there are six or more people, there is no longer any constraint on Betsy!) So the maximum possible number is seven, as shown below.

$$A, B, C, D, E, F, G, H + Z$$

$$A \rightarrow \begin{matrix} D \\ \text{and} \\ E \end{matrix} \qquad \begin{matrix} \text{if} \\ \text{total} < 6 \end{matrix} \rightarrow B$$

$$H \rightarrow \cancel{A} \qquad C, G : \text{Yes}$$
$$\qquad\qquad\qquad F : \text{No}$$

$$\cancel{A} \rightarrow H$$

yes:	Z	C	G	A/H	D	E	B
no:	F	H/A					

The answer for the first column is 5. The answer for the second column is 7.

Number Properties and More

In this unit, you will learn all about number properties, including how to handle divisibility, primes, odds and evens, positives and negatives, combinatorics, and probability. You'll also learn advanced strategies for testing cases on number properties problems.

In This Unit

Divisibility and Primes

In This Chapter...

In this chapter, you will learn number property rules specific to positive integers, including a special subset of positive integers called primes. You'll learn how to find multiples, factor pairs, and prime factors of integers and how to address divisibility topics. Finally, you'll learn different ways that the GMAT will present this information and how the test might disguise the information—as well as how to strip away the disguise!

CHAPTER 27 Divisibility and Primes

The special properties of integers form the basis of most number properties problems on the GMAT. **Integers** are whole numbers, such as 0, 1, 2, and 3, that have no fractional part. Integers include positive numbers (1, 2, 3 …), negative numbers (−1, −2, −3 …), and the number 0.

Arithmetic Rules

Most arithmetic operations on integers will result in an integer. For example:

$4 + 5 = 9$ $(−2) + 1 = −1$ The sum of two integers is always an integer.

$4 − 5 = −1$ $(−2) − (−3) = 1$ The difference of two integers is always an integer.

$4 \times 5 = 20$ $(−2) \times 3 = −6$ The product of two integers is always an integer.

Division, however, is different. Sometimes the result is an integer, and sometimes it is not:

$8 \div 2 = 4$ This result is an integer …

$2 \div 8 = \dfrac{1}{4}$ … but this one isn't. (By the way, the result of division is called the **quotient**.)

An integer is said to be **divisible** by another number if the result, or quotient, is an integer.

For example, 21 is divisible by 3, because 21 divided by 3 results in an integer ($21 \div 3 = 7$). However, 21 is not divisible by 4, because 21 divided by 4 results in a non-integer ($21 \div 4 = 5.25$).

You can also talk about divisibility in terms of remainders. One number is divisible by another if the result has a remainder of 0. For example, 21 is divisible by 3, because 21 divided by 3 yields 7 with a remainder of 0. On the other hand, 21 is not divisible by 4, because 21 divided by 4 yields 5 with a remainder of 1.

Here are some more examples:

$8 \div 2 = 4$ Therefore, 8 is divisible by 2.

You can also say that 2 is a **divisor** or **factor** of 8.

$2 \div 8 = 0.25$ Therefore, 2 is *not* divisible by 8.

$(−6) \div 2 = −3$ Therefore, −6 is divisible by 2.

$(−6) \div (−4) = 1.5$ Therefore, −6 is *not* divisible by −4.

Rules of Divisibility by Certain Integers

The **divisibility rules** are very useful shortcuts to determine whether an integer is divisible by 2, 3, 4, 5, 6, 8, 9, and 10.

An integer is divisible by:

2 if the integer is even.

For example, 12 is divisible by 2, but 13 is not. Integers that are divisible by 2 are called **even**, and integers that are not divisible by 2 are called **odd**. You can tell whether a number is even by checking to see whether the units (ones) digit is 0, 2, 4, 6, or 8. For example, 1,234,567 is odd, because 7 is odd, whereas 2,345,678 is even, because 8 is even.

3 if the sum of the integer's digits is divisible by 3.

For example, 72 is divisible by 3, because the sum of its digits is $7 + 2 = 9$, which is divisible by 3. By contrast, 83 is not divisible by 3, because the sum of its digits is 11, which is not divisible by 3.

4 if the integer is divisible by 2 *twice* or if the last two digits are divisible by 4.

For example, 28 is divisible by 4, because you can divide it by 2 twice and get an integer result ($28 \div 2 = 14$ and $14 \div 2 = 7$). For larger numbers, check only the last two digits. For example, 23,456 is divisible by 4, because 56 is divisible by 4, but 25,678 is not divisible by 4, because 78 is not divisible by 4.

5 if the integer ends in 0 or 5.

For example, 75 and 80 are divisible by 5, but 77 and 83 are not.

6 if the integer is divisible by *both* 2 and 3.

For example, 48 is divisible by 6, since it is divisible by 2 (it ends with an 8, which is even) AND by 3 ($4 + 8 = 12$, which is divisible by 3).

8 if the integer is divisible by 2 three times or if the last three digits are divisible by 8.

For example, 32 is divisible by 8, since you can divide it by 2 three times and get an integer result ($32 \div 2 = 16$, $16 \div 2 = 8$, and $8 \div 2 = 4$). For larger numbers, check only the last three digits. For example, 23,456 is divisible by 8, because 456 is divisible by 8, whereas 23,556 is not divisible by 8, because 556 is not divisible by 8.

9 if the sum of the integer's digits is divisible by 9.

Since the sum of the digits of 4,185 is $4 + 1 + 8 + 5 = 18$, it is divisible by 9. By contrast, 3,459 is not divisible by 9, because the sum of its digits is 21, which is not divisible by 9.

10 if the integer ends in 0.

Because it ends in a zero, 670 is divisible by 10, but 675 is not.

The GMAT can also test these divisibility rules in reverse. For example, if you are told that a number has a ones digit equal to 0, you can infer that this number is divisible by 2, by 5, and by 10. Similarly, if you are told that the sum of the digits of x is equal to 21, you can infer that x is divisible by 3 but *not* by 9.

There is no rule listed for divisibility by 7, because there isn't a relatively easy rule for this. The simplest way to check for divisibility by 7, or by any other number not found in this list, is to perform long division—that is, if you have to divide at all. First, check whether you can estimate or otherwise avoid annoying math!

27

Factors and Multiples

Factors and multiples are essentially opposite terms.

A **factor** is a positive integer that divides evenly into an integer. For example, what are the factors of 8? The factors (or divisors) are 1, 2, 4, and 8. A factor of an integer is smaller than or equal to that integer.

A **multiple** of an integer is formed by multiplying that integer by any integer. What are the multiples of 8? The multiples include 8, 16, 24, and 32 (and keep going forever). On the GMAT, multiples of an integer are equal to or larger than that integer.

Note that an integer is always both a factor and a multiple of itself; for example, 8 is both a factor of and a multiple of 8. In addition, 1 is a factor of *every* integer.

An easy way to find all the factors of *small* integers is to use **factor pairs**. Factor pairs for any integer are the pairs of factors that, when multiplied together, yield that integer. For example, the factor pairs of 8 are (1, 8) and (2, 4).

To find the factor pairs of a number such as 72, start with the most basic factors: 1 and 72. Then, "walk upwards" from 1, testing to see whether different numbers are factors of 72. Once you find a number that is a factor of 72, find its partner by dividing 72 by the factor. Keep walking upwards until all factors are exhausted.

Here's how to find factor pairs, step-by-step:

1. Make a table with two columns labeled *Small* and *Large*.

2. Start with 1 in the Small column and 72 in the Large column.

3. Test the next possible factor of 72 (which is 2); 2 is a factor of 72, so write 2 underneath the 1 in your table. Divide 72 by 2 to find the factor pair: 36. Write 36 in the Large column.

4. Repeat this process until the numbers in the Small and the Large columns run into each other. In this case, once you have tested 8 and found that 9 is its paired factor, you can stop.

Small	Large
1	72
2	36
3	24
4	18
6	12
8	9

Fewer Factors, More Multiples

It can be easy to confuse factors and multiples. Use the mnemonic **Fewer Factors, More Multiples** to help remember the difference. Every positive integer has a limited number of factors. Factors divide into the integer and are therefore less than or equal to the integer. For example, there are only four factors of 8: 1, 2, 4, and 8.

By contrast, every positive integer has infinite multiples. These multiply out from the integer and are therefore greater than or equal to the integer. For example, the first five multiples of 8 are 8, 16, 24, 32, and 40, but you could go on listing multiples of 8 forever.

Factors, multiples, and divisibility are very closely related concepts. For example, 3 is a factor (or a divisor) of 12. This is the same as saying that 12 is a multiple of 3 or that 12 is divisible by 3.

On the GMAT, this terminology is often used interchangeably in order to make the problem seem harder than it actually is. Be aware of the different ways that the GMAT can phrase information about divisibility. Moreover, try to convert all such statements to the same terminology. For example, all of the following statements *say exactly the same thing*:

- 12 is divisible by 3.
- 12 is a multiple of 3.
- $\frac{12}{3}$ is an integer.
- 12 is equal to $3n$, where n is an integer.
- 12 items can be shared among 3 people so that each person has the same number of items.
- 3 is a divisor of 12, or 3 is a factor of 12.
- 3 divides 12.
- $\frac{12}{3}$ yields a remainder of 0.
- 3 goes into 12 evenly.

When you see language similar to the above, you can translate it and write it down in whatever form works best for you. Practice recognizing that all of these forms are really telling you the same piece of information.

Divisibility and Addition/Subtraction

If you add two multiples of 7, you get another multiple of 7. Try it: $35 + 21 = 56$. This is always mathematically valid because this is the math that's happening: $(5 \times 7) + (3 \times 7) = (5 + 3) \times 7 = 8 \times 7$.

Likewise, if you subtract two multiples of 7, you get another multiple of 7. Try it: $35 - 21 = 14$. Again, this is what's happening with the math: $(5 \times 7) - (3 \times 7) = (5 - 3) \times 7 = 2 \times 7$.

This pattern holds true for the multiples of any integer N. If you add or subtract multiples of N, the result is a multiple of N. You can restate this principle using any of the disguises noted earlier: For example, if N is a divisor of x and of y, then N is a divisor of $x + y$.

Primes

Prime numbers are a very important topic on the GMAT. A prime number is any positive integer with *exactly two* different factors: 1 and itself. In other words, a prime number has *no* factors *other* than 1 and itself. For example, 7 is prime because the only factors of 7 are 1 and 7. However, 8 is not prime because it has more than two factors: 1, 2, 4, and 8.

The number 1 is a special case. It has exactly one factor (itself), so it does not qualify as prime (which needs exactly two factors). The number 1 is unique in that 1 has just one factor, while all the other non-prime positive integers (officially known as *composite* numbers) have three or more factors.

27

1	Primes (2, 3, 5, 7, ...)	Composites (4, 6, 8, 9, ...)
Exactly one factor:	Exactly two factors:	Three or more factors:
1	1	1
	Itself	Itself
		Other(s) between 1 and itself

The first prime number is 2, which is also the only even prime. The first ten prime numbers are 2, 3, 5, 7, 11, 13, 17, 19, 23, and 29. Memorizing these primes will save you time on the test.

Prime Factorization

Earlier, you learned how to find the factor pairs of a number. You can also find the **prime factors** of a number. Every number has its own unique mix of prime factors, so breaking a number down to its prime factors can be very useful on the GMAT.

Create a prime factor tree, as shown below with the number 72. Test different numbers to find one that goes into 72 without leaving a remainder. Once you find such a number, split 72 into factors, as shown here:

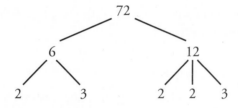

For example, 72 is divisible by 6, so it can be split into 6 and $72 \div 6 = 12$. Then, repeat this process on 6 and 12 until every branch on the tree ends at a prime number. Once you have only primes, stop, because you cannot split prime numbers into two smaller factors. In this example, 72 splits into 5 total prime factors (including repeats): $2 \times 2 \times 2 \times 3 \times 3$. In general, write prime factors for a number in increasing order, as shown.

Prime factorization is an extremely important tool to use on the GMAT. Once you know the prime factors of a number, you can determine *all* the factors of that number, even for large numbers. The factors can be found by building all the possible products of the prime factors; the next section shows how.

Factor Foundation Rule

The GMAT expects you to know the factor foundation rule: **If *a* is a factor of *b*, and *b* is a factor of *c*, then *a* is a factor of *c*.** In other words, any integer is divisible by all of its factors—and it is also divisible by all of the factors of its factors.

For example, if 72 is divisible by 12, then 72 is also divisible by all the factors of 12 (1, 2, 3, 4, 6, and 12). Written another way, if 12 is a factor of 72, then all the factors of 12 are also factors of 72. The factor foundation rule allows you to conceive of factors as building blocks in a foundation; for example, 12 and 6 are factors, or building blocks, of 72 (because 12×6 builds 72).

27

The number 12, in turn, is built from its own factors; for example, 4×3 builds 12. Thus, if 12 is part of the foundation of 72 and 12 in turn rests on the foundation built by its prime factors (2, 2, and 3), then 72 is also built on the foundation of 2, 2, and 3.

You can use the bottom level—the prime building blocks—to find (almost) any factor of 72. First, write them in increasing order: $2 \times 2 \times 2 \times 3 \times 3$. (The one factor you won't find here is the factor of 1. Just remember that all numbers always have 1 as a factor.)

Back to the building blocks. First, 2 and 3 are factors of 72. Next, you can multiply any combination of the building blocks to find larger factors. For example, $2 \times 2 = 4$ is a factor of 72. So is $2 \times 3 = 6$.

You can combine any of the prime factors you like to find any factors of 72. For example, if the test asks you whether 24 is a factor of 72, you could divide to find out—but that would get annoying as the numbers get larger. Instead, find the prime factors of 24 (which are 2, 2, 2, and 3), and check whether they're on the list for 72. They are, so 24 is also a factor of 72.

The Prime Box

You can organize this information with a tool called a prime box. A **prime box** is exactly what its name implies: a box that holds all the prime factors of a number (in other words, the lowest-level building blocks). Here are prime boxes for 72, 12, and 125:

Do repeat copies of the prime factors if the number has multiple copies of that prime factor. What goes in the box should actually multiply up to the main number.

You can use the prime box to test whether or not a specific number is a factor of another number. For example:

Is 27 a factor of 72?

$27 = 3 \times 3 \times 3$, but 72 only has *two* 3's in its prime box. It's not possible to make 27 from the prime factors of 72, so 27 is not a factor of 72.

Now, try another example:

If the integer *n* is divisible by 8 and 15, is *n* divisible by 12 ?

$$\boxed{\begin{array}{c} n \\ 2, 2, 2, \\ 3, 5, \\ \dots ? \end{array}}$$

First, factor both numbers: $8 = 2 \times 2 \times 2$ and $15 = 3 \times 5$. Although you don't know what *n* is, *n* has to be divisible by any number made up of those primes.

$12 = 2 \times 2 \times 3$. All of those factors appear in *n*'s box, so yes, *n* is also divisible by 12.

What if integer *k* is divisible by 8 and by 10? First, factor: $8 = 2 \times 2 \times 2$ and $10 = 2 \times 5$. Next, combine ... actually, wait. Don't combine yet. If the two numbers have any *overlapping* factors, then you first have to strip out any overlap. The number 10 has one factor of 2 and the number 8 has three factors of 2, so they overlap on one factor of 2. Strip out that one factor. The prime box for *k* is $2 \times 2 \times 2 \times 5$.

Notice the ellipses and question mark ("... ?") in the prime box of *n*. This indicates that you have created a **partial prime box** of *n*. Whereas the *complete* set of prime factors of 72 can be calculated and put into its prime box, you only have a *partial* list of prime factors of *n*, because *n* is an unknown number. You know that *n* is divisible by 8 and 15, but you do *not* know what additional primes, if any, *n* has in its prime box.

Most of the time, when building a prime box for a *variable*, you will use a partial prime box, but when building a prime box for a *number*, you will use a complete prime box.

Remainders

Most of this chapter has focused on numbers that are divisible by other numbers (factors)—that is, numbers that have an integer result. This section, however, discusses what happens when a number, such as 8, is divided by a *non*-factor, such as 5.

Every division has four parts:

1. The **dividend** is the number being divided. In $8 \div 5$, the dividend is 8.
2. The **divisor** is the number that is dividing. In $8 \div 5$, the divisor is 5.
3. The **quotient** is the number of times that the divisor goes into the dividend *completely*. The quotient is always an integer. In $8 \div 5$, the quotient is 1, because 5 goes into 8 one (1) time completely.
4. The **remainder** is what is left over. In $8 \div 5$, the remainder is 3, because 3 is left over after 5 goes into 8 once.

Putting it all together, you have $8 \div 5 = 1$, with a remainder of 3.

On the GMAT, it's not unusual to see the word *remainder*. The other terms (*dividend, divisor,* and *quotient*) are much less common; they could appear but most people won't see them. Factor that knowledge into your decision as to whether to memorize these terms.

As another example, the number 17 is not divisible by 5. When you divide 17 by 5 using long division, you get 3 with a remainder of 2:

$$\begin{array}{r} 3 \\ 5\overline{)17} \\ -15 \\ \hline 2 \end{array}$$

The quotient is 3, because 15 is the largest multiple of 5 smaller than 17, and $15 \div 5 = 3$. The remainder is 2, because 17 is 2 more than a multiple of 5 (15).

You can also express this relationship as a general formula:

Dividend = Quotient × Divisor + Remainder
(or, Dividend = Multiple of Divisor + Remainder)

Finally, it is possible to have a remainder of 0. A remainder of 0 occurs when one number actually is divisible by another. For example, $20 \div 5 = 4$ remainder 0. Most of the time, you won't need to notice that something has a remainder of 0, but the GMAT might use this to disguise information. If the test tells you that n divided by 5 has a remainder of 0, it's really telling you that n is divisible by 5. (You could also say it's telling you that n is a multiple of 5.)

Problem Set

For questions 1–6, answer each question with one of three responses: Always Yes, Always No, or Sometimes Yes/Sometimes No. If your answer is Sometimes Yes/Sometimes No, use two numerical examples to show how to get a Yes and a No.

All variables in problems 1–6 are integers.

1. If a is divided by 7 or by 18, an integer results. Is $\frac{a}{42}$ an integer?

2. If 80 is a factor of r, is 15 a factor of r ?

3. If 7 is a factor of n and 7 is a factor of p, is $n + p$ divisible by 7 ?

4. If j is divisible by 12 and 10, is j divisible by 24 ?

5. If 6 is a divisor of r and r is a factor of s, is 6 a factor of s ?

6. If s is a multiple of 12 and t is a multiple of 12, is $7s + 5t$ a multiple of 12 ?

Save the following problems for review after you finish this entire guide.

7. Mayumi invited her colleagues to a party. In preparation, she prepared a bowl of punch that she then divided into $\frac{1}{2}$ cup portions. She believes that if 12 people show up, there will be 6 portions left over, and that if 10 people show up, there will be 4 portions left over. If Mayumi prepared fewer than 50 total cups of punch, and she believes that all of her colleagues will drink the same amount, then how many total cups of punch did she prepare?

    (A) 18
    (B) 27
    (C) 30
    (D) 36
    (E) 45

8. A university badminton club has both students and professors as members. Is the number of students in the club at least 45 ?

    (1) The number of professors in the club is a multiple of 8.

    (2) The number of students in the club is exactly 20% greater than the number of professors in the club.

27

9. A skeet shooting competition awards points for each round as follows: The first-place finisher receives 11 points, the second-place finisher receives 7 points, the third-place finisher receives 5 points, and the fourth-place finisher receives 2 points. No other points are awarded. Jordan competes in several rounds of the skeet shooting competition and receives points in each round. If the product of all of the points Jordan receives equals 84,700, in how many rounds does Jordan participate?

   (A)   2
   (B)   3
   (C)   7
   (D)   9
   (E)   11

27

Solutions

1. **Always Yes:**

   a

2, 3, 3,
7, . . . ?

   If *a* is divisible by 7 and by 18, its prime factors include all of the factors of those two numbers: 2, 3, 3, and 7, as shown in the prime box. Therefore, any integer that can be constructed as a product of any of these prime factors is also a factor of *a*. $42 = 2 \times 3 \times 7$, all of which are in the prime box, so 42 is also a factor of *a*.

2. **Sometimes Yes/Sometimes No:**

   r

2, 2, 2,
2, 5, . . . ?

   If *r* is divisible by 80, its prime factors include 2, 2, 2, 2, and 5, as shown in the prime box. Therefore, any integer that can be constructed as a product of any of these prime factors is also a factor of *r*. $15 = 3 \times 5$. The factor 5 is in the prime box, but the 3 may or may not be. For example, if $r = 80$, then No, 15 is *not* a factor of *r*, but if $r = 240$ (which is 80×3), then Yes, 15 *is* a factor of *r*.

3. **Always Yes:** If two numbers are both multiples of the same number, then their *sum* is also a multiple of that same number. Since *n* and *p* share the common factor 7, the sum of *n* and *p* must also be divisible by 7.

4. **Sometimes Yes/Sometimes No:**

j		*j*		*j*
2, 2, 3, . . . ?		2, 5, . . . ?		2, 2, 3, 5, . . . ?

   Careful! The number 12 contains 2, 2, and 3. The number 10 contains 2 and 5. But you can't (necessarily) put all of those numbers in the combined prime box for *j*. First, check for overlap. The two boxes overlap on one factor of 2, so strip out one 2, leaving you with $2 \times 2 \times 3 \times 5$ for *j*'s prime box.

   Next, the question asks whether *j* is divisible by 24, which equals $2 \times 2 \times 2 \times 3$. The prime box of *j* contains at least two 2's and *could* contain more, but it doesn't have to. The number 24 requires three 2's. Therefore, you may or may not be able to create 24 from *j*'s prime box; 24 is not necessarily a factor of *j*.

   Prove it with numbers. The smallest possible value of *j* is $2 \times 2 \times 3 \times 5 = 60$. This number is *not* divisible by 24, so if $j = 60$, the answer is No. Alternatively, *j* could equal 120 (which is 60×2), in which case *j* is divisible by 24 and the answer is Yes.

5. **Always Yes:** By the factor foundation rule, if 6 is a factor of *r* and *r* is a factor of *s*, then 6 is a factor of *s*.

6. **Always Yes:** If *s* is a multiple of 12, then so is $7s$. If *t* is a multiple of 12, then so is $5t$. Since $7s$ and $5t$ are both multiples of 12, then their sum ($7s + 5t$) is also a multiple of 12.

7. **(B) 27:** First, Understand. Mayumi prepares a giant bowl of punch and then estimates how much will be left over, depending on how many guests arrive. That makes this a remainder problem. The question asks for the total number of cups of punch that were prepared, so translate the given information about portions into cups whenever possible.

    Start with the first situation: There are 12 guests who each drink the same amount, with 6 servings left over. The remainder is the easier part to deal with. If there are 6 portions left over, that will be $6 \times \frac{1}{2} = 3$ cups left over.

    The amount that the guests will drink is a little trickier. You know they will all drink the same amount, but you don't know what that amount will be. If they all drink one portion, they will drink $12 \text{ people} \times 1\frac{\text{portion}}{\text{person}} \times \frac{1}{2}\frac{\text{cups}}{\text{portion}} = 6$ cups of punch. If they all drink 2 portions, they will drink $12 \times 2 \times \frac{1}{2} = 12$ cups. What's the pattern here? Every portion they each drink equals 6 cups of punch. So no matter how many portions they all drink, the final amount of punch will be a multiple of 6. Combined with the 3 cups of punch that are left over, the final amount of punch must be 3 more than a multiple of 6.

    Take a look at the answer choices, and eliminate any that don't match this information. Only (B) 27 and (E) 45 are 3 more than a multiple of 6.

    Apply the same logic above to the second situation described in the problem. If 10 people show up, there will be 4 portions left over. 4 portions will be 2 cups left over. And if 10 people drink one portion of punch, that will be 5 total cups of punch. So no matter how many portions each guest drinks, the total amount they drink will be a multiple of 5. That means the correct answer must be 2 more than a multiple of 5.

    Only choice **(B)** is also 2 more than a multiple of 5.

8. **(C):** Let s and p be the number of students and professors in the club, respectively. The question asks whether $s \geq 45$.

    (1) INSUFFICIENT: This statement provides information about the professors but not the students. The question stem did not provide any additional information about the relationship between p and s, so this statement is not sufficient to answer the question.

    (2) INSUFFICIENT: This statement provides a *relative* relationship between the number of professors and the number of students but no actual values. There is a hidden integer constraint here—both p and s must be integers—so this limits the values that could work for the given relationship. What integers will allow you to take 20% and get another integer?

    Case 1: Try 100 first since this is a percent problem. Let $p = 100$ and $s = 120$. (To find 20%, take 10% and double it.) In this case, Yes, $s \geq 45$.

    A No case would require an integer less than 45 that will still yield an integer when you take 20%. Benchmark your way to the smallest possible integer that will work: If 20% = 1, then 100% = (1)(5) = 5. Now put this number formally through the test to make sure the logic worked.

    Case 2: Try $p = 5$. In this case, 20% of 5 is 1, so $s = 6$. In this case, s is less than 45, so the answer is No.

(1) AND (2) SUFFICIENT: According to statement (1), the value of p has to be 8, 16, 24, 32, and so on. According to statement (2), the smallest possible value of p is 5; the other possible values of p will be multiples of 5, or 5, 10, 15, 20, and so on.

Put the information together. The first value that is both a multiple of 8 and a multiple of 5 is $p = 40$. Now find s: 20% of 40 $= 4 + 4 = 8$, so $s = 48$. This is the smallest possible value for s, so the answer is always Yes, $s \geq 45$.

The correct answer is **(C)**: Both statements together are sufficient, but neither one works alone.

9. **(C) 7:** The values for scoring first, second, third, and fourth place in the competition are all prime numbers—when this happens, it is never a coincidence. Notice also that the problem mentions a *product* involving those prime numbers. Those two pieces together signal a prime factor problem. Take that ugly number and break it down into its prime factors:

$$84,700 = 847 \times 100$$

847 is a pretty annoying number to have to break down. But the problem indicates that it must be some combination of 2, 5, 7, and 11. It doesn't contain any 2s or 5s, so it must be some combination of 7 and/or 11.

Break the number into parts that are more easily divisible by 7:

$$700 = 7 \times 100$$
$$140 = 7 \times 20$$
$$7 = 7 \times 1$$

$700 + 140 + 7$ adds up to 847. To get there, you need a total of $100 + 20 + 1 = 121 \times 7$. The 7 part of that is a prime, but the 121 can be broken down further. (And don't forget about the initial value of 100—that still needs to be broken down, too!)

$$847 = 7 \times 121 = 7 \times 11 \times 11$$
$$100 = 10 \times 10 = 2 \times 2 \times 5 \times 5$$

Thus, Jordan received first place twice (11 points each), second place once (7 points each), third place twice (5 points each), and fourth place twice (2 points each). Jordan competed in a total of 7 rounds.

27

Odds, Evens, Positives, and Negatives

In This Chapter...

- Arithmetic Rules of Odds and Evens

- Positives and Negatives

- Absolute Value: Absolutely Positive

- A Double Negative = A Positive

- Multiplying and Dividing Signed Numbers

- Number Property Disguises

- The Sum of Two Primes

In this chapter, you will learn how positive and negative concepts are tested on the exam for both integers and non-integers. You will also learn about odd and even rules, which apply only to integers. Finally, you'll learn how to recognize these topics when the GMAT disguises them at times.

CHAPTER 28 Odds, Evens, Positives, and Negatives

Even numbers are integers that are divisible by 2. Odd numbers are integers that are not divisible by 2. All integers are either even or odd. For example:

Evens: 0, 2, 4, 6, 8, 10, 12 ...   Odds: 1, 3, 5, 7, 9, 11 ...

Note that 0 is an even integer. When 0 is divided by 2, the result is an integer—so 0 is even.

Consecutive integers alternate between even and odd: 9, 10, 11, 12, 13 ...

                                                         O, E, O, E, O ...

Negative integers are also either even or odd:

Evens: −2, −4, −6, −8, −10, −12 ...   Odds: −1, −3, −5, −7, −9, −11 ...

Arithmetic Rules of Odds and Evens

The GMAT tests your knowledge of how odd and even numbers combine through addition, subtraction, multiplication, and division. Rules for adding, subtracting, multiplying, and dividing odd and even numbers can be derived by testing out simple numbers, but it pays to memorize the following rules for operating with odds and evens, as they are extremely useful for certain GMAT math questions.

Addition and subtraction:

     Even $\pm$ Even = Even $8 + 6 = 14$

     Odd $\pm$ Odd = Even $7 + 9 = 16$

     Even $\pm$ Odd = Odd $7 + 8 = 15$

If they're the same, the sum (or difference) will be even. If they're different, the sum (or difference) will be odd.

Multiplication:

     Even $\times$ Even = Even $2 \times 4 = 8$

     Even $\times$ Odd = Even $4 \times 3 = 12$

     Odd $\times$ Odd = Odd $3 \times 5 = 15$

If one even number is present, the product will be even. If you have only odd numbers, the product will be odd.

If you multiply together several even integers, the result will be divisible by higher and higher powers of 2 because each even number will contribute at least one 2 to the factors of the product.

For example, if there are two even integers in a set of integers being multiplied together, the result will be divisible by (at least) 4:

$$\mathbf{2} \times 5 \times \mathbf{6} = 60 \qquad \text{(divisible by 4)}$$

If there are three even integers in a set of integers being multiplied together, the result will be divisible by (at least) 8:

$$\mathbf{2} \times 5 \times \mathbf{6} \times \mathbf{10} = 600 \qquad \text{(divisible by 8)}$$

Division:

There are no guaranteed outcomes in division, because the division of two integers may not yield an integer result. In these cases, you'll have to try the actual numbers given. The divisibility rules outlined in Chapter 27, Divisibility and Primes, can help you determine the outcome.

Positives and Negatives

Numbers can be either positive or negative (except the number 0, which is neither):

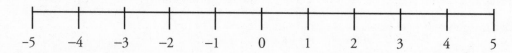

On the number line, negative numbers are all to the left of the number 0. Positive numbers are all to the right of the number 0.

Note that a variable (such as x) can have either a positive or a negative value, unless there is evidence otherwise. The variable x is not necessarily positive, nor is $-x$ necessarily negative. For example, if $x = -3$, then $-x = 3$.

Absolute Value: Absolutely Positive

Absolute value can be a component of positive/negative problems. The **absolute value** of a number answers this question: How far away is the number from 0 on the number line? For example, the number 5 is exactly 5 units away from 0, so the absolute value of 5 equals 5. Mathematically, this is written using the symbol for absolute value: $|5| = 5$. To find the absolute value of -5, look at the number line again: -5 is also exactly 5 units away from 0. Thus, the absolute value of -5 equals 5, or, in mathematical symbols, $|-5| = 5$.

Absolute value is always positive because it disregards the direction (positive or negative) from which the number approaches 0 on the number line. When you interpret a number in an absolute value sign, just think: absolutely positive! (Except, of course, for 0, because $|0| = 0$. This is the smallest possible absolute value.)

One more thing: 5 and -5 are the same distance from 0; in other words, 0 is located halfway between them. In general, if two numbers are opposites of each other, then they have the same absolute value, and 0 is halfway between. If $x = -y$, then one of the two scenarios below is true:

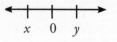 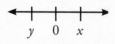

It's not possible to tell which variable is positive and which is negative without more information.

A Double Negative = A Positive

A **double negative** occurs when a minus sign is in front of a negative number (which already has its own negative sign). For example:

What is $7 - (-3)$?

As you learned in English class, two negatives yield a positive:

$7 - (-3) = 7 + 3 = 10$

This is a very easy step to miss, especially when the double negative is somewhat hidden. For example:

What is $7 - (12 - x)$?

Many people will make the mistake of computing this as $7 - 12 - x$. However, notice the first minus sign has to be distributed to both terms in the parentheses, so the second term ends up with a double minus sign. This expression is simplified as $7 - 12 - (-x) = 7 - 12 + x$.

Multiplying and Dividing Signed Numbers

When you multiply or divide numbers, positive or negative, follow these rules to keep the signs straight:

Even number of negative signs = **positive**	0 negative signs: $7 \times 8 = 56$	2 negative signs: $(-7) \times (-2) = 14$
Odd number of negative signs = **negative**	1 negative sign: $-7 \times 8 = -56$	3 negative signs: $(-1) \times (-2) \times (-3) = -6$

Try this Data Sufficiency problem:

Is the product of all of the elements in set S negative?

(1) All of the elements in set S are negative.

(2) There are 5 negative numbers in set S.

The problem asks whether the product of all of the elements is negative. Based on the rule above, it seems as though you just need to know whether there are an odd or even number of negative numbers in the set. There is one other number, though, to consider: 0. If you forgot about that while doing the problem, try it again right now.

Statement (1) indicates that everything in set S is negative, but you don't know whether there are an odd or even number of terms in the set, so this information is not sufficient to answer the question.

Statement (2) indicates that there are 5 negative numbers in the set. When the GMAT says something like this, you *can* conclude that there are exactly 5 negative numbers in the set (and no more). There could also be other numbers in the set (such as 0 or positive numbers). If there are 5 negative numbers and no others, then the product would be negative. If there are 5 negative numbers and other positive numbers, then the product would still be negative. But if 0 is in the mix, then the product is 0, which is not negative. So this statement is also not sufficient by itself.

Combined, set S contains 5 negative numbers *and nothing else*, so this information is sufficient to know that the product of the elements in set S must be negative. The correct answer is (C): The two statements are sufficient together, but neither one works alone.

28

Number Property Disguises

Sometimes, the test will deliberately disguise information about positives, negatives, odds, and evens.

For example, what does this sentence mean?

$m = 2k + 1$, where k is an integer.

The variable k is defined as an integer. Then k gets multiplied by 2. Any integer multiplied by 2 results in an even integer, so $2k$ is even. Finally, the equation adds 1. Take any even integer and add 1 and you'll end up with an odd integer. So, this information is telling you that m is an odd integer.

Extrapolate to any generic scenario. Any even number can be represented as $2n$, where n is an integer. When you see that language, make a note that they're really telling you $2n$ is even. An odd number is always one more than an even number, so $2n + 1$ must be odd. The same would be true if you subtracted 1 from an even integer. When you see this notation in future (even if the variable is different, as it is in the given problem), note that the problem is signaling that something is even or odd.

Here's another example:

$$\frac{a - b}{c} < 0$$

Hmm, that whole thing on the left is less than zero. First, less than zero is the same thing as negative, so the first part of this disguise is pretty straightforward. When you see < 0, interpret that as negative. And when you see > 0, interpret that as positive.

Next, the numerator $(a - b)$ divided by the denominator (c) is negative. This is a more complex version of something like $\frac{x}{y} < 0$. In order for that to be true, the numerator and denominator need to have *different* signs. That is, either the numerator is positive and the denominator is negative, or vice versa.

So, in the original statement, either $(a - b)$ is positive and c is negative, or vice versa.

Generally speaking, whenever you see inequalities with the number 0 on one side of the inequality, consider how to approach the problem using positive and negative principles.

Here's a third example:

If m and n are positive integers and $\frac{16}{m} = n$ . . . (and then it asks you some question)

That equation probably doesn't look like it's conveying anything particularly special—but it is. First, fractions are annoying, so multiply to get rid of the fraction: $16 = mn$. And the question stem also said that m and n are positive integers.

That equation is actually disguising really useful information! The two variables are positive integers and they multiply to 16. There are only a few pairs of possible values that would work: 1 and 16; 2 and 8; 4 and 4.

In fact, this setup is disguising the fact that m and n are *factors* of 16. Sure, they could have just said that—but they can make the problem a lot more challenging by disguising the information in this way.

The GMAT will sometimes use the above notations to disguise information about number properties; add them to your growing list of "GMAT codes" to know for the test. And keep an eye out for others as you keep studying. Any time you find yourself exclaiming, "Wait, *that* was what this really meant?," pull out a flash card and distill that realization into a "Next time I see X, I'll know they're *really* saying Y" takeaway.

28

The Sum of Two Primes

All prime numbers are odd, except the number 2. (All even numbers greater than 2 are divisible by 2, so they cannot be prime.) Thus, the sum of any two primes will be even (odd + odd = even), *unless* one of those primes is the number 2.

If a problem tells you that the sum of two primes is odd, one of those primes must be the number 2 and the other prime must not be 2. Conversely, if you know that 2 *cannot* be one of the primes in the sum, then the sum of the two primes must be even. Try an example:

> If a and b are both prime numbers greater than 10, which of the following CANNOT be true?
>
> I. ab is an even number.
> II. The difference between a and b equals 117.
> III. The sum of a and b is even.
>
> (A) I only
> (B) I and II only
> (C) I and III only
> (D) II and III only
> (E) I, II, and III

The question asks what cannot be true; jot that down. Since a and b are both prime numbers greater than 10, they must both be odd. Therefore, ab must be an odd number, so statement I cannot be true. This statement has to be included in the correct answer, so eliminate answer (D).

Similarly, if a and b are both odd, then $a - b$ cannot equal 117 (an odd number). The difference between two odd numbers must be even. Therefore, statement II cannot be true. Eliminate answers (A) and (C).

Finally, since a and b are both odd, $a + b$ must be even, so statement III will always be true. Statements I and II cannot be true, so the correct answer is (B).

Problem Set

For questions 1–6, answer each question with one of three responses: Always Yes, Always No, or Sometimes Yes/Sometimes No. Try to explain each answer using the rules you learned in this section.

All variables in questions 1–6 are integers.

1. If $x \div y$ yields an odd integer, is x odd?

2. If $a + b$ is even, is ab even?

3. If c, d, and e are consecutive integers, is cde even?

4. If h is even, j is odd, and k is odd, is $k(h + j)$ odd?

5. If n, p, q, and r are consecutive integers, is their sum even?

6. If xy is even and z is even, is $x + z$ even?

Save the following problems for review after you finish this entire guide.

7. Simplify $\dfrac{-30}{5} - \dfrac{18 - 9}{-3}$.

8. Simplify $\dfrac{20 \times (-7)}{-35 \times (-2)}$.

28

Answers and explanations follow on the next page. ▶ ▶ ▶

Solutions

1. **Sometimes Yes/Sometimes No:** There are no guaranteed outcomes in division. For example, if $x = 6$ and $y = 2$, then $6 \div 2 = 3$ and x is even. Alternatively, if $x = 9$ and $y = 3$, then $9 \div 3 = 3$ and x is odd.

2. **Sometimes Yes/Sometimes No:** If $a + b$ is even, a and b are either both odd or both even. If they are both odd, ab is odd. If they are both even, ab is even.

3. **Always Yes:** Since all integers alternate between even and odd, at least one of the consecutive integers, c, d, or e, must be even. Therefore, the product cde must be even.

4. **Always Yes:** If h is even and j is odd, then $h + j$ must be odd, since E + O = O. Therefore, $k(h + j) = \text{odd(odd)}$, which is always odd.

5. **Always Yes:** If n, p, q, and r are consecutive integers, two of them must be odd and two of them must be even. Pair them up to add them: O + O = E and E + E = E. Finally, add those two results: E + E = E.

6. **Sometimes Yes/Sometimes No:** If xy is even, then either x or y (or both x and y) must be even. Given that z is even, $x + z$ could be either O + E or E + E. If $x + z = $ O + E = O, the answer is No. If $x + z = $ E + E = E, the answer is Yes.

7. **-3:** This is a two-step subtraction problem. First, simplify each fraction. The first fraction simplifies to $\frac{-30}{5} = -6$, and the second fraction simplifies to $\frac{9}{-3} = -3$. The final answer is $-6 - (-3) = -6 + 3 = -3$.

8. **-2:** The sign of the first product, $20 \times (-7)$, is negative. The sign of the second product, $-35 \times (-2)$, is positive. Therefore, -140 divided by 70 is -2.

Combinatorics

In This Chapter...

- The Words *OR* and *AND*

- Arranging Groups

- Arranging Groups Using the Anagram Grid

- Multiple Groups

In this chapter, you will learn how to set up and solve combination, or counting, problems. These questions are not very common on the GMAT and many people dislike them, so you may choose not to study certain material; the chapter will guide you in making this choice.

CHAPTER 29 Combinatorics

The Words *OR* and *AND*

Suppose you are at a restaurant that offers a free side dish of soup or salad with any main dish. How many possible side dishes can you order?

You have two options: the soup OR the salad. The most important part of the example is this: The word *or* means *add*. You will see this word show up again and again in both combinatorics and probability problems.

If the same restaurant offers three main dishes (steak, salmon, or pasta), then how many possible combinations of main dish and side dish are there?

There are two decisions that need to be made: a main dish AND a side dish. List out all the possible combinations:

Steak – Soup	Steak – Salad	Salmon – Soup
Salmon – Salad	Pasta – Soup	Pasta – Salad

There are six possible combinations. For a problem without many options, you can literally just write out the possibilities. You can also do some math if you know that the word *and* means *multiply*.

When you make two decisions, you make decision 1 AND decision 2. This is true whether the decisions are simultaneous (e.g., choosing a main dish and a side dish) or sequential (e.g., choosing among routes between successive towns on a road trip).

In this example, you have three options for main dishes AND two options for side dishes:

$$\text{(steak OR chicken OR salmon)} \quad \text{AND} \quad \text{(soup OR salad)}$$
$$(\quad 1 \quad + \quad 1 \quad + \quad 1 \quad) \quad \times \quad (\quad 1 \quad + \quad 1 \quad) \quad = \quad 6$$
$$3 \quad\quad \times \quad\quad 2 \quad\quad = \quad 6$$

More straightforward combinatorics (also known as counting) problems can be solved using these two principles:

1. *OR* means *add*.

2. *AND* means *multiply*.

GMAT questions will get more complicated, of course. Try the following example:

> An office manager must choose a four-digit lock code for the office door. The first and last digits of the code must be odd, and no repetition of digits is allowed. How many different lock codes are possible?

When a question asks how many possible ways something can happen, you have a combinatorics or counting problem. In this case, the manager has to make four decisions to get a four-digit lock code. To keep track, make a slot for each digit:

$$\underset{\text{Digit 1}}{\underline{\hspace{1.5cm}}} \times \underset{\text{AND}}{} \underset{\text{Digit 2}}{\underline{\hspace{1.5cm}}} \times \underset{\text{AND}}{} \underset{\text{Digit 3}}{\underline{\hspace{1.5cm}}} \times \underset{\text{AND}}{} \underset{\text{Digit 4}}{\underline{\hspace{1.5cm}}}$$

Next, fill in the number of options for each slot. This is known as the **slot method**.

How many options are there for each digit? Start with the most constrained decisions first. There are restrictions on the first and last numbers so start there.

The first digit must be odd, so it can be 1 OR 3 OR 5 OR 7 OR 9. There are five options for the first digit. The problem also indicated that there can be no repeated numbers. Now that you have chosen the first digit (even though you don't know what the actual value will be), there are only four odd numbers remaining for the last digit. Fill in both slots:

$$\underset{\text{Digit 1}}{\underline{\hspace{0.6cm}5\hspace{0.6cm}}} \times \underset{\text{AND}}{} \underset{\text{Digit 2}}{\underline{\hspace{1.5cm}}} \times \underset{\text{AND}}{} \underset{\text{Digit 3}}{\underline{\hspace{1.5cm}}} \times \underset{\text{AND}}{} \underset{\text{Digit 4}}{\underline{\hspace{0.6cm}4\hspace{0.6cm}}}$$

Now, fill in the other two slots. Make sure to account for the lack of repetition. Ten digits exist in total (0 through 9), but two have already been used, so there are eight options remaining for the second digit and seven options for the third digit:

$$\underset{\text{Digit 1}}{\underline{\hspace{0.6cm}5\hspace{0.6cm}}} \times \underset{\text{AND}}{} \underset{\text{Digit 2}}{\underline{\hspace{0.6cm}8\hspace{0.6cm}}} \times \underset{\text{AND}}{} \underset{\text{Digit 3}}{\underline{\hspace{0.6cm}7\hspace{0.6cm}}} \times \underset{\text{AND}}{} \underset{\text{Digit 4}}{\underline{\hspace{0.6cm}4\hspace{0.6cm}}}$$

Finally, multiply this out. Look to multiply multiples of 5s and 2s together (because $5 \times 2 = 10$, and 10 is easier to multiply into other numbers). In this case, $5 \times 4 = 20$ and $8 \times 7 = 56$. The number 20 can be thought of as 2×10, so multiply $(56)(2)(10) = 1{,}120$.

When making decisions, there are two main cases:

1.   Decision 1 OR Decision 2: ADD the possibilities.

2.   Decision 1 AND Decision 2: MULTIPLY the possibilities.

Finally, the rest of this chapter deals with more complex scenarios. Many test-takers really dislike combinatorics; if you are one of them, you can decide to bail (guess immediately) on most combinatorics problems on the GMAT. It is possible to score well into the 700s while bailing on most combinatorics problems on the test.

If you see a straightforward problem for which you can write out a small number of combinations, go ahead and logic it out. If you see a more complicated problem, you may want to choose your favorite letter and move on. (And, if you decide to do that, you don't have to learn how to do anything else in this chapter.)

29

Arranging Groups

Another very common type of combinatorics problem asks how many different ways there are to arrange a group.

The number of ways of arranging n distinct objects, if there are no restrictions, is $n!$ (n factorial).

The term **n factorial** ($n!$) refers to the product of all the integers from 1 to n, inclusive. If you are going to go for it on medium to harder combinatorics questions, memorize the first six factorials, shown here:

$$1! = 1 \qquad\qquad 4! = 4 \times 3 \times 2 \times 1 = 24$$
$$2! = 2 \times 1 = 2 \qquad\qquad 5! = 5 \times 4 \times 3 \times 2 \times 1 = 120$$
$$3! = 3 \times 2 \times 1 = 6 \qquad\qquad 6! = 6 \times 5 \times 4 \times 3 \times 2 \times 1 = 720$$

For example, how many ways are there to arrange four people in four chairs in a row? Using the **slot method**, there is one slot for each position in the row. If you place any one of four people in the first chair, then you can place any one of the remaining three people in the second chair. For the third and fourth chairs, you have two choices and then one choice.

$$\underline{\ 4\ } \times \underline{\ 3\ } \times \underline{\ 2\ } \times \underline{\ 1\ } = 24 \text{ arrangements}$$

If you know how to think that through, you can just say, "The number of ways to arrange four people equals 4 factorial, which equals 24."

Arranging Groups Using the Anagram Grid

How many arrangements are there of the letters in the word EEL?

There are three letters, so according to the factorial formula, there should be $3! = 6$ arrangements, as follows (the two E's have subscripts to keep them straight):

$$E_1E_2L \qquad E_1LE_2 \qquad LE_1E_2$$
$$E_2E_1L \qquad E_2LE_1 \qquad LE_2E_1$$

The two arrangements in each column are considered identical. For example, E_1E_2L is the same thing as E_2E_1L; they're both EEL. There are really only three distinct arrangements:

$$EEL \qquad ELE \qquad LEE$$

Sometimes, you have to divide out a subset of the possible arrangements because they are identical to others in the set.

Here's how that would play out on a more GMAT-like problem:

> Seven people enter a race. There are 4 types of medals given as prizes for completing the race. The winner gets a platinum medal, the runner-up gets a gold medal, the next 2 racers each get a silver medal, and the last 3 racers all get bronze medals. What is the number of different ways the medals can be awarded?

In order to keep track of all the different categories, create an **anagram grid**. Anagram grids can be used whenever you are arranging members of a group.

The number of columns in the grid will always be equal to the number of members of the group. There are 7 runners in the race, so make 7 columns (labeled 1 through 7). Next, categorize each member of the group. There are 1 platinum medal, 1 gold medal, 2 silver medals, and 3 bronze medals. Note: Use only letters for the bottom row, never numbers (you'll see why in a minute).

1	2	3	4	5	6	7
P	G	S	S	B	B	B

Just as the two E's in EEL were indistinguishable, the 2 silver medals and the 3 bronze medals are indistinguishable, so 7! is not the answer. Use the top and bottom rows to create a fraction:

$$\frac{\text{Top row}}{\text{Bottom row}} = \frac{7!}{1!1!2!3!}$$

The numerator of the fraction is always the factorial of the largest number in the top row (in this case, 7!). The denominator is the product of the factorials of each *different* kind of letter in the bottom row. In this case, there are one P, one G, two S's, and three B's. (Use only letters in the bottom row to avoid mixing up the number of repeats with the numbers themselves.)

The bottom row of the fraction shows the 1! terms for both P and G, but in practice, you don't have to write out any 1! terms, since they don't make a difference to the calculation. As you simplify the fraction, look for ways to cancel out numbers in the denominator with numbers in the numerator:

$$\frac{7!}{2!3!} = \frac{7 \times 6 \times 5 \times \overset{2}{\cancel{4}} \times \cancel{3!}}{\underset{1}{\cancel{2}} \times 1 \times \cancel{3!}} = 7 \times 6 \times 5 \times 2 = 420$$

Try another problem:

A local card club will send 3 representatives to the national conference. If the local club has 8 members, how many different groups of representatives could the club send?

The problem talks about 8 members, so draw 8 columns for the anagram grid. There are 3 representatives chosen; represent them with Y. Use N to represent the 5 members of the group who are not chosen.

1	2	3	4	5	6	7	8
Y	Y	Y	N	N	N	N	N

Set up your fraction:

$$\frac{8!}{3!5!} = \frac{8 \times 7 \times \cancel{6} \times \cancel{5!}}{(\cancel{3} \times \cancel{2} \times 1)\cancel{5!}} = 8 \times 7 = 56$$

On the top of the fraction, only write out the numbers down to the largest factorial that also appears on the bottom of the fraction. In the fraction above, you can cancel out the two 5! terms without having to write them out.

Multiple Groups

So far, the discussion has revolved around two main themes: (1) making decisions and (2) arranging groups. More difficult combinatorics problems will actually combine the two topics. In other words, you may have to make multiple decisions, each of which will involve arranging different groups.

Try the following problem:

> The I Eta Pi fraternity must choose a delegation of 3 senior members and 2 junior members for an annual interfraternity conference. If I Eta Pi has 6 senior members and 5 junior members, how many different delegations are possible?

First, note that you are choosing senior members AND junior members. These are different decisions, so determine each separately and then multiply the possible arrangements.

You have to pick 3 seniors out of a group of 6. That means that 3 are chosen (and identical) and the remaining 3 are not chosen (and also identical):

$$\frac{6!}{3!3!} = \frac{\cancel{6} \times 5 \times 4 \times \cancel{3!}}{(\cancel{3} \times \cancel{2} \times 1)\cancel{3!}} = 5 \times 4 = 20$$

Similarly, pick 2 juniors out of a group of 5, where 2 members are chosen (and identical) and the remaining 3 members are not chosen (and also identical):

$$\frac{5!}{2!3!} = \frac{5 \times \cancel{4}^{2} \times \cancel{3!}}{(\cancel{2} \times 1)\cancel{3!}}_{1} = 5 \times 2 = 10$$

There are 20 possible senior delegations AND 10 possible junior delegations. Since *AND* means *multiply*, there are $20 \times 10 = 200$ possible delegations.

Problems will not always make it clear that you are dealing with multiple decisions. Try the following problem:

> The yearbook committee has to pick a color scheme for this year's yearbook. There are 7 colors to choose from (red, orange, yellow, green, blue, indigo, and violet). How many different color schemes are possible if the committee can select at most 2 colors?

Although this question concerns only one group (colors), it also involves multiple decisions. The question states there can be *at most* 2 colors chosen. In other words, the color scheme can contain 1 color OR 2 colors.

Figure out how many combinations are possible if 1 color is chosen, as well as how many are possible if 2 colors are chosen, and then add them together:

$$\text{1 color chosen and 6 colors not chosen} = \frac{7!}{1!6!} = 7$$

$$\text{2 colors chosen and 5 colors not chosen} = \frac{7!}{2!5!} = 21$$

Together, there are $7 + 21 = 28$ possible color schemes.

Problem Set

Now that you've finished the chapter, try the following problems.

1. In how many different ways can the letters in the word *LEVEL* be arranged?

2. A company makes 5 different types of truffles. If one package contains exactly 2 truffles of different types, how may different combinations are possible?

3. A pod of 6 dolphins always swims single file, with 3 females at the front and 3 males in the rear. In how many different arrangements can the dolphins swim?

Save the following problems for review after you finish this entire guide.

4. Mario's Pizza offers a choice of 2 types of crust, 2 types of cheese, and 5 different types of vegetables. If Linda's volleyball team decides to order a pizza with 4 types of vegetables, how many different choices do the teammates have at Mario's Pizza?

5. What is the sum of all the possible three-digit numbers that can be constructed using the digits 3, 4, and 5 if each digit can be used only once in each number?

29

Answers and explanations follow on the next page. ▶ ▶ ▶

Solutions

1. **30 ways:** There are two repeated E's and two repeated L's in the word *LEVEL*. To find the number of ways this word can be arranged, set up a fraction in which the numerator is the factorial of the number of letters and the denominator is the factorial of the number of each repeated letter:

$$\frac{5!}{2!2!} = \frac{5 \times \overset{2}{\cancel{4}} \times 3 \times \cancel{2!}}{\underset{1}{\cancel{2}} \times 1 \times \cancel{2!}} = 5 \times 2 \times 3 = 30$$

    Alternatively, you can solve this problem using the slot method, as long as you correct for over-counting (since there are some identical elements). There are five choices for the first letter, four for the second, and so on, making the product $5 \times 4 \times 3 \times 2 \times 1 = 120$. However, there are two sets of two indistinguishable elements each, so you must divide by 2! to account for each of these. Thus, the total number of combinations is as shown in the calculation above.

2. **10:** In every combination, 2 types of truffles will be in the package and 3 types of truffles will not. Therefore, this problem is a question about the number of anagrams that can be made from the "word" YYNNN:

1	2	3	4	5
Y	Y	N	N	N

$$\frac{5!}{2!3!} = \frac{5 \times \overset{2}{\cancel{4}} \times \cancel{3!}}{\underset{1}{\cancel{2}} \times \cancel{3!}} = 5 \times 2 = 10$$

3. **36:** This is a multiple arrangements problem, in which you have two separate pools (females AND males). There are 3! ways in which the 3 females can swim. There are 3! ways in which the 3 males can swim. Therefore, there are $3! \times 3!$ ways in which the entire pod can swim:

$$3! \times 3! = 6 \times 6 = 36$$

4. **20 choices:** Consider the vegetables first. Model them with the "word" YYYYN, in which four of the types are on the pizza and one is not. The number of anagrams for this "word" is in the table below:

1	2	3	4	5
Y	Y	Y	Y	N

$$\frac{5!}{4!} = 5$$

    If each of these pizzas can also be offered in 2 choices of crust, there are $5 \times 2 = 10$ choices of pizza. The same logic applies for the cheese so there are $10 \times 2 = 20$ choices.

5. **2,664:** There are six ways in which to arrange these digits:

    $$3 \quad 4 \quad 5$$
    $$3 \quad 5 \quad 4$$
    $$4 \quad 3 \quad 5$$
    $$4 \quad 5 \quad 3$$
    $$5 \quad 3 \quad 4$$
    $$5 \quad 4 \quad 3$$

Notice that each digit appears twice in the hundreds column, twice in the tens column, and twice in the ones column. Use place value to find the sum. The sum of each digit in the hundreds column is $3 + 3 + 4 + 4 + 5 + 5 = 24$. Since this is the hundreds column, multiply this sum by 100 to get the sum of only the hundreds part of each number. Repeat this reasoning for the tens column and the ones column:

$$100(24) + 10(24) + 1(24) = 2,400 + 240 + 24 = 2,664$$

Probability

In This Chapter...

- Calculate the Numerator and Denominator Separately

- More Than One Event: AND vs. OR

- P(A) + P(Not A) = 1

- The 1 − x Probability Trick

In this chapter, you will learn how to set up and solve probability problems for both single and multiple events. You'll also learn a very useful shortcut for tackling multi-part probabilities: calculating the probability of the outcome that you *don't* want (otherwise known as the $1 - x$ trick).

CHAPTER 30 Probability

Probability is a quantity that expresses the chance, or likelihood, of an event.

Think of probability as a fraction:

$$\text{Probability} = \frac{\text{Number of } \textit{desired} \text{ or } \textit{successful} \text{ outcomes}}{\text{Total number of } \textit{possible} \text{ outcomes}}$$

For instance, if you flip a coin (one side heads, the other tails), what is the probability that heads turns up? There are two possible outcomes (heads or tails), but only one of them is considered desirable (heads), so the probability is $\frac{1}{2}$.

Notice that the numerator of the fraction is *always* a subset of the denominator. If there are n possible outcomes, then the number of desirable outcomes must be between 0 and n (the number of outcomes cannot be negative). As a result, *any probability will be between 0 and 1.*

An impossible event has a probability of 0 when the desired outcome cannot happen. For example, if you flip a coin (one side heads, the other tails), what is the probability that a dragon turns up? There are no dragons on the coin, so $\frac{0}{2} = 0$. By contrast, a certain event has a probability of 1 when the number of desired outcomes is equal to the number of possible outcomes. If you flip a coin (heads or tails), what is the probability that either heads or tails turns up? $\frac{2}{2} = 1$. Those are the only two possible outcomes.

Additionally, probability can be expressed as a fraction, a decimal, or a percent. For example, $\frac{3}{4} = 0.75 = 75\%$. Depending on the problem, you can solve in any one of these forms; sometimes, you'll need to use the percent form in order to think about the number of desired outcomes and the number of possible outcomes.

Calculate the Numerator and Denominator Separately

Numerators and denominators of probabilities are related, but they must be calculated separately. Often, it will be easier to begin by calculating the denominator.

There are two ways to calculate a number of outcomes for either the numerator or the denominator:

1. Manually count the number of outcomes (if there aren't that many).

2. Use an appropriate combinatorics formula. These problems tend to be harder; if you dislike probability, you may decide to bail immediately on these kinds of problems (as there aren't typically that many on the test).

Try the following problem:

> Two number cubes with faces numbered 1 to 6 are rolled. What is the probability that the sum of the rolls is 8 ?

Start with the total number of possible outcomes (the denominator). For this calculation, you can use combinatorics. Notice that rolling two number cubes is like rolling cube 1 AND rolling cube 2. For each of these rolls, there are six possible outcomes (the numbers 1 to 6). Since AND equals multiply, there are $6 \times 6 = 36$ possible outcomes. This is the denominator of the fraction.

Next, figure out how many of those 36 possible rolls represent the desired outcome (a sum of 8). It would be complicated to come up with an appropriate combinatorics formula—and not worth the time it would take because only a limited number of combinations would work. Count them up! If the first cube turns up a 1, the other cube would need to roll a 7. This isn't possible, so eliminate that possibility. Keep counting; here are the rolls that work, in order (first roll and second roll):

2 and 6	3 and 5	4 and 4	5 and 3	6 and 2

You do actually need to include the final two in that list; a roll of 3 and then 5 is a different outcome than a roll of 5 and then 3 because both of those outcomes were counted separately in the 6×6 calculation.

There are 5 combinations that work, so the probability of a sum of 8 is $\frac{5}{36}$.

More Than One Event: AND vs. OR

Combinatorics and probability have another connection: the meaning of the words *AND* and *OR*. In probability, as well as in combinatorics, the word *AND* means multiply, and the word *OR* means add. Try this example:

> There is a $\frac{1}{2}$ probability that a certain coin will turn up heads on any given toss. What is the probability that two tosses of the coin will yield heads both times?

To answer this question, calculate the probability that the coin lands on heads on the first flip AND heads on the second flip. The probability of heads on the first flip is $\frac{1}{2}$. The probability of heads on the second flip is also $\frac{1}{2}$. Since AND means multiply, the probability is $\frac{1}{2} \times \frac{1}{2} = \frac{1}{4}$.

Try another example:

> The weather report for today states that there is a 40% chance of sun, a 25% chance of rain, and a 35% chance of hail. Assuming only one of the three outcomes can happen, what is the probability that it rains or hails today?

The question is asking for the probability of rain OR hail. Therefore, the probability is $25\% + 35\% = 60\%$. The calculation would change if *both* rain and hail can happen, but don't worry about that for now.

P(A) + P(Not A) = 1

P(A) + P(Not A) = 1 is a fancy way of saying that the probability of something happening plus the probability of that thing *not* happening must sum to 1. For example, the probability that it either rains or does not rain is equal to 1: If there's a 25% chance of rain, then there must be a 75% chance that it will *not* rain. Try an example:

> A person has a 40% chance of winning a game every time he or she plays it. If there are no ties, what is the probability that Asha loses the first game played and wins the second game?

If the probability of winning the game is 40%, then the probability of *not* winning the game (losing) is $100\% - 40\% = 60\%$. Calculate the probability that Asha loses the game the first time AND wins the game the second time:

$$(60\%) \times (40\%) = 0.6 \times 0.4 = 0.24$$

The probability is 0.24, or 24%.

The 1 − *x* Probability Trick

Suppose that a salesperson makes 5 sales calls, and you want to find the likelihood that he or she makes *at least 1* sale. If you try to calculate this probability directly, you will have to confront 5 separate possibilities that constitute "success": exactly 1 sale, exactly 2 sales, exactly 3 sales, exactly 4 sales, or exactly 5 sales. This would almost certainly be more work than you can reasonably do in two minutes.

There is, however, another option. Instead of calculating the probability that the salesperson makes at least 1 sale, you can calculate the probability that the salesperson does *not* make at least 1 sale.

$$\text{Prob of at least 1 sale} + \text{Prob of 0 sales} = 1$$
$$P(\geq 1) \quad + \quad P(0) \quad = 1$$
$$P(\geq 1) \quad\quad\quad = 1 - P(0)$$

These two outcomes (at least 1 sale or 0 sales) make up all of the possible outcomes. So if you know the probability of making 0 sales, you can subtract that from 1 to find the probability of making at least 1 sale. This is the **1 − *x* shortcut**.

Calculating just a single probability and subtracting from 1 is a lot faster than calculating 5 probabilities and adding them up. When a probability problem sets up an *at least* or *at most* scenario, look for this 1 − *x* shortcut.

For complicated probability problems, decide whether it is easier to calculate the probability you want or the probability you do *not* want. On the GMAT, most of the time, it will be faster to calculate the probability that the problem did not ask for. Try an example:

> A bag contains equal numbers of red, green, and yellow marbles. If Gurdeep pulls three marbles out of the bag, replacing each marble after picking it, what is the probability that at least one will be red?

Since the question asks for the probability that at least one will be red, there are three possible cases to calculate: one red, two red, or three red. Instead, calculate the probability that *none* of the marbles are red. Each time Gurdeep picks a marble, there is a $\frac{2}{3}$ probability that the marble will *not* be red. The probability that all three marbles will not be red is $\frac{2}{3} \times \frac{2}{3} \times \frac{2}{3} = \frac{8}{27}$.

If the probability that *none* of the marbles is red is $\frac{8}{27}$, then the probability that at least one marble is red is $1 - \frac{8}{27} = \frac{19}{27}$.

If you need to calculate the probability of an event (P(A)), there are two ways to calculate the probability:

$$P(A) \quad \text{or} \quad 1 - P(\text{Not A})$$

When the question includes *at least* or *at most* language, the 1 − P(Not A) method is usually faster.

Problem Set

Now that you've finished the chapter, try the following problems. For problems 1 and 2, assume that each number cube has six sides with faces numbered 1 to 6.

1. Two number cubes are rolled. What is the probability that the sum of the two numbers will yield a 10 or lower?

2. What is the probability that the sum of two number cubes will yield a 7 on their first roll, and then when both are rolled again, their sum will again yield a 7 ?

3. On the planned day of a picnic, there is a 30% chance of rain. If it rains, there is a 50% chance that the picnic will be canceled, but if it doesn't rain, the picnic will take place. What is the chance that the picnic will take place?

Save the following problems for review after you finish this entire guide.

4. In a diving competition, each diver has a 20% chance of a perfect dive. The first perfect dive of the competition, but no subsequent dives, will receive a perfect score. What are the chances that the third diver will receive a perfect score on that dive? (Assume that each diver can perform only one dive.)

5. A magician has five animals in a magic hat: 3 doves and 2 rabbits. If the magician pulls two animals out of the hat at random, what is the chance that the two will be the same type of animal?

Answers and explanations follow on the next page. ▶ ▶ ▶

Solutions

1. $\frac{11}{12}$: There are a total of $6 \times 6 = 36$ possible outcomes. There are many possible ways to get the desired outcome of a sum of 10 or lower. Solve this problem by calculating the probability that the sum will be *higher* than 10 and subtracting that probability from 1. There are three combinations of two number cubes that yield a sum higher than 10: $5 + 6$, $6 + 5$, and $6 + 6$. Therefore, the probability that the sum will be higher than 10 is $\frac{3}{36}$, or $\frac{1}{12}$. The probability that the sum will be 10 or lower is $1 - \frac{1}{12} = \frac{11}{12}$.

2. $\frac{1}{36}$: There are 36 ways in which two number cubes can be thrown ($6 \times 6 = 36$). The combinations that yield a sum of 7 are $1 + 6$, $2 + 5$, $3 + 4$, $4 + 3$, $5 + 2$, and $6 + 1$, or six different combinations. Therefore, the probability of rolling a 7 is $\frac{6}{36}$, or $\frac{1}{6}$. To find the probability that this will happen twice in a row (an outcome of 7 AND 7), multiply: $\frac{1}{6} \times \frac{1}{6} = \frac{1}{36}$.

3. **85%:** There are two possible ways in which the picnic can take place:

   1. One: It doesn't rain: $P = 70\%$ OR

   2. Two: It rains AND the picnic is held anyway:

   $$P = 30\%\left(\frac{1}{2}\right) = 15\%$$

   Add the probabilities together to find the total probability that the picnic will take place:

   $$70\% + 15\% = 85\%$$

4. $\frac{16}{125}$: In order for the third diver to receive a perfect score, neither of the previous two divers can receive one. Therefore, you are finding the probability of a chain of three events: that diver one will *not* get a perfect score AND diver two will *not* get a perfect score AND diver three *will* get a perfect score. Multiply the probabilities: $\frac{4}{5} \times \frac{4}{5} \times \frac{1}{5} = \frac{16}{125}$.

   The probability is $\frac{16}{125}$ that the third diver will receive a perfect score.

5. $\frac{4}{10}$ **or 40%:** Use an anagram model to determine the total number of different pairs the magician can pull out of the hat. Since two animals will be in the pair and the other three will not, use the "word" YYNNN.

A	B	C	D	E
Y	Y	N	N	N

   $\frac{5!}{2!3!} = \frac{5 \times 4}{2 \times 1} = 10$

   Thus, there are 10 possible pairs; this is the bottom of the probability fraction.

Then, list the pairs in which the animals will match. Represent the rabbits with the subscript letters *a* and *b*, and the doves with the letters *x*, *y*, and *z*.

Matched Pairs: R_aR_b D_xD_y There are four pairs in which the animals will be
D_xD_z D_yD_z a matched set: one way in which the rabbits can
be chosen and three ways in which the doves can
be chosen.

Therefore, the probability that the magician will randomly draw a matched set is $\frac{4}{10} = 40\%$.

Coordinate Plane

In This Chapter...

- Positive and Negative Quadrants

- The Slope of a Line

- The Four Types of Slopes

- The Intercepts of a Line

- Slope-Intercept Equation: $y = mx + b$

- Horizontal and Vertical Lines

- The Distance Between Two Points

In this chapter, you will learn how to find the slope of a line and how to map a line onto a coordinate plane. You'll learn how to use the slope-intercept form of the equation of a line, as well as how to find the distance between any two points in a coordinate plane.

CHAPTER 31 Coordinate Plane

The **coordinate plane** is formed by a horizontal axis or reference line (the **x-axis**) and a vertical axis (the **y-axis**), as shown below. These axes are each marked off like a number line, with both positive and negative numbers. The axes cross at right angles at the number zero.

Points in the plane are identified by using an ordered pair of numbers, such as the point shown, which is written as $(2, -3)$. The first number in the ordered pair, (2), is the **x-coordinate**, which corresponds to the point's horizontal location, as measured by the x-axis. The second number in the ordered pair, (-3), is the **y-coordinate**, which corresponds to the point's vertical location, as indicated by the y-axis. The point $(0, 0)$, where the axes cross, is called the **origin**.

A line in the plane is formed by the connection of two or more points. Also, along the x-axis line, the y-coordinate is 0. Likewise, along the y-axis line, the x-coordinate is 0.

If the GMAT gives you coordinates with other variables, match them to x and y. For instance, if you have point (a, b), a is the x-coordinate and b is the y-coordinate.

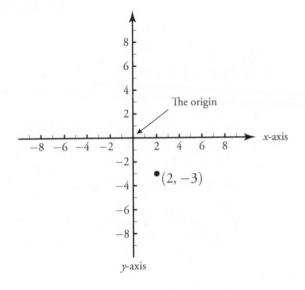

Positive and Negative Quadrants

31

There are four quadrants in the coordinate plane, as shown in the figure below. Start in the upper-right corner and move *counter*clockwise.

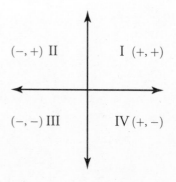

Quadrant I contains only those points with a **positive** *x*-coordinate and a **positive** *y*-coordinate.

Quadrant II contains only those points with a **negative** *x*-coordinate and a **positive** *y*-coordinate.

Quadrant III contains only those points with a **negative** *x*-coordinate and a **negative** *y*-coordinate.

Quadrant IV contains only those points with a **positive** *x*-coordinate and a **negative** *y*-coordinate.

The Slope of a Line

The **slope** of a line is defined as *rise over run*—that is, how much the line *rises* vertically divided by how much the line *runs* horizontally.

The slope of a line can be determined by taking any two points on the line and (1) determining the **rise**, or difference between their *y*-coordinates, and (2) determining the **run**, or difference between their *x*-coordinates. You can use the formula below to find a slope:

$$\text{Slope} = \frac{\text{Rise}}{\text{Run}}$$

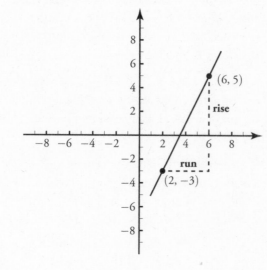

For example, in the graph shown, the line rises vertically from −3 to +5. To find the vertical distance, subtract the *y*-coordinates: $5 - (-3) = 8$. Thus, the line rises 8 units. The line also runs horizontally from 2 to 6. To find the horizontal distance, subtract the *x*-coordinates: $6 - 2 = 4$. Thus, the line runs 4 units.

Put the results together to find the slope of the line: $\frac{\text{Rise}}{\text{Run}} = \frac{8}{4} = 2$.

Two other points on the same line may have a different rise and run, but the slope will be the same. The rise over run will always be 2 because a line has a constant slope.

The slope of a line is equal to $\frac{y_2 - y_1}{x_2 - x_1}$.

For a different line, if you are given the two points (2, 3) and (4, −1), then you can find the slope:

$$\frac{-1 - 3}{4 - 2} = \frac{-4}{2} = -2$$

You can use the two points in either order, but make sure that y_2 and x_2 always come from the same point (and that y_1 and x_1 always come from the same point). Here's the slope for the same two points but used in reverse order, $(4, -1)$ and $(2, 3)$:

$$\frac{3 - (-1)}{2 - 4} = \frac{4}{-2} = -2$$

Either way, the slope is the same.

The Four Types of Slopes

A line can have one of four types of slopes:

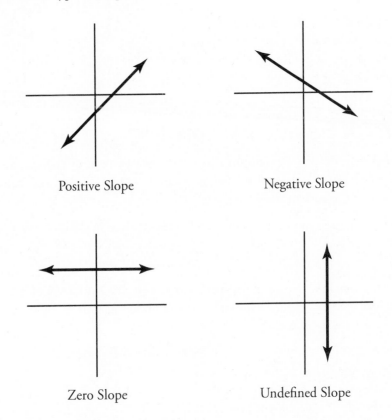

Positive Slope

Negative Slope

Zero Slope

Undefined Slope

A line with positive slope rises upward from left to right. A line with negative slope falls downward from left to right. A horizontal line has zero slope. A vertical line has undefined slope. Notice that the x-axis has zero slope, while the y-axis has undefined slope.

31

The Intercepts of a Line

A point where a line intersects a coordinate axis is called an **intercept**. There are two types of intercepts: the x-intercept, where the line intersects the x-axis, and the y-intercept, where the line intersects the y-axis.

The x-intercept is expressed using the ordered pair $(x, 0)$, where x is the point at which the line intersects the x-axis. **The x-intercept is the point on the line at which $y = 0$.** In this graph, the x-intercept is -4, as expressed by the ordered pair $(-4, 0)$.

The y-intercept is expressed using the ordered pair $(0, y)$, where y is the point at which the line intersects the y-axis. **The y-intercept is the point on the line at which $x = 0$.** In this graph, the y-intercept is 6, as expressed by the ordered pair $(0, 6)$.

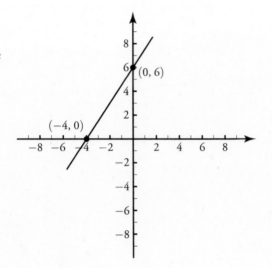

Slope-Intercept Equation: $y = mx + b$

Linear equations represent lines in the coordinate plane. Linear equations often look like this: $Ax + By = C$, where A, B, and C are numbers. For instance, $6x + 3y = 18$ is a linear equation. Linear equations never involve terms such as x^2, $\sqrt{x}$, or xy.

In coordinate plane problems, it can be useful to write linear equations in slope-intercept form:

$$y = mx + b$$

In this equation, m represents the slope of the line and b represents the y-intercept of the line, or the point at which the line crosses the y-axis. When you want to graph a linear equation, rewrite the equation in slope-intercept form. Try this example:

What is the slope-intercept form for a line with the equation $6x + 3y = 18$?

Rewrite the equation by solving for y as follows:

$$6x + 3y = 18$$

$3y = 18 - 6x$	Subtract $6x$ from both sides.
$y = 6 - 2x$	Divide both sides by 3.
$y = -2x + 6$	Rearrange. The y-intercept is $(0, 6)$, and the slope is -2.

To graph this line, first put a point at +6 on the *y*-axis (because the *y*-intercept, *b*, equals 6).

Then, count down 2 units (because the slope is negative) and to the right 1 unit. Place another point.

Now, draw a line between the two points.

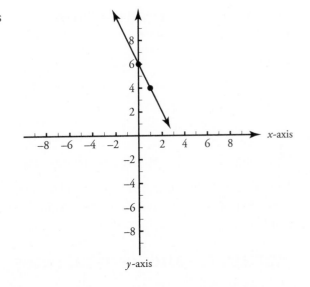

The GMAT sometimes asks you to determine which quadrants a given line passes through. For example:

Which quadrants does the line $2x + y = 5$ pass through?

First, rewrite the line in the form $y = mx + b$:

$$2x + y = 5$$
$$y = 5 - 2x$$
$$y = -2x + 5$$

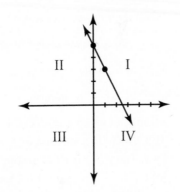

Next, sketch the line. Since $b = 5$, the *y*-intercept is the point $(0, 5)$. The slope is -2, so the line slopes downward to the right from the *y*-intercept. A slope of -2 is the equivalent of $\frac{-2}{1}$. Count two places down from the intercept (the rise of a negative slope) and one place to the right (the run). Draw a second point, then connect the two points with a line. You can now see that the line passes through quadrants I, II, and IV.

Alternatively, find two points on the line by setting x and y equal to 0 in the original equation. In this way, you find the x- and y-intercepts:

$x = 0$	$y = 0$
$2x + y = 5$	$2x + y = 5$
$2(0) + y = 5$	$2x + (0) = 5$
$y = 5$	$x = 2.5$

The points $(0, 5)$ and $(2.5, 0)$ are both on the line.

Now, sketch the line using the points you have identified. If you plot $(0, 5)$ and $(2.5, 0)$ on the coordinate plane, you can connect them to see the position of the line. Again, the line passes through quadrants I, II, and IV.

Horizontal and Vertical Lines

Horizontal and vertical lines are not expressed in the $y = mx + b$ form. Instead, they are expressed as simpler one-variable equations.

Horizontal lines are expressed in the form:

$y = some\ number$, such as $y = 2$ or $y = -7$

Vertical lines are expressed in the form:

$x = some\ number$, such as $x = 3$ or $x = 5$

All the points on a vertical line have the same x-coordinate. This is why the equation of a vertical line is defined only by x. The y-axis itself corresponds to the equation $x = 0$. Likewise, all the points on a horizontal line have the same y-coordinate. This is why the equation of a horizontal line is defined only by y. The x-axis itself corresponds to the equation $y = 0$.

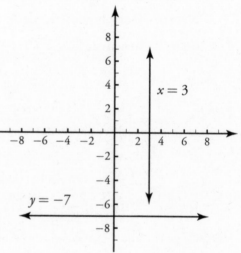

The Distance Between Two Points

The distance between any two points in the coordinate plane can be calculated by using the Pythagorean theorem. For example:

What is the distance between the points $(1, 3)$ and $(7, -5)$?

(A)   6
(B)   8
(C)   10
(D)   15
(E)   18

Start by drawing a right triangle connecting the points, as shown here:

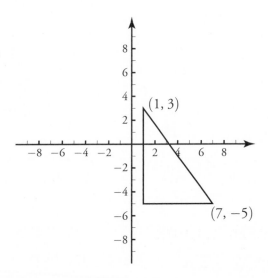

Next, find the lengths of the two legs of the triangle by figuring out the rise and the run.

The y-coordinate (rise) changes from 3 to -5, a difference of 8 (the vertical leg).

The x-coordinate (run) changes from 1 to 7, a difference of 6 (the horizontal leg).

Though there is a formula to calculate distance, first try to estimate. The rise is 8, and the desired distance is definitely longer, so eliminate answers (A) and (B).

Check the remaining answers. While the distance is longer than 8, it's not *that* much longer. 15 would be almost double 8, which is way too long. Eliminate (D) and (E), leaving the correct answer, (C).

Every once in a while, you may have to actually calculate the distance. The rise and the run are the two legs of the triangle (called a and b); the desired distance is the hypotenuse (called c). Plug the two legs into the Pythagorean theorem formula, $a^2 + b^2 = c^2$, and solve for the hypotenuse:

$$a^2 + b^2 = c^2$$
$$6^2 + 8^2 = c^2$$
$$36 + 64 = c^2$$
$$100 = c^2$$
$$10 = c$$

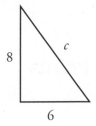

Problem Set

Now that you've finished the chapter, try these problems.

1. A line has the equation $y = 3x + 7$. At which point does this line intersect the y-axis?

2. A line has the equation $x = -2y + z$. If (3, 2) is a point on the line, what is z ?

3. Which quadrants, if any, do NOT contain any points on the line represented by $x - y = 18$?

4. A line has a slope of $\frac{1}{6}$ and intersects the x-axis at (−24, 0). At which point does this line intersect the y-axis?

Save the following problems for review after you finish this entire guide.

5. A line has the equation $x = \frac{y}{80} - 20$. At which point does this line intersect the x-axis?

6. Which quadrants, if any, do NOT contain any points on the line represented by $x = 10y$?

7. Which quadrants, if any, contain points on the line represented by $x + 18 = 2y$?

8. A line has a slope of $\frac{3}{4}$ and intersects the point (−12, −39). At which point does this line intersect the x-axis?

Answers and explanations follow on the next page. ▶ ▶ ▶

Solutions

1. **(0, 7):** A line intersects the y-axis at the y-intercept. Since this equation is written in slope-intercept form, $y = mx + b$, the y-intercept is the b portion of the equation: 7. Thus, the line intersects the y-axis at the point (0, 7).

2. **7:** Substitute the coordinates (3, 2) for x and y and solve for z:

    $$3 = -2(2) + z$$
    $$3 = -4 + z$$
    $$z = 7$$

3. **Quadrant II:** First, rewrite the line in slope-intercept form:

    $$y = x - 18$$

    Find the intercepts by setting x equal to 0 and y equal to 0:

$y = 0 - 18$	$0 = x - 18$
$y = -18$	$x = 18$

    Plot the points: $(0, -18)$ and $(18, 0)$. (In the diagram shown, each tick mark represents three units: 3, 6, 9, ...) The line does not pass through quadrant II.

4. **(0, 4):** Plug the slope in for m. Then, use the given point to find the value of b:

    $$y = \frac{1}{6}x + b$$
    $$0 = \frac{1}{6}(-24) + b$$
    $$0 = -4 + b$$
    $$b = 4$$

    The variable b represents the y-intercept. Therefore, the line intersects the y-axis at (0, 4).

5. **(−20, 0):** A line intersects the x-axis at the x-intercept, or when the y-coordinate is equal to 0. Substitute 0 for y and solve for x:

    $$x = 0 - 20$$
    $$x = -20$$

    The line crosses the x-intercept at the point $(-20, 0)$.

6. **Quadrants II and IV:** First, rewrite the line in slope-intercept form: $y = \frac{x}{10}$

    If you plug in 0 for either variable, the other variable will also equal 0. The line crosses the *y*-intercept at the origin (0, 0). To find another point on the line, substitute any convenient number for *x*; given the equation, 10 would be a good number to choose:

    $$y = \frac{10}{10} = 1 \qquad \text{The point (10, 1) is on the line.}$$

    Plot the points: (0, 0) and (10, 1). The line does not pass through quadrants II or IV.

7. **Quadrants I, II, and III:** First, rewrite the line in slope-intercept form: $y = \frac{x}{2} + 9$

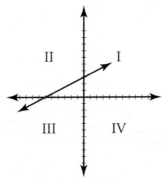

    Find the intercepts by setting *x* equal to 0 and *y* equal to 0:

    $$0 = \frac{x}{2} + 9 \qquad\qquad y = \frac{0}{2} + 9$$
    $$x = -18 \qquad\qquad\quad y = 9$$

    Plot the points: (−18, 0) and (0, 9). (In the diagram shown, each tick mark represents three units: 3, 6, 9, ...) The line passes through quadrants I, II, and III.

8. **(40, 0):** First, plug the information given into the slope-intercept equation to find the value of b:

$$y = \frac{3}{4}x + b$$

$$-39 = \frac{3}{4}(-12) + b$$

$$-39 = -9 + b$$

$$b = -30$$

This allows you to write the equation of this line:

$$y = \frac{3}{4}x - 30$$

The line intersects the x-axis when $y = 0$. Set y equal to 0 and solve for x:

$$0 = \frac{3}{4}x - 30$$

$$\frac{3}{4}x = 30$$

$$x = 40$$

The line intersects the x-axis at (40, 0).

Applying to Business School?

Prep made personal.

Whether you're looking to enroll in a comprehensive course or get personalized 1-on-1 instruction, we've got you covered.

Our Manhattan Prep instructors aren't just 99th-percentile scoring **GMAT experts**—they're experienced teachers who will go the extra mile to help you hit your top score.

Check out what our students have to say about Manhattan Prep:

"Deciding to take this class was the best decision I made in my GMAT journey.... I would strongly recommend anyone take a class at Manhattan Prep..."

Allison, Manhattan Prep GMAT Student 10/17/23

"I've recommended Manhattan Prep to many friends and coworkers looking to study for the GMAT and truly think it is the best decision to get through this phase!"

Aman, Manhattan Prep GMAT Student 6/27/23

"Hands down best materials / course on the market."

Sam, Manhattan Prep GMAT Student 5/25/23

"Highly recommend taking GMAT Manhattan Prep. They do an amazing job breaking down the test and giving you the tools to be successful."

Glodie, Manhattan Prep GMAT Student 1/10/22

"There are SO many useful strategies that are covered on the Manhattan Prep online portal and during class. ... These are game changers, since it really helps you structure your studies."

Neil, Manhattan Prep GMAT Student 3/29/23

POWERED BY KAPLAN

Contacts us at 800-576-4628 or gmat@manhattanprep.com
for more information about your GMAT study options.